The O'Doherty Papers
(Volume II)

William Maginn

Alpha Editions

This Edition Published in 2021

ISBN: 9789354506215

Design and Setting By
Alpha Editions
www.alphaedis.com
Email – info@alphaedis.com

As per information held with us this book is in Public Domain.
This book is a reproduction of an important historical work. Alpha Editions uses the best technology to reproduce historical work in the same manner it was first published to preserve its original nature. Any marks or number seen are left intentionally to preserve its true form.

THE
ODOHERTY PAPERS

BY THE LATE

WILLIAM MAGINN, LL.D.

ANNOTATED BY

Dr. SHELTON MACKENZIE

EDITOR OF "SHEIL'S SKETCHES OF THE IRISH BAR"—"THE NOCTES
AMBROSIANÆ," ETC.

IN TWO VOLUMES
VOL. II

REDFIELD
34 BEEKMAN STREET, NEW YORK
1855

CONTENTS OF VOLUME II

	PAGE
PANDEMUS POLYGLOTT	7
THREE GOBLETS OF WINE (from the Greek)	25
JUDY CALLAGHAN (rendered into Latin Verse)	26
MONSIEUR JUDAS (after Béranger)	28
ROGER GOODFELLOW (after Béranger)	30
BACKE AND SIDE GO BARE (in Latin Verse)	32
AT MY TIME OF DAY	33
FAREWELL, BEGGARLY SCOTLAND (in Latin Verse)	34
FRENCH SLANG SONG FROM VIDOCQ	36
DEATH IN THE POT	41
LUCTUS ON THE DEATH OF SIR DANIEL DONNELLY	47
Child Daniel, by Lord Byron. — Sorrow is Dry, by Dr. Scott, the Odontist. — Letter from Wordsworth; Extract from a Great Auto-Biographical Poem: Sir Daniel Donnelly, a Ballad. — Letter from Odoherty; Odonnelly, an Ode by Morgan Odoherty. — Letter from Mr. Seward; Ullaloo, a Greek Elegy. — Latin Version of the Ullaloo. — Hebrew Dirge, by Dr. John Barrett. — Jenning's Dirge over Donnelly. — Greek Epitaph on the Bruiser. — Dowden's Lamentation. — Speech at the Cork Institution	50
JOHN GILPIN AND MAZEPPA	83
THE EMBALMER (Latin Translations)	93
Take thy Old Cloak about Thee. — July the First. — The Groves of Blarney. — Mary Ambree — Sir Tristrem. — Epitaphs	96
IRISH MELODIES	103
St. Patrick ("A fig for St. Dennis of France.") — Lament of a Connaught Ranger. — Rafferty's Advice. — The Gathering of the Mahonys. — A Real Irish "Fly not yet." — The Impassioned Wave	108
LETTER-WRITING	118
BYRON TO MURRAY	125
ODE TO MRS. FLANAGAN	127
ODE TO MARSHAL GROUCHY	130

CONTENTS OF VOLUME II.

	PAGE
SEMIHORÆ BIOGRAPHICÆ	133
No. 1. — Winifred Jenkins	133
No. 2. — Dicky Gossip	139
No. 3. — Author of Waverley	145
DRINK AWAY!	152
DROUTHINESS (a Parody)	153
A LADLEFUL FROM THE DEVIL'S PUNCH BOWL	156
A Festal Ode. — What constitutes a Feast? — Lord Byron's Combolio.	157
ROYAL VISIT TO IRELAND (August, MDCCCXXI) —	
The King's Landing. — A Welcome to His Majesty. — Odoherty's Impromptu. — Translation of the Royal Adventus.	164
WHO WROTE "THE GROVES OF BLARNEY"?	181
FREE AND EASY TRANSLATIONS OF HORACE	182
REMARKS ON SHELLEY'S "ADONAIS".	190
FIRST NOTES OF AN INCIPIENT BALLAD-METRE-MONGER	201
THE WINE-BIBBER'S GLORY — A NEW SONG	205
LATIN TRANSLATION OF THE SAME	206
A RUNNING COMMENTARY ON THE RITTER BANN	210
CRITIQUE ON LORD BYRON	219
MODERN ENGLISH BALLADS —	
Spring's Return. — The Lament for Thurtell	226
MOORE-ISH MELODIES —	
The Last Lamp of the Alley. — 'Tis the Last Glass of Claret. — Rich and Rare. — Tom Stokes Lived Once. — Billingsgate Music. — To a Bottle of Old Port. — To the Finish I Went	230
ANECDOTES AND FACETIÆ	234
THE ROUTE	245
A HAPPY NEW-YEAR	248
HENDERSON THE HISTORIAN	250
PARODY ON WORDSWORTH	263
A TRAVELLER'S WEEK	264
LETTER FROM A WASHERWOMAN	279
THE NIGHT WALKER	292
SONG OF THE SEA	300
NEW HORATIAN READINGS	301
FIRST LOVE	304
THE CRABSTICK	313
SONNET	314
PANEGYRIC ON COLONEL PRIDE	315
THE EQUALITY OF THE SEXES	323
LETTERS FROM THE DEAD TO THE LIVING	327
THE LAST WORDS OF CHARLES EDWARDS, ESQ.	343

DR. MAGINN'S
MISCELLANEOUS WRITINGS.

The Odoherty Papers.

Pandemus Polyglott.*

IT has been well observed by somebody, that any man could make an interesting book if he would only give, honestly and without reserve, an account of such things as he himself had seen and heard; but if a man should add to this a candid history of his remarkable friends and acquaintance, how infinitely would he enhance the interest of his own! Some folks call this method of biography prosy—Heaven help their unphilosophical short-sightedness! Wherein consists the charm of Benvenuto Cellini's account of himself, which nobody can deny to be the *ne plus ultra* of all conceivable autobiographies? Why, it clearly arises from these two sources: first, from his not scrupling to give a straightforward narrative of every shadow of an adventure he lighted upon, not hesitating a moment to tell the whole truth at least, however often he may be so obliging as to favour us with a matter of ten times as much as that same; and, secondly, from the number of persons and personages he introduces his reader to, from the magnificent Francis to the unhappy engraver (I think), whom he despatched in so judicious a manner by that memorable thrust of his dagger into the back of the poor man's

* This article, evidently suggested by Father Prout's admirable translations and paraphrases, appeared in *Blackwood* for October, 1837.— M.

neck, whereby he so scientifically separated the vertebræ, and interrupted the succession of the spinal marrow, to the immediate attainment of his laudable object — to wit, the release of his fellow-sinner from his worldly sorrows. Again, in the other sex, from the lovely and capricious Duchess of Florence, with her rings and cameos and trumpery, down to the frail fair one whose fondness for Benvenuto so repeatedly jeopardized his capacity for enjoying the same. But there is a third charm about the good artist's book, and this may, perhaps, outweigh the other two — namely, his introduction of the heroes and magnates of his age *en déshabille*. Truly, if he who can show us a king, two popes, a reigning duke or two, duchesses, nobles, courtiers, and cardinals by the squadron, all in dressing-gowns and slippers, be not set up in the high places among those who have delighted their fellows, wherewithal shall a man claim that distinction? But I flatter myself, that charming as Benvenuto is, I must even supersede him by as much as learning is of more account than throat or marble-cutting, and learned men than heroes, &c.

But the world is not going at this time to enjoy the full benefit of my experiences. Let it suffice for the present that I afford mankind a glimpse of one of the most remarkable of men; one of those who leave their reputation as a legacy to their species, having had the uncommon forbearance to abstain from impairing the same in any degree by enjoying it themselves.

Without farther preface then, reader, give me leave to present to you Doctor Pandemus Polyglott, LL.D., Lugd. Bat. Olim. Soc., member of no end of societies, literary, and antiquarian, historical, philosophical, &c. &c. I would give you his tail of initials at full length, if it were not that I have generally found the dullest people take most pains in this behalf — and the Doctor is not dull — and, moreover, he has won by his pen a tail so considerable that it could not be doubled up in less than twice the space of that which the great Hero of the age, Wellington, has carved out with his sword, and which may be found occupying a good half page of the Army List. Besides, Dr. Polyglott is a living character; and though now as fine a specimen of an octogenarian as may be met with in a June day's march, yet he has not done winning to himself those bright scholarly honours which so safely ensure to their possessers an enviable obscurity with reference to the generality of people.

The Doctor, though a colossus of mind, has had the firmness through life to forego all those mundane advantages which his wondrous powers must have obtained for him, had such been his pleasure; and as in early life he gave himself up to the allurements of classical literature, so with a constancy seldom rivalled did he in manhood, and in age still does he adhere to the same sweet mistress. The fruits of this affection are manifold, as some forty MS. folios testify; but while the Doctor lives, his intimates alone will have the benefit of their acquaintance; for he is far too chary of his own personal comfort, too sensible of his own dignity, to sacrifice the one, or diminish his own proud sense of the other, by trusting the smallest of his learned labours to the caprice or indifference of a world engaged for the most part in pursuits which he looks down upon with pity, and would regard, if he were less good than he is, with contempt.

But these limits will not allow me to do justice to a tithe of the merits of my worthy Nestor; so, reader, we (you and I) must be content with what the allotted space will admit. You will not be surprised, after the slight insight I have given you into the character of Dr. Polyglott's mind, and the extent of his erudition, to learn that the good cheerful old man is altogether "wrapt and throwly lapt" in reminiscences and thoughts, the beginning, middle, and end whereof are classical.

"Ay, ay, boy," said he to me (I am forty-five) one day, when I had been lauding and magnifying sundry of our own poets in his presence, "Ay, ay, boy, call 'em poets if you will—mere mushrooms—Shakspere—didst ever hear of Sophocles?—Jonson—Bah!—poor neoteric stuff—vernacular. There is but one good couplet in the language, only one."

"And whose is that, sir?" I ventured to ask.

"Pope's."

I was thunderstruck, so often had I heard the old man revile "Pope, the Anti-Homeric," as he delighted to call him, "the clipper of the old Greek's solid coin, to reduce it to the beggarly standard of wit's understanding."

"Pope's, sir," said I, in wonder; "pray, repeat it."

Slowly and deliberately did the Doctor recite—

"They who a living marble seek,
Must carve in Latin or in Greek."

Never till this hour had I dreamt of the possibility of the Doctor having read a line of English poetry, except in a translation, and I ventured to hint thus much.

"Not read English poetry!" said he, "why, half my amusements would be at an end were it not for your so-called poets—common plagiarists. Not one of them but goes out on the highway to plunder the old Greeks and Romans. Oh! how I love to nab the filchers."

Here was new ground broken between me and the Doctor, and right well have I profited by it; in almost every branch of modern poetry have I tried him, and almost invariably has he shown me that our great men are but pickers-up of the crumbs that have fallen from the tables of their masters, of old parallel passages that most men can quote. But what astonishes me most, is the readiness with which the Doctor detects whole pieces translated from the more obscure ancients; many of them, indeed, whose works are generally believed to be lost entirely. Having been frequently startled at this, I thought I would *set* him with a poem, for which he could have no ancient parallel; accordingly, one evening, I read him, from the Anti-Jacobin, Canning's Knifegrinder.

"The varlet!" cried the Doctor, "reach me vol. 17 of the MSS."

I gave it him, and forthwith did he spread before my eyes the following:

Σαπφικα.	Sapphica.
ὁ φιλανθρωπος και ὁ σιδηροτεκτων.	Philanthropus et Faber Ferrarius.
Φιλανθρωπος.	Dialogus.
	Philanthropus.
πη βαδιζεις, πτωχε σιδηροτεκτον ;	"Hinc ita quônam, Faber o egene ?
ἠ θ' ὁδος στυφλη, σφαλερος θ' ὁ κυκλος·	Et via horrescit, rota claudicatque ;
ψυχρος εἰ, κἀχουσι περισκελη, και τρημα γαληρος.	Flat notus ; rimis petasus laborat, Tritaque bracca.
οὐκ ἀγανος οἰδε, σιδηροτεκτον, ὁστις ἐν διφροις μαλακοισι κλινει, δεινον ὡς κραξαι "ψαλιδας τε ϶ηγω ἠδε μαχαιρας."	"O Father languens, patet haud superbis, Appia ut rhedis habet otiantes, Quid sit ad cotem vocitare cultros Fissaque ferra.

τις δε σ', ὦ'ταν, ὦσε σιδηροθηγειν ;
τις τυραννος σ' ἀφνεος ἠδικη εν ;
ἠ μεγας σ' ὁ γαιοκρατωρ ; ὁ πρεσβυς ;
    ἠ κδικος αἰσχρως ;

ἠδικης' ὁ γαιοκρατωρ σε θηρων
κειμενων ; ἠ σ' ἐκδεκατευς' ὁ πρεσβυς ;
ἠ 'κδικος λῃστης ἀπενεγκε σου το
    παν δι' ἀγωνα ;

(οἰσθα Τομπανου "Μεροπων τα χρη-
    στα ;")
σταγματ' οἰκτοι' ἐν βλεφαροιν τρεουσιν,
ἐκπεσοντ' ἐιπῃς ὁποταν συ πικρας
    μυθον ἀνιας.

    Σιδηροτεκτων.

μυθον ; ὠποποι· ἐπος οὐκ ἔχω τι·
ἐν καπηλειῳ δ' ὁτ' ἐπινον ἐχθες,
μου γαληρον ἠδε περισκελη τις
    δρυψ' ἐν ἀγωνι.

ἀλλα ῥαβδουχοι τοτε μ' εἱλον ἀνδρες,
ἠγαγον δε μ' αὐτικα προς δικαστην·
χὠ δικαστης ποδοκακῃ μ' ἐθηκεν
    ὥστε πλανητα.

νυν δε χαιροιην μεγα σοι προπινων,
δεσποτα, ζυθου δεπας, εἰ συ δοιης
δραχμ' ἐμοιγ'· ἀλλ' οὐποτε μοι τα μεν
    πολιτικα μελλει.

    Φιλανθρωπος.

δραχμα σοι ; ταχ' εἰς ἀϊδην ἀπελθε,
σχετλι', ὁς τινειν κακα τοσσ' ἀβουλεις,
φαυλ', ἀναισθητ', ἀδοκιμαστ', ἀεικες,
    ἐκβολιμ', αφρον.

"Dic, Faber, cultros acuisse quis te
Egit? anne in te locuples tyrannus
Sævii? terræ dominus? sacerdos?
    Causidicusve?

"Ob feras terræ dominus necatus?
Aut tenax poscens decumas sacerdos?
Lite vel rem causidicus malignè
    Abstulit omnem?

"Nonne nôsti 'Jura Hominum' Païni?
Ecce! palpebris lacrymæ tremiscunt,
Inde casuræ simul explicâris
    Tristia fata."

    Faber.

"Fata — Dii magni! nihil est quod
    edam,
Ni quòd hesternâ ut biberem in popinâ
Nocte lis orta! heu! periere braccæ
    Atque galerus.

"Pacis occurrunt mihi tum ministri,
Meque Prætoris rapiunt ad aulam:
Prætor erronis properat numellâ
    Figere plantas."

"Jamque gaudebo tibi si propinem
Poculum, tete mihi dante nummum;
Me tamen stringo, neque, pro virili,
    Publica curo."

    Philanthropus.

"An tibi nummum? potius ruinam;
Perdite, ulcisci mala tanta nolens;
Sordide, infelix, inhoneste, prave
    Turpis et excors."

Sapphics.

The Friend of Humanity and the Knifegrinder

Friend of Humanity.

"Needy Knifegrinder! whither art thou going?
Rough is the road; thy wheel is out of order;
Bleak blows the blast; your hat has got a hole in't,
    So have your breeches.

"Weary knifegrinder, little know the proud ones,
Who in their coaches roll along the turnpike-
Road, what hard work 'tis crying all day, 'Knives and
    Scissors to grind O.'

"Tell me, Knifegrinder, how came you to grind knives?
Did some rich man tyrannically use you?
Was it the 'squire? or parson of the parish?
    Or the attorney?

"Was it the 'squire for killing of his game? or
Covetous parson for his tithes destraining?
Or roguish lawyer made you lose your little
    All in a lawsuit?

"Have you not read the 'Rights of Man' by Tom Paine?
Drops of compassion tremble on my eyelids,
Ready to fall as soon as you have told your
    Pitiful story."

Knifegrinder.

"Story! God bless you? I have none to tell, sir;
Only last night a-drinking at the Chequers,
This poor old hat and breeches, as you see, were
    Torn in a scuffle.

"Constables came up for to take me into
Custody; they took me before the justice;
Justice Oldmixon put me in the parish
    Stocks for a vagrant.

"I should be glad to drink your honor's health in
A pot of beer, if you will give me sixpence;
But for my part I never love to meddle
    With politics, sir."

Friend of Humanity.

"*I* give thee sixpence! I will see thee damn'd first,
Wretch, whom no sense of wrongs can rouse to vengeance;
Sordid, unfeeling, reprobate, degraded,
    Spiritless outcast."

"There, sir," cried the Doctor; "even George Canning's hands were not quite so clean, you see; now I will tell you how, as I take it, he came by the original. In the University Library at Leyden, where I first got my fellowship, were near a cart-load of MSS. of various ages and languages. The greater part of these had, as far as I could learn, never been examined, and they were indeed considered as little better than lumber.

Fired by the success which had attended Angelo Mai's researches in a similar field, I diligently set about examining, collating, and transcribing these MSS. Among the rest was a small volume of tattered parchment, of singularly ancient appearance, and grievously decayed by the action of damp and vermin. To this, which was apparently a MS. of the tenth century, I devoted my most serious attention, and succeeded in deciphering the present very curious dialogue, which is, I believe, unique, and two other poems. The Latin version was made by Professor Groetbaum, who printed the three poems, and circulated an impression of five copies among his most select friends. One of these copies was purchased at the sale of Professor Krautstuffer's library, after his death, by an Englishman named Heber, I think, who came express from London upon the occasion, and gave for the tract a sum equal to about forty-two pounds English. From this copy, I doubt not, arose George Canning's translation."

Turning over the leaves of the folio the Doctor had bid me reach for him, my eye lighted upon the following anacreontic, which I very easily recollected as an old English acquaintance, in spite of his present Greek costume. I named this fact to the Doctor, and ventured to suggest the possibility of his having been imposed upon by some of his scholarly friends at Leyden : but I will first transcribe the poems, Greek and English, and then give the reader Dr. Polyglott's highly interesting account:—

εἰς μυιαν πινουσαν οἰνον.
πολυεργε, πολυπραγμων,
καταδιψοωσα μυια,
ἀγε δητα, συμπιωμεν·
μεγα χαιρε· σοι μεν ἐστι
μεθυ παν τοδ᾽, ἠν δυνησῃ
ῥοφεειν νιν εκροφειν τε.
δρεπε νυν βιου τα τερπνα,
ὀλιγος βιος, βραχυς τε.
ὁ δ᾽ ἐμος τε σος θ᾽ ὁμοιω,
τελος ἀμφω εἰστρεχοντε.
θερος ἐν σος ἐστ᾽ ἐμος δε
πλεον οὐδεν ἐστιν, εἰ και
τρις ἐνεστιν εἰκοσ᾽ αὐτῳ.
θερε᾽ ὡς τρις εἰκοσ᾽ εἰσαν,
βραχε᾽ ὡς και ἐν φανοῦνται.

Written extempore by a Gentleman, occasioned by a fly drinking out of his cup.

" Busy, curious, thirsty fly,
Drink with me and drink as I ;
Freely welcome to my cup,
Couldst thou sip, and sip it up.
Make the most of life you may,
Life is short and fades away.

" Both alike are mine and thine,
Hastening quick to their decline ;
Thine's a summer, mine no more,
Though repeated to threescore.
Threescore summers, when they're gone,
Will appear as short as one !

"Marvellous!" cried the Doctor, when I had recited to him this well-known song—"Marvellous! That ode, sir, I doubt not, was written by Anacreon himself. That the Λ>υγεσιν αί γυναικες' should be admitted into all collections, while this is rejected, appears to me the consummation of critical injustice."

"As how, sir?"

"Why, you know, the λεγειν κ. λ. τ.' was discovered by Henri Estienne on an old book-cover."

"Assuredly, sir," continued the Doctor. "When the vellum came to be stripped from the cover, and strictly examined, on the *other side* appeared the ode, of which this unknown translator has tried to palm off his version upon us for an original drinking-song. Too bad—too bad! No doubt, copies of both odes were taken, and, less doubt, they were distributed among the literati of that time, by which means some stray copy having in a later age fallen into the hands of our anonymous plagiary, he has done this evil thing."

The Doctor, like most other persons of taste, is much addicted to music, and in his early days was no mean proficient therein; but his great age now materially interferes with his enjoyment of this pleasure, for he is somewhat deaf, and, as he facetiously observes, there are *trumpeters* enough in concert-rooms without him. However, he does not altogether abstain from the delights of harmony, for it is his rule to attend one concert, and only one, during the season. On these occasions I am always his companion; and in the course of this duty last season, I had a very striking proof of his readiness in detecting plagiarism. We were at the Hanover Square Rooms, and it was a benefit concert, I forget whose, but all the musical magnates in London were there. Presently appeared Henry Phillips[*] to sing his admirable ditty, "Woman." During the song I observed that the Doctor appeared surprised and somewhat puzzled; when it was over, he desired me to refer to the *libretto*, and tell him the author's name; it was written down as by Geo. Withers.

"It is a robbery," said the Doctor.

"It is a mutilation," said I. "Some hod-and-mortar litera-

[*] The celebrated baritone singer.—M.

teur has been paring down to concert-room dimensions one of the few lyrics that give Withers a claim to the title of poet."

"Oh ho!" cried the Doctor; "then when we get home I will show you what a thief even a puritan may be."

Our conversation was here interrupted by the appearance of an elegant young lady, who came forward and sung the following song, which, to my no small amusement, and the equal annoyance of sundry of his neighbors, the Doctor actually accompanied with its monkish original; thus—

Dr. Polyglott.	Young Lady.
O Terræ puella,	Child of Earth,
Auricoma, bella,	With the golden hair!
Mens puraque, et ora	Thy soul is too pure,
Te vetant decora	And thy face too fair,
Incolere tribus	To dwell with creatures
Mortalium, quibus	Of mortal mould,
Sunt verba fervoris	Whose lips are warm
At corda rigoris.	As their hearts are cold.
Nobiscum vagare,	Roam, Roam
Fit domus in aere;	To our fairy home.
O Terræ puella,	Child of Earth,
Auricoma, bella!	With the golden hair!
Sis pars chorearum	Thou shalt dance
Cum summa nympharum	With the Fairy Queen
In nocte æstiva,	O' summer nights
Sub Cynthia viva,	On the moon-lit green,
Dum Musica tales	To music murmuring
Dat sonitus quales	Sweeter far
Non quisquam audivit	Than ever was heard
Sub sole qui vivit	'Neath the morning star.
	Roam, roam, &c.

Great was the Doctor's glee at this detection, and greater was mine at his mode of making it known. Indeed all was glee with us that evening; and when we had returned home, and disposed of that *sine quâ non* of all sensible amusement-hunters, a light supper after the play or concert, or whatever it may be, and the Doctor's meerschaum (one of his Leyden habits) was in high puff, we naturally took to talking over the evening's entertainment. Of course the various performers passed in review, and, among the rest, Phillips escaped not the hearty commendations of both of us.

"By the by," said the Doctor, "you called his 'Woman' a mutilation—have you the ballad as written by Withers?"

"I have," said I, producing a volume of Ritson's Collection.

"And here is its original," said the Doctor, laying his hand on one of the aforenamed vols. of his MSS. "Now let us read—begin thou"—and I began—

Dr. Polyglott.	Myself.
Anne ego depositis tabescam viribus exspes,	Shall I wasting in despair,
Et patiar cum sit fœmina pulcra mori?	Die because a woman's fair?
Anne meas pallore genas cura anxia tinget,	Or make pale my cheek with care,
Quod petit alterius mala colore rosam?	Because another's rosy are?
Exsuperet splendore diem sine labe venustas,	Be she fairer than the day,
Florigerumve parit quod nova Maia decus;	Or the flowery fields in May;
Illi ni videar qui sim bene dignus amatu,	If she think not well of me,
Egregium refert quid decus omne mihi?	What care I how fair she be?
Anne ego collabi patiar mea corda dolore,	Should my heart be grieved or pine,
Quod mansueta fuit fœmina visa mihi?	'Cause I see a woman kind?
Ingenio vel quæ cùm sit bene prædita culto,	Or a well-disposed nature
Ora simul monstret qualia adoret amor?	Joined with a lovely feature?
Si pietate suâ, si mansuetudine laudes	Be she meeker, kinder than
Turturis exsuperet, vel, pelicane, tuas;	Turtle-dove or pelican;
Ia me ni pia sit, ni sit mansueta puella,	If she be not so to me,
Quid refert pietas officiosa mihi?	What care I how kind she be?
Fœmina quòd præstat reliquis bonitate, movebit	Shall a woman's virtues move
Ergone dum peream me muliebris amor?	Me to perish for her love?
Sint merita illius summâ dignissima laude,	Or her well-deservings known
Nonne igitur meriti sim memor ipse mei?	Make me quite forget my own?
Actu si bonitas ita conspiciatur in omni,	Be she with such goodness blest
Ut ductum e meritis Optima nomen erit;	As may gain her name of Best:
Me nisi participem placeat bonitatis habere,	If she be not such to me,
Quid refert quantâ sit bonitate mihi?	What care I how good she be?
Quòd Fortuna nimis videatur larga puellæ,	'Cause her fortune seems too high,
Anne ego desipiens in mala fata ruam?	Shall I play the fool and die?
Mos est ingenium queis nobile, puraque mens est,	Those that bear a noble mind, When they want of riches find,
Exiguæ quandō comperiuntur opes,	Think what with them they would do,
Quid cum divitiis facerent reputare salaces	Who without them dare to woo;
Qui guzâ fiunt deficiente proci.	
Et nisi fas in eâ talem mihi cernere mentem	And unless that mind I see,
Quid refert, quamvis magna puella mihi?	What care I though great she be?

Magna sit, aut bona, sit mansueta aut denique
    pulchra,
Spem me non igitur destituisse sinam;
In me, crede mihi, foveat si pectus amorem,
Ipse prius patiar quàm gemat illa mori;
Quod si sincerè parvi me pendat amantem,
    In rem contemptæ fas sit abire malam:
Scilicet ut placeat mihi ni sit facta puella,
Quid refert cui sit facta puella mihi?

Great, or good, or kind, or fair,
    I will ne'er the more despair —
If she love me, this believe,
I will die ere she shall grieve;
If she slight me when I woo,
I can scorn and let her go;
    If she be not made for me,
    What care I for whom she be?

"A pretty tolerable proof of disregard to the Eighth Commandment, I think," continued the Doctor; "but don't let us be too hard upon poor George; he was a fine fellow in his way, and, sorry as was the rubbish he perpetrated in after time, this song must be admitted to be far above much of the same kind of poetry at that day;—it is, at least, a most excellent translation."

"Surely, sir," said I, "the author of that poem must have been proud of his translator."

"Possibly," replied the Doctor, "if he understood English; but I suspect two bars to the author's enjoyment — first, his not understanding the language; and, secondly, his not having lived to Withers's time. In short, the author is unknown. I take him to have been some one of the Belgic writers of the earlier part of the 16th century — Hadrian Marius, perhaps, or one of those bright satellites, revolving round the planet of Julius Cæsar Scaliger."

I ventured to suggest to Dr. Polyglott the possibility of some more modern bard having translated Withers's English into Latin; and reminded the Doctor of the great number of excellent songs produced about the date of that under discussion, viz. 1620. I remember particularly specifying Waller's "Rose," as of surpassing excellence in its line. But I had taken an unfortunate view of the matter: my first suggestion called forth from the Doctor a most vigorous expression of contempt for my judgment. Good old man! I think I see him now, as, ὑπ' ὀφρύσ' ἰδών, and emitting a fog of reek from both ends of his *écume de mer*, he curled his lip and cried, "Translate English into Latin! Fie, oh, fie! The world never yet held a fool capable of such absurdity. Why sir, it would be to dress a lazar in a royal robe.

But it is too gross a notion to be entertained — pooh!" and forth rushed another eruption of smoke and sparks from the bowl; for his pipe was finished, and the act of refilling it alone restored him to sufficient composure to notice my mention of Waller.

"That 'Rose' you talk of," said the Doctor, "I know it well: that robbery of Waller's was the death of a professor at Leyden."

"How, sir?" asked I, modestly.

"Thus," replied the Doctor. "Wätinstern, in those days Professor of Humanity, foolishly fell in love; and disdaining, as in duty bound, if not in taste, the vernacular, wrote the original of the 'Rose,' upon the obdurate Frau Jacqueline von Krakertsting; and it was rumored, would have won her by it, had she chanced to have understood the language it was written in. Copies were multiplied among the literati, and much fame resulted to the Professor, who, upon the ill success of his forlorn hope upon the damsel, pined and became consumptive. One day a friend, thinking to delight him (for he was what is called an excellent English scholar) brought him Waller's version, which was just then in high vogue; Wätinstern read and admired it; but finding that the Briton had not acknowledged the Batavian origin of his poemation, and, moreover, had omitted the fine pair of moral couplets which close it, fell into so violent a train of angry objurgation upon his meanness, that excessive wrath produced an attack of hæmophthysis, which, in a few days carried off the Professor, who is reported to have expired muttering Martial's line:—

'Stat contrà dicitque tibi tua pagina fur es.'

But here is Wätinstern's poem: place Waller's alongside it, and judge for yourself what cause the former had for his wrath.

WATINSTERN.	WALLER.
I, Rosa, purpurei flos jocundissime prati,	Go, lovely Rose,
Dic cui labe pari tempora meque terit,	Tell her, that wastes her time and me,
Illius laudes tecum persæpe paranti,	That now she knows,
Quam pulchra et dulcis visa sit illa mihi.	When I resemble her to thee, How sweet and fair she seems to be.
Dic cui flore datur primo gaudere juventæ,	Tell her that's young,
Gratia quæ verò ne videatur avet;	And shuns to have her beauties spied, That hadst thou sprung

Nescia fortè virum si te genuisset cremus,
Mortem tu laudis nescia passa fores.
Nil valet omninò lucem male passa venustas.
In lucem veniat protenus illa, jube.
Quam petit omnis amor virgo patiatur amorem,
Nec, cum miretur, quis stet in ore rubor.

Tum morere, ut rerum videat communia fata
Rararum, fato conscia facta tuo.
Parte frui fas est quam parvâ temporis illis,
Queis tantum veneris tantaque forma datur.

Sed quamvis moriare, tamen post fata peracta
Qui fuit ante tuis frondibus adsit odor.
Temnere sic discat Pietatem Temporis arma;
Vivere Virtutem cum mera Forma perit.

In valleys where no men abide,
Thou might'st have uncommended died.
Small is the worth
Of Beauty from the light retired;
Bid her come forth,
Suffer herself to be desired,
And not blush so to be admired.

Then die; that she
The common fate of all things rare
May read in thee;
How small a part of time they share,
That are so wondrous bright and fair.

Yet though they fade,
From thy dead leaves let fragrance rise,
And teach the maid
That goodness Time's rude hand defies,
And virtue lives when beauty dies.

"Hold thee," cried the Doctor, as I read the last stanza of the "Rose;" "why, how is this? Surely Waller did not translate Wätinstern's four last lines after all?"

I replied, by showing the Doctor how Kirke White had added that stanza, and how it was found, in his autograph, upon the margin of his copy of Waller.

"There again!" cried my learned friend, "you see they are all alike; not one will acknowledge that he is a mere translator. I dare be sworn Ben Jonson, if he were alive, would deny his obligations to Joannes Secundus, Muretus, &c., for some of his best amatory pieces. You know of course how much he is their debtor?"

I confessed my ignorance of the matter.

"I thought as much," said Dr. Polyglott. "I was led to suspect it, when I lighted the other day in a collection upon a little poem, professing to be an original of Ben's and beginning,

'Take, oh take those lips away,' &c."

"Surely," said I, "that is genuine."

"Oh, surely!" replied the Doctor, with a smile, "as genuine a translation as possible of this poem of Secundus."

He handed me a volume of his MSS., and I began, according to his direction, to read.

"Stop!" interrupted the Doctor, "Do you know the English?"

"I do," said I.

"Well, then, repeat it, line for line, with the original, and you will be better able to judge how far the Englishman is indebted to him of the Hague."

I read as follows:—

CARMEN:—AUCTORE JOANNE SECUNDO HAGENSI.

Hinc ista, hinc procul amove labella,
Quæ tam dulcè fuere perjurata;
Auroræ et radiis pares ocellos,
Luces mane novum e viâ trahentes.
At refer mihi basia huc, sigilla,
Frustrâ impressa tamen, sigilla amoris.
Oh! cela nivis ista colla, cela,
Ornant quæ gremium tibi gelatum;
Quorum in culminibus rosæ vigentes
Sunt quales referunt Aprilis horæ;
At primùm mea corda liberato,
His a te gelidis ligata vinclis.

SONG BY BEN JONSON.

TAKE, oh take those lips away,
   That so sweetly were forsworn;
And those eyes, the break of day,
   Lights that do mislead the morn:
But my kisses bring again,
   Seals of love, but seal'd in vain.

Hide, oh hide those hills of snow,
   Which thy frozen bosom bears;
On whose tops the pinks that grow
   Are of those that April wears;
But first set my poor heart free,
Bound in these icy chains by thee.

"It is very strange," murmured I, reluctantly forced to admit the Doctor's charge against "Rare Ben." "But how does it happen that this poem does not appear in any of the numerous editions of Secundus?"

"Oh! that is easily accounted for," answered the Doctor; "none of Secundus's works were published during his life. Indeed it was probably owing to the piracy of a German bookseller of the 16th century that they were not suffered to perish."

I begged the Doctor to relate the story to me; and he continued—"Upon the execution of Sir Thomas More, you know, all Europe rung with indignant reproaches against the royal monster of England; and Secundus, then a spirited youth of two-and-twenty or so, wrote an epitaph and nenia upon the murdered ex-Chancellor. These were only circulated among his private friends (being considered somewhat too hard upon his patron, the Emperor's uncle, for publication), until a copy fell into the hands of the above-mentioned bibliopole, who printed and published the two poems in the early part of the year 1536; but the pirated copy was so unlike that which Secundus had written, that Hadrian Marius, in vindication of his brother's scholarship, had the poems printed from his own copy; and they were published during the same year at Louvain. Much posthumous fame accrued to Secundus from this publication; and in 1538 the men of Leyden gave the world the first edition of the same author's justly celebrated Basia. Secundus's works were now much sought after by the scholars of Leyden, and there are still several pieces of his preserved among the MSS. in the University Library. You will find copies of them all in that volume. This is among the number, and I, at least, have no doubt whatever of its authenticity."

I thanked the Doctor for his narrative, and hazarded an expression of surprise at his peculiar readiness in detecting this kind of literary buccaneering.

"My dear boy," replied he, "you can have no idea how general the evil practice is. Indeed I wonder other scholars have not taken up the cudgels in defence of the plundered Grecians and Latinists. Now you yourself might do the state some service in this respect if you would, and you cannot conceive how entertaining the pursuit is."

I modestly professed my incapability.

"Why, truly," said the Doctor, "you are not at present quick at detecting a plagiarism; but by practice and the aid of my volumes, you would in a few years become capable of filling my place in the learned world when I shall vacate it. But you must devote yourself to a severe course of study, ere you can hope to attain the requisite amount of proficiency. Why, it is a curious fact that I heard you not many days ago unconsciously chanting a bacchanalian ode of Cæsius Bassus."

"Me, sir!" cried I, in amazement; "Why I thought there were no remains of that lyrist extant?"

"So think many," said the Doctor; "but I know the reverse. Among the shockingly mutilated MSS. whence I rescued the

Greek Sapphics, which I showed you the other day, beginning ηι θαϊζεις; κ. τ. λ. was a very much injured paper MS. containing several fragments of lyric odes, one only of which I was enabled to make out entirely; and that only after much toil, and by the aid of a good deal of conjecture. That ode I heard you vocalizing in its Anglicised condition, as 'The Glasses sparkle on the Board.' Come now, chant it again, and I will reward you with the Alcaic original as an accompaniment."

I did as I was bid: and after this manner was the Doctor's assertion proved:—

CARMEN: AUCTORE CÆSIO BASSO.

SONG: THE GLASSES SPARKLE.

En! pocla mensis compositis micant;
  Vini refulget purpureus color;
    Regnant voluptates, feruntque
      Gaudia deliciasque secum.
Invitat Euhoe! nox; absit dies;
  Indulgeamus nunc genium mero,
    Mergamus et curæ vel atri
      Quod superest cyatho doloris.

THE glasses sparkle on the board,
  The wine is ruby bright;
    The reign of pleasure is restored,
      Of ease and gay delight:
The day is gone; the night's our own,
  Then let us feast the soul;
    Should any pain or care remain,
      Why drown it in the bowl.

Sunt qui gravari tristitiâ ferunt
  Vitam; sed o! ne credite fabulam—
    An Liber effundit dolorem?
      An Veneris lacrymas ocelli?
Omnis Catonum copia desipit
  Vinclis volentum stringere gaudia;—
    Si vita fert luctum, sodales,
      Heus iterum! cyatho lavemus.

This world they say 's a world of wo;
  But that I do deny;
    Can sorrow from the goblet flow?
      Or pain from beauty's eye?
The wise are fools with all their rules,
  Who would our joys control—
    If life's a pain, I say't again,
      Why drown it in the bowl.

Poeta labi quàm rapidè monet
  Tempus; quid ergò, quid sapientius
    Quàm spargere in pennis Falernum,
      Cùmque movet celeres morari?
Hæc nostra nox est; nos quoque floribus
Spargemus horas usque volubiles;
    Mergemus et curæ vel atri
      Quod superest cyatho Doloris.

That time flies fast the poet sings,
  Then surely 'twould be wise
    In rosy wine to dip his wings,
      And catch him as he flies.
This night is ours: then strew with flow'rs
  The moments as they roll;
    If any pain or care remain,
      Why drown it in the bowl.

"And is that an ode of Cæsius Bassus, sir?" asked I; "what a pity you could not recover any more."

"Ah!" cried the Doctor, "it was a pity; the more so, as the MS. is unique."

"By the by," said I, "how did you discover it to belong to Bassus?"

"Why, thus:—Upon a very much tattered leaf, detached from the rest (the MS. was in the form of a book), I found the letters C . . . s B . . . i C . . . na; the hiatus are obviously to be filled up thus: Cæsii Bassi Carmina."

I own I was hardly satisfied; but I did not like to hazard offending my friend by a doubt; so I drew his attention to a copy of choriambics, with a translation appended, being the only specimen of English poetry contained in the volume.

"Those poems," said the Doctor, in reply to my enquiries, "were a joint tribute from myself and our excellent and talented friend, Matthew Child, to the widow Schwartz, upon the loss of her only son, a youth of the highest promise. The lady was an Englishwoman; so, remembering the fate of Wätinstern's poem in former days, I determined to procure an English translation to present with my poem to my friend's widow. I selected my old friend Mat. for this office, and right well did he respond to my application. Come, indulge me by reading the poems, Latin and English." I read them thus:—

FILIOLUM MORIBUNDUM VIDUA ALLOQUITUR—AUCTORE P. P.

EHEU! hi gemitus, nate, tibi; vita relabitur;
Jamque olim roseis pallida Mors insidet in genis.
Amisere oculi jam radios; vocis abest melos;
Et fractus quasi flos turbinibus, præteriit decus.
Actum est. Amplius haud corda micant—cum lacrymis parens,
Haud ingrata tamen, quod tribuit Jupiter, accipit:
Luctus corda premit; gutta frequens ex oculis cadit
Matris, dum tibi post fata patent æthereæ domus.
Ridentem genetricem assoliti sæpe pedes sequi,
Nomen blæsa loqui murmuribus lingua puertiæ;
Auratæ niveus quas modo frons exhibuit comæ;
Par labrumque rosæ; pallida Mors! hæc ubi jam latent?
Dextrâ cæsa tuâ, quem facis heu! cuncta tenet sopor;
Dum matri superest nil, tacitæ nil nisi lachrymæ,
Aut vocem simulans hei mihi! vox Fantaseos tuam;
Aut frustrâ in pueri, dum repeto, flere cadavera.
Mox condet tumulus reliquias ex oculis meis,
Dum vitæ miseram mæsta viam solaque persequar!
Manes inter amans sedem habitat primus et unicus,
Extremæque hodie tecum abeunt deliciæ, puer.

The Widow to her Dying Child—by Matthew Child.

That sigh's for thee, thou precious one; life's tide is ebbing fast,
And o'er thy once all-joyous face death's sickly hue is cast.
Thine azure eye hath lost its ray, thy voice its buoyant tone,
And, like a flower the storm has crush'd, thy beauty's past and gone.

Another pang, and all is o'er—the pulseless heart is still,
Meekly, though sad, thy mother bows to the Almighty's will;
Grief presses heavy on my heart, my tears fall thick and fast,
But thou—thou art in heaven, my child, life's chequer'd dream is past.

The busy feet that gladly ran thy mother's smile to greet;
The prattling tongue that lisp'd her name in childhood's accents sweet;
The glossy curl that beam'd like gold upon thy snowy brow;
The lip, meet rival of the rose, O Death! where are they now?

Wither'd beneath thine icy touch; lock'd in thy dull cold sleep;
While all the joy a mother knows is silently to weep;
Or start as Fancy's echo wakes thy voice to mock her pain,
Then turn to gaze upon thy corse, and feel her grief is vain.

The grave, the dark cold grave, full soon will hide thee from my view,
While I my weary way through life in solitude pursue;
My early and my only love is number'd with the dead,
And thou—my last sole joy on earth—thou too, my boy, hast fled.

"I read somewhere but a few days ago this very translation, without any hint of its being so."

"Impossible!" cried the Doctor, "Mat. is too honourable a man for that, and you may well be sure I did not publish it."

"Nevertheless," persisted I, "I could swear I saw it; and now I come to recollect, it is in this book." Taking up a volume of the Saturday Magazine, I searched, and lo! there it was at page ——, vol. ——, signed, K. D. W.

"That beats all," cried Dr. Polyglott, "K. D. W. then has robbed us both—hocus-pocusing Mat.'s translation into an original of his own, and plundering me at the same moment."

The Doctor was seriously affected; seeing which I recommended his pillow to him, the rather as daylight was breaking in—for, what with the meerschaum and the Latin, the Doctor had lost all ken of time, and the night had sped away like a winged dream. My young-hearted old patron took my hint and went to bed, and so our conversation ended—from the which, if our reader have derived neither pleasure nor profit. Heaven help him! If, however he have enjoyed either the one or the other, or both, let him rejoice in the gratifying expectancy of farther revelations, in future days, of the learned lucubrations of Dr. Pandemus Polyglott.

Three Goblets of Wine.*

Τρεῖς γάρ μόνους κρατῆρας ἐγκεραννύω
Τοῖς εὖ φρονοῦσι· τὸν μὲν ὑγιείας ἕνα.
Ὃν πρῶτον ἐκπίνουσι· τὸν δὲ δεύτερον
Ἔρωτος ἡδονῆς τε· τὸν δὲ τρίτον δ᾽
ὕπνου,
Ὃν εἰς πίοντες οἱ σοφοὶ κεκλημένοι
Οἴκαδε βαδίζουσ᾽. ὁ δὲ τέταρτος οὐκέτι
Ἡμέτερός ἐστ᾽, ἀλλ᾽ ὕβρεως. ὁ δὲ τέμπτος, βοῆς.
Ἕκτος δὲ μανίας, ὥστε καὶ βάλλειν ποιεῖν.
Πολὺς γὰρ εἰς ἓν μικρὸν ἀγγεῖον χυθεὶς
Ὑποσκελίζει ῥᾶστα τοὺς πεπωκότας.

THREE goblets of wine
Alone should comprise
The extent of the tipple
Of those that are wise.

The first is for health;
And the second I measure,
To be quaffed for the sake
Of love, and of pleasure.

The third is for sleep;
And, while it is ending,
The prudent will homeward
Be thinking of wending.

The fourth, not our own,
Makes insolence glorious;
And the fifth ends in shouting,
And clamour uproarious

And those who a sixth
Down their weasands are pouring,
Already are bruising,
And fighting, and flooring.

Oh! the tight little vessel,
If often we fill it,
How it trips up the heels
Of those who may swill it!

---

* This was published in *Blackwood* for May, 1834, as sung at THE NOCTES. The Greek was there represented as written by Eubulus, a comic poet, contemporary with Eubilides of Miletus, the preceptor of Demosthenes. I suspect that Maginn wrote the Greek as well as the English. — M.

Judy Callaghan.*

I.

'Twas on a windy night,
  About two o'clock in the morning,
An Irish lad so tight,
  All wind and weather scorning,
At Judy Callaghan's door,
  Sitting upon the palings,
His love-tale he did pour,
  And this in part his wailings:
      Only say
You'll be Mrs. Brallaghan;
      Don't say nay,
Charming Judy Callaghan.

II.

Oh! list to what I say,
  Charms you've got like Venus;
Own your love you may,
  There's the wall between us.
You lie fast asleep,
  Snug in bed a-snoring;
Round the house I creep,
  Your hard heart imploring.
      Only say
You'll have Mr. Brallaghan;
      Don't say nay,
Charming Judy Callaghan.

I.

Erat turbida nox
  Hora secunda mane,
Quando proruit vox
  Carmen in hoc inane;
Viri miseri mens
  Meditabatur hymen,
Hinc puellæ flens
  Stabat obsidens limen.
      Semel tantum dic
Eris nostra Lalage;
      Ne recuses sic,
Dulcis Julia Calage.

II.

Planctibus aurem fer,
  Venere tu formosior;
Dic hos muros per,
  Tuo favore potior!
Voce beatum fac;
  En, dum dormis, vigilo,
Nocte obambulans hac
  Domum planctu stridulo.
      Semel tantum dic
Eris nostra Lalage;
      Ne recuses sic,
Dulcis Julia Calage.

---

* After much search, (having vainly sent to England for a copy,) I have found this Latin translation of the well known Irish Ballad of "Judy Callaghan," in an old number of the *Southern Literary Messenger*. It is there stated to have been given to the Editor by the late Mr. Reynolds, the eminent classical teacher in the Richmond Academy, and is credited to "a Kerry Latinist." It is very true that all the County Kerry men ("conticuere omnes") are excellent Latin scholars, but equally true that Maginn wrote the version which I here present. It was affiliated on him, in his life-time, and even named as his before his face. Besides, it has Maginn's peculiar mark—it imitates the very rythm of the original. The air of "Judy Callaghan" was composed, in Dublin, by the late Jonathan Blewitt, who died in 1854. He was an Englishman, but had accurately caught the particular characteristics of an Irish jig tune. The words were written long after the music—authorship unknown.—In the magazine, the Latin translation is given as "The Sabine Farmer's Serenade. Being a newly-recovered fragment of a Latin opera."—M.

JUDY CALLAGHAN.

III.

I've got a pig and a sow,
   I've got a stye to sleep 'em,
A calf and a brindled cow,
   And cabin, too, to keep 'em:
Sunday hat and coat,
   An old gray mare to ride on;
Saddle and bridle to boot,
   That you may ride astride on.
        Only say
   You'll be Mrs. Brallaghan;
            Don't say nay,
Charming Judy Callaghan.

IV.

I've got an acre of ground,
   I've got it set with praties;
I've got of 'baccy a pound,
   I've got some tea for ladies:
I've got the ring to wed,
   Whiskey to make us gaily;
I've got a feather bed,
   And handsome new shilelagh.
        Only say
   You'll have Mr. Brallaghan;
            Don't say nay,
Charming Judy Callaghan.

V.

You've got a charming eye;
   You've got spelling and reading,
You've got, and so have I,
   A taste for gentle breeding;
You're rich, and fair, and young,
   As every body's knowing,
You've got a dacent tongue
   Whene'er 'tis set a-going.
        Only say
   You'll have Mr. Brallaghan;
            Don't say nay,
Charming Judy Callaghan.

VI.

For a wife till death,
   I am willing to take ye

III.

Est mihi prægnans sus,
   Et porcellis stabulum;
Villula, grex, et rus
   Ad vaccarum pabulum;
Feriis cerneres me
   Splendido vestimento,
Tunc heus, quam bene te
   Veherem in jumento!
Semel tantum dic
   Eris nostra Lalage,
Ne recuses sic,
   Dulcis Julia Calage.

IV.

Vis poma terræ? sum
   Uno dives jugere;
Vis lac et mella, cum
   Bacchi succo, sugere?
Vis aquæ vitæ vim?
   Plumoso somnum sacculo?
Vis ut paratus sim
   Vel annulo vel baculo?
Semel tantum dic
   Eris nostra Lalage;
Ne recuses sic,
   Dulcis Julia Calage.

V.

Litteris operam das;
   Lucido fulges oculo;
Dotes insuper quas
   Nummi sunt in loculo.
Novi quod apta sis
   Ad procreandam sobolem!
Possides (nesciat quis?)
   Linguam satis mobilem.
Semel tantum dic
   Eris nostra Laluge;
Ne recuses sic,
   Dulcis Julia Calage.

VI.

Conjux utinam tu
   Fieres, lepidum cor, mi!

But, och, I waste my breath,
　The devil sure can't wake ye.
'Tis just beginning to rain,
　So I'll get under cover;
To-morrow I'll come again,
　And be your constant lover.
　　　　Only say
　You'll be Mrs. Bradlaghan;
　　　　Don't say nay,
　Charming Judy Callaghan.

Halitum perdimus, heu,
　Te soper urget. Dormi
Ingruit imber trux —
　Jam sub tecto pellitur
Is quem crastina lux
　Referet huc fideliter.
　　　　Semel tantum dic
　Eris nostra Lalage;
　　　　Ne recuses sic,
　Dulcis Julia Calage.

Monsieur Judas.*

Monsieur Judas est un drôle
　Qui soutient avec chaleur
Qu'il n'a joué qu'un seul rôle
　Et n'a pris qu'une couleur.
Nous qui détestons les gens
Tantôt rouges, tantôt blancs,
　　Parlons bas,
　　Parlons bas,
　Ici près j'ai vu Judas,
J'ai vu Judas, j'ai vu Judas.

Curieux et nouvelliste,
　Cet observateur moral
Parfois se dit journaliste,
　Et tranche du libéral;
Mais voulons-nous réclamer
Le droit de tout imprimer,
　　Parlons bas,
　　Parlons bas,
　Ici près j'ai vu Judas,
J'ai vu Judas, j'ai vu Judas.

Here Judas, with a face where shame
　Or honor ne'er was known to be,
Maintaining he is still the same,
　That he ne'er rattled — no — not he.
But we must spurn the grovelling hack,
To-day all white — to-morrow black,
　　But hush! he'll hear,
　　He'll hear, he'll hear;
　Iscariot's near — Iscariot's near!

The moral Surface swears to-day
　Defiance to the priest and Pope;
To-morrow, ready to betray
　His brother churchmen to the rope.
But let us trust the hangman's string
Is spun for him — the recreant thing!
　　But hush! he'll hear,
　　He'll hear, he'll hear;
　Iscariot's near — Iscariot's near!

---

* This parody upon one of Béranger's most popular satires, was sung by Odoherty at The Noctes, and was published in *Blackwood* for July, 1829. It was republished by every ultra-Protestant journal in the United Kingdom, as levelled at Sir Robert Peel, who had brought in and carried Catholic Emancipation, to which the whole of his preceding twenty years of public life had been constantly and energetically opposed. Peel's own plea was that he was as Anti-Catholic as ever, but the crisis arose when he had to choose between Emancipation and Civil War, and he preferred the former. — M.

Sans respect du caractère.
Souvent ce lâche effronté
Porte l'habit militaire
Avec la croix au côté.
Nous qui faisons volontiers
L'éloge de nos guerriers,
  Parlons bas,
  Parlons bas,
Ici près j'a vu Judas,
J'ai vu Judas, j'ai vu Judas.

Enfin, sa bouche flétrie
Ose prendre un noble accent,
Et des maux de la patrie
Ne parle qu'en gémissant.
Nous qui faisons le procès
A tous les mauvais Français,
  Parlons bas,
  Parlons bas,
Ici près j'ai vu Judas.
J'ai vu Judas, j'ai vu Judas.

Monsieur Judas, sans malice,
Tout haut vous dit; " Mes amis,
Les limiers de la police
Sont à craindre en ce pays."
Mais nous, qui de mains brocards
Poursuivons jusqu'aux mouchards,
  Parlons bas,
  Parlons bas,
Ici près j'ai vu Judas,
J'ai vu Judas, j'ai vu Judas.

All character that knave has lost;—
Soon will the Neophyte appear,
By priestly hands bedipp'd, be-cross'd,
Begreased, bechrism'd, with holy
  smear,
Soon may he reach his final home,
" A member of the Church of Rome."*
  But hush! he'll hear,
  He'll hear, he'll hear;
Iscariot's near—Iscariot's near!

Now from his mouth polluted flows—
Snufflled in Joseph Surface tone—
Laments o'er hapless Ireland's woes,
O'er England's dangerous state a
  groan.
Ere long beneath the hands of Ketch,
Sigh for thyself, degraded wretch!
  But hush! he'll hear,
  He'll hear, he'll hear;
Iscariot's near—Iscariot's near!

Judas! till then the public fleece,
For kin and cousins scheme and job,
Rail against watchmen and police,†
Inferior swindlers scourge or rob.
At last, another crowd before,
Thou shalt speak once—and speak on
  more!
  But hush! he'll hear,
  He'll hear, he'll hear;
Iscariot's near—Iscariot's near!

---

* The ordinary conclusion of a gallows speech in Ireland,—" I die an unworthy member of the Church of Rome."—M. OD.

† When Irish Secretary, Peel established the constabulary force, by which Ireland is governed,—the members of it are familiarly called " Peelers." In 1829-'30, when Home Secretary, he organized the present excellent police of London.—M.

Roger Goodfellow.

A SONG.

*To be sung to all sorry rascals.**

1.

Aux gens atrabilaires
Pour exemple donné,
En un temps de misères
Roger Bontemps est né.
Vivre obscur à sa guise,
Narguer les mécontents ;
Eh gai ! c'est la devise
Du gros Roger Bontemps.

2.

Du chapeau de son père,
Coiffé dans de grands jours,
De roses ou de lierre
Le rajeunir toujours :
Mettre un manteau de bure,
Vieil ami de vingt ans :
Eh gai ! c'est la parure
Du gros Roger Bontemps.

3.

Posséder dans sa hutte
Une table, un vieux lit,
Des cartes, une flûte,
Un broc que Dieu remplit,
Un portrait de maîtresse,
Un coffre et rien dedans ;
Eh gai ! c'est la richesse
Du gros Roger Bontemps.

4.

Aux enfants de la ville
Montrer de petits jeux,
Etre un faiseur habile
De contes graveleux ;

1.

Small sirs, so melancholy
In patriotic wo,—
To cure your carking folly
Comes Roger Goodfellow ;
To live as best it list him,
To scorn who does not so —
Ha, ha, this is the system
Of Roger Goodfellow.

2.

At field the earliest whistling ;
At kirk the doucest seen ;
On holydays a-wrestling
The stoutest on the green ;
Thus on in frank enjoyment
And grateful glee to go —
Ha, ha, 'tis the employment
Of Roger Goodfellow.

3.

Round Roger's cabin dangle,
From curious carved pins,
All wonders of the angle,
All mysteries of gins ;
While in his cupboard niche, is
A pewter pot or so —
Ha, ha, these are the riches
Of Roger Goodfellow.

4.

To know the wind and weather
Will make the salmon spring ;
To know the spot of heather
That hides the strongest wing ;

---

* This parody upon Béranger's " Roger Bontemps," to the air of " Ronde du camp de Grandpré," sung at *The Noctes*, was published in *Blackwood* for February, 1832.—M.

Ne par er que de danse
Et d'almanachs chantants ;
Eh gai ! c'est la science
Du gros Roger Bontemps.

5.

Faute de vin d'élite,
Sabler ceux du canton :
Préférer Marguerite
Aux dames du grand ton ;
De joie et de tendresse
Remplir tous ses instants ;
Eh gai ! c'est la sagesse
Du gros Roger Bontemps.

6.

Dire au ciel : Je me fie,
Mon père, à ta bonté ;
De ma philosophie
Pardonnez la gaité ;
Que ma saison dernière
Soit encore un printemps :
Eh gai ! c'est la prière
Du gros Roger Bontemps.

7.

Vous, pauvres pleins d'envie,
Vous, riches désireux ;
Vous, dont la char dévie
Après un cours heureux ;
Vous, qui perdoez peut-être
Des titres éclatants,
Eh gai ! prenez pour maitre
Le gros Roger Bontemps.

To tell the moon's compliance
With hail, rain, wind, and snow —
Ha, ha, this is the science
Of Roger Goodfellow.

5.

For wine to think nought of it,
With jolly good ale when lined ;
Nor ma'am my lady covet,
So housewife Joan be kind ;
While of each old state-housewife he
Doth nothing ask to know —
Ha, ha, 'tis the philosophy
Of Roger Goodfellow.

6.

To say, " O mighty Maker,
I bless thee, that thou here
Hast made me thus partaker
Of love and lusty cheer :
As older still, oh, gayer,
And jollier may I grow," —
Ha, 'tis a worthy prayer
Of Roger Goodfellow.

7.

Ho, ho, ye wheezing whiners ;
Ye kill-joys of the land !
State-malady-diviners ;
Yarus-pinners out of sand !
On common-sense who'd trample,
And lay religion low ;
For God's sake take example
By Roger Goodfellow.

Backe and Side go Bare, go Bare.*

1.

Backe and side go bare, go bare,
 Both foot and hande go colde :
But, bellye, God sende thee good ale yenough,
 Whether it be newe or olde.
I cannot eat but lytle meate.
 My stomacke is not good ;
But sure I thinke that I can drynke
 With him that weares a hood.
Though I go bare, take ye no care,
 I am nothing a colde ;
I stuff my skyn so full within,
 Of jolly good ale and olde.
Backe and side go bare, go bare,
 Both foote and hande go colde ;
But, bellye, God sende thee good ale enoughe,
 Whether it be newe or olde.

2.

I love no rost, but a nut-browne toste,
 And a crab laid in the fyre ;
A little breade shall do me stead,
 Much breade I not desyre.
No frost nor snow, nor winde, nor trowe,
 Can hurt me if I wolde ;
I am so wrapt, and throwly lapt,
 Of jolly good ale and olde,
  Backe and side go bare, &c.

3.

And Tyb, my wyfe, that, as her lyfe,
 Loveth well good ale to seeke ;
Full of drynkes shee, tyll ye may see
 The teares run down her cheeke :

1.

Sint nuda dorsum, latera —
 Pes, manus, algens sit ;
Dum ventri veteris copia
 Zythi novive fit.
Non possum multum edere,
 Quia stomachus est nullus ;
Sed volo vel monacho bibere
 Quanquam sit huic cucullus.
Et quamvis nudus ambulo,
 De frigore non est metus ;
Quia semper Zytho vetulo
 Ventriculus est impletus.
Sint nuda dorsum, latera —
 Pes, manus, algens sit ;
Dum ventri veteris copia
 Zythi novive fit.

2.

Assatum nolo — tostum volo —
 Vel pomum igni situm ;
Nil pane careo — pavum habeo
 Pro pane appetitum.
Me gelu, nix, vel ventus vix
 Afficerent injuriâ ;
Hæc sperno, ni adesset mi
 Zythi veteris penurin.
  Sint nuda, &c.

3.

Et uxor Tybie, qui semper sibi
 Vult quærere Zythum bene,
Ebibit hæc persæpe, nec
 Sistit, dum madeant genæ.

---

* This chant, (curiously rendered into Latin verse, in the exact measure of the original, with its single and double rhymes,) was sung by Odoherty, at *The Noctes*, and published in *Blackwood*, for July, 1822. — The original English ballad was written by John Still, Bishop of Bath and Wells, who flourished in the reign of Elizabeth, and died in 1607. He is the reputed author of "Gammer Gurton's Needle," a dramatic piece of low humor, very characteristic of the manners of the English in that day. The chant, " Back and side go bare," is introduced into this drama. — M.

AT MY TIME OF DAY.

Then dowth she trowle to mee the boule,
   Even as a mault-worme shuld;
And sayth, "Sweete hart, I took my parte
   Of this jolly good ale and olde."
     Backe and side go bare, &c.

4.

Now let them drynke, till they nod and wynke,
   Even as good felowes should doe :
They shall not mysse to have the blysse
   Good ale doth bringe men to.
And all poore soules that have scrowr'd boules,
   Or have them lustely trolde,
God save the lyves of them and their wyves,
   Whether they be yonge or old.
     Backe and syde go bare, &c.

Et mihi tum dat cantharum,
   Sic mores sunt bibosi;
Et dicit " Cor, en! impleor
   Zythi dulcis et annosi."
     Sint nuda, &c.

4.

Nunc ebibant, donec nictant
   Ut decet virum bonum;
Felicitatis habebunt satis,
   Nam Zythi hoc est donum.
Et omnes hi, qui canthari
   Sunt haustibus lætati,
Atque uxores vel juniores
   Vel senes, Diis sint grati.
     Sint nuda, &c.

At my Time of Day.*

Je vou drois à mon âge.
   (Il en seroit temps,)
Etre moins volage
   Que les jeunes gens,
Et mettre en usage
   D'un vaillard bien sage
Tous le sentimens.
Je vou drois du vieil homme
   Etre separé ;
Les morceau de pomme
   N'est pas digé ;
Gens de bien, gens d'honneur.
   A votre scavoir faire
Je livre mon cœur ;
   Mais laissez en tiere
Et libre carriere
A ma belle humeur.

At *my* time o' day
   It were proper, in truth,
If I *could* be less gay
   Than your frolicsome youth,
And now, old and gray
   To plod on my way
Like a senior, in sooth.
I wish my old tricks
   I could wholly forget ;
But the apple here sticks,
   Undigested as yet.
Let the good folks who will
   With my plan disagree,
They may scold me their fill,
   If I only am free
To retain in full glee
All my good humor still.

---

* This was sung at the Noctes, and published in *Blackwood* for September, 1825. North, (into whose mouth it was put,) said : " I shall give you a song written by Coulanges, when he was about eighty, and I heard it first sung by a man of the same age who heard Coulanges himself singing it a very short time before he died, which was in 1715, or perhaps 1716. I heard it perhaps sixty years after, if not more." — The original was sung by North, and the translation chanted, as improvised by Odoherty. — M.

Farewell, Beggarly Scotland.

RENDERED INTO LATIN.*

1.

Valedico, Scotia, tibi,
  Mendica, egens, frigida gens
Diabolus me reportet ibi
  Si unquam tibi sum rediens.
Arbor unus nascitur ibi,
  Isque patibulus est decens,
Bos ipse Austrum suspicit, sibi
  Alas ut fugeret cupiens.

2.

Vale, vale, Scotia mendica,
  Avenæ, siliquæ, crambe, far!
Ridentes virgines, Anglia antiqua,
  Salvete, at zythum cui nil est par!

---

* The original English song, as well as the above translation, was sung by Odoherty at The Noctes, and published in *Blackwood*, for November, 1824. As an attack on Scotland, it gave great offence to many readers of Maga. It appeared, however, that Odoherty was innocent of the authorship of the English original, which belonged to Allan Cunningham. In a tale of his, called "Corporal Colville," published in the *London Magazine*, for February, 1823, this very "Farewell to Scotland" had first appeared. It is subjoined, to test the accuracy of Maginn's Latin translation.—

1.

Farewell, farewell, beggarly Scotland,
  Cold and beggarly poor countrie;
If ever I cross thy border again,
  The muckle deil must carry me.
There's but one tree in a' the land,
  And that's the bonny gallows tree;
The very nowte look to the south,
  And wish that they had wings to flee.

2.

Farewell, farewell, beggarly Scotland,
  Brose and Bannocks, crowdy and kale!
Welcome, welcome, jolly old England,
  Laughing lasses and foaming ale!

FAREWELL, BEGGARLY SCOTLAND.

Cum redirem Carlilam lætam
  Risu excepi effuso ter,
Si unquam Sarcam rediens petam
  Diabole ingens! tu me fer!

2.

Vale popellus tunicatus
  Crinibus crassis, et cum his
Tibicen precans si quid afflatûs
  Famelici emere asse vis!
Capros pascerem Cadwalladero,
  Cui cibus ex cepis et caseo fit,
Potius quam degam cum populo fero,
  Cui vestis sine fundo sit.

'Twas when I came to merry Carlisle,
  That out I laughed loud laughters three,
And if I cross the Sark again,
  The muckle deil maun carry me.

3.

Farewell, farewell, beggarly Scotland,
  Kilted kimmers, wi' carroty hair,
Pipers, who beg that your honors would buy
  A bawbee's worth of their famished air.
I'd rather keep Cadwallader's goats,
  And feast upon toasted cheese and leeks,
Than go back again to the beggarly North,
  To herd 'mang loons with bottomless breeks.

French Slang Song from Vidocq.*

As from ken¹ to ken I was going,†
Doing a bit on the prigging lay;²
Who should I meet but a jolly blowen,³
Tol lol, lol lol, tol derol, ay;
Who should I meet but a jolly blowen,
Who was fly⁴ to the time o' day.⁵

Who should I meet but a jolly blowen,
Who was fly to the time o' day;
I pattered in flash⁶ like a covey,⁷ knowing,
Tol lol, &c.
"Ay, bub or grubby,⁸ I say."

I pattered in flash, like a covey, knowing,
"Ay, bub or grubby, I say." —

¹ *Ken* — shop, house.
² *Prigging lay* — thieving business.
³ *Blowen* — girl, strumpet, sweetheart.
⁴ *Fly* — (contraction of *flash*) awake, up to, practised in.
⁵ *Time o' day* — knowledge of business, thieving, &c.
⁶ *Pattered in flash* — spoke in slang.
⁷ *Covey* — man.
⁸ *Bub, grub* — drink, food.

---

* Maginn prided himself upon this paraphrase, on a song in Vidocq's Memoirs, in which he had brought his intimate knowledge of London slang to interpret that of Paris. It was given in *Blackwood* for July, 1829, as sung at THE NOCTES. — M.

† Here is subjoined the original slang song, to show the fidelity and spirit of the translation. — M.

En roulant de vergne en vergne.¹
Pour apprendre a goupiner,²
J'ai rencontré la mercandière,³
Lonfa malura dondaine,
Qui du pivois solisait,⁴
Lonfa malura dondé.

J'ai rencontré la mercandière,
Qui du pivois solisait.
Je lui jaspine en bigorne,⁵
Lonfa malura dondaine,
Qu'as-tu donc à morfiller ?⁶
Lonfa malura dondé.

Je lui jaspine en bigorne
Qu'as-tu donc à morfiller?
J'ai du chenu pivois sans lance⁷
Lonfa malura dondaine,
Et du larton savonné,⁸
Lonfa malura dondé.

¹ *City to city.*
² *To work.*
³ *The Shopkeeper.*

⁴ *Sold wine.*

⁵ *I ask him in slang.*

⁶ *To eat.*

⁷ *Good wine without water.*

⁸ *White bread.*

FRENCH SLANG SONG FROM VIDOCQ.

"Lots of gatter,"⁹ quo she, "are flowing,
 Tol lol, &c.
Lend me a lift in the family way.¹⁰

"Lots of gatter," quo she, "are flowing,
 Lend me a lift in the family way.
You may have a crib¹¹ to stow in,
 Tol lol, &c.
Welcome, my pal,¹² as the flowers in May.

"You may have a bed to stow in;
 Welcome, my pal, as the flowers in May."
To her ken at once I go in,
 Tol lol, &c.
Where in a corner out of the way.

To her ken at once I go in,
 Where in a corner out of the way,
With his smeller,¹³ a trumpet blowing,
 Tol lol, &c.
A regular swell-cove¹⁴ lushy¹⁵ lay.

With his smeller a trumpet blowing,
A regular swell-cove lushy lay:

J'ai du chenu pivois sans lance
Et du larton savonné
Une lourde, une tournante⁹
Lonfa malura dondaine,
Et un pieu pour roupiller¹⁰
Lonfa malura dondé.

Une lourde, une tournante
Et un pieu pour roupiller,
J'enquille dans sa cambriole¹¹
Lonfa malura dondaine,
Espérant de l'entifler¹²
Lonfa malura dondé.

J'enquille dans sa cambriole
Espérant de l'entifler
Je rembroque au coin du rifle¹³
Lonfa malura dondaine,
Un messière qui pionçait¹⁴
Lonfa malura dondé.

Je rembroque au coin du rifle
Un messière qui pionçait;

⁹ *Gatter*—porter.

¹⁰ *Family*—the thieves in general. *The Family Way*—the thieving line.

¹¹ *Crib*—bed.

¹² *Pal*—friend, companion, paramour.

¹³ *Smeller*—nose. *Trumpet blowing* here is not slang, but poetry for snoring.
¹⁴ *Swell cove*—gentleman, dandy.
¹⁵ *Lushy* — drunk.

⁹ *A door and a key.*

¹⁰ *A bed to sleep upon.*

¹¹ *I enter her chamber.*

¹² *To make myself agreeable to her.*

¹³ *I observe in the corner of the room.*
¹⁴ *A man lying asleep.*

To his clies[16] my hooks[17] I throw in,   [16] *Clies* — pockets.
  Tol lol, &c.   [17] *Hooks* — fingers; in full, *thiev-*
And collar his dragons[18] clear away.   *ing hooks.*

     [18] *Collar his dragons* — take his sovereigns; on the obverse of a sovereign is, or was, a figure of St. George and the *dragon.* The etymon of collar is obvious to all persons who know the taking-ways of Bow-street, and elsewhere. It is a whimsical coincidence, that the motto of the Marquis of Londonderry is "Metuenda *coralla draconis.*" Ask the city of London, if "I fear I may not collar the dragons," would not be a fair translation.

To his clies my hooks I throw in,
  And collar his dragons clear away;
Then his ticker[19] I set agoing,   [19] *Ticker* — watch. The French
  Tol lol, &c.   slang is *tocquanta.*
And his onions,[20] chain, and key.   [20] *Onions* — seals.

Then his ticker I set agoing,
  With his onions, chain, and key.
Next slipt off his bottom clo'ing,
  Tol lol, &c.
And his gingerbread topper gay.

Next slipt off his bottom clo'ing,
  And his gingerbread topper gay,

J'ai sondé dans ses vallades,[15]   [15]*Search his pockets.*
Lonfa malura dondaine,
Son carle j'ai pessigué[16]   [16]*I took his money.*
Lonfa malura dondé.

J'ai sondé dans ses vallades,
Son carle j'ai pessigué
Son carle, aussi sa tocquante[17]   [17]*His money and watch.*
Lonfa malura dondaine,
Et ses attaches de cé[18]   [18]*His silver buckles.*
Lonfa malura dondé.

Son carle, aussi sa tocquante
Et ses attaches de cé,
Son coulant et sa montante[19]   [19]*His chain and breeches.*
Lonfa malura dondaine.
Et son combre galuché[20]   [20]*Gold-edged hat.*
Lonfa malura dondé.

Son coulant et sa montante
Et son combre galuché,

FRENCH SLANG SONG FROM VIDOCQ.

Then his other toggery[21] stowing,
  Tol lol, &c.
All with the swag,[22] I sneak away.

Then his other toggery stowing,
  All with the swag I sneak away.
" Tramp it, tramp it, my jolly blowen,
  Tol lol, &c.
Or be grabbed[23] by the beaks[24] we may.

" Tramp it, tramp it, my jolly blowen,
  Or be grabbed by the beaks we may;
And we shall caper a-heel-and-toeing,
  Tol lol, &c.
A Newgate hornpipe some fine day.

" And we shall caper a-heel-and-toeing,
  A Newgate hornpipe some fine day;
With the mots,[25] their ogles[26] throwing,
  Tol lol, &c.
And old Cotton[27] humming his pray.[28]

[21] *Toggery* — clothes [from *toga*.]
[22] *Swag* — plunder.

[23] *Grabbed* — taken.
[24] *Beaks* — police-officers.

[25] *Mots* — girls.
[26] *Ogles* — eyes.
[27] *Old Cotton* — then Ordinary of Newgate.
[28] *Humming his pray* — saying his prayers.

Son frusque, aussi sa lisette[21]
Lonfa malura dondaine,
Et ses tirants brodanchés[22]
Lonfa malura dondé.

Son frusque, aussi sa lisette
Et ses tirants brodanchés,
Crompe, crompe, mercandière[23]
Lonfa malura dondaine,
Car nous serions bequillés[24]
Lonfa malura dondé.

Crompe, crompe, mercandière,
Car nous serions bequillés
Sur la placarde de vergne[25]
Lonfa malura dondaine,
Il nous faudrait gambiller[26]
Lonfa malura dondé.

Sur la placarde de vergne
Il nous faudrait gambiller
Allumés de toutes ces largues[27]
Lonfa malura dondaine,
Et du trepe rassemblé[28]
Lonfa malura dondé.

[21] *His coat and waistcoat.*

[22] *Embroidered stockings.*

[23] *Take care of yourself, shopkeeper.*
[24] *Hanged.*

[25] *On the Place de Ville.*

[26] *To dance.*

[27] *Looked at by all these women.*

[28] *People.*

"With the mots their ogles throwing,
And old Cotton humming his pray;
And the fogle-hunters[29] doing,   [29] *Fogle-hunters* — pickpockets.
Tol lol, &c.
Their morning fake[30] in the prigging lay.   [30] *Morning fake* — morning thievery.

Allumés de toutes ces largues
Et du trepe rassemblé,
Et de ces charlato bons drilles,[29]   [29] *Thieves; good fellows.*
Lonfa malura doudaine,
Tous abolant goupiner[30]   [30] *All coming to rob.*
Lonfa malura dondé.

Death in the Pot.

(LETTER FROM AN ELDERLY GENTLEWOMAN TO MR. CHRISTOPHER NORTH.*)

MY DEAR MR. NORTH,

I MUCH fear that this is the last letter you will ever receive from your old friend. "I'm wearin' awa, Kit! to the land o' the leal!" and that, too, under the influence of a complication of disorders, which have been undermining my constitution (originally a sound and stout one) for upwards of half a century. Look to yourself, my much respected lad—and think no more of your rheumatism. That, believe me, is a mere trifle —but think of what you have been doing, since the peace of 1763, (in that year were you born,) in the eating and drinking way, and tremble. I know, my dear Kit, that you never were a gormandizer, nor a sot; neither surely was I—but it matters not,—the most abstemious of us all have gone through fearful trials, and I have not skill in figures to cast up the poisonous contents of my hapless stomach for nearly threescore years. You would not know me now; I had not the slightest suspicion of myself in the looking-glass this morning. Such a face! so wan and wo-begone! No such person drew Priam's curtains at dead of night, or could have told him half his Troy was burned.

* In 1820, Mr. Frederick Accum, of old Compton Street, Soho, London, (self-described as "Operative Chemist, Lecturer on Practical Chemistry, Mineralogy, &c. &c.") published a startling Treatise on Adulterations of Food, and Culinary Poisons, exhibiting the Fraudulent Sophistications of Bread, Beer, Wine, spirituous Liquors, Tea, Coffee, Cream, Confectionary, Vinegar, Mustard, Pepper, Cheese, Olive Oil, Pickles, and other articles employed in domestic economy, and methods of detecting them. The book told many household, if not home truths and had a large sale. (Mr. Accum, it may be added, was subsequently detected in the act of cutting out leaves from valuable books in the British Museum, to save the trouble of transcribing their contents, and only escaped trial in a criminal Court, by returning to his native Germany, where he died.) Accum's book was quizzically reviewed in *Blackwood* for February, 1820, with copious extracts, showing the adulterations upon articles of food in ordinary consumption. The review, (which was called "There is Death in the Pot: 2 Kings—chap. vi, verse 11,") was followed up, in the next number of Maga, by this affecting epistle from Mrs. Susanna Trollope. —M.

Well—hear me come to the point. I remember now, perfectly well, that I have been out of sorts all my lifetime; and the causes of my continual illness have this day been revealed to me. May my melancholy fate be a warning to you, and all your dear contributors, a set of men whom the world could ill spare at this crisis. Mr. Editor—I HAVE BEEN POISONED.

You must know that I became personally acquainted, a few weeks ago, quite accidentally, with that distinguished chemist, well known in our metropolis by the name of "Death in the Pot." He volunteered a visit to me at breakfast, last Thursday, and I accepted him. Just as I had poured out the first cup of tea, and was extending it graciously towards him, he looked at me, and with a low, hoarse, husky voice, like Mr. Kean's, asked me if I were not excessively ill: I had not had the least suspicion of being so—but there was a terrible something in "Death in the Pot's" face which told me I was a dead woman. I immediately got up—I mean strove to get up, to ring the bell for a clergyman—but I fainted away. On awaking from my swoon, I beheld "Death in the Pot" still staring with his fateful eyes—and croaking out, half in soliloquy, half in tête-à-tête, "There is not a life in London worth ten years' purchase." I implored him to speak plainly, and for God's sake not to look at me so malagrugorously—and plainly enough he did then speak to be sure—"MRS. TROLLOPE, YOU ARE POISONED."

"Who," cried I out convulsively, "who has perpetrated the foul deed? On whose guilty head will lie my innocent blood? Has it been from motives of private revenge? Speak, Mr. Accum—speak! Have you any proofs of a conspiracy?" "Yes, Madam, I have proofs, damning proofs. Your wine-merchant, your brewer, your baker, your confectioner, your grocer, ay, your very butcher are in league against you; and, Mrs. Trollope, YOU ARE POISONED!" "When—Oh! when was the fatal dose administered? Would an emetic be of no avail? Could you not yet administer a——" But here my voice was choked, and nothing was audible, Mr. North, but the sighs and sobs of your poor Trollope.

At last I became more composed—and Mr. Accum asked me what was, in general, the first thing I did on rising from bed in the morning. Alas! I felt that it was no time for delicacy, and I told him at once, that it was to take off a bumper of brandy for a complaint in my stomach. He asked to look at the bottle. I brought it forth from the press in my own number, that tall square tower-like bottle, Mr. North, so green to the eye and smooth to the grasp. You know the bottle well—it belonged to my mother before me. He put it to his nose—he poured out a driblet into a tea-spoon as cautiously as if it had been the blackdrop,—he tasted it—and again repeated these terrible words, "MRS. TROLLOPE, YOU ARE POISONED.—It has," he continued, " a peculiar disagreeable smell, like the breath of habitual drunkards."——"Oh! thought I, has it come to this! The smell ever seemed to my unsuspecting soul most fragrant and delicious." Death in the Pot then told me, that the liquid I had been innocently drinking every morn for thirty years was not brandy at all, but a vile distillation of British molasses over wine lees, rectified over quick-lime, and mixed with saw-dust. And this a sad solitary unsuspecting spinster had been imbibing as brandy for so many years! A gleam of comfort now shot across my brain—I told Mr. Accum that I had, during my whole life, been in the habit of taking a smallish glass of Hollands before going to bed, which I fain hoped might have the effect of counteracting the bad effects of the forgery that had been committed against me. I produced the bottle—the white globular one you know. Death in the Pot tried and tasted—and alas! instead of Hollands, he pronounced it vile British malt spirit, fined by a solution of sub-acetate of lead, and then a solution of alum—and strengthened with grains of paradise, Guinea, pepper, capsicum, and other acrid and aromatic substances. These are learned words—but they made a terrible impression upon my memory. Mr. Accum is a most amiable man, I well believe—but he is a stranger to pity. "Mrs. Trollope, YOU HAVE BEEN POISONED," was all he would utter. Had the brandy and Hollands been genuine there would have been no harm—but they were *imitation*, and " YOU ARE POISONED."

Feeling myself very faint, I asked, naturally enough for a woman in my situation, for a glass of wine. It was brought—but Mr. Accum was at hand to snatch the deadly draught from my lips. He tasted what used to be called my genuine old port,

> And in the scowl of heaven his face
> Grew black as he was sipping.

"It is spoiled elder wine—rendered astringent by oak-wood saw-dust, and the husks of filberts—lead and arsenic, Madam, are——" but my ears tingled and I heard no more. I confessed to the amount of six glasses a-day of this hellish liquor—pardon my warmth—and that such had been my allowance for many years. My thirst was now intolerable, and I beseeched a glass of beer. It came, and Death in the Pot detected at once the murderous designs of the brewer. Cocnlus indicus, Spanish juice, hartshorn shavings, orange powder, copperas, opium, tobacco, nux vomica—such were the shocking words he kept repeating to himself—and then again, "MRS. TROLLOPE IS POISONED." "May I not have a single cup of tea, Mr. Accum," I asked imploringly, and the chemist shook his head. He then opened the tea-caddy, and emptying its contents, rubbed my best green tea between his hard horny palms. "Sloe-leaves, and white-thorn leaves, Madam, coloured with Dutch pink, and with the fine green bloom of verdigris! Much, in the course of your regular life, you must have swallowed!" "Might I try the coffee?" Oh! Mr. North, Mr. North, you know my age, and never once, during my whole existence, have I tasted coffee. I have been deluded by pease and beans, sand, gravel, and vegetable powder! Mr. Accum called it sham coffee, most infamous stuff, and unfit for human food! Alas! the day that I was born!

In despair I asked for a glass of water, and just as the sparkling beverage was about to touch my pale quivering lips, my friend, for I must call him so in spite of every thing, interfered, and tasting it, squirted it out of his mouth, with a most alarming countenance. "It comes out of a lead cistern—it is a deadly poison." Here I threw myself on my knees before this inexorable man, and cried, "Mr. Death in the Pot, is there in heaven, on earth, or the waters under the earth, any one particle of matter that is not impregnated with death? What means this desperate mockery? For mercy's sake give me the very smallest piece of bread and cheese, or I can support myself no longer. Are we, or are we not, to have a morsel of breakfast this day?" He cut off about an inch long piece of cheese from that identical double Gloucester that you yourself, Mr. North, chose for me, on your last visit to London, and declared that it had been rendered most poisonous by the anotta used to colour it. " There is here, Mrs. Trollope, a quantity of red lead. Have you, madam, never experienced, after devouring half a pound of this cheese, an indescribable pain in the region of the abdomen and of the stomach, accompanied with a feeling of tension, which occasioned much restlessness, anxiety, and repugnance to food? Have you never felt, after a Welch rabbit of it, a very violent cholic?" "Yes! yes—often, often, I exclaimed." "And did you use pepper and mustard?" "I did even so." "Let me see the castors." I rose from my knees —and brought them out. He puffed out a little pepper into the palm of his hand, and went on as usual, "This, madam, is spurious pepper altogether—it is made up of oil cakes, (the residue of linseed, from which the oil has been pressed,) common clay, and, perhaps, a small portion of Cayenne pepper (itself probably artificial or adulterated) to make it pungent. But now for the mustard,"—at this juncture the servant maid came in, and I told her that I was poisoned—she set up a prodigious scream, and Mr. Accum let fall the mustard pot on the carpet.

But it is needless for me to prolong the shocking narrative. They assisted me to get into bed, from which I never more expect to rise. My eyes have been opened, and I see the horrors of my situation. I now remember the most excruciating cholic, and divers other pangs which I thought nothing of at the time, but which must have been the effect of the deleterious solids and liquids which I was daily introducing into my stomach. It appears that I have never, so much as once, either eat or drank a real thing—that is, a thing being what it pretended to be. Oh! the weight of lead and of copper that has passed through my body! Oh! too, the gravel and the sand! But it is impossible to deceive me now. This very evening some bread was brought to me. Bread! I cried out indignantly—Take the vile deception out of my sight. Yes, my dear Kit, it was a villanous loaf of clay and alum! But my resolution is fixed, and I hope to die in peace. Henceforth, I shall not allow one particle of matter to descend into my stomach! Already I feel myself "of the earth, earthy." Mr. Accum seldom leaves my bedside—and yesterday brought with him several eatables and drinkables, which he assured me he had analyzed, subjected to the test-act, and found them to be conformists. But I have no trust in chemistry. His quarter-loaf looked like a chip cut off the corner of a stone block. It was a manifest *sham loaf*. After being deluded in my Hollands, bit in my brandy, and having found my muffins a mockery, never more shall I be thrown off my guard. I am waxing weaker and weaker—so farewell! Bewildering indeed has been the destiny of

Susanna Trollope.

P. S.—I have opened my mistress's letter to add, that she died this evening about a quarter past eight, in excruciating torments.

Sally Rogers.

"Luctus" on the Death of Sir Daniel Donnelly.

LATE CHAMPION OF IRELAND.*

[WE felt too deep sympathy with the afflicted population of a sister kingdom, to venture the publication of the following Luctus, till time had in some measure alleviated the national suffering — and, to borrow a figure from an oration attributed to Coun-

* For the proper understanding of the " Luctus" on Donnelly, it is necessary to state a few particulars relative to the career and character of that pugilistic worthy. Daniel Donnelly was an Irishman by birth and a carpenter by trade. He possessed lofty stature, great agility, and powerful strength. His skill in throwing was great. His straight-forward blow would almost fell an ox. But he was deficient in science. He fought only two great battles. The first, with Cooper, on the Curragh of Kildare, was a great victory over the English pugilist. Donnelly, on this occasion, had been trained by the celebrated Captain Kelly, and was in fine condition, — Pierce Egan said "strong as a lion, and active as a prize-fighter." The reputation this encounter procured for him caused him to visit London, where he was pitted against Oliver, who had some pretensions to the Championship. Donnelly was in very bad training for this battle, and, though he beat Oliver, displayed inferior science — not even sufficiently availing himself of his known power with the right hand. This fight came off in July, 1819. He declined further contests, at that time; extravagantly wasted the battle-money which he had won; injured his health by drinking and other excesses; and actually returned to Ireland with only forty shillings in his pocket. A great reception awaited him on the green sod. A ridiculous report that the Prince Regent (afterward George IV.) had knighted him, obtained currency and credence among the mob of Dublin, and about 20,000 persons assembled at Dunleary, to receive "Sir Daniel Donnelly," and, mounting him on a white horse, escorted him to his house in Townshend street, where he made them a speech and drank to their health in a noggin of the native. — Donnybrook Fair, (then a fact and now little more than a tradition,) commenced, (on August 27, 1819,) shortly after his arrival, and Sir Daniel exhibited himself in one of the tents or booths — sparring with Gregson and Cooper, and realizing a good deal of money thereby. After this Sir Daniel retired into private life, in "the public" line, as landlord of The Shining Daisy in Pill Lane, where he flourished for several months, making friends and money. But in February, 1820, having drank an almost incredible number of tumblers of punch at one sitting, (out of mere bravado,) and swallowed half a bucket of cold water, while in a state of profuse perspiration, after the aforesaid tumblers, he burst a blood vessel and departed this life in the 44th year of his age. His funeral, on a Sunday, was quite a " monster demonstration," as regards the num-

sellor Phillips, "wiped off with his passing pinions the daily dews which a sympathetic people had poured on the shining daisy that sprung through the unshaven shamrock, round the gloomy grave of the demolishing Donnelly!" But as the moon has thrice renewed her horns since the demise of Sir Daniel, we trust that we shall not now be thought to be interfering "with the sacred silence of a nation's sorrow," by publishing a selection from the "numbers without number, numberless," of Luctus that have been for the last quarter pouring in upon us from every part of the united empire. We confess, that we are not of that school of philosophy, which considers the loss sustained by Ireland in the death of Donnelly altogether and for ever irreparable. Surely a successor will step into his shoes. But what although centuries should pass by, without an Irishman willing

bers who followed him to his last resting-place, in Bully's Acre. It was calculated that 100 carriages, 400 horsemen, and over 50,000 of the "rag, tag, and bobtail" were in the procession. The horses were unyoked from the hearse, which was drawn to the burial ground by the crowd, and most prominent among the trappings of woe were the Gloves (demonstrative of his Championship,) borne on a cushion in front of the hearse. There was a report that the Resurrectionists had exhumed Donnelly's body, but this was strongly denied, eight of his friends having visited his grave on February 24, 1820, and having opened it found that the body was untouched. They reported accordingly, and kept nightly watch until March 2, when a regular grave was built. A subscription was made to raise a monument to Sir Daniel, and a large sum was obtained, but I believe that the monument never was erected. — In the sporting article entitled "Boxiana, No. VI." which opened *Blackwood* for March, 1820, the death of Donnelly was thus alluded to: — "We feel that it is utterly impossible for us to conclude this article, without adverting, in such terms as are becoming the melancholy occasion, to the great, indeed irreparable, loss which the boxing world has lately sustained in the death of Sir Daniel Donnelly. Ireland, we understand, is inconsolable. Since the heroic age of Corcoran and Ryan no such leveller had appeared. Happy and contented with the fame he had enjoyed under his native skies, it never had been the desire of Sir Daniel to fight on this side of the Channel. Accordingly, he past his prime in and about Dublin, satisfied with being held the most formidable Buffer (so our good Irish friends denominate Pugilists) among a potato-fed population of upwards of five millions. No one who has been in Ireland will suppose that Sir Daniel Donnelly walked up to the "good eminence" of the championship, with his hands in his breeches-pockets. We are not in possession of the facts of his early career — we know not when he dropped the sprig of shillelah, and restricted himself to the unweaponed fist. It must have been deeply interesting to have to contend with the Champion of England? What are centuries but short links in the long chain of time? For ourselves, we shall be satisfied with the destinies of Ireland, should a Donnelly appear once in a thousand years. Whoever may be the Editor of this Magazine in the year 2820, let him pay particular attention to our words,—and, if our views on the subject prove to be correct, we hope that all the subscribers to our work at that period, will purchase "sets" from the beginning. But these are idle speculations,—so let us address ourselves to graver matter. To prove our strict impartiality, we wrote the titles of their respective authors on separate slips of paper, which were all shaken strenuously in the Adjutant's old foraging cap, and as the titles came out in the hand of Mr. Blackwood, (whom we occasionally admit into the divan,) so are they now printed. It is singular

marked the transition. We have heard it said, and are inclined to think the theory true, that Sir Daniel's style of boxing showed, perhaps too strikingly, that he had excelled at the miscellaneous fighting of Donnybrook Fair. He was not a straight—nor yet a quick hitter. His education certainly had not been neglected, but it had been irregular. There were not only Iricisms in his style—but even provincialisms which were corrected in the London ring, not without danger to the success of his first prize essay. But the native vigour of the man prevailed over the imperfect institutions of his country—and with all the disadvantages of an irregular, imperfect, and unfinished education, Sir Daniel Donnelly not only triumphed over all his compatriots, but sustained the honour of Ireland in a country, perhaps, too much disposed to disparage her; and, in his last battle, with the renowned Oliver, the shamrock sprang up beneath his feet, rejoicing in the blood that died its threefold beauty, more proudly than it ever rejoiced, when, sprinkled with the dews of morning, it waved its verdant locks to the breezes that swept the level expanse of the Bog of Allen, or the rugged magnificence of Macgillicuddy's reeks. The death of this illustrious man has left unsolved a great problem, Was England or Ireland to have taken precedence in the rank of nations? Could Donnelly have beat Cribb? Could Carter have beat Donnelly! Alas! vain interrogatories! The glory of Ireland is eclipsed—and ages may elapse before another sun shine in, what Mr. Egan beautifully calls, her pugilistic hemisphere. We have just received a vast number of Elegies on his death—from Cork, Limerick, Waterford, and Dublin —some of them eminently beautiful. It was not to be thought that such a man would be permitted to leave us, without the meed of some melodious tear; and we are happy to see among the "Luctus," the names of Moore, Maturin, Croly, and Anster. Of these—anon." It happened, however, that Moore, Maturin, Croly, and Anster, did *not* figure in "The Luctus," published in May, 1820.—M.

that the names of the two greatest poets of the day, Lord Byron and Dr. Scott, should have followed each other.]

LETTER FROM LORD BYRON, ENCLOSING THE COMMENCEMENT OF "CHILD DANIEL."

MY DEAR NORTH,

MY old Armenian has come in upon me, just as the afflatus was rising, like a blast along Loch-na-gar, and I should as soon think of offending my Lord Carlisle* as the gentleman now stroking his aged beard. I break abruptly off with the words "Beggar's dust." What the devil is Hobhouse† about since he left Newgate? After all, there is no place like London for fun and frolic —yet I am at Venice. This sounds oddly.—Skimble Scamble stuff.——BYRON.

CHILD DANIEL.

In Fancy-land there is a burst of wo,
 The spirit's tribute to the fallen; see
On each scarr'd front the clouds of sorrow grow,
 Bloating its sprightly shine. But what is he
For whom grief's mighty butt is broach'd so free?

---

* The Earl of Carlisle (born 1748) was guardian of Lord Byron, who dedicated the "Hours of Idleness" to him, but afterwards quarrelled with him, and spoke, in "English Bard," of

"The paralytic puling of Carlisle."

The Earl, however, had some poetical taste, and wrote several tragedies — two of which, at least, are above mediocrity. He died in 1825.—M.

† John Cam Hobhouse, (created Lord Broughton in 1851,) had been committed to Newgate for a libel on the House of Commons, and the result was his return, in conjunction with Sir Francis Burdett, by the electors of Westminster, as one of their representatives in Parliament. In those days he was fiercely radical, but subsequently became a cabinet minister (in the Whig administration) and finally hid his head in a coronet. He will be best remembered, as Byron's early, and, perhaps, truest, friend. It was he who replied in the *Westminster Review*, to Captain Medwin's gossiping book on Byron. He was the literary executor of the poet, (who little expected that his liberal friend would end his political career in the House of Lords,) and was the best qualified to have w tten his life.—M.

Were his brows shadow'd by the awful crown,
    The Bishop's mitre, or high plumery
Of the mail'd warrior? Won he his renown
On pulpit, throne, or field, whom death hath now struck down?

He won it in the field where arms are none,
    Save those the mother gives to us. He was
A climbing star which had not fully shone,
    Yet promised in its glory to surpass
Our champion star ascendant; but alas!
The sceptred shade that values earthly might,
    And pow'r and pith, and bottom, as the grass,
Gave with his fleshless fist a buffet slight; ——
Say, bottle-holding Leach, why ends so soon the fight?

What boots t' inquire?—'Tis done. Green mantled Erin
    May weep her hopes of milling sway past by,
And Cribb, sublime, no lowlier rival fearing,
    Repose, sole Ammon of the fistic sky,
    Conceited, quaffing his blue ruin high,
Till comes the Swell, that come to all men must,
    By whose foul blows Sir Daniel low doth lie,
Summons the Champion to resign his trust,
And mingles his with Kings, Slaves, Chieftains, Beggars' dust!

*   *   *   *   *   *   *

"*In Fancy-land there is a burst of wo.*"

Why will Coleridge and Wordsworth continue to bother the world with their metaphysics? FANCY and IMAGINATIOM! Neither of them can tell the difference. Sam, write another Christabel—but William, thou Sylvan Sage, no more Excursions, though, joking apart, thou art the best of all the Pond poets. Moulsey Hurst is the "green navel" of Fancy-land.—BYRON.

"*For whom grief's mighty butt is broached so free.*"

I owe this line to my friend, Meux.*—BYRON.

"*The bishop's mitre, or high plumery*
"*Of the mail'd warrior?*"

I have no doubt that Donnelly would have made a very excellent bishop. He would have been powerful in the pulpit. The finest-armed man I ever saw was a bishop of the Greek Church, who had been a robber in his youth. Milo himself could not have shown nobler knuckles. Spirit of Pollux! Donnelly

---

* Meux and Company, brewers, at the corner of Tottenham Court Road and New Oxford Street, London. Sir Henry Meux, Baronet, who is the head of the firm, has represented Hertfordshire in Parliament since 1847.—M.

was not a soldier—a hired blood-shedder! He did not, like Shaw, close a life of honour by a disgraceful death at the carnage of Mont St. Jean, fighting against the Man of the Age, who may yet be destined to be the liberator of Europe.—BYRON.

"*Our champion star ascendant.*"

I am no enemy of Cribb's! But lives there a man so base as to say that he has not been indebted more to fortune than to bravery or skill in all his battles? Was he not fast losing his first fight with Jem Belcher, when that finished pugilist's hands gave way? Was not the Monops out of condition in the second contest? When Gregson, by a chance fall, could not come to time, Cribb was dead-beat; and "Bob of Wigan, ring-honoured Lancaster," was comparatively fresh, and able to have renewed the combat. What Briton will dare to say, that Molyneux did not win his first battle with the Champion? It seemed otherwise to the Umpires; but neither Europe nor America was to be so satisfied; and as my friend, Leigh Hunt, (he *is* my friend according to common speech, and I have no fault to find with his dedication of Rimini,) has lately expressed a wish that Napoleon may be liberated from St. Helena, that he may fight the battle of Waterloo over again with Wellington, so do I wish that Pluto would send us back Molyneux to try his fortune once more with Tom Cribb. My own opinion is, that judgment would be reversed in both cases.—BYRON.

"*Say, bottle-holding Leach, why ends so soon the fight?*"

There is no allusion here to the Vice Chancellor of England, which the reader may have suspected from the previous note about reversals of judgment. Neither is there any allusion to William Elford Leach of the British Museum. Had there been, the epithet would have been more apt, "beetle-holding Leach."*—BYRON.

"*And mingles with his Kings, Slaves, Chieftains, Beggars' dust!*"

The reader will pardon the tautology of this line. Where is the difference between them all?—BYRON.

---

* The late Sir John Leach, (who obtained the Vice Chancellorship of England, in 1818, as a reward for his endeavors to obtain a divorce of the Prince Regent from Caroline, Princess of Wales,) became Master of the Rolls in 1827, when Copley was made Lord Chancellor. It was Leach who advised the appointment of the infamous Milan Commission, (to establish a system of espionage, with bribery of her attendants, over the actions of Caroline of Brunswick,) and supervised the proceedings against her, when she became Queen. His decisions in Chancery were so frequently reversed, on appeal, that they have no weight. Romilly said that he preferred the tardy justice of Chancellor Eldon to the swift injustice of Vice Chancellor Leach. It was said, contrasting the delays of Eldon with the rapidity of Leach, that one had a Court of *oyer sans terminer*, and the other that of *terminer sans oyer*.—M

LETTER FROM DR. SCOTT,* ENCLOSING A "DIRGE ON DONNELLY."

Dear Mr. North—Understanding that your No. is to contain the "*Luctus Variorum*" on the late champion of Ireland, I take the liberty of adding my small contribution in the shape of the following song, which has had the honour of being sung at the HODGE-PODGE, the JUMBLE, and the MILLENIUM, with great applause. It is adapted to your own favourite tune, *The Sneddon March*, or "*The Paisley Weavers*," one of the finest manufacturing airs in our Scottish music. It is confidently asserted in the first circles here, that you and the Contributors are to be all West in a few weeks. Take the Tug to Grangemouth—track it thence in the Canal-boat—enjoy a week's cold punch here—and then steam it to Fort William or Belfast. But my pen, as usual, is running away with—Your faithful friend and coadjutor, JAMES SCOTT, D. G. L. H. V.
Glasgow, 7, *Millar-Street, May 1st.*

SORROW IS DRY.

Being a New Song, by Dr. James Scott.

When to Peggy Bauldie's daughter, first I told Sir Daniel's death,
Like a glass of soda-water it took away her breath;
It took away your breath, my dear, and it sorely dimm'd your sight,
And ay ye let the salt, salt tear, down fall for Erin's knight;
For he was a knight of glory bright, the spur ne'er deck'd a bolder,
Great George's blade itself was laid upon Sir Daniel's shoulder.
  Sing, Hey ho, the Sneddon, &c.

I took a turn along the street, to breathe the Trongate† air,
Carnegie's lass I chanced to meet, with a bag of lemons fair;

---

* James Scott, a dentist in Glasgow, who never wrote a line in his life, was selected by Lockhart to father sundry *skits*, in prose and verse, which it was not quite convenient to have affiliated on the real author. Among other productions thus attributed to "Doctor" Scott, was Lockhart's now well-known "Captain Paton's Lament," given, as "by James Scott, Esquire," in the lively article called *Christopher in the Tent*, which preceded The Noctes Ambrosianæ.—I have considerable doubt whether the communication from Dr. Scott, introduced into the "Luctus" was really written and interpolated by Lockhart, or an imitation by Maginn. I include it, however,—giving the reader what lawyers call "the benefit of the doubt.'—M.

† The Trongate:—one of the principal streets in the more antique portion of the City of Glasgow.—M.

Says I, "Gude Meg, ohon! ohon! you've heard of Dan's disaster—
If I'm alive, I'll come at five, and feed upon your master—
A glass or two no harm will do to either saint or sinner,
And a bowl with friends will make amends for a so so sort of dinner."
    Sing, Hey ho, the Sneddon, &c.

I found Carnegie in his nook, upon the old settee,
And dark and dismal was his look, as black as black might be,
Then suddenly the blood did fly, and leave his face so pale,
That scarce I knew, in alter'd hue, the bard of Largo's vale;
But Meg was winding up the jack, so off flew all my pains,
For, large as cocks, two fat carocks I knew were hung in chains.
    Sing, Hey ho, the Sneddon, &c.

Nevertheless, he did express his joy to see me there—
Meg laid the cloth, and, nothing loath, I soon pull'd in my chair;
The mutton broth and bouilli both came up in season due—
The grace is said—when Provan's head at the door appears in view—
The bard at work like any Turk, first nods an invitation;
For who so free as all the three from priggish botheration?
    Sing, Hey ho, the Sneddon, &c.

Ere long the Towddies deck the board with a cod's head and shoulders,
And the oyster-sauce it surely was great joy to all beholders.
To George our king a jolly cann of royal port is poured—
Our gracious king, who knighted Dan with his own shining sword—
The next we sip with trembling lip—'tis of the claret clear—
To the hero dead that cup we shed, and mix it with a tear.
    Sing, Hey ho, the Sneddon, &c.

'Tis now your servant's turn to mix the nectar of the bowl:
Still on the Ring our thoughts we fix, while round the goblets roll,
Great Jackson, Belcher, Scroggins, Gas, we celebrate in turns,
Each Christian, Jew, and Pagan, with the Fancy's flame that burns;
Carnegie's finger on the board a mimic circle draws,
And, Egan-like, h' expounds the rounds, and pugilistic laws.
    Sing, Hey ho the Sneddon, &c.

'Tis thus that worth heroic is suitably lamented.—
Great Daniel's shade, I know it, dry grief had much resented—
What signify your tear and sigh?—A bumper is the thing
Will gladden most the generous ghost of a champion of the King,
The tear and sigh from voice and eye must quickly pass away,
But the bumper good may be renewed until our dying day!
    Sing, Hey ho, the Sneddon, &c.

LETTER FROM MR. W. W. TO MR. CHRISTOPHER NORTH.*

Dear Sir,
Had it not been one of the deepest convictions of my mind, even from very early youth, that there was something in periodical literature radically and essentially wrong, *in rerum naturâ*, as Bacon Lord Verulam has wisely observed of a subject somewhat different, I should certainly, before the commencement of the present portion of time, have sent divers valuable communications unto your Miscellany. For, concerning both the matter and manner of Blackwood's Edinborough Magazine, it hath fallen to my lot in life, on six, eight, or ten different occasions —some of them not without their importance, considered in relation to the ordinary on-goings of the world which we inhabit, and others of them, peradventure, utterly and thoroughly worthless;—I say, that it hath fallen to my lot in life to hear the Work, of which you are the Editor, spoken of in words of commendation and praise. It appeareth manifest, however, that to form a philosophical, that is, a true character of a work published periodically, it behooveth a man to peruse the whole series of the above-mentioned work seriatim, that is, in continuous and uninterrupted succession, inasmuch as that various articles, on literature, philosophy, and the fine arts, being by their respective authors left unfinished in one number, are mayhap brought to a conclusion in a second—nay, peradventure, continued in a second, and even a third—yea, often not finished until a tenth, and after the intervention of divers Numbers free wholly and altogether from any discussion on that specific subject, but composed, it may be, either of nobler or of baser matter. Thus, it often fareth ill with one particular Number of a periodical work —say for June or January—because, that although both the imaginative and reasoning faculties may be manifested and bodied forth visibly and palpably, so that, as I have remarked on another occasion, they may "lie like surfaces," nevertheless, if there shall be the intervention of a chasm of time between

---

* This diffuse introduction, so much after the manner of Wordsworth, was considered very well executed, and the Bard of Rydal told me, long after, that he had been greatly amused with it. — M.

the first portion of the embodied act and the visible manifestation of the second — or again, between the second and third, and so on according to any imaginable or unimaginable series, — then I aver, that he will greatly err, who, from such knowledge of any work, (that is, a periodical work, for indeed it is of such only that it can be so predicated,) shall venture to bestow or to inflict upon it a decided and permanent character, either for good or for evil. Thus, for example, I have observed in divers Numbers of Blackwood's Edinborough Magazine, sarcasms rather witty than wise, in my apprehension, directed against myself, on the score of the Lyrical Ballads, and my Quarto Poem entitled the Excursion. In other Numbers again — I cannot charge my memory for what months or in what year, nor, indeed, is it of vital importance to this question — methinks I have read disquisitions on my poetry, and on those great and immutable principles in human nature on which it is built, and in virtue of which I do not feel as if I were arrogating to myself any peculiar gift of prophecy, when I declare my belief that these my poems will be immortal ; — I repeat, that in such and such Numbers I have perused such and such articles and compositions, in which I have not been slow to discern a fineness of tact and a depth of thought and feeling not elsewhere to be found, unless I be greatly deceived, in the criticism of this in many things degenerate, because too intellectual age. Between the folly of some Numbers, therefore, and the wisdom of others — or in other words of still more perspicuous signification, between the falsehood of one writer, and the truth of another, there must exist many shades by which such opposite extremes are brought, without a painful sense of contrariety, before the eyes of what Mr. Coleridge has called the "Reading Public." Of all such shades — if any such there be — I am wholly unapprized — because I see the work but rarely, as I have already observed, for I am not, to the best of my recollection, a subscriber to the Kendal Book-Club; such institutions being, in small towns, where the spirit of literature is generally bad in itself and fatally misdirected, conducted upon a principle, or rather a want of principle, which cannot be too much discommended.

 The upshot of the whole is this, that it is contrary both to my theory and my practice to become a regular contributor to any periodical work whatsoever, forasmuch as such habits of composition are inimical to the growth and sanity of original genius, and therefore unworthy of him who writes for "all time" except the present.

Nevertheless, it hath so happened, that in seasons prior to this, I have transmitted to the Editors of divers periodical Miscellanies, small portions of large works, and even small works perfect in themselves; nor would it be altogether consistent with those benign feelings which I am disposed to cherish towards your Miscellany, as a Periodical that occasionally aimeth at excellence, and may even without any flagrant violation of truth, be said occasionally to approximate thereto, to withhold from it such slight marks of my esteem, as, upon former occasions, I have not scrupled to bestow upon others haply less worthy of them. I therefore send you first, an Extract from my Great Poem on my Own Life, and it is a passage which I have greatly elaborated;—and, secondly, Sir Daniel Donnelly, a Ballad, which, in the next edition of my works, must be included under the general class of "Poems of the Imagination and the Affections."

EXTRACT FROM MY GREAT AUTO-BIOGRAPHICAL POEM.

It is most veritable,—that sage law
Which tells that, at the wane of mightiness,
Yea even of colossal guilt, or power
That, like the iron man by poets feign'd,
Can with uplifted arm draw from above
The ministering lightnings, all insensible
To touch of other feeling, we do find
That which our hearts have cherish'd but as fear,
Is mingled still with love; and we must weep
The very loss of that which caused our tears.—
E'en so it happeneth when Donnelly dies.
Cheeks are besullied with unused brine,
And eyes disguis'd in tumid wretchedness,
That oft have put such seeming on for him,
But not at Pity's bidding!—Yea, even I,
Albeit, who never "ruffian'd" in the ring,
Nor know of "challenge," save the echoing hills;
Nor "fibbing," save that poesy doth feign;

Nor heard his fame, but as the mutterings
Of clouds contentious on Helvellyn's side,
Distant, yet deep, agnize a strange regret,
And mourn Donnelly—Honourable Sir Daniel:—
(Blessings be on them, and eternal praise,*
The Knighter and the Knighted.) Love doth dwell
Here in these solitudes, and our corporal clay
Doth for its season bear the self-same fire,
Impregnate with the same humanities,
Moulded and mixed like others.
　　　　　　　I remember,
Once on a time,—'twas when I was a boy,
For I was childish once, and often since
Have, with a cheerful resignation, learned
How soon the boy doth prophecy the man,—
I chanced, with one whom I could never love,
Yet seldom left, to thread a thorny wood,
To seek the stock-doves' sacred domicile;—
Like thieves, we did contend about our crime,
I and that young companion. Of that child
His brief coevals still had stood in awe,
And Fear did do him menial offices,
While Silence walk'd beside, and word breath'd none.
Howbeit, mine arm, which oft in vassal wise
Had borne his satchel, and but ill defended
From buffets, half in sport, half tyrannous,
With which I was reguerdon'd,—chanced prevail.

His soul was then subdued, and much and sore
He wept, convulsive; nay, his firm breast heav'd,
As doth the bosom of the troublous lake
After the whirlwind goeth; and so sad
Did seem the ruins of his very pride,
I could not choose but weep with him, so long
We sobb'd together, till a smile 'gan dry
The human rain, and he once more was calm;—
For sorrow, like all else, hath end. Albeit,
Those tears, however boyish, were more fit,
Since nature's self did draw them from their source,
Than aught that cunning'st poet can distil,
By potent alchemy, from human eye,
To consecrate Donnelly's grave. Even so;
For they discours'd with a dumb eloquence,

---

* " Blessings be on them, and eternal praise,
　The poets."—WORDSWORTH.

Beyond the tongue of dirge or epitaph,
Of that which passeth in man's heart, when Power,
Like Babylon, hath fall'n, and pass'd away.

SIR DANIEL DONNELLY.—A BALLAD.

I came down to breakfast — And why all this sobbing,
This weeping and wailing? I hastily cried;
Has Grimalkin, my boy, ta'en away your tame Robin?
Has Duckling, or Pullet, or White Coney died?

'Twas thus the short list of his joys I ran over,
While the tears were fast coursing down Timothy's face,
And strove the small darling his red cheek to cover.—
What is this? — thought my soul — Is it grief or disgrace?

I looked on the Courier, my weekly newspaper,
For I felt that the cause of his sorrow was there;
So quick is grief's eye that no word could escape her—
"Dead is Daniel, the hero of Donnybrooke fair!"

O mournful was then the low song of the kettle,
And long look'd my face in the bright polish'd grate;
Dull, dull clank'd the tongs, though composed of true metal,
They seemed to my fancy the long shears of fate.

I sought the fresh air, but the sun, like a firebrand
In my dark bosom kindled grief's faggotty pile:
Ah, me! ye five Catholic millions of Ireland,
What now will become of your bull-breeding isle?

Mine eyes met the earth, in their wand'ring uneasy;
And I thought, as I saw through the vanishing snow
The flower of Sir Daniel, the bright shining Daisy,
On that beautiful poem I wrote long ago.

By the stroke of the thunder-stone split in its glory,
On the earth lay extended a green-crested pine;
Then I dreamt, poor Sir Dan, of thy pitiful story,
For the trunk was as straight and as knotty as thine!

Thus sun, flower, and tree all, in blaze, blight, or blossom,
The same sombre image of sorrow supplied,
While Nature breath'd forth from her mountainous bosom,
'Weep, weep for the day when Dan Donnelly died!"

LETTER FROM ODOHERTY.

Killarney, May 9th.

MY DEAREST KIT,—Here am I, living at rack and manger, with my old schoolfellow, Blennerhasset; and you and your Magazine may go to the devil, for any thing I care about either of you. We embark on the lake about 11 o'clock, after a decent breakfast, and contrive to kill the evening till about five, soon after which, we enter ourselves for the sweepstakes, and, to use the phraseology of my friend, the Reverend Hamilton Paul, generally contrive to stow away under our belt, a bottle of blackstrap, before tumbling in. You may think this monotonous; but you are quite wrong. One day we fish trout, another eels, and another salmon, which produces an agreeable variety; and it was only last Thursday, that Rowan Cashel and myself swam across the Devil's Punch Bowl,* on the top of Mangerton. We also attend wakes, fairs, funerals, and patrons, and go to church as regular as clock-work. In short, I have some intention of marrying again, and settling for the remainder of my life, at least for a year or two, somewhere in Kerry. I hear Mullcocky blowing his horn for us to join a batch of young ladies, on a party of pleasure, to the upper lake, and we are going to dine on cold provisions on Ronayne's Island, which is as beautiful and romantic a spot as ever you clapt eyes on. I enclose for you the only piece of poetry I have composed since I passed through Cork. I jotted it down with a black-lead pencil, in a silver case, belonging to a young gentleman with a good-natured face, on the outside of the coach; and I am sorry to say, that on parting from us, he forgot to ask it back again; so I keep it for the sake of an agreeable travelling companion. You will observe, from its stopping short all at once, that the Poem is only a fragment. Mullcocky

---

* Popular tradition relates that the great hollow on the top of Mangerton, at Killarney, (called "The Devil's Punch-Bowl," and filled with ice-cold water,) was caused by the devil's having bitten a good mouthful from the summit of said mountain, and that, having slightly injured one of his wisdom-teeth thereby, he dropped the said mouthful in the heart of Tipperary, where it remains, to the present day, as "The Rock of Cashel."—M.

is in a big passion, I hear, so good-b'ye Kit, prays ever your hearty chum, MORGAN ODOHERTY.

P. S. Something seems to have gone wrong with the barge, so I have time for a P. S. I encountered the Champion's funeral; and it was the biggest I ever witnessed. It was duly celebrated by games too; for, as the story went, certain persons suspected of being young surgeons or their jackalls, were met and severely beaten by some of the champions of the fist, who jaloused, as your Scottish peasantry say, that they were on the watch for the hero's remains. Another version of the story is, that the designs of the scalpel were all along suspected by the knights of the daddle, who appointed a trusty band to watch, for two days and nights, the holy shrine where their saint was laid. Having gone, however, to indulge themselves in a funeral libation for an hour or two, at the "honour" (a drinking bout at a burial) they found, on repairing to their post, that the enemy had been before them, and had, with infinite judgment, effected the resurrection, before the champion was well warm in his grave. A deputation of very respectable gentlemen waited on the corpse, next day, to ascertain the fact: but it is absolutely impossible to ascertain any fact in Dublin; and you meet thousands and tens of thousands every day, and in every company, who maintain that the champion is now in Edinburgh. If you have seen him on any of your dissecting tables there, pray let me know.— But I hear the ladies giggling, so I must be after joining the water-party.

ODONNELLY, AN ODE BY MORGAN ODOHERTY.

I.

WHEN green Erin laments for her hero, removed
From the Isle where he flourished, the Isle that he loved,
Where he entered so often the twenty foot lists,
And, twinkling like meteors, he flourished his fists,
And gave to his foes more set downs and toss overs,
Than ever was done by the greatest philosophers,
 In folio, in twelves, or in quarto,
Shall the harp of Odoherty silent remain,
 And shall he not waken its music again?
  Oh! yes, with his soul and his heart too!

II.

Majestic Odonnelly! proud as thou art,
Like a cedar on top of Mount Hermon,
We lament that death shamelessly made thee depart,
In the gripes, like a blacksmith or chairman.
Oh! hadst thou been felled by Tom Cribb in the ring,
Or by Carter* been milled to a jelly,
Oh! sure that had been a more dignified thing,
Than to kick for a pain in your belly!

III.

A curse on the belly that robbed us of thee,
And the bowels unfit for their office;
A curse on the potyeen you swallowed too free,
For a stomach complaint, all the doctors agree,
Far worse than a headach or cough is.
Death, who like a cruel and insolent bully, drubs
All those he thinks fit to attack,
Cried Dan, my tight lad, try a touch of my mulligrubs,
Which soon laid him flat on his back!

IV.

Great Spirits of Broughton, Jem Belcher, and Fig,
Of Corcoran, Pierce, and Dutch Sam;
Whether up stairs or down, you kick up a rig,
And at intervals pause your blue ruin to swig,
Or with grub, your bread baskets to cram.
Or, whether for quiet you're placed all alone
In some charming retired little heaven of your own,
Where the turf is elastic, in short just the thing
That Bill Gibbons would choose when he's forming a ring,
That wherever you wander you still may turn to,
And thrash and be thrashed till you're all black and blue;
Where your favourite enjoyments for ever are near,
And you eat and you drink, and you fight all the year;
Ah! receive then to join in your milling delight,
The shade of Sir Daniel Donnelly, knight;
With whom a turn up is no frolic;
His is no white or cold liver,
For he beat Oliver,
Challenged Carter, and died of the colic.

---

* John Carter was a rival pugilist who repeatedly challenged Donnelly, but always failed to " post the coal," at the place and time appointed for paying the deposite or the battle-money. Like Sir Daniel, he settled down in Dublin, as a publican. — M.

V.

Bad luck to my soul,
But I'll fill the punch bowl,
To the brim with good stingo; and so, Nelly,
Don't let the toast pass you,
But fill up your glass to
Demolishing Daniel Donnelly.

LETTER FROM MR. SEWARD.

Ch: Ch: April 1, 1820.

MY DEAR SIR,

FOR the fuller explication of the subjoined Threne, the reader is referred to the conclusion of the last book of the Iliad, which has supplied a great part of the *exequial* diction — who, indeed, so fit as the mourners of a Hector to furnish with funeral-phrases those of a Donnelly? — and to the notes upon that unrivalled sketch of the manners of the Emerald Isle, Castle Rackrent. For more immediate use, i. e. (to borrow Miss Edgeworth's own terms) "for the advantage of *lazy* readers, who would rather read a page than walk a yard, and from compassion, not to say sympathy with their infirmity," I have transcribed a small portion of the latter.

Buller has just run up to town for his Easter holidays, or you should have had the whole of the notes in the customary language of classical commentary. As it is, you will come off with more text than annotation. We shall neither of us soon forget the cordial hospitality of the Tent last August.* — Yours ever very truly, W. SEWARD.

"ULLALOO, GOL, OR LAMENTATION OVER THE DEAD."

——*Magnoque ululante tumultu.*—VIRG.
————————*ululatibus omne*
Implevére nemus.—OV.

THE body of the deceased, dressed in grave-clothes, and ornamented with flowers, was placed on a bier, or some elevated

* Mr. Seward, of Christ Church, (in connection with Mr. Buller of Brazennose,) was originally introduced as an interlocutor with Christopher in the Tent, in 1819, — occasionally appeared at THE NOCTES, and was kept on hand through the Dies Boreales, as late as 1849-50. — M.

spot. The relations and keeners (*singing mourners*) ranged themselves in two divisions, one at the head and the other at the feet of the corpse. The bards and eroteries had before prepared the funeral "caoinan," or song. The chief bard of the head-chorus began by singing the first stanza in a low doleful tone, which was softly accompanied by the harp: at the conclusion the foot-semichorus began the lamentation, or "Ullaloo" (Ελελευ) from the first note of the preceding stanza, in which they were answered by the head-semichorus; then both united in one general chorus. The chorus of the first stanza being ended, the chief bard of the foot semichorus began the second " Gol," or lamentation, in which he was answered by that of the head ; and then, as before, both united in the general full chorus. Thus, alternately, were the song and choruses performed during the night. The genealogy, rank, possessions, virtues, and vices of the dead were rehearsed, and a number of interrogations were addressed to the deceased ; as, " Why did he die ?" if married, " Whether his wife was faithful to him, his sons dutiful, or good hunters or warriors ?" if a young man, " Whether he had been crossed in love ?" or, " If the blue-eyed maids of Erin treated him with scorn."— *Transactions of the Royal Irish Academy*, IV.)

The crowd of people, who assemble at these funerals, sometimes amounts to a thousand, often to four or five hundred. (N. B. Sixty thousand, it is said, attended Donnelly to his grave !) They gather, as the bearers of the hearse proceed on their way ; and when they pass through any village, or when they come near any houses, they begin to cry, " Oh ! Oh ! Oh ! Oh ! Oh ! Agh ! Agh !" raising their notes from the first *Oh !* to the last *Agh !* in a kind of mournful howl.

P. S. Scholars, with more of leisure and literature than belongs to myself, might have found in Pindar, what I have sought in Homer—the appropriate archetype for a sublime choral ode. Was the " huge Diagoras of Rhodes, indeed, with all his accompaniment of pugilist sons and grandsons—Damagetus, and Doreus, and Acusilaus, and Euclon, Pisirrothius—better entitled to the πυγμας αποινα bestowed in the seventh Olympic Hymn, than Sir Daniel Donnelly ? By the bye, from the reception at first given to the claim preferred by his daughter, Aristopatira, to the

honours of "a sitting" at the grand *spectacle* of Pisa, (for we must carefully distinguish the θεα of the scholiast from the Chinese beverage mentioned in the elegy,) we may infer that the γυμνικος αγων of the ancients, as the epithet implies, involved somewhat more or an exposure even than is witnessed in our modern ball-rooms. See Blackwood's Magazine, XXXVI. 699.*
In one respect the Rhodian, πυξ αρεταν εύρων, appears to have differed from our illustrious Irishman; as Pindar calls him ευθυμαχαν, and Donnelly (we are told by the author of the "Boxiana," ib. 615.) was "not a straight hitter." Neither have we any authority for applying the πατερων ορθαι φρενες of v. 168, to the intellects of the genuine sons of St. *Patrick*. *Hactenus proleptices*.

P. S. To my utter amazement, Buller has burst in upon me, all covered with mud, a well-booted Grecian. Heaven knows what has brought him back so suddenly to Oxford. Something is in the wind, no doubt. Hearing that I am writing to you, he begs to add a scrawl, though he has to cross and recross my letter, like that of a boarding-school Miss. Once more fare thee well. W. S.

ULLALOO!

Ελεγειον.

———*illum superare pugnis*
Nobilem.—Hor.
Non hæc jocosæ conveniunt lyræ.—Ibid.

Φευ πυκτων πολυ φερτατε, φευ τριποθητε ΔΟΝΕΛΛΕ,
Ωλε᾽ άη᾽ αιωνος φευ μαλα τουδε νεος.
Ουδε τι σοι πατρης απιοντι μεμηλεν Ιερνης,
Ουδ᾽ εξ μυριαδων (φευ ελελευ ελελευ)
Οί σουγ᾽ αμφιεπον ταφον ασμασιν ανδροδαμοιο†

---

* In the Boxiana, No. 6, which is here referred to, it was decided "that, in the ball-room, a waltzing-match is a more indecent exhibition than a boxing-match,"—which it certainly is.—M.

† Ανδροδαμοιο, though not at present to be found in any Greek writer, may perhaps be justified by the analogy of ίπποδαμοιο, an epithet once deemed of so much consequence in the last line of the Iliad, by a scrupulous translator, that for Pope's closing couplet,

Such honours Ilion to her hero paid,
And peaceful slept the mighty Hector's shade;

Θρηνων εξαρχοις (φευ ελελευ ελελευ).
Οἱ μεν αρ' εθρηνεον, επι δε στεναχοντο γυναικες,
Και πιον* αμφοτεροι (φευ ελελευ ελελευ)

which certainly somewhat embellishes the simplicity of the original, ὑπερ τον αληθη λογον ἐεδαιδαλμενος ψευδεσι ποικιλοις, he proposed to substitute,

Such honours Ilion to her prince decreed,
To the great tamer of the gallant steed!—W. S.

* Πιον. "All night there were tea-drinkings for the women, and punch for the men." (Edgeworth's Ormond, II. 375.) I remember to have seen a Greek ode, Εις την Οεαν, and many Latin disquisitions upon the same fragrant leaf, nearly coeval with its first introduction into Europe; in all of which, as in its French appellation, the aspirate is preserved. I cannot but suspect that, in the *nigrum vitiis præfigere Theta*, which I would read *nigram viti præponere Theian*, the preference of bohea to black-strap (αιθοπι ειν·) is sub-obscurely adumbrated.

Indeed, if I were not afraid of attempting to tread in steps to which I feel myself unequal, I would Bullerize so far as to conjecture, on the principle of the English proverb, "grief is thirsty," that *pious, pine, repine*, &c. in our semi-Greek language may be taken from πινω, and its deflections; and would farther connect the French *feu*, "deceased," with the φευ of Grecian lamentation.

Shall I, before I close this hariolating note, give you one of our absent friend's scraps of erudition? Buller, you are aware, is one of those black swans at Oxford, a Whig; and you will be but too ready to say politically, whatever share he may possess of your personal regard, *Hic niger est*—But to his commentary. Upon Iliad, Ω. 751, &c. he asks, in that modest tone of query, which ushered Newton's optics into the world:—"May not the poet, in the true spirit of vaticination, here point to Lord C-stl-r-gh, (he is very delicate, you will observe, in involving his allusion, by omitting the vowels,) as the modern Achilles, where he says,

Περνασχ' ὁντιν' ἐλεσκε (leg. ελεξε, *clegi, eligi, curavit*) περην ἁλος ατρυγετοιο.

ι. e. Clarkio interprete, *vendere solebat*, ON THE OTHER SIDE OF THE CHANNEL?" The familiarity of the practice, he adds, was certified by that *minimus maximus* of men, the late Speaker [Abbot]: and in ὁντιν, he thinks it not difficult to trace the rudiments of a well-known and associated name, Quintin (sc. Dick.) He then proceeds to corroborative quotations, in which his talent of conjectural emendation is largely exercised;

Pulcrum est digito monstrari, et " Dick-buyer *hic est!"*
Ten, cirratorum centum dictata fuisse
Pro nihilo pendes?

points out, with his usual felicity, the peculiar beauty of the vernacular *sobriquet*, "Dick-buyer;" since, in some cases, (e. g. Saumaise's famous *Hundreda*, &c.) classical language does not furnish a full equivalent; and then, after observing that the influencing of the votes of a hundred Right Honourable dandies (*Cirratorum, ι. e. nobilium puerorum*, Lubin.) is no light matter! rejects a proposed reading, *senatorum*, though of some plausibility, as the *centum* in

LUCTUS ON THE DEATH OF DONNELLY. 67

Ανδρες υδωρ τε βιου* το κριθινον, άι δε γυναικες
'Ην καλευυσι Θεαν (φευ ελελευ ελελευ)·
"Τιπτε φαος λειπειν, τοσσων νικητερ αγωνων,"
Εξερεους', "εθελες; (φευ ελελευ ελελευ)
" Μων τινος αλλου ερᾷ γυνη, ειπ'; η υίος απεδρα,
" Ουδε μαχην ανετλη ; (φευ ελελευ ελελευ)
" Η σε φιλουντα κοραι γλαυκωπιδες, ευχος, Ιερνες,
" Ουκ ετ' αρ' αντεφιλουν; (φευ ελελευ ελελευ)
" Αγγλων ου τι λοχον μεγαλοφρων εν δαϊ λυγρῃ
" Πυκτικον† εδδεισας (φευ ελελευ ελελευ).
" Αλλ' ειτις σε μεν 'Αλλος,‡ η Ουλιβαροιος ενιπτοι,
" Ηε Κοώπηρος (φευ ελελευ ελελευ)
" Αλλα συ τοιγ' επεεσσι‖ παραιφαμενος κατερυκες,

that combination would so greatly underrate his lordship's range of "dictation" — not that he calls him "a dictator!" — next cites
Hic (Dick) *est quem legis,* i. e. eligis;
slily subjoins, *Non meus hic sermo, sed quem præcepit Ofallus,*
intimating that the suggestion had originated with the Irish Whig Duke of Leinster, Earl and Baron Ofalley ; and summons the aid of happier guessers to restore the true reading of the very *corrupt* person — pshaw, I mean passage — *Monstor digito* (Qu. Canning's ?) *prætereuntium * * * FIDICEN. * * — W. S.

* Ύδωρ βιυ, almost *literatim* usquebagh, "an Irish and Erse word," says Johnson, "which signifies *the water of life.*" The French have the same metaphor in their *Eau de Vie.* — W. S.

† Πυκτικον. See Il. Ω. 779. By a similar substitution of πυκτικος for πυκινος we read elsewhere,

Πυκτικη ως ὅταν ανδρ 'ατη λαβῃ—

Qu. Does ατη. A. T. represent, αινιγματωδως, Turner or Tring? I don't know their Christian names, but I observe you call the latter Athletic.

Πυκτικον ἀέε τι μοι ειπες επος.

Where the reader will note well the last two emphatic words. — W. S.

‡ 'Αλλος κ. τ. γ. This, by a slight deflection from Homer's

Αλλ' ειτις; με και αλλος ενι μεγαροισιν ενιπτοι, IL. Ω. 768.

gives the very names of the English pugilists, whom Donnelly caused to "bite the dust." — W. S.

‖ Επεεσσι alludes to the phrase *speaking* to a man, παραιφαμενος is literally rendered *admonishing,* and κατερυκες means *giving a check;* all, I believe, cant terms in the noble science of boxing. For κατερυκες, could I have gotten over the two slight objections of absolute non-resemblance and violated metre, I should have wished to substitute εκολαζες, *punishedst,* especially as connected with κολαφος, *colaphus,* and κολαπτω *tundo, tundendo excavo,* which, when applied (as it is by Aristotle) to the eyes, gives in its first sense the "peepers queered" of English pugilists, and the American "gouging" in the latter. But you will have remarked, that I am particularly nice in what regards the *ductus*

"Ου γαρ μειλιχος ης (φευ ελελευ ελελευ)
"Και συν γ' εν παλαμησιν οδαξ ελεν ασπετον ουδας·
"—Νυν δε σε μοιρα κιχεν (φευ ελελευ ελελευ)."
Ως εφασαν κλαιοντες· επεστενε δημος απειρων,
"Οι, οι, οι, οι, οι, αι, ε, ε, αι, ε, ε, αι."*

My dear Kit,—Fearing you have forgotten your Greek, I favour you with a Latin version of Will's "Ullaloo." I have had glorious fun in town; but am off like a shot to Cheltenham. I am sick of Brazenose.—She is an Irish girl, with 700 per annum, in the vicinity of the Bog of Allen. Keep a look out, and you will see me in the marriage-list.—Special license.—You old boy. These εισαιωνα. Bob Buller.

Heu! pugilum multò validissime, heu ter lugende Donelle!
Excidisti vitâ heu! valdè hâc juvenis.
Neque quidquam tibi patria abeunti curæ fuit Iërne,
Neque sex myriades (heu! &c.)
Qui tui curaverunt funus cantibus virûm-domitoris,
Nærias auspicantibus (heu! &c.)
Hi quidem lugubre canebant, adgemebantque mulieres,
Bibebantque ambo (heu! &c.)
Viri quidem Aquam vitæ hordeaceam, fæminæ verò
Quam vocant Theam (heu! &c.)
"Cur lucem relinquere, tot victor certaminum,"
Rogant, "voluisti? (heu! &c.)
"Num aliquem alium amat uxor, dic? vel filius aufugit
"Neque pugnam sustinuit? (heu! &c.)
"Vel te amantem virgines cæsiis-oculis, decus Iërnes,
"Non redamabant? (heu! &c.)
"Anglorum nunquam cohortem magnanimus in pugnâ tiisti
"Pugilum timuisti (heu! &c.)
"Sed si quis te vel Hallus, vel Olivarius in creparet,
"Vel Coöperus (heu! &c.)
"Tu contrà illum verbis (Qu. verberibus) admonens cohibebas,
"Neque enim mitis eras (heu! &c.)
"Et tuis manibus mordicùs prehendit immensum solum
—"Nunc vèro te fatum consecutum est (heu! &c.")
Sic dixerunt flentes; adgemuit plebs immensa:
"Oh! Oh! Oh! Oh! Oh! Agh! &c."

literarum, &c. in my emendations; and κατερυκες and εκολαξες approach very little nearer than Macedon and Monmouth. Even in its present reading, however, the line is—what Buller would have called versus verè πυκτικος.—W. S.
* Crescendo.

A HEBREW DIRGE OVER SIR DANIEL DONNELLY.

(By the Rev. J. BARRETT, D. D. S. F. T. C. D. Professor of Hebrew in Trinity College, Dublin.)

MR. NORTH,

Do you see me now,* my feelings were never so much hurted as when I heard of the death of the man of the strong hand— ὡς ἀγαθὸν—Dan, or Daniel, or Sir Daniel Donnelly. At Commons that day, I ate nothing to speak of, do you see me now nothing to speak of, only a matter of four pounds avoirdupois of beef; no delicacy, except the half, or perhaps 3–5ths of a custard pudding, and drank nothing but three pints of October. Ἆς, ἆ, said I, ἀπώλετο καλὸς.—though I know not whether he was καλὸς or callous—Ἀπώλετο, ἆ, ὂ, ay, ay, said Dr. Kyle,† for he is a man facetious in himself. Cheer up, doctor, said he, and take this cut of mutton. Κάτθανε καὶ Πάτροκλος—Damn Patroclus, said I, Lord pardon me, do you see me now, for swearing,‡ what was he to Donnelly, Ἰβέρνικος ἱππότα Δανιήλ.

At chapel next Sunday, I slept through three quarters of an hour, though Dr. Wall§ was preaching—for grief produceth somnolency. There was I inspired with a poetical effusion— nam me Phoebus amat—in the Hebrew tongue—the tongue despised by the ambubaiarum collegia Pharmacopolæ mendici mimæ balatrones—but dear to me, seeing that it bringeth me in a neat salary. Having heard then, O most learned Mr. North, that you had summoned your bold bards to send their verses to Auld Reekie's town, I send you this. I hate long prefaces, and have ere now fined a refractory scholar for saying grace too tediously, and thereby keeping the meat cooling—a thing, most

---

* Dr. Barrett, was Vice Provost of Trinity College, Dublin, and Professor of Hebrew also.—His spoken English was *sui generis*. "Do you see me now" prefaced almost every sentence he uttered. But he will figure more largely in print, by and by, and all about him is reserved.—M.

† Provost of Trinity College, Dublin, and afterwards Bishop of Cork and Ross. He had been Maginn's College tutor.—M.

‡ Barrett, albeit a Protestant Clergyman, was rather addicted to swearing. —M.

§ The Rev. Dr. C. W. Wall, then a Fellow and (since 1847) Vice Provost of Trinity.—M.

erudite Star of Edinburgh, hateful to my soul. Therefore, do you see me now, I shall not keep your expectation cooling, but let you fall to. Print my Hebrew properly. Mind the points. Put not a Patach for a Kametz, a Chateph Sægol for a Tzere, a Kibbutz for a Sheva. Masoretically print it, diacritically compose it. So farewell. Vive valeque.

J. BARRETT.

DUBLIN, *April*, 1, 1820.

[By some accident, which we cannot explain, Dr. Barrett's dirge has come to us much mutilated. We hasten, however, to print the fragments. It is a remarkable circumstance, that Dr. Barrett's lament bears a resemblance to a lament of Mr. Hyman Hurwitz's published in 1817. It must be accidental. EDIT.]

Translated by the Rev. E. Hincks,* F. T. C. D.

I.

אֱלִי אִירִין וּבְנֶיהָ!
כְּמוֹ אִשָּׁה בְּחֶבְלֵי־הּ;
וְכִבְתוּלָה, חֲגוּרַת־שָׂק
עֲלֵי בַּעַל נְעוּרֶיהָ,
אֱלִי וכו׳

1.

Mourn Erin, sons of Erin mourn,
Give utterance to the inward throe,
As wails of her first love forlorn,
The virgin clad in robes of wo.

II.

עֲלֵי גֶבֶר, אֲשֶׁר נִסְפַּד
בַּעֲוֹדָה בִּנְעִירִירוֹ
וְעַל בֶּן דַּד, אֲשֶׁר נִלְקַח,
וְעַל הַלּוּשֶׁת חָפָנָיו.
אֱלִי וכו׳

2.

Mourn for our Champion snatched away
From the fair Currag's verdant ring;
Mourn for his fist now wrapt in clay,
No more the ponderous thump to fling.

---

* Author of Bonaparte, a poem; I fear not extant. Mr. H. has made Mr. Coleridge's translation of Hurwitz's dirge the basis of his.—M. OD. [Dr. Edward Hincks, (whose father was Professor of Hebrew in the Belfast Institution, and whose brother Francis was Prime-Minister of Canada as late as 1854,) was one of the Fellows of Trinity, in Barrett's time, and vacated his Fellowship on taking a rich college living in the north of Ireland. As an Oriental scholar his reputation has long been great, and he ranks very high indeed as a decypherer of hieroglyphics and of the peculiar writing discovered by Layard and others at Nineveh.—M.]

III.

Lost.

IV.

כְּלִי בַלְעָה, אֲשֶׁר עָשָׂה
פְּנֵי אָרֶץ וְיֹשְׁבֵיו,
בְּמוֹת שׂוֹר דָּנִיאֵל הִזּלִי
בְּטֶרֶם מְלֹאת יָמָיו
אלי וכ׳

Cetera desunt.

3.

Mourn for the daisy* flower that went,
Ere half disclosed its boxing powers;
Mourn the green bud so rudely rent
From Ireland's pugilistic bowers.

4.

Mourn for the universal wo,
With solemn dirge and faltering tongue,
For Ireland's champion is laid low,
So stout, so hearty, and so strong.

Of Mr. Hinck's translation we shall only give in addition the 9th, 11th, and 12th verses.

9.

Mourn for old Ireland's hopes decayed,
Her bruisers weep in mournful strain,
Their fair example prostrate laid,
By seven-and-forty tumblers slain.

* * * * *

11.

Long as the Commons-hall is trod,
Will I the yearly dirge renew,
Mourn for the nursling of the sod,†
Our darling hurried from our view.

12.

The proud shall pass forgot; the chill,
Damp, trickling vault their only mourner,
Not so our daisy; no, that still
Clings to the breast which first had worn her.

* * * * *

LETTER FROM MR. JENNINGS.

Mr. Editor:

GRIEF drives poetry from my mouth with as vehement an explosion as that with which a bottle of soda water, in summer, expels the cork. Sir Daniel Donnelly's death has had this effect

* The daisy was the flower of Sir Daniel, just as the violet was that of Bonaparte. After his signal defeat of Oliver, he went home singing, "Down among the Daisies." — J. B.

† The sod, κατ' ἐξοχήν, is Ireland. — J. B.

on me; it has impregnated me with the gas of sorrow, and I effervesce in rhyme. My stanzas on the death of that great man may not be so good as those of others, but they are as sincere as the sincerest. Put them into your Boxiana collection. If you ever come to Cork, I shall be happy to supply you with soda water (quart bottles at 12d., pint ditto at 6d.,) with the utmost despatch, and of the best quality. Don't be afraid of any of Mr. Death-in-the-Pot's nostrums. I remain, sir, your obedient servant, THOMAS JENNINGS,*

CORK, *March 26th*, 1820, 7 *Brown Street.*   *Soda Water Manufacturer.*

A DIRGE OVER SIR DANIEL DONNELLY; BY THOMAS JENNINGS.

Tune—"Molly Astore."

1.

As down Exchequer Street† I strayed,
  A little time ago,
I chanced to meet an honest blade,
  His face brimful of wo;
I asked him why he seemed so sad,
  Or why he sighed so sore;
O Grammachree, och Tom, says he,
  Sir Daniel is no more!

2.

With that he took me straight away,
  And pensively we went,
To where poor Daniel's body lay,
  In wooden waistcoat pent;
And many a yard before we reached
  The threshold of his door,
We heard the keeners as they screeched,
  Sir Daniel is no more!

3.

We entered soft, for feelings sad
  Were stirring in our breast,
To take our farewell of the lad,
  Who now was gone to rest;

---

* Mr. Thomas Jennings, who was an extensive and very scientific soda-water manufacturer in "the beautiful city of Cork," never perpetrated a line of poetry in his life. The greater the fun in presenting him, in the "Luctus," as tuneful and tearful over the death of Donnelly.—M.

† In Dublin.—T. J.

We took a drop of Dan's potheen,
    And joined the piteous roar;
O, where shall be his fellow seen,
    Since Daniel is no more!

4.

His was the fist whose weighty dint
    Did Oliver defeat,
His was the fist that gave the hint
    It need not oft repeat,
His was the fist that overthrew
    His rivals o'er and o'er;
But now we cry in pillalu,
    Sir Daniel is no more!

5.

Cribb, Cooper, Carter, need not fear
    Great Donnelly's renown,
For at his wake we're seated here,
    While he is lying down;
For Death, that primest swell of all,
    Has laid him on the floor,
And left us here, alas! to bawl,
    Sir Daniel is no more!

EPITAPH.

Here lies Sir Daniel Donnelly,
    A pugilist of fame;
In Ireland bred and born was he,
    And he was genuine game;
Then if an Irishman you be,
    When you have read this o'er,
Go home and drink the memory
    Of him who is no more.

⁎ Mr. Jennings' Epitaph is no doubt very beautiful, but we have been informed, by letter, from the committee, in Townes' Street, Dublin, appointed to erect the Donnelly testimonial (which, we are happy to say, will shortly be raised near the Wellington testimonial in that city,) that another epitaph has been decided on. We intend soon to devote a paper to the "Donnelly testimonial," in which we shall probably enter into a comparison between the two great Irishmen, for whom the gratitude of their country is raising these tributes—Wellington and Donnelly. Meanwhile, we subjoin the Epitaph. It may

not be amiss to state, that the committee laudably requested permission from the Earl of Huntingdon, to imitate the Epitaph on his great ancestor,* which his Lordship, an Irishman himself, was most graciously pleased to grant.

> Underneath this pillar high
> Lies Sir Daniel Donnelly;
> He was a stout and handy man,
> And people called him "Buffing Dan;"
> Knighthood he took from George's sword,
> And well he wore it, by my word!
> He died at last from forty-seven
> Tumblers of punch he drank one even;
> O'erthrown by punch, unharmed by fist,
> He died unbeaten Pugilist!
> Such a buffer as Donnelly,
> Ireland never again will see.
>   Obiit xiii° Kal. Martii MDCCCXX.

LETTER FROM MR. RICHARD DOWDEN.†

Mr. Editor,

I send you my mite, to join the other poets of Ireland in the universal wail over Sir Daniel Donnelly. The song I transmit is to the tune of the Groves of Blarney. If you have never heard the original words, which were written by the late Mr. Richard Millikin‡ of this city, go get Terry Magrath, my good friend and fellow citizen, who is at present in Edinburgh, to sing it for you. It is an excellent song, and he sings it divinely.§ I am sure, that after you have heard him you will participate in my indignation against Mr. Thomas Moore, poet and melodist,

---

* Robin Hood. See the epitaph in Percy's Reliques, vol. i. p. 82, and elsewhere.—T. J.

† This gentleman, who, to distinguish himself from all others of the same name, has adopted the peculiar signature of "Richard Dowden (Richard)" was the son-in-law, if I recollect rightly, of Thomas Jennings, whose business he conducted.—M.

‡ Richard Millikin, well-known as author of "The Groves of Blarney," was an attorney in Cork.—M.

§ Mr. Magrath who resided in Edinburgh, for many years as professor of music, was a native of Cork. Sir Walter Scott greatly admired his singing.—M.

for having travestied so delightful a poem in his song beginning with, " 'Tis the last rose of Summer."—I am, Sir, your very humble Servant, RICHARD DOWDEN.
CORK INSTITUTION, *March* 31, 1820.

P. S.— If you wish for minutes of the interesting proceedings of this Institute, where I am bibliothecical assistant, I can help you. Or if you have any desire for the memoirs of the Cork Philosophical and Literary Society, I could give you some aid in that respect also.

A New Song, to the tune of the Groves of Blarney, being in Lamentation for the unhappy death of Sir Daniel Donnelly, Kt. C. I.* By RICHARD DOWDEN.

1.

" WHAT is it ails you, †ye beauteous people
Why are ye dropping the salt, salt tear,
Why does your tipple stand like a steeple,
None of ye stirring about the beer?"
'Twas thus I spoke to some honest fellows,
Sitting in grief in Cork's own town,
At Judy Kelly's, sign of the bellows,
Over the best of ‡Beamish's brown.
   Hulla, hulla, hulla, hulla, hulla, mulla-gone.

2.

'Twas they that answered me in a minute,
" Where do you come from, my honest man?
If from Ireland, the devil's in it
If you don't know 'tis all for Dan!
For brave Sir Daniel, that was no spaniel,
But a true bull-dog of Irish game,
Who laid his whacks on the bullying Saxon §
All for the honour of Ireland's name.
   Hulla, hulla, &c.

---

* C. I. Champion of Ireland, not Cork Institution. Sir Daniel never was a professor here.— R. D.

† The beauteous people, or rather the beautiful people, is the classic appellation for Irishmen, as the "beautiful city" is Cork.— R. D.

‡ Brown stout, brewed by Messrs. Beamish and Crawford, in the South Main Street, Cork, and good stuff it is.— R. D.

§ An Englishman, or a man of English descent, is called in Ireland (as in the Highlands of Scotland) a Sussenugh, or Saxon.— R. D.

3.

"He treated Oliver, just as Gulliver*
Treated the Lilliputian's house;
For he was a buffer that would not suffer
Crossbuttock, cuff, or thump like a mouse;
But like a lion, or bright Orion,
Or ould King Brian, surnamed Boro',
Who made the Danes, Sir, quit Clontarf's plains, Sir,
As fast as Boney quit Waterloo.
Hulla, hulla, &c.

4.

"Our worthy Regent was so delighted
With the great valour he did evince,
That Dan was cited, ay, and invited
To come be knighted by his own Prince;
Sir Richard Phillips, or Sir Bob Wilson,†
Could not compare with him in worth;
For this transaction, may satisfaction
Crown every action of George the Fourth.
Hulla, hulla, &c.

5.

"Was I a poet, 'tis I would show it,
And all should know it this cruel night;
I'd give the nation a bold oration
In declamation and letters bright
From Cork and Kerry to Londonderry
A mullagone I'd sadly roar,
With sweet Poll Cleary, and Judy Leary,‡
The blood-relations of my Lord Donoughmore.
Hulla, hulla, &c.

6.

"O Counsellor Connell, Æneas M'Donnel,§
And Charley Phillips, my speaking man,

---

* Vide Gulliver's travels. Verbum Sap.— R. D.

† Two *true* knights.— R. D. [Sir R. Phillips, a publisher and author, knighted by George III., when Sheriff of London, and Sir Robert Wilson, dismissed from the British Army, for interfering, on behalf of the people, at Queen Caroline's funeral, (in 1821) but subsequently restored, raised to the rank of General and Governorship of Gibraltar, and died in 1849.— M.]

‡ Borrowed from a MS. addition, (which, though never published, is always in singing put) to the Groves of Blarney, to the great comfort of the noble Lord.— R. D.

§ Three Irish orators.— R. D.

How you would swagger in trope and figure,
  If you were paid for praising Dan!
But without money, none of 'em, honey,
  Can bear to wag their humbugging jaw;
They're not worth naming, the set of scheming,
  Roguish, make-gaming limbs of the law."
    Hulla, hulla, &c.

7.

So sung this sporter, over his porter,
  Chanting as sweet as a nightingale;
Even Nebuchadnezzar, or Julius Cæsar,
  Would gladly stay Sir, to hear the tale.
I bet a penny, that Mr. Rennie,*
  And Mr. Davy,† himself beside,
Wouldn't make a ditty one half so pretty,
  On brave Sir Daniel, our Irish pride,
    Hulla, hulla, &c.

SPEECH DELIVERED AT THE CORK INSTITUTION.

Cork, *May 14th,* 1820.

Mr. Editor,—The Article Boxiana, in your Magazine for March last, afforded me as much satisfaction as ever I recollect to have experienced in the perusal of any periodical paper. Your heartfelt interest in the grand national quere, " Could Donnelly have beat Cribb? Could Carter have beat Donnelly?" has induced me, as Secretary to the Cork Philosophical and Literary Society, to communicate to you the truly eloquent and pathetic éloge, delivered before that society, immediately subsequent to the notification of the Death of the never-to-be-sufficiently lamented Sir Daniel Donnelly. The Cork Philosophical and Literary Society justly ranks as the first public institution in the South of Ireland, and is *inferior* to none in the British Dominions in general utility; its proceedings, therefore, can not but be acceptable to every true lover of science. (*a*)—Early

* A Glasgow lecturer on metaphysics, &c. in Cork.— R. D.
† Professor of Chemistry, and secretary to the Cork Institution.— R. D.
[Dr. John Davy, brother and biographer of Sir Humphrey Davy, P. R. S.—M.]
a, A quarto volume of its transactions is in the press, and will speedily be published under the superintendence of J. Rennie of Glasgow, A. M. who lately arrived in Cork. From the high literary fame of Mr. Rennie, and the innate value of the papers themselves, it is expected the philosophical world will be furnished with a treat, unparalleled in any transactions of modern days.—W. H.

on the evening of Wednesday, the 22d March, the assembly of talent and beauty, (*b*) in the Hall, (*c*) belonging to the society, was unprecedented in the memory of the oldest member; the chair was richly ornamented with crape and other funereal emblems, and the lamps and a superb lustre were decorated with

b, For the further elucidation of this subject, it may be necessary to inform you that *ladies* are admitted to our Society, provided, for the three hours they sit there, they remain *silent;* this, by some of the members, is conceived to be a very great hardship, that ladies who are capable of delivering their sentiments, and contributing to the interest of the discussion, should be restricted from that privilege which so peculiarly belongs to the sex. This law has been transgressed in one solitary instance, (mirabile dictu!) when, during the reading of a paper a short time since on the obstetric art, a respectable widow lady begged to offer a few remarks in opposition to the theory brought forward by the learned author of the paper. She was instantly called to order, and severely censured; this was certainly carrying the restriction too far, as one practical observation, connected with the subject, was worth folios of theory.—W. H.

c, As an illustration of the above, I transmit you a drawing of the hall, and shall feel particularly obliged, if you yourself will attend to its execution.

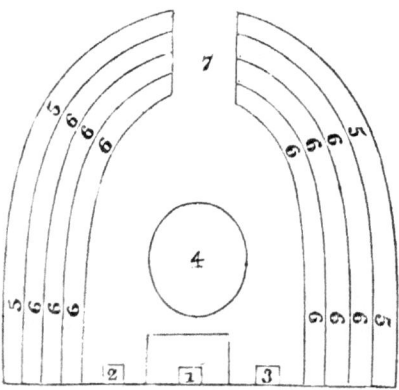

No. 1, The chair, a little elevated above the floor, and strewed round with shamrocks, emblematical of the country that gave "the Donnelly" birth. No. 2, The treasurer's seat and a desk, a large willow branch waving over him. No. 3, The secretary, with a similar desk, &c., a branch of cypress. No. 4, A circular table at which the reader sits, and *fronts* the president, the table covered with a black cloth, and furnished with wax candles, decanters of water, rummers, &c. No. 5, 5, 5, 5, The ladies' seats. No. 6, 6, 6, 6, The gentlemen's seats. No. 7. The entrance.

festoons of cypress and willow, producing an effect solemn and impressive beyond description, and the dead and awful silence that prevailed was only interrupted at broken intervals by the long drawn breath and suppressed sigh; (*d*) at length the President, having taken the Chair, Mr. Richard Dowden arose, and in a tremulous tone of voice, that evidently betrayed the inward tumult and agitation of his soul, addressed the meeting as follows:

"Mr. President!—Never have I so forcibly experienced my utter incapacity to do justice to an important subject—never have I felt myself so truly embarrassed as on the present distressing occasion.* (*hear! hear!*) When I look around, and behold the galaxy of genius that surrounds me, (*hear! hear!*) my heart sinks within me, and my faltering tongue almost denies its office. I confess my weakness. I declare my inability. I throw myself upon your candour. I confide in the liberality of a generous, an enlightened public. (*hear! hear!*) Yes, I experience by anticipation that indulgence from you, that will kindle a flame of gratitude in my breast, never to be extinguished but by death! (*hear! hear!*) Mr. President! How vain are all things here below! The gay smiling morn of life is the dark gloomy evening of Death! The dawn of intellect is the twilight of the grave! 'The cloud-capt towers, the gorgeous palaces, the solemn temples, the great globe itself, yea, all that it inhabit, shall dissolve, and like the baseless fabric of a vision, leave not a wreck behind!' 'Pallida morse æquo pulsat pede pauperum tabernas regumque turres.' He! (*hear!*)

d, Amongst the decorations mentioned above, I had almost forgotten to notice a beautiful transparent full length portrait of Sir Daniel, elevated considerably above the chair, illuminated from behind by six argand patent lamps, and forming an exquisite contrast with the gloom and sorrow that reigned below. It was executed for the occasion by Mr. Topp, portrait painter to the Society, and reflects equal honour on that gentleman for his talents as an artist, and his feelings as a man. After it had been exposed for a sufficient time in the Exhibition Gallery, it is the benevolent intention of Mr. Topp, to present it to the sorrowing widow, as a "sweet remembrancer" of her never-to-be-forgotten partner.—W. H.

* Mr. Dowden is one of the most eminent speakers in our Society, I may say the Demosthenes of the Society: He was much attached to the late Sir Daniel, and had the benefit of his instruction several years.—W. H.

who but a few short days since was the glory of our land; He! (*hear!*) whose intellectual and corporeal energies were the theme of every tongue; He! (*hear* HIM!) who basked in all the sunshine of prosperity; He! (*hear!*) who, in all the pride of conscious dignity, stood on the loftiest pinnacle of fame and honour; He! (*hear!*) whose virtues were as the refreshing dews of Heaven; He!——is gone!!! The inexorable arm of the King of Terrors has widowed every heart of sensibility. The chilling gloom of despair has frozen every soul. Cribb is glad; Carter rejoices; Hall, Cooper, and Oliver, are avenged! England triumphs. 'Don'ly is dead, and Erin is no more!' (*a general burst of feeling; the sobs of the ladies greatly predominating!!*)

"Great Shade!* where art thou now? O! that the thin airy presence of thy spirituality were hovering round us, to hear the humble tribute paid to thy departed worth—to behold thy memory watered with a nation's tears!† (*hear* HIM!) Sir Daniel was descended, by the mother's side, from the illustrious Peter Corcoran, a hero, beneath whose arm proud Albion oft did crouch, and through his father, from the mighty Ryan, the formidable opponent of the irresistible Johnson. The blood of heroes circulated in his veins; the acts of his forefathers fired his imagination; the genius of Erin presided at his birth, and nursed him with a parent's care! Of his deeds what shall we say? His actions, who shall record? Who amongst us is adequate to the task of speaking his praise? What language is capable of conveying, even in the faintest degree, any just conception of his more than human talents!!‡ Unpossessed of the advantages which a regular education affords, relying solely on

---

* Here the learned gentleman addressed the full length portrait of Sir Daniel before alluded to.—W. H.

† Mr. Dowden's voice was now completely overpowered by the sobbing of the ladies; it gained such an ascendency, that it required the united efforts of president, vice, censors, and myself, to restore order.—W. H.

‡ Sir Daniel's great abilities were known but to few; he was a remarkably modest man, and dreaded publicity; he was a warm and passionate admirer of the fine arts, particularly poetry and music, which often "soothed his soul to melancholy;" he was deeply skilled in Oriental literature, and is supposed by many to have been the author of Anastasius.—W. H.

the gigantic force of his own stupendous capabilities, like the blazing comet, he arose before the astonished world, remained a short period above the horizon, eclipsing all competition, dazzling every eye with the brilliancy of his career, and at length sunk to rest amidst the acclamations of an applauding country! (*hear! hear!*) As when the sun, arising in the morning, quickly dispels the dark clouds, thick mists and vapours, which surrounded him, and which vainly attempted to obscure his rays and dim his brightness, breaks forth in all the meridian blaze of unclouded noon, spreading around him life, and light, and gladness; then at the approach of evening, he calmly sinks, with inconceivable splendour, into the western wave, leaving the world, it is true, in tenfold darkness, but still living and existing in the memory of those who were crowned with his blessings, who were supported and nourished by his beneficent bounties! (*hear! hear!*)

"The domestic life of Sir Daniel was marked by all the most endearing features that characterize the tender husband, the fond father, the sincere, the generous friend. Early in life he formed a connexion with an amiable and enlightened female of the Society of Friends, who was the balm of every wound in life, the soft and pleasing pillow upon which he reclined his head in the awful hour of death. During all the conquests which diffused such lustre round his manly brow, she (*hear* HIM!) was ever the object of his thoughts; and though the *leveller* of a Cooper, and the *facer* of an Oliver, might for a moment have interrupted the train of his reflections, the remembrance of his beloved Rebecca recalled his fainting powers, stimulated him to fresh exertions, and finally enabled him to prostrate in the dust his haughty foe!!! (*tumultuous applause.*)*

"At daybreak, on the morning of his interment, the inhabitants of Dublin manifested their attachment to their adored champion, by every mark of attention and respect. The bells of the several parish churches were muffled, minute guns were fired in the Park; and the concourse of people assembled in the streets was beyond all precedent. During that eventful day,

---

* Here the reading of the paper was again partially interrupted, by the removal of two female friends, whose philosophy was completely subdued by feeling.— W. H.

the shops remained shut, public business was suspended, the theatres were closed, and the gloom of sorrow and the depression of anguish pervaded every countenance.

"At ten o'clock the procession moved from Sir Daniel's mansion in Sackville-street, towards St. Patrick's Cathedral. At twelve the coffin was lowered into the silent vault, and Mozart's celebrated Requiem was performed under the immediate direction of Sir John Stevenson, with an uncommon and impressive effect.

> Such honours Erin to her hero paid,
> And peaceful slept the mighty Don'ly's shade.

"It was the dying request of Sir Daniel that no external pomp should adorn his grave. A plain marble slab marks the spot where *he* is laid, 'who once had beauty, titles, wealth, and fame.'

> 'Yet shall thy grave with rising flowers be dressed,
> And the green turf lie lightly on thy breast;
> There shall the morn her earliest tears bestow,
> There the first roses of the year shall blow;
> While angels with their silver wings o'ershade
> The ground now sacred by thy reliques made.'*

But let us drop the curtain, the feelings of humanity forbid us to dwell longer on the harrowing scene!! (*hear! hear!*)

> 'Jamque opus exegi: quod nec Jovis ire, nec ignes,
> Nec poterit ferrum, nec edax abolere vetustas.'"

Mr. Dowden then sat down, cheered from all sides of the room.

The publication of the above will probably induce me to favour you with the proceedings of our Society.—I remain your obedient Servant,   Wm. Holt.†

P. S.—I will thank you to present my compliments to Dr. Thompson, when you see him, and tell him I have nearly finished the Meteorological Table for the next month's Annals.

---

* The anticipations of the writer have been agreeably realized. We understand, since his interment, some respectable ladies who knew him, and valued the deceased, have adorned his grave with "rising flowers," among which the *Narcissus* appears predominant. We also understand that the Royal Society have directed the Marquis Canova, to exert his superior abilities in the production of a statue of Sir Daniel in his favourite attitude.—C. North.

† William Holt, a bookseller in Cork, calculated and published an almanack there, and was known as a profound mathematician.—M.

John Gilpin and Mazeppa.*

Had the poem of John Gilpin appeared immediately after that of Mazeppa, we should have believed, in this age of parody, that Cowper wished to have his joke upon Lord Byron. As it is, we cannot help suspecting that his Lordship has been aiming a sly hit at the bard of Olney; and though his satire is occasionally rather stiff and formal, it cannot be denied that, on the whole, the Hetman of the Cossacks is a very amusing double of the train-band captain of the Cockneys.

"John Gilpin" has always appeared to us a very fine chivalrous poem. Unquestionably, the author sometimes indulges in a strain of humour which, to fastidious minds, lessens the sublimity of the principal character, and of his destinies; yet, we believe, that by more philosophical readers, this mixture of the ludicrous with the terrible, is felt to present a more true and affecting picture of human life.

In childhood and early youth we are, after all, the best judges of representation of human passion. We see objects, incidents, and events, as they really are; we estimate their effect on the agents engaged with them, free from all bias; and mere words, mere poetry, however much they may delight us, are, during that wise and blessed age, unable to pervert our judgment, or mislead the natural affections of our heart.

Accordingly, "John Gilpin" is that poem which has drawn from youth more tears and smiles than, perhaps, any other in the whole range of English poetry. It is treasured up in every amiable and sensitive heart, and that man is little to be envied whose conjugal affection would not kindle at the inn of Edmonston, or whose filial piety would not grow warmer at the Callender's house at Ware.

It is not our intention to give an elaborate analysis of "John Gilpin," or a philosophical exposition of the principles on which that great poem is constructed. This would necessarily lead us

---

* Mazeppa, written in the autumn of 1818, at Ravenna, was published in 1819. This article, treating it as a parody on, or imitation of, Cowper's ballad of John Gilpin, appeared in *Blackwood* in July, 1819.—M.

into a discussion of the principles of all poetry, which we prefer giving some months hence, in a separate treatise. Mr. Wordsworth has, to be sure, done this already, in his preface to the "Lyrical Ballads;" but, unless we are greatly mistaken, (ni fallor) he has not exhausted the subject—and we do not fear that among the numerous quartos yet to be written thereupon, ours can fail of attracting some portion of that public regard, which we gratefully acknowledge to have hitherto been so lavishly bestowed on our lucubrations.

It seems to have been Lord Byron's intention to shew what John Gilpin's feeling would, in all probability, have been, had he been placed in circumstances different from those in which he found himself on the anniversary of his marriage with Mrs. Gilpin; and surely the least imaginative reader will be of opinion that the noble lord has attained this difficult object in Mazeppa. After the perusal of the two works, we all feel that if John Gilpin's stars had permitted it, he was just the man to have become the monarch of the Ukraine; and *vice versa*, that Mazeppa, but for the accident of his birth, &c. might have established a highly respectable firm in Cheapside.

Cowper has not given us any account of the antenuptial loves of John Gilpin, but introduced him at once to our acquaintance, as a married man, with a considerable family, and in a thriving trade. Mazeppa, on the other hand, had involved himself, early in life and the poem, in a very improper intrigue. But human nature is the same in all countries; and no good objection could have been brought against either bard, though John Gilpin had been described as gallanting a citizen's wife on a water-party to Richmond, and Mazeppa comfortably settled with a wife and family in some mercantile town on the frontiers of Poland. As Mr. Wordsworth remarks, "similitude dissimilitude," is one of the chief sources of the sublime in poetry.

That principle being once admitted, Mazeppa will probably seem to every one sufficiently like John Gilpin, in character and situation in life. Let us next look at the two gentlemen after they are fairly mounted. There is no occasion to quote the whole description of John, for it is probably familiar to our readers. Suffice it to remind them that

> "John Gilpin, at his horse's side,
> Fast seized the flowing mane."

And that afterwards,

> "Then over all, that he might be
> Equipped from top to toe,
> His long red cloak, well brushed and neat,
> He manfully did throw."

Lord Byron is more minute in his description; and from it we suspect that, on the whole, Mazeppa was better mounted than John Gilpin.

> "Bring forth the horse — the horse was brought —
> In truth he was a noble steed,
> A Tartar of the Ukraine breed."

John Gilpin's horse was, we have reason to know, an Irishman — his friend the Callender having imported him from the county of Tipperary.* On the other hand, though better mounted, Mazeppa was worse dressed, for he was

> "In nature's nakedness."

This being the case, he was probably in the long run no better off than John Gilpin, of whom it is written that

> "The snorting beast began to trot,
> Which galled him in his seat."

Hitherto the similarity between the Hetman and the Linen-draper has been sufficiently apparent; but it is much more striking after they have fairly started.

> "So, fair and softly, John he cried,
> But John he cried in vain,
> That trot became a gallop soon,
> In spite of curb or rein.
>
> "So stooping down, as needs he must,
> Who cannot sit upright,
> He grasped the mane with both his hands,
> And eke with all his might.
>
> "His horse, who never in that sort
> Had handled been before,
> What thing upon his back had got,
> Did wonder more and more."

---

* He was bred by —— Blennerhasset, Esq. — See Sporting Magazine for that year. — M. OD.

Nothing can be finer and more headlong than this, except what follows:—

> "'Away, away! my breath had gone
> I saw not where he hurried on!
> Twas scarcely yet the break of day,
> And on he foamed, away, away!'"

In one very remarkable particular, John Gilpin is distinguished from Mazeppa.

> "So stooping down, as needs he must,
> Who cannot sit upright,
> He grasped the mane with both his hands,
> And eke with all his might."

On the contrary, Mazeppa says,

> "With sudden wrath I wrenched my hand,
> And snapped the cord, which to the mane
> Had bound my neck in lieu of rein."

It would appear, therefore, that on first starting, Mazeppa (it will, no doubt, be said *involuntarily*) had his arms round his horse's neck, but afterwards held them more like a gentleman who had taken lessons in riding, whereas John Gilpin, first of all, probably attempted to elevate his bridle-hand, but afterwards conceived it more salutary to embrace the neck of his Bucephalus. This, however, is a circumstance scarcely worth mentioning. Lord Byron then goes on to say,

> "Away, away, my steed and I,
> Upon the pinions of the wind!"

And Cowper in like manner writes,

> "Away went Gilpin neck or nought,
> Away went hat and wig,"

Which last line does, we confess, convey to our mind a more lively idea of the rapidity of motion, than any single image in Mazeppa.

It is impossible, however, to admire sufficiently the skill with which Lord Byron has contrasted the general features of Mazeppa's ride with those of John Gilpin's. John's steed gallops along the king's highway, and Mazeppa's through the desert. Yet, if danger or terror be one source of the sublime, we humbly hold that there is a sublimity in the situation of the London cit, far beyond that of the Polish gentleman. For, in the first place,

Mazeppa being securely bound to his horse, need entertain no apprehensions of a severe fall, whereas John's adhesion to his nag seems to the reader almost in the light of a continued miracle, little accustomed as he must have been to that sort of exercise. Secondly, would not any person whatever prefer gallopping along turf, sand, or dust, to a causeway leading from the metropolis of a great empire? Nothing surprises us so much in the poem of John Gilpin, as that the Callender's horse does not come down, which would almost force us to suspect that John was a better horseman than the world in general give him credit for. Indeed, though not much of a metaphysician ourselves, having read little on that subject, save some of the works of the celebrated Macvey Napier, Esq., we think that we may venture to assert, that a considerable portion of the delight with which we peruse or rather pursue John Gilpin, arises from our admiration of his skill in horsemanship. This admiration of the rider is also blended with affection for the man.

"We love him for the dangers he is passing,
And he loves us because we pity them."

And this leads us, in the third place, to remark that those dangers are of the most formidable kind. We may safely assert that before he reached Edmonton, he had brushed by at least 200 carriages, coming and going, of all sorts, from the broad-wheeled waggon to the shandrydan. Yet it does not appear that he drove any of them into pieces, or in any one instance transfixed his friend's galloway on the pole of a carriage coming up to town. He seems to us to be a man under the protection of Providence. And then, what majestic calmness and composure are his! Why, not two men in eight millions, that is to say, no other man but John Gilpin, in the whole then population of England, would have exhibited such heroism.—Mazeppa, too, no doubt, had his difficulties to contend with—but they were not of so formidable a description. His feelings must have been very uncomfortable as he "neared the wild wood," "studded with old sturdy trees," and he probably laid his account with many a bang on the shins;—but Lord Byron ought not to have told us that the trees "were few and far between;" for, in that case, the forest must have been very pretty riding.

> "He rustled through the leaves like wind,
> Left shrubs, and trees, and wolves behind."

It would almost seem from these lines, as if Mazeppa were under such alarm, as to imagine the shrubs and trees to be chasing him, as well as the wolves. This is a touch of poetry beyond any thing to be found in John Gilpin. His dangers were of another sort.

> "The dogs did bark, the children screamed,
> Up flew the windows all" —

The extreme folly of thus suddenly throwing open their windows (an ugly trick by which many an honest man has come to an untimely end,) is almost redeemed by the deep interest which these worthy but thoughtless people take in the fortunes of the flying Cockney.

> "And every one cried out — well done!
> As loud as he could bawl."

We never read this agonising poem (for the interest is so intensely kept up as to be indeed agonising) without blessing ourselves for the fortunate delusion of the various turnpikemen by which John Gilpin was saved the necessity of taking many dangerous leaps, one or other of which would, in all human probability, have proved fatal.

> "He carries weight — he rides a race."

This exclamation, borne before him, and just before him, on the wings of the wind, gives one a truly awful idea of velocity, and well might Cowper exclaim,

> "'Twas wonderful to view
> How in a trice the turnpikemen
> Their gates wide open flew."

No sooner did the public mind take up the belief "he rides a race," than by a wonderful process of thought, it discovers the amount of the wager he had laid,

> "'Tis for a thousand pound."

an immense sum at that time, when horse-racing had not nearly reached its meridian splendour, and when only a very few numbers, if any, of the Sporting Magazine had been published. In all this, Cowper has manifestly the advantage over Byron.

Compared with the fine passages now quoted from Gilpin, how tame are the following words of Mazeppa.

> "Untired, untamed, and worse than wild,
> All furious as a favoured child
> Balked of its wish — or fiercer still,
> A woman piqued, who has her will."

Here Mazeppa's gallantry altogether forsakes him, nor can we imagine a more inelegant compliment to the mistress whom he was then leaving, than to compare her, or indeed any of her sex, to a wild Tartar horse, on whom he was then tied "in nature's nakedness."

It does not appear that Gilpin lost his senses or his presence of mind during any portion of the Excursion, a Poem. Mazeppa, on the other hand, was completely done up, and absolutely fainted.

> "He who dies,
> Can die no more than then I died,
> O'er-tortured by that ghastly ride."

Presence of mind is a quality indispensable in the character of a true hero. We pity Mazeppa, but we admire Gilpin.

Mazeppa complains frequently of hunger during his ride — but no such weakness degrades Gilpin, who seems almost raised above all the ordinary wants of nature.

> "Stop! stop! John Gilpin — here's the house,
> They all at once did cry —
> The dinner waits, and we are tired;
> Said Gilpin — so am I!"

Not a single word of regret does he utter for the want of that dinner which has so long waited for him, but which, from the impatient appetites of Mrs. Gilpin and the children, he well knows is then trembling on the brink of destruction. One solitary exclamation is all that proceeds from his lips, as he hurries by below the balcony,

> "So am I!"

An ordinary writer would have filled his mouth with many needless words. Lord Byron has evidently very closely copied this sublime passage in an early part of Mazeppa's career.

> "Writhing half my form about,
> Howl'd back my curse; but 'midst the tread,

> The thunder of my courser's speed,
> Perchance they did not hear nor heed."

It may be questioned, however, if this, fine as it is, does not want the concise energy of the original.

The dangers which Gilpin and Mazeppa encounter, arise not only from land but water. Thus quoth the Pole:

> "Methought the dash of waves was nigh,
> The wild horse swims the wilder stream."

In like manner, we are told by Cowper,

> "Thus all through merry Islington,
> These gambols did he play
> Until he came unto the Wash
> Of Edmonton so gay.
>
> And there he threw the wash about
> On both sides of the way,
> Just like unto a trundling mop,
> Or a wild goose at play."

These images are homely, but they are not, on that account, the less expressive. That of the "trundling mop," simply expresses the appearance of the "Wash," thrown off on both sides of the way by the poney *en passant;* that of the wild goose at play, makes a direct appeal to the imaginative faculty, and suggests to our minds at least, a much more poetical feeling of a good gallopper, than his Lordship's images of the crying baby, or the scolding mistress. It gives one a momentary flash of the higher and hidden powers of that roadster, and convinces us that his owner would not part with him for a very considerable sum of money. This is one of those sudden and unexpected touches so characteristic of Cowper, and that prove what great things he might have accomplished, had he turned his genius more systematically to the cultivation of the higher provinces of poetry.

After swimming the river, Mazeppa's horse is not in the least degree tired, but

> "With glossy skin, and dripping mane,
> And reeling limbs and reeking flank,
> The wild steed's sinewy nerves still strain
> Up the repelling bank."

Here Lord Byron strictly follows the original.

> "But yet his horse was not a whit
> Inclined to tarry there, &c.

and what is still more strikingly similar, the two horses have the very same motives for their conduct.

> "For why? his owner had a house
> Full ten miles off at Ware."

Mazeppa's horse had hitherto been accustomed to lead a free and easy life, rather more than ten miles off in the Ukraine — and thither accordingly he set off at score, making play all the way, pretty much after the fashion of a steeple-hunt. It may perhaps be worth while to quote, for a particular reason, the following verse:

> "So like an arrow swift he flew,
> Shot by an archer strong;
> So did he fly, which brings me to
> The middle of my song."

Now, it is very remarkable — and we think the coincidence cannot be accidental — that the corresponding passage in Mazeppa also occurs just about the middle of the poem, which satisfactorily shews, that the original structures of the two great works do in their dimensions exactly coincide.

The termination of Gilpin's excursion therefore, evidently suggested that of Mazeppa's. But Byron has contrived to give quite a new turn to his poem — so that in the final catastrophe he almost seems to lose sight of the original. At Ware Gilpin's horse stands stock still at the door of his master's house, which, by the by, proves that he had not that unchancy trick of bolting into the stable, "*sans ceremonie*," which has incommoded many a sober-headed gentleman. Mazeppa's horse, in like manner, falls down the instant he reaches home, so we observe that the transition from motion to repose is in both cases equally abrupt. Mazeppa's sufferings are now at an end — and being put instantly into a good warm bed, he soon comes to himself — marries — and in good time becomes the father of many children, and Hetman of the Cossacks. Gilpin, on the other hand, has scarcely had leisure to put on a new hat and wig, than off he sets again without ever drawing a bit — but it is unnecessary to follow him farther with any minuteness. Conclude we cannot without recalling to the memory of our readers one stanza which ever awakens in our minds a profound sense of the depth of Mrs.

Gilpin's conjugal affection, and of the illimitable range of the
imagination when flying on the wings of terrified love.

> "Now Mrs. Gilpin, when she saw
> Her husband posting down
> Into the country far away,
> She pull'd out half a crown."

That one line, "into the country far away," gives to us a vaster
idea of distance — of time and space — that the whole 1000 lines
of Mazeppa. The reader at once feels how little chance there
is of the post-boy overtaking Gilpin — and owns that the worthy
man ought to be left entirely to himself and his wild destinies.

We need pursue the parallel no farther. But we may remark,
that though we have now proved John Gilpin to have been the
prototype of Mazeppa, yet the noble author has likewise had in
his recollection the punishment which used sometimes to be inflicted on criminals in Russia. They were bound on the back
of an elk, and sent into Siberia or elsewhere. We refer our
readers to the Sporting Magazine, where they will find a very
affecting picture of a gentleman on his elk. It was always the
practice to shave the criminal before he mounted, and in the picture we speak of, he has a beard of about six inches long, which
informs us that he had been on his travels probably several
weeks. *Ut pictura poesis.*

The Embalmer.*

Pero con todo esto me parece, que el traducir de una lengua en otra, como no sea de las Reynas de las lenguas, Griega y Latina, es como quien mira los tapices Flamencos por el revés que aunque se veén las figuras son llenas de hilos que las obscurecen, y no se ven con la lisura y tez de la haz; y el traducir de lenguas faciles ni arguye ingenio, ni elocucion, como no le arguye el que traslada ni el que copia un papel de otro papel; y no por esto quiero inferir que no sea loable este excercicio del traducir porque en otras cosas peores se podria occupar el hombre, y que menos provecho le truxessen.

Don Quixote, p. 2, c. 62.

IN spite of the angry motto against translators which I have here prefixed, I yet must say I look upon them as a very valuable body of men, and you may take my word for it, that my respect for the corps is not at all diminished by the circumstance of my having occasionally figured in it myself. But I do not much value those of our brotherhood who are contented with oversetting, as the Germans phrase it, works into the mere vernacular. They are only writers for a day—nothing but ephemerals. *Non sic itur ad astra.* If the original be worth knowing, people will read it in its native tongue, so that there is no good done for any but the ignorant or lazy part of mankind.

My department, I flatter myself, is rather higher. It has been long complained, that all living languages are in a state of such continual flux, that it is almost wasting a man's talents to write in them. Geoffry Crayon, if I do not mistake, most pathetically laments this affair in his Sketch Book. Chaucer strikes us as more antique reading than Homer; and a man finds more difficulty in getting through Gawain Douglas than through Virgil. It is a melancholy reflection for the thousand-and-one writers of the present day, that even such of them as have the good luck to survive half a dozen centuries, must submit to the misfortune of being read through the musty medium of comments and glossaries.

I have often turned my thoughts towards the prevention of

* This appeared in *Blackwood*, for July, 1821.—M.

this calamitous event, but, until a few days ago, in vain. An idea then suddenly struck me, as I lay in bed one morning, so felicitous, that I instantly jumped up, and set about putting it into execution. My project is, to translate all works of modern tongues at once into ancient;—a dead language, as my Lord Byron very properly remarks, in his late pamphlet on Pope, being the only immortal thing in this world. By this means we should embalm our authors; and I intend to take upon me at once the office of EMBALMER GENERAL, in which capacity I may perhaps appear at the coronation, and offer the King a mummy case, as an appropriate homage fee. The works of our poets— for our prose writers I leave to Dr. Bellendenus—will, I trust, be preserved by my preparations, at least as effectually as bodies are by the antiseptic drugs, or gross unguents of Sir Everard Home,* or that most magnificence personage, William Thomas Brande, Esquire, Secretary to the Royal Institution, and chief concocter of that highly amusing and agreeably authentic miscellany, the Quarterly Journal of Science.

It may be said, that translations always fall far short of the original, and sacrifice numberless graces. Perhaps this is true of all other translators now extant; but in my particular case, all that I am afraid of is, that I may beautify the original too much, and that the charms of my style and composition may make the readers of my translations apt to value inferior productions too highly, from the beauty of the amber in which I shall enwrap them. However, as in such cases the originals will perish, the world will be the better for having my versions in their place; and a regard to the general interest of mankind ought to pervade the breast of every good and benevolent person.

I had some doubt as to what language I should patronize. Hebrew is by far too crabbed to write, and is, besides, lying under high professional censure. I understand, indeed, that a gentleman in Italy has translated the Satires of Horace successfully into the language of Zion; and that it is capable of beautiful and harmonious melody, every body who has read the pa-

---

* Sir Everard Home, a Scottish surgeon who obtained reputation and practice in London, was born in 1756, and died in 1832. His "Lectures on Comparative Anatomy" are in high esteem.—M.

thetic dirge,* in the thirty-eighth Number of *Blackwood*, by the vice-provost of Trinity College, Dublin, must acknowledge. But, in spite of all this, a man's fingers get horribly cramped in jotting and dotting. It is tiresome work to be meddling with the kings and emperors of Hebrew accentuation—with Zakeph-Katons, Telisha Gedolas, Schalschelets, and other grim-titled little flourishes. And if the thing were to be done at all, it should be done Masoretically; for I look on the Anti-Masorites to be complete Whigs (*i. e.* very contemptible persons) in literature. With respect to Greek, it is a very fit language. We all remember Porson's elegant translation of Three Children Sliding on the Ice; and I have read two or three neat versions of Shakspere, done by Cambridge men for the prize founded by him. God save the King, too, has been done for the Classical Journal passably; and Mr. Cæcilius Metellus has given the commencement of John Gilpin so well, in the same periodical, that I wish he would finish it; after which, he might try his hand at the celebrated imitation of Cowper's philosophical poem, Lord Byron's Mazeppa. I was inclined to follow these examples, but it most unluckily happened, that in the very first poem I took up, I had occasion to look for the precise signification of a word beginning with omega, which I wanted to use; and not being quite satisfied with Stephanus's interpretation, I am obliged to wait until I see the opinion of the new *Thes.* on the point, which will delay my Greekish intentions, until somewhere in the year 1835. Latin, then, being all that remained, I have commenced operations on a grand scale. Vincent Bourne, honest dear fellow, has done a great deal already in that way, but I shall soon surpass his labours.

I was dubious, too, with respect to the metres, whether I should only use those of ancient Rome, or conform myself to the modern versification. There are great authorities on both sides, Dr. Aldrich translated

A soldier and a sailor,
A tinker and a tailor, &c.

into Latin of similar structure with the English, and Chevy-Chase has been done in the same. Many inferior names might

* *Vide ante*, in the "Luctus on the Death of Donnelly."—M.

be also adduced. The objection to it is, that Latin lines to English tunes, are as much out of place, as English lines of Latin form.

I send a few fragments, sweepings of my portfolios, as samples. The great works I am employed in, I shall keep for your private inspection. Below are a part of "Take thy old cloak about thee," of "July the First," of "The Groves of Blarney," of "Mary Ambree," of "Sir Tristrem," and the epitaphs on Sir Patrick Sarsfield, John, Duke of Marlborough, Henry, Duke of Grafton, Robin Hood, Earl of Huntingdon, and Sir Daniel Donnelly, champion of Ireland. I have used both Latin and English metres.

I.

VERSE OF "TAKE THY OLD CLOAK ABOUT THEE."*

Sung by Iago in the Second Act of Othello.

King Stephen was a worthy peer,
   His breeches cost him but a crown,
He held them sixpence all too dear,
   And so he call'd the tailor loon.
He was a king, and wore a crown,
   Thou art a squire of low degree;
'Tis pride that pulls the country down,
   So take thy old cloak about thee.

Rex Stephanus princeps fuit illustrissimus olim,
   Sexque decem braccæ constiterunt obolis.
Assibus hoc pretium reputans sex charius æquo,
   Sartorem jurgat nomine furciferi.
Ille fuit dominus celso diademate cinctus,
   Et tu demissi nil nisi verna loci;
Eheu! sternit humi nunc nostra superbia regnum,
   Veste igitur trita contege terga precor.

II.

VERSES OF JULY THE FIRST, THE GREAT ORANGE SONG IN IRELAND.

July the first, in old Bridge town,
   There was a grievous battle,—

---

* After a diligent collation of MSS. I have fixed on readings which differ somewhat from the received text of his poem.—M. OD.

Where many a man lay on the ground,
 And the cannon they did rattle.
King James, he pitch'd his tents between,
 His lines for to retire,*
But William threw his bomb-balls in,
 And set them all on fire.*
   *   *   *   *
The horse and cannon cross'd the stream,
 And the foot came following a'ter,
But brave Duke Schomberg lost his life
 In crossing the Boyne Water.
   *   *   *   *
A bullet from the Irish came,
 And grazed King William's arm —*
They thought his majesty was slain,
 But it did him little harm.*
   *   *   *   *
The Protestants of Drogheda
 Have reason to be thankful,
That they were all preserved that day,
 Though they were but a handful.

In veteris pontis vico, Juliique calendis
Atrox pugna fuit, morientia millia campum
Sternebant: Sonitum horribilem tormenta dedere.
In medio spatio tendebat rex Iacobus,
Posset ut ex acie subducere longius,† autem
Igniferos jecit glandes Gulielmus in hostem,
Exussitque statim flammis tentoria cuncta.
   *   *   *   *
Flumen transivere equites tormentaque primum,
His instant pedites; Dux Schonenbergius acer,
Dum transit, vitam deperdit in amne Bubinda.
   *   *   *   *
Strinxit mox humerum Gulielmi glans ab Hibernis;
Nil nocuit, quanquam de regis morte timerent.
   *   *   *   *
Sint Protestantes Drohediæ super omnia læti,
Quod parvi numero, salvi tunc Marte fuerunt.

---

* To be pronounced — more Hibernico — reti-er, fi-er, ar-rum, har-rum. — M. OD.

† I fear I may have misunderstood this line — the original being rather obscure — something like Sir R. Phillip's common sense. — M. OD.

III.

GROVES OF BLARNEY.*

The groves of Blarney they are most charming——
Blarnæi nemorat sunt jucundissima visu.

But I prefer the next verse.

'Tis lady Jeffries, that owns this station,
Like Alexander or Helen fair;
There is no lady in all the nation
For emulation can with her compare.
She has castles round her, that no nine-pounder
Can dare to plunder her place of strength,
But Oliver Cromwell he did her pummel,
And made a hole in her battlement.

Jeffries castellum regit, perpulchra virago,
Par et Alexandro pulchræ Helenæque simul,
Cui cunctas inter peperit quas dulcis Ierne,
Dicere se similem fœmina nulla potest.
Hæc castella tenet quæ non tormenta timerent,
Quæ ter tres libras horrida ferre solent.
Sed Cromwellus eam graviter concussit, hiatum
In nido patulum conficiens dominæ.

---

* Blarney certainly is a most interesting part of the world. Its famous old castle—"the statues gracing this noble place in"—its Charles the Twelfth, &c.—the various stories connected with it—but, above all, its celebrated stone, render it highly worthy of public attention. The stone is on the top of the battlements of the castle, and is bound with iron; being struck, as it is mentioned in the above quoted verse, by a cannon shot, when Oliver Cromwell attacked the place; but we believe the story of his being there rests on rather weak foundations. Any person who kisses that stone, is privileged to talk blarney all his life; and many a gentleman has been seen from Ireland who has proved the efficacy of the ceremony. It is said, but the doctrine is not quite so authentic, that a dip in the Shannon gives the privilege of never blushing while in the act of committing blarney. Certain specimens, however, have come under our notice of ingenious Irishmen, who, all unbaptized, were quiet free from the sin of changing complexion. Blarney (not the place, but the thing) is quite a distinct affair from humbug, as lexicographers must well know. Its fame is widely extended all over the world, as it was the only English word that the King of Abyssinia was acquainted with, as you may see by Salt's Travels. — M. OD.

† Nemorā — *a* long by cæsura. — See Dr. Carey. — M. OD.

IV.

VERSE OF MARY AMBREE.*

When our brave commanders, whom death could not daunt,
March'd off to the siege of the city of Gaunt;
They counted their forces by two and by three,
But the foremost in battle was Mary Ambree.

Cum nostri ductores qui mortem spernebant,
Ad Gantii turres cingendas pergebant,
Et copias legebant per duos et tres,
Fuit prima in pugna Maria Ambres.

V.

VERSE OF SIR TRISTREM.

[*I have translated the entire poem.*]

Geten and born was so,
   The child was fair and white,
Nas never Rohand so wo,
   He wist not what to wite;
To childbed ded he go,
   His owhen wiif al so tite,
Said he had children to,
   On hem was his delite,
     Bi Crist,
In court men cleped him so,
   Tho Tram bifor the Trist.

Sic genitus et satus,
   In mundum infans it;
Rohantius contristatus
   Quid facere non scit.
In lecto qui fuit stratus,
   Partus uxoris fit,
Quasi filius fuit natus
   Quem multum dilexit.
     Per Christum
Et fuit appellatus
   Cum Tramo ante Tristum.

---

* In Percy's Reliques. The lady is mentioned also by Ben Jonson, as Mary Ambree, who marched so free, &c. — M. OD.

VI.
ON SIR P. SARSFIELD.*

Oh! Patrick Sarsfield, Ireland's wonder,
Who fought in field like any thunder,
One of King James's chief commanders,
Now lies the food of crows in Flanders.
    Ohone!

O! Patrici Sarsfield, decus mirantis Iernes,
Cui tonitru simili cernere usus erat:
Jacobi heroas quo non præstantior inter,
Belgarum corvis mortuus esca jaces.
    Eheu!

VII.
ON JOHN, DUKE OF MARLBOROUGH.
By Doctor Evans.

Here lies John, Duke of Marlborough,
Who ran the Frenchman thorough and thorough;
Married Sarah Jennings, spinster,
Died in Saint James's, and was buried in Westminster.

Hic jacet Dux Marleburiensis,
Qui Gallos secuit tanquam ensis,
Virginem duxit Jenningiam Saram,
Mortuus Jacobi ad regiam claram,
Sepultus ad Stephani Martyris aram!

I must apologize for introducing a supernumerary line, and also for bringing "regiam claram" rhythmi gratiâ. Both practices, however, are justifiable by high poetic authority in this and other countries.

VIII.
CONCLUSION OF THE EPITAPH ON HENRY, DUKE OF GRAFTON, SON OF CHARLES II. KILLED AT THE SIEGE OF CORK, 1690.†

Yet a bullet of Cork
It did his work,

---

* Under a very fine print of Sir Patrick, engraved, if I do not mistake, by Lady Bingham, his daughter. If she also wrote the epitaph, it reflects great credit on her poetical powers. Sir Patrick fought gallantly for James II. in Ireland, and left it on the overthrow of his party. On the continent he continued his aversion to William III., and was killed in the battle of Landen, in which that monarch was defeated. He was a brave man. — M. OD.

† Shot by a blacksmith, who turned out, quoth the Cork Remembrancer, from a forge in the Old Post Office lane, as he was crossing the river Lee. The

THE EMBALMER.

Unhappy pellet!
With grief I tell it,
It has undone
Great Cæsar's son!
A statesman's spoil'd;
A soldier foil'd;
God rot him
Who shot him,—
A son of a ——,*
I say no more.
Here lies Henry, the Duke of Grafton!

Sed glans Corcensis stravit, miserabile telum,
 Heu! natum rapuit Cæsaris egregrii,
Excelsum pariter vel bello consiliisve:—
 Cædentis manus occupet atra lues!
Dispereat scorti soboles.—Nil amplius addam.
 Hic sunt Henrici Graftonis ossa Ducis.

IX.

ON ROBIN HOOD.†

Underneath this little stone,
Lies Robert, Earl of Huntingdon;
He was in truth an archer good,
And people call'd him Robin Hood.
Such outlaws as he and his men
England never will see again.

[*Alcaics.*]

Parvo Robertus hic situs est comes
Huntingdonensis sub lapide obrutus;
 Nemo negabit quam peritus,
  Missilibus fuerit sagittis.
Vulgo vocatus Robin-a-Hoodius
Exlex in agris vivere maluit,
 In Anglia nunquam Roberto
  Vel sociis similes videbis.

---

place where he fell is called Grafton's alley. The epitaph is taken from a book published in 1702, called Poems on Affairs of State, &c. 2 vols. It is written by Sir F. S——d.—M. OD.

* There is a pleasant equivoque here. We are left in the dark whether this opprobrious name is applied to the blacksmith, or the Duke, of whom we know it was quite true. Verbruggen, the comedian, cracked a similar joke on the Duke of Saint Albans, which I believe is in Joe Millar. I have endeavored to preserve the equivoque.—M. OD.

† In Percy's Reliques.—M. OD.

X.

ON SIR DANIEL DONNELLY, C. I.[*]

Underneath this pillar high,
Lies Sir Daniel Donnelly;
He was a stout and handy man,
And people call'd him buffing Dan.
Knighthood he took from George's sword,
And well he wore it by my word!
He died at last, from forty-seven
Tumblers of punch he drank one even.
O'erthrown by punch, unharm'd by fist,
He died unbeaten pugilist.
Such a buffer as Donnelly,
Ireland never again will see.

Hic jacet sub columnâ stratus,
Daniel Donnellius eques auratus;
Fortis et acer ab omnibus ratus,
Plagosus Daniel cognominatus,
Eques a Georgio fuit creatus,
Ornavitque ordinem equitatus;
Quadraginta septem trucidatus,
Cantharis punchi hic est allatus;
Potu, non pugno, ita domatus,[†]
Cecidit heros nunquam æquatus;
Hiberniæ insulæ quâ fuit natus
Vir talis non erit posthac datus.

Enough of these. *Manum quod aiunt de tabula.*

I strongly recommend any poet who wishes for immortality, to take advantage of my recipe. I am ready to translate for any gentleman at a fair and reasonable rate. Nor shall I be over hard in requiring any conditions from him, except that there be a slight degree of intelligibility in what he writes—say about four degrees above Maturin's Universe,[‡]—which, I hope, is not too much.

[*] From that great work "Blackwood's Magazine," No. XXXVIII.—M. OD.
[†] More antique for *domitus*.—M. OD.
[‡] A poem, in blank verse, written by Maturin, author of the tragedy of "Bertram," and now quite forgotten.—M.

Irish Melodies.*

Dear North,

It has often struck me with astonishment, that the people of Ireland should have so tamely submitted to Mr. Thomas Moore's audacity, in prefixing the title of Irish to his melodies. That the tunes are Irish, I admit; but as for the songs, they in general have as much to do with Ireland, as with Nova Scotia. What an Irish affair, for example—"Go where glory waits thee," &c. Might not it have been sung by a cheesemonger's daughter of High Holborn when her master's apprentice was going in a fit of valour to list himself in the third Buffs, or by any other such amatory person, as well as a Hibernian Virgin? And if so, where is the Irishism of the thing at all? Again,

> When in death I shall calm recline,
> Bear my heart to my mistress dear;†
> Tell her it fed upon smiles and wine——

Tell her it fed upon fiddlesticks! Pretty food for an Irishman's heart for the ladies! Not a man of us from Carnsore Point to Bloody Forland would give a penny a pound for smiles; and as for wine, in the name of decency, is *that* a Milesian beverage? Far from it indeed; it is not to be imagined that I should give five or six shillings for a bottle of grape juice, which would not be within five quarts of relieving me from the horrors of sobriety, when for the self-same sum I could stow under my belt a full gallon of Roscrea, drink beyond comparison superior. The idea is in fact absurd. But there would be no end were I to point out all the un-Irish points of Moore's poetry. Allusions to our localities, it is true, we sometimes meet with, as thinly scattered as plumbs in the holiday puddings of a Yorkshire boarding school, and scattered, for the same reason, just to save appearances, and give a title to the assumed name. There's the Vale

---

* This article, intended to commence a series, appeared in *Blackwood*, for December, 1821.—M.

† This expression, I own, *is* Irish; but it is lost by the common punctuation, *mistress dear*, which is just as bald an epithet as any man would wish to meet with on a day's journey—M. OD.

of Ovoca, for instance, a song upon a valley in Wicklow, but which would suit any other valley in the world, provided always it had three syllables, and the middle one of due length.

Were I in a savage mood, I could cut him up with as much ease as a butcher in Ormond market dissects an ox from the county of Tipperary; but I shall spare him for this time, intending, if I have leisure, to devote an entire paper to prove his utter incompetence; at present I shall only ask, whether, in these pseudo-Irish Melodies, there is one song about our saints, fairs, wakes, rows, patrons, or any other diversion among us? Is there one drinking song which decent individuals would willingly roar forth after dinner in soul-subduing soloes, or give to the winds in the full swell of a thirty-man chorus? Not one—no —not one. Here am I,—who, any night these twenty years, might have been discovered by him whom it concerned, discussing my four-and-twentieth tumbler, and giving the side of the festive board, or the chair presiding o'er the sons of light, with songs fit to draw nine souls out of one weaver, and, of course, hearing others in my turn—ready to declare that never was song of Moore's sung in my company; and that is decisive. If any one should appeal from my long experience—let such unbelieving person leave the case to any independent jury, selected indifferently from all districts,—from the honest Inishowen consumers of the north, down to the wet gulletted devourers of Tommy Walker* in the south, and he will be convinced. In fact, my dear North, read over his "Fill the bumper fair," and you will find, that instead of giving us a real hearty chanson-a-boire, as we say in Dunkirk, you have a parcel of mythological botheration about Prometheus, and other stale personages, which, in the days of heathenism, would be laughed at for its ignorance, as it is now, in the days of Christianity, voted a bore for its impertinence. And is this the national song-writer for this much injured and hard drinking island?—Perish the idea!—As an oratorical friend of mine once said at an aggregate meeting in Fishamble Street, such a thought is a stigma upon humanity- and a taint upon the finer feelings of man!

A fair sort of young man, the Hon. Mr. O'Callaghan, of the

* Thomas Walker and Co., extensive whiskey-distillers in Cork.—M.

White Knight's family,* has been so struck with this deficiency of Mr. T. Moore, that he is going to give us a number of melodies in opposition to those of our little bard. I wish him success, but I am afraid that, though he is an ingenious person, he is not possessed of that ideal faculty which is requisite for the task. For fear he should fail, I have determined to start, and show the world a real specimen of true Irish melody, in a series of songs symphonious to the feelings of my countrymen. Neither Moore nor O'Callaghan will, I flatter myself, be much read after this series of mine. I hate boasting; but,—pocas polabras—as Christopher Sly observes.

We were talking about the business last Thursday, at the Cork in Mary-street, while Talbot was playing most divinely on the Union pipes. There were present Terence Flanagan, Pat. Moriarty, Jerry O'Geogheghan, Phelim Macgillicuddy, Callaghan O'Shaughnessy, and some other equally well known and respected characters, who are to a man good judges of punch, porter, and poetry; and they agreed it would be a sin if I did not publish a half-dozen of melodies, four of which I wrote in the tap-room the night before, just to get rid of a quarter of an hour or so, while I was finishing a few pints in solitary reflection. No man can resist pressing of the kind, and I yielded. Talbot, in the handsomest manner, volunteered to set the airs—for which, though I offered him instant payment, he would not suffer me to remunerate him in any other manner than by permitting me to treat him to a hot glass. When it was asked what would be the best vehicle for giving them to the public, we voted that the only Irish Magazine, [Blackwood,] was the fit soil for the planting of Irish melodies; and it was carried unanimously that they should be instantly transmitted to Mr. North.

I have not aimed, or rather Talbot has not aimed, at bothering the plain and simple melody by any adventitious airs and graces. You have them, unadorned, adorned the most—that is, stark naked. The piano trashery has bedevilled the tunes given by Moore; and this is another instance of the man's in-

* There are yet, in Limerick and Kerry, three branches of one of the old Irish families, respectively headed by the White Knight, the Knight of Glyn, and the Knight of Kerry.—M.

sufficiency. Just think of the piano being chosen as the instrument for Irish airs, when he had, as a southern correspondent of yours sings,

> The harp or bagpipe, which you please,

to melodize with! Moore first had Sir John Stephenson as his composer, (who now is at work for Mr. O'Callaghan,) and then he took up Bishop—both friends of mine, with whom I often have cleaned out a bottle, and therefore I shall not say any thing derogatory of either. In short, let the public judge between Moore, myself, and O'Callaghan—Bishop, Talbot, and Stephenson—and God defend the right. I shall make a few remarks on the melodies I send, and then conclude. Indeed I had not an idea of writing half so much when I began.

Melody the first is *theological*, containing the principal acts of our national Saint—his coming to Ireland on a stone—his never-emptying can, commonly called St. Patrick's pot—his changing a leg of mutton into a salmon in Lent time—and his banishment of the snakes. Consult Jocelyn.*

Melody the second is *pathetic*, being the Lamentation of a Connaught Ranger, discharged. I had eleven cousins in that regiment. I may as well give it as my opinion, that the only cure for our present difficulties, is to go to war without delay; and I venture to say, if an aggregate meeting of the seven millions of us could be called any where, a war would be voted *nem. con.* I don't much care with whom, that being an afterthought, but I certainly would prefer having a shaking of those ugly-looking garlic-eaters, the Spaniards, who are now so impudent as to imagine they could have fought the French without us. I heard one Pedro Apodaca say as much, and I just knocked him down, to show him I did not agree with him in opinion. I would engage that 200,000 men would be raised in a day in this country, and if we would not batter the Dons———, I leave it to the reader.

The third is *amatory*. Compare this with the best of Tom

* The tune to which these words are put is a great favourite in Ireland. It is said the original words (" The night before Larry was stretched") were written by a very learned gentleman, who is now a dignitary of the established church in Ireland. It is a first-rate slang song.—M. OD. [The Rev. Dr. Burrowes, Dean of Cork, wrote the song in question.—M.]

IRISH MELODIES.   107

Moore's ditties. But to be sure it is absurd to think of a man of his inches talking of making love to half the girls in the country, as he does in Little's poems.

The fourth is *warlike*—something in the manner of Sir Walter Scott's Gatherings. It relates to a feud in Kerry.*

The fifth is *convivial*, and was extempore. I did not write it with the other four, but actually chanted it on the spur of the occasion this morning, at the time noted. It is to the famous tune of Lillebullero—my uncle Toby's favourite; and the tune, as you may see, by Burnet, with which Lord Wharton whistled King James, of the unsavoury surname, out of three kingdoms. It is among us a party air, and called the Protestant Boys; but honest men of all parties must approve of my words. They come home to every man's feelings.

The last is *sentimental*. I wrote it merely to prove I could write fine if I liked; but it cost me a lot of trouble. I actually had to go to the Commercial Buildings, and swallow seven cups of the most sloppish Bohea I could get, and eat a quartern loaf cut into thin slices, before I was in a fit mood to write such stuff. If I were to continue that diet, I should be the first of your pretty song writers in the empire; but it would be the death of me in a week. I am not quite recovered from that breakfast yet—and I do not wonder at the unfortunate figure the poor Cockneys cut, who are everlastingly suffering under the deleterious effects of tea-drinking.

I have scribbled to the end of my paper, so must conclude.

Song I.
SAINT PATRICK.

A   fig   for   St.   Den - nis   of France,   He's   a

* The tune of this ("The Groves of the Pool") is indigenous of the South of Ireland. There is a capital song to this tune, by R. Millikin, of Cork, beginning with "Now the war, dearest Nancy, is ended, and peace is come over from France." Millikin is the author of the Groves of Blarney, which Mathews sings with so much effect.—M. OD. There is a sort of sketch of his in Ryan's Worthies of Ireland.—C. NORTH.

THE ODOHERTY PAPERS.

trum-pe-ry fellow to brag on; A fig for St. George and his lance, Which

spitted a heathenish dragon: And the saints of the Welshman and Scot Are a

pi-ti-ful couple of pipers, Both of whom may just travel to pot, If com-

pared with the patron of swipers, St. Patrick of Ireland, my dear!

1.

A fig for St. Dennis of France,
  He's a trumpery fellow to brag on;
A fig for St. George and his lance,
  Which spitted a heathenish dragon;
And the Saints of the Welshman or Scot
  Are a couple of pitiful pipers,
Both of whom may just travel to pot,
  Compared with the patron of swipers,
    St. Patrick of Ireland, my dear!

2.

He came to the Emerald Isle
  On a lump of a paving-stone mounted;
The steam-boat he beat to a mile,
  Which mighty good sailing was counted:
Says he, "The salt water, I think,
  Has made me most bloodily thirsty,
So bring me a flagon of drink,
  To keep down the mulligrubs, burst ye,
    Of drink that is fit for a saint."

3.

He preach'd then with wonderful force,
  The ignorant natives a-teaching;
With a pint he wash'd down his discourse,
  "For," says he, "I detest your dry preaching."
The people, with wonderment struck,

At a pastor so pious and civil,
Exclaim'd "We're for you, my old buck,
And we pitch our blind gods to the devil,
    Who dwells in hot water below."

4.

This ended, our worshipful spoon
    Went to visit an elegant fellow,
Whose practice each cool afternoon
    Was to get most delightfully mellow.
That day, with a black jack of beer,
    It chanced he was treating a party;
Says the saint, "This good day, do you hear,
    I drank nothing to speak of, my hearty,
        So give me a pull at the pot."

5.

The pewter he lifted in sport,
    (Believe me, I tell you no fable,)
A gallon he drank from the quart,
    And then planted it full on the table.
"A miracle!" every one said,
    And they all took a haul at the stingo;
They were capital hands at the trade,
    And drank till they fell; yet, by jingo!
        The pot still frothed over the brim.

6.

Next day quoth his host, "'Tis a fast,
    But I've nought in my larder but mutton,
And on Fridays who'd make such repast,
    Except an unchristian-like glutton?"
Says Pat, "Cease your nonsense, I beg,
    What you tell me is nothing but gammon;
Take my compliments down to the leg,
    And bid it come hither a salmon!"
        And the leg most politely complied.

7.

You've heard, I suppose, long ago,
    How the snakes in a manner most antic,
He march'd to the county Mayo,
    And trundled them into th' Atlantic.
Hence not to use water for drink
    The people of Ireland determine;
With mighty good reason, I think,
    Since St. Patrick has fill'd it with vermin,
        And vipers, and other such stuff.

8.

O! he was an elegant blade,
  As you'd meet from Fair Head to Kilcrumper,
And though under the sod he is laid,
  Yet here goes his health in a bumper!
I wish he was here, that my glass
  He might by art magic replenish;
But as he is not, why, alas!
  My ditty must come to a finish —
    Because all the liquor is out!

Song II.

LAMENT OF A CONNAUGHT RANGER.

Air. — *Lamentation over Sir Dan.*

With the melancholy expression of days gone by.

I wish to St. Patrick we had a new war, I'd not care who t'was

with, nor what it was for; With the French, or the Yankees, or

bet-ter again, With the yel-low mulattoes of Lisbon or Spain.

1.

I wish to St. Patrick we had a new war,
I'd not care who 'twas with, nor what it was for:
With the French, or the Yankees — or, better again,
With the yellow Mulattoes of Lisbon or Spain!

2.

My heart is half broke when I think of the fun
We had before Boney, poor fellow, was done;
Oh! 'twas I who was sore when I heard he was dead,
For I thought on the days when he got me good bread.

3.

When he, who, God rest him! was never afraid,
Sir Thomas,* commanded the Fighting Brigade;

---

* Sir T. Picton, who commanded the 4th division in the Peninsular War. It was chiefly composed of Irishmen, and was called the "fighting division,"

And the Rangers of Connaught — to see them was life —
Made game of the Frenchmen,* and gave them the knife.

4.

When abroad and at home we had sport and content —
Who cared then a damn for tithe, taxes, or rent?
When each dashing fine fellow who wish'd to enlist,
Might be off to the wars with his gun in his fist.

5.

Now the landlord is bother'd, and tenant bereft —
The soldier's discharged, — and the sailor adrift, —
Half-pays to our captains poor living afford,
And the Duke is no more than a Government Lord!

6.

And our active light-bobs, and our bold grenadiers,
Must dirty their fingers with plough, loom, or shears;
Or if, just out of fun, we would venture a snap
At no more than a proctor, we're thrown into trap.

7.

So bad luck to the minute that brought us the peace,
For it almost has ground the nose out of our face;
And I wish to St. Patrick we had a new war,
Och! no matter with whom, no, nor what it is for!

Song III.

RAFFERTY'S ADVICE.

Air. — *Limerick Glove.*

With uproarious jollity.

When you go courting a neat or a dainty lass, Don't you be sighing or

ready to faint, alas! Little she'd care for such pluckless philandering,

---

from its constant activity in engaging. The Connaught Rangers (the 88th) was one regiment of this most dashing brigade; and many a saying of Sir T.'s is treasured up by them, for he was a great favourite, from his gallant habits. — M. OD.

* A common phrase among the Irish soldiery for charging with the bayonet. — M. OD.

And to Old Nick she would send you a wandering. But, you thief, you

rogue, you rap-pa-ree, Arrah, have at her like Paddy O' Raf-fer-ty.

1.

When you go courting a neat or a dainty lass,
Don't you be sighing or ready to faint, alas!
Little she'd care for such pluckless philandering,
And to Old Nick she would send you a wandering.
  But, you thief, you rogue, you rapparee!
  Arrah, have at her like Paddy O'Rafferty.

2.

Tip her the wink, and take hold of the fist of her;
Kiss her before she'd have time to say Christopher;
She may cry out, " You're an impudent fellow, sir!"
But her eye will unsay what her tongue it may tell you, sir.
  Oh, you thief, you rogue, you rapparee,
  You're a devil of a fellow, Paddy O'Rafferty.

3.

Give her another, or rather a score of 'em,
Still you will find her ready for more of 'em;
Press her, caress her, my dear, like a stylish man,
For that is the way to go court like an Irishman.
  Oh, you, &c.

4.

Pitch to the devil sighings and " well-a-days,"
Oglings and singing of piperly melodies;
When in your arms you fairly have got her, sir,
Her heart it will melt like a lump of fresh butter, sir!
  Oh, you, &c.

5.

Oh, the dear creatures — sure I am kill'd with 'em!
My heart, was it big as the sea, would be fill'd with 'em;
Far have I truff'd it, and surely where'er I went,
'Twas with the girls I had fun and merriment.
  Oh, you thief, you rogue, you rapparee,
  You're a devil of a fellow, Paddy O'Rafferty.

IRISH MELODIES.   113

Song IV.
THE GATHERING OF THE MAHONYS.
Tune — Groves of the Pool.

With indignant energy.

Jerry Mahony, arrah, my jewel, Come, let us be off to the fair, For the Donovans, all in their glory, Most certainly mean to be there. Says they, "The whole Mahony faction we'll banish 'em out clear and clean;" But it never was yet in their breeches, their bullaboo words to maintain.

1.

JERRY MAHONY, arrah, my jewel, come, let us be off to the fair,
For the Donovans all in their glory most certainly mean to be there;
Says they, " The whole Mahony faction we'll banish 'em out clear and clean."
But it never was yet in their breeches, their bullaboo words to maintain.

2.

There's Darby to head us, and Barney, as civil a man as yet spoke,
'Twould make your mouth water to see him, just giving a bit of a stroke;
There's Corney, the bandy-legg'd tailor, a boy of the true sort of stuff,
Who'd fight though the black blood was flowing like buttermilk out of his buff.

3.

There's broken-nos'd Bat from the mountain — last week he burst out of the jail,
And Murty the beautiful Tory,* who'd scorn in a row to turn tail;

---

* Tory, in Ireland, is a kind of pet name, "Oh! you Tory," is the same as "Oh! you rogue," used sportively. If a man wishes to call another a rogue seriously, he calls him Whig, the terms being convertible. — M. OD.

Bloody Bill will be there like a darling, and Jerry, och! let him alone,
For giving his blackthorn a flourish, or lifting a lump of a stone.

4.

And Tim, who serv'd in the militia, his bayonet has stuck on a pole;
Foxy Dick has his scythe in good order, a neat sort of tool on the whole;
A cudgel, I see, is your weapon, and never I knew it to fail;
But I think that a man is more handy, who fights, as I do, with a flail.

5.

We muster a hundred shillelahs, all handled by elegant men,
Who batter'd the Donovans often, and now will go do it again;
To-day we will teach them some manners, and show that, in spite of their talk,
We still, like our fathers before us, are surely the cocks of the walk.

6.

After cutting out work for the sexton, by smashing a dozen or so,
We'll quit in the utmost of splendour, and down to Peg Slattery's go;
In gallons we'll wash down the battle, and drink to the next merry day;
When must'ring again in a body, we all shall go leathering away.

Song V.

A REAL IRISH "FLY NOT YET."

[*Tune*—*Lillibullero*. Time, four o'clock in the morning, or thereabouts.]

Solo.

Hark! hark! from below, The rascal-ly row Of watchmen in chorus

bawling "Four!" But spite of their noise, My rol-licking boys, We'll

Grand Chorus.
With practical accompaniments.

stay till we've emptied one bottle more. Bumpers, bumpers, flowing bumpers,

Bumper your glasses high up to the brim, And he who is talking A

word a-bout walk-ing, Out of the win-dow at once with him.

1.

Hark! hark! from below,
The rascally row
Of watchmen, in chorus, bawling "Four!"
But spite of their noise,
My rollocking boys!
We'll stay till we've emptied *one bottle more.

Chorus.†

Bumpers—bumpers—flowing bumpers!
Bumper your glasses high up to the brim!
And he who is talking
A word about walking,
Out of the window at once with him!

2.

Our whiskey is good,
As ever yet stood,
Steaming on table from glass or pot:
It came from a still,
Snug under a hill,
Where the eye of the gauger saw it not.
Bumpers, &c.

3.

Then why should we run
Away from the sun—
Here's to his health, my own elegant men!
We drank to his rest
Last night in the west,
And we'll welcome him now that he wakes again.
Bumpers, &c.

4.

And here we shall stop,
Until every drop,
That charges our bottles, is gone, clean gone;

---

* Of whiskey, viz. about thirteen tumblers.—M. OD.
† We pronounce the word generally in Ireland as we sound the *ch* in church—Tchorus.—I think it is a prettier way.—M. OD.

And then, sallying out,
We'll leather the rout,*
Who've dared to remind us how time has run.
Bumpers, &c.

Song VI.

THE IMPASSIONED WAVE.

[*Tune* — " *Thomon um Though.*"]

'Tis sweet up-on th'impassion'd wave To hear the voice of mu-sic stealing, And while the dark winds wildly rave, To catch the genuine soul of feeling; While all around, the ether blue Its dim ma-jes-tic beam is shedding, And ro-sy tints of heavenly hue Are thro' the mid-night dark-ness spreading.

1.

'Tis sweet upon the impassion'd wave
To hear the voice of music stealing,
And while the dark winds wildly rave,
To catch the genuine soul of feeling!

---

* Beating the watch is a pleasant and usual finale to a social party in Dublin. I am compelled myself now and then to castigate them, merely for the impertinent clamour they make at night about the hours. Our ancestors must have been in the depths of barbarity, when they established this ungentlemanlike custom.— M. OD.

While all around, the ether blue
  Its dim, majestic beam is shedding,
And roseate tints of heavenly hue
  Are through the midnight darkness spreading!

2.

So is it when the thrill of love
  Through every burning pulse is flowing;
And like the foliage of the grove,
  A holy light on all bestowing!
O! never from this fever'd heart
  Shall dreams on wings of gold be flying;
But e'en when life itself shall part,
  I'll think on thee, sweet maid, though dying!

3.

'Twas thus, upon the mountain's height,
  Young Dermod sung his plaint of sorrow,
Regardless of the evening light,
  That ushers in the gay to-morrow!
For love had of his cheek bereft
  That smile — that glow — of joyous gladness,
And sympathy's cold sting had left
  Nought there — but pale and gloomy sadness!

Letter-Writing.*

EPISTOLARY as well as personal intercourse is, according to the mode in which it is carried on, one of the pleasantest or most irksome things in the world. It is delightful to drop in on a friend without the solemn prelude of invitation and acceptance — to join a social circle, where we may suffer our minds and hearts to relax and expand in the happy consciousness of perfect security from invidious remark and carping criticism; where we may give the reins to the sportiveness of innocent fancy, or the enthusiasm of warm-hearted feeling; where we may talk sense or nonsense, (I pity people who *cannot* talk nonsense,) without fear of being looked into icicles by the coldness of unimaginative people, living pieces of clock-work, who dare not themselves utter a word, or lift up a little finger, without first weighing the important point, in the hair balance of propriety and good breeding. It is equally delightful to *let* the pen talk freely, and unpremeditatedly, and to one by whom we are sure of being understood; but a formal letter, like a ceremonious morning visit, is tedious alike to the writer and receiver — for the most part spun out with unmeaning phrases, trite observations, complimentary flourishes, and protestations of respect and attachment, so far not deceitful, as they never deceive any body. Oh the misery of having to compose a set, proper, well worded, correctly pointed, polite, elegant epistle! — one that must have a beginning, a middle, and an end, as methodically arranged and portioned out as the several parts of a sermon under three heads, or the three gradations of shade in a school-girl's first landscape! For my part, I would rather be set to beat hemp, or weed in a turnip field, than to write such a letter exactly every month, or every fortnight, at the precise point of time from the date of our correspondent's last letter, that he or she wrote after the reception of ours — as if one's thoughts bubbled up to the well-head at regular periods, a pint at a time, to be bottled off for immediate use. Thought! what has thought to do in such a corre

* From *Blackwood* for March, 1822. — M.

spondence? It murders thought, quenches fancy, wastes time, spoils paper, wears out innocent goose-quills — "I'd rather be a kitten and cry mew! than one of those same" prosing letter-mongers. Surely in this age of invention something may be struck out to obviate the necessity (if such necessity exists) of so tasking, degrading the human intellect. Why should not a sort of mute barrel-organ be constructed on the plan of those that play sets of tunes and country dances, to indite a catalogue of polite epistles calculated for all the ceremonious observances of good-breeding? Oh the unspeakable relief (could such a machine be invented) of having only to *grind* an answer to one of one's "dear five hundred friends!" Or, suppose there were to be an epistolary steam-engine — Aye, that's the thing — Steam does every thing now-a-days. Dear Mr. Brunel, set about it, I beseech you, and achieve the most glorious of your undertakings. The block machine at Portsmouth would be nothing to it — *That* spares manual labor — *this* would relieve mental drudgery, and thousands yet unborn - - - - But hold! I am not so sure that the female sex in general may quite enter into my views of the subject.

Those who pique themselves on excelling in "l'eloquence du billét," or those fair scribblerinas just emancipated from boarding-school restraints, or the dragonism of their governesses, just beginning to taste the refined enjoyments of sentimental, confidential, soul-breathing correspondence with some Angelina, Seraphina, or Laura Matilda; to indite beautiful little notes, with long-tailed letters, upon vellum paper with pink margins, sealed with sweet mottos, and dainty devices — "Je ne change qu'en mourant" — "Forget me not," or Cupid with a rose, "L'une seule me suffit" — the whole deliciously perfumed with musk and attar of roses — Young ladies who collect "copies of verses," and charades — keep albums — copy patterns — make bread seals — work little dogs upon footstools, and paint flowers without shadow — Oh! no — the epistolary steam-engine will never come into vogue with those dear creatures — *They* must enjoy the "feast of reason, and the flow of soul," and they must write — Ye Gods! how they *do* write!

But for another genus of female scribes — Unhappy innocents!

who groan in spirit at the dire necessity of having to hammer out one of those aforesaid terrible epistles—who having in due form dated the gilt-edged sheet that lies outspread before them in appalling whiteness—having also felicitously achieved the graceful exordium, "My dear Mrs. P." or "My dear Lady V." or "My dear —— any thing else else," feel that they are *in for it*, and must say something—Oh, that something that must come of nothing! those bricks that must be made without straw! those pages that must be filled with words! Yea, with words that must be sewed into sentences! Yea, with sentences that must *seem* to mean something; the whole to be tacked together, all neatly fitted and dove-tailed, so as to form one smooth polished surface! What were the labours of Hercules to such a task! The very thought of it puts me into a mental perspiration; and, from my inmost soul, I compassionate the unfortunates now (at this very moment, perhaps,) screwed up perpendicular in the seat of torture, having in the right hand a fresh-nibbed patent pen, dipped ever and anon into the ink bottle, as if to hook up ideas, and under the outspread palm of the left hand a fair sheet of best Bath post, (ready to receive thoughts yet unhatched,) on which their eyes are rivetted with a stare of disconsolate perplexity, infinitely touching to a feeling mind. To such unhappy persons, in whose miseries I deeply sympathize - - - -

Have I not groaned under similar horrors, from the hour when I was first shut up (under lock and key, I believe) to indite a dutiful epistle to an honoured aunt? I remember as if it were yesterday, the moment when she who had enjoined the task entered to inspect the performance, which, by her calculation, should have been fully completed—I remember how sheepishly I hung down my head, when she snatched from before me the paper, (on which I had made no further progress than "My dear *ant*,") angrily exclaiming, "What, child! have you been shut up here three hours to call your aunt a pismire?" From that hour of humiliation I have too often groaned under the endurance of similar penance, and I have learnt from my own sufferings to compassionate those of my dear sisters in affliction. To such unhappy persons, then, I would fain offer a few hints, (the fruit of long experience,) which, if they have not already been suggested by their own observation, may prove serviceable in the hour of emergency.

Let them - - - or suppose I address myself to *one* particular sufferer—there is something more confidential in that manner of communicating one's ideas—As Moore says, "Heart speaks to heart"—I say, then, take always special care to write by candlelight, for not only is the apparently unimportant operation of snuffing the candle in itself a momentary relief to the depressing consciousness of mental vacuum, but not unfrequently that trifling act, or the brightening flame of the taper, elicits, as it were, from the dull embers of fancy, a sympathetic spark of fortunate conception—When such a one occurs, seize it quickly and dexterously, but, at the same time, with such cautious prudence as not to huddle up and contract in one short, paltry sentence, that which, if ingeniously handled, may be wire-drawn, so as to undulate gracefully and smoothly over a whole page.

For the more ready practice of this invaluable art of dilating, it will be expedient to stock your memory with a large assortment of those precious words of many syllables, that fill whole lines at once; "incomprehensibly, amazingly, decidedly, solicitously, inconceivably, incontrovertibly." An opportunity of using these, is, to a distressed spinner, as delightful as a copy all m's and n's to a child. "Command you may, your mind from play." They run on with such delicious smoothness!

I have known a judicious selection of such, cunningly arranged, and neatly linked together, with a few mono-syllables, interjections, and well-chosen epithets, (which may be liberally inserted with good general effect,) so worked up, as to form altogether a very respectable and even elegant composition, such as amongst the best judges of that peculiar style is pronounced to be "a charming letter!" Then the pause—the break—has altogether a picturesque effect. Long-tailed letters are not only beautiful in themselves, but the use of them necessarily creates such a space between the lines, as helps one honourably and expeditiously over the ground to be filled up. The tails of your g's and y's in particular, may be boldly flourished with a "down-sweeping" curve, so as beautifully to obscure the line underneath, without rendering it wholly illegible. This last, however, is but a minor grace, a mere illumination of the manuscript, on which I have touched rather by accident than design. I pass on to remarks of greater moment. There is another expedient of infinite efficacy, but requiring to be employed with such nice *tact*, that none but an experienced spinner should venture on the practice of it. You may continue, by the help of a little alteration, amplification, and transposition of the precise terms, to amuse your correspondent with a recapitulation of the very matter that formed the groundwork of his, or her last epistle to yourself. Should he detect you in this retort, (against which the chances are equal,) he will be restrained by good breeding from making any observations to yourself on the subject, and in fact he will (if a candid and reasonable person) find no just cause of complaint against you, for refreshing his memory, and thus impressing more indelibly on his mind a subject he had conceived of sufficient importance to be imparted to you. Again—you need not fear that he shall turn your own arms against you—their loading is spent in your retort, so that it will still be his business to furnish fresh matter, every thing (you perceive) in this game depending on the first throw.

This species of manœuvre, as I before observed, should by no means be rashly ventured, but it is an art well worth the trouble of acquiring, at the expense of some pains and study, one (in which you are so fortunate as to become a proficient) that will relieve you from all further anxiety, furnishing you (at the expense of your correspondents) with ample materials for your own epistolary compositions. As to the strict honesty of this proceeding, no conscience need, I think, be so squeamish as to hesitate on the subject, for, in fact, what has conscience to do with the style of correspondence now under consideration? It were well if a fine lady's letter were oftener made up of such innocent ingredients, for (generally speaking) would not the abstract of such a one fairly translated run thus?

My dear Lady D——	You tiresome old toad:
With feelings of the most inexpressibly affectionate inter-	You've manœuvred off one of your gawky frights at last,

est, I take up my pen to congratulate you on the marriage of your lovely and accomplished Alethea.

To you who know every thought of my heart, it is almost unnecessary to say, that next to the maternal tenderness with which I watch over my own girls, I feel the most anxious solicitude in every thing that relates to your charming family.

That sweet love Alethea has always, you know, been my peculiar favourite, and tears of the sweetest exultation swell into my eyes, when I think of the brilliant establishment you have secured for her.

Our long friendship, my beloved friend, and my maternal affection for the dear creature, are pleas which I shall urge in claiming the delightful office of presenting her at the next drawing-room.

Soon, very soon, my dearest friend, may I have to congratulate you on some equally advantageous establishment for your sweet delicate Anna Maria.

I earnestly hope that foolish story (which *you* of course have heard) about Lord V.'s keeping a lady at Paris, and having lost and I must say something on the occasion.

How the deuce! did you contrive to hook in that moodle of a lord, when I have been spreading my nets ever since he came of age, to catch him for my eldest girl?

That pert minx Alethea has always been my particular aversion, and I am ready to cry with spite, at the idea of her being a countess.

As you can't hobble to court on your crutches, I shall be expected to present her *ladyship*, and I *must* do it, though I know I shall expire with vexation at the sight of the V. diamonds in her odious red hair.

One comfort is — you'll never be able to get off that little hump-backed thing Anna Maria, and you know well enough there is no hope of it, so hate to be talked to about her.

You won't care much about it, even if it was true, but I can think of nothing else to plague the old cat. I'll take care the

£20,000 at the Salon, at one sitting, will not reach the ear of our sweet sensitive girl — But people are so malicious!

Where are your two lovely boys? Dear fellows! we have not seen them since they left Eton, and you know how I delight in their charming spirits.

&c. &c. &c. &c. &c.

And remains ever,
With the most inviolable attachment,
My dearest Lady D.'s
Most sincerely affectionate
Friend,   M. G.

young one shall know it *somehow*.

I'd as lieve have a couple of wild cats turned loose into the drawing room, as let in those two riotous cubs; but I've nine girls to bring out yet, and the young D.'s will be tolerably good catches, though only honourable.

Fudge, fudge, fudge, fudge, fudge.

I think, I've given you enough for one dose, though I'm afraid you're up to me. I hate you cordially; *that's certain*.

M. G.

Byron to Murray.*

Attacks on me were what I look'd for, Murray,
    But why the devil do they badger you?
These godly newspapers seem hot as curry,
    But don't, dear Publisher, be in a stew.
They'll be so glad to see you in a flurry —
    I mean those canting Quacks of your Review —
They fain would have you all to their own Set;
    But never mind them — we're not parted yet.
They surely don't suspect you, Mr. John,
    Of being more than *accoucheur* to Cain;
What mortal ever said you wrote the Don?
    I dig the mine — you only fire the train!
But here — why, really, no great lengths I've gone —
    Big wigs and buzz were always my disdain —
But my poor shoulders why throw *all* the guilt on?
    There's as much blasphemy, or more, in Milton.

The thing's a drama, not a sermon-book;
    Here stands the murderer — that's *the old one* there
In gown and cassock how would Satan look?
    Should Fratricides discourse like Doctor Blair?
The puritanic Milton freedom took,
    Which now-a-days would make a bishop stare;

---

* This versified paraphrase of the letter written by Byron, to his publisher, (John Murray) on the excitement caused by the appearance of "Cain a Mystery," was delivered by Odoherty at The Noctes, in March, 1822. I subjoin the original: —

    Letter from Lord Byron to Mr. Murray.

                          Pisa, *Feb.* 8, 1822.

Dear Sir — Attacks upon me were to be expected; but I perceive one upon *you* in the papers, which, I confess, that I did not expect. How, or in what manner *you* can be considered responsible for what *I* publish, I am at a loss to conceive. If "Cain," be "blasphemous," Paradise Lost is blasphemous; and the very words of the Oxford Gentleman, "Evil be thou, my good," are from that very poem, from the mouth of Satan; and is there any thing more in that of Lucifer in the Mystery? Cain is nothing more than a drama, not a piece of argument. If Lucifer and Cain speak as the first murderer and the first rebel may be supposed to speak, surely all the rest of the personages talk also according to their characters; and the stronger passions have ever been permitted to the drama. I have even avoided introducing the Deity, as in Scripture (though Milton does, and not very wisely either;) but have adopted his angel, as sent to Cain, instead, on purpose to avoid shocking any feelings on the sub-

But not to shock the feelings of the age,
    I only bring you angels on the stage.
To bully You — yet shrink from battling Me,
    Is baseness. Nothing baser stains "The Times,"
While Jeffrey in each catalogue I see,
    While no one talks of priestly Playfair's crimes,
While Drummond, at Marseilles, blasphemes with glee,
    Why all this row about my harmless rhymes?
Depend on't, Piso, 'tis some private pique
    'Mong those that cram your Quarterly with Greek.

If this goes on, I wish you'd plainly tell 'em,
    'Twere quite a treat *to me* to be indicted;
Is it less sin to write such books than sell 'em?
    There's muscle! — I'm resolved I'll see you righted.
In me, great Sharpe, in me converte telum!
    Come, Doctor Sewell, show you *have* been knighted.
— On my account you never shall be dunn'd,
The copyright, in part, I will refund.

You may tell all who come into your shop,
    You and your Bull-dog both remonstrated;
My Jackall did the same, you hints may drop,
    (All which, perhaps, you have already said.)
Just speak the word, I'll fly to be your prop,
    They shall not touch a hair, man, in your head.
You're free to print this letter; you're a fool
If you don't send it first to the JOHN BULL.

---

ject, by falling short of, what all uninspired men must fall short in, viz., giving an adequate notion of the effect of the presence of Jehovah. The old mysteries introduced him liberally enough, and all this is avoided in the new one.

The attempt to *bully you*, because they think it will not succeed with me, seems to me as atrocious an attempt as ever disgraced the times. What! when Gibbon's, Hume's, Priestley's, and Drummond's publishers have been allowed to rest in peace for seventy years, are *you* to be singled out for a work of *fiction*, not of history or argument? There must be something at the bottom of this — some private enemy of your own — it is otherwise incredible.

I can only say, "*Me — me adsum qui feci*," that any proceeding directed against you, I beg may be transferred to me, who am willing and *ought* to endure them all; that if you have lost money by the publication, I will refund any, or all of the copyright; that I desire you will say, that both *you* and Mr. Gifford remonstrated against the publication, as also Mr. Hobhouse; that I alone occasioned it, and I alone am the person who either legally or otherwise should bear the burthen. If they prosecute, I will come to England; that is, if by meeting it in my own person, I can save yours. Let me know — you sha'n't suffer for me, if I can help it. Make any use of this letter which you please. Yours ever,   BYRON.

Ode to Mrs. Flanagan.

By an Irish Gentleman, lately deceased.*

Mr. North,—A friend of mine died last month in Tralee, *sit illi terra levis.* He left behind him a large quantity of MSS. His wife, a woman of singular judgment, appointed me to prepare them for the press; and before I finally commit them entire to the public, I think it right to give a specimen of the poetical part. The public in this incredulous age might not wish to purchase a couple of folios without some sample of their contents. I give, therefore, the first that comes to hand.

It happens to be a poem, written about 1817, to a Mrs. Flanagan of Youghall. Every gentleman who assisted me in my commentary is duly mentioned, after the laudable custom of those *viri clarissimi*, the variorum editors.

I remain, sir, your most obedient, and very humble servant,

PHILIP FORAGER.

DRUMANIGILLIBEG, *Feb.* 29, 1820.

P. S.—I understand, that it is conceived by some of the critics who have perused this piece, that the hint is taken from Horace. Perhaps so—I accordingly subjoin the ode.

HORATII, *Carm. Lib.* iii. *Od.* 7.	MSS. No. I.
Asterien consolatur de Gygis absentia, et ad fidem hortatur.	To Mrs. Kitty Flanagan, comforts her on the absence of her husband, Jerry Flanagan, mate of the Jolly Jupiter, and drops a hint about a light dragoon.

QUID fles, Asterie, quem tibi candidi
Primo restituent vere Favonii,
    Thynâ merce beatum,
        Constantis juvenem fide,
	WHY do cry, my sweet Mrs. Flanagan,
	When you will soon have your own dear man again,
	Whom the first wind will bring home from the Delaware,
	Brimful of sovereigns, and such other yellow ware?

---

* This paraphrase appeared in *Blackwood* for March, 1820.—M.

Gygen? ille, Notes actus ad Oricum
Post insana Capræ sidera, frigidas
 Noctes, non sine multis
  Insomnis, lacrimis, agit.

Atqui sollicitæ nuncius hospitæ,
Suspirare Cloén, et miseram tuis
 Dicens ignibus uri,
  Tentat mille vafer modis.
Ut Prœtum mulier perfida credulum
Falsis impulerit criminibus, nimis
 Casto Bellerophonti
  Maturare necem, refert.

Narrat penè datum Pelea Tartaro,
Magnessam Hippolyten dum fugit abstinens:

He's driven in to some port to the west of us,*
(A thing that might happen, dear, to the best of us,)
Where he is sighing, sobbing, and chattering,
Night and day long, of his own dear Catherine :
Although his landlady, one Mrs. Gallagher,†
Wants him to quit you, the rogue, and to follow her.
She tells him the tale of the wife of old Potiphar,‡
(Relating a fact that will ne'er be forgot of her,)
Who, from a feeling malignant and sultery,
Had Joseph near hanged for eschewing adultery :
And from this basest, this vilest of women, he
Gets Mr. Hunt's smutty story of Rimini,‖

---

* Dingle-i-couch, a celebrated harbour in the kingdom of Kerry.—P. F.

† Mrs. Gallagher (pronounced more Hibernico, Gollagher) keeps the sign of the cat-and-bagpipes in Dingle,—a woman irreproachable in her conduct, amatory in her disposition, fair in her dealings, and a good hand in *running spirits*. Touching the colour of her hair, it is red, and she was a widow (at the time of this poem,) of her third husband for nearly three months—she has been since married. Miss Skinandbone, a maiden lady in Dingle, tells me that her treatment of Flanagan was kind, and that he was *no* Joseph—but this may not be authenticated.—P. F. She appears to be a woman of taste and reading, by having my poem in her house.—LEIGH HUNT. It was left at her house by a Cockney barber, who was running away from his creditors, and taking ship on board the Yankiedoodle in Dingle; he left it with Mrs. G. as pledge for a tumbler of punch.—RODERICK MULSHENAN. Perhaps he found it too *heavy* to carry it any farther.—Z.

‡ This allusion to Scripture, I think profane and reprehensible, LEIGH HUNT. So do I, BYRON. So do I, WM. HONE. So do I, BEDFORD. So do I, SUSSEX. So do I, T. MOORE. So also many more Whig wits, men conspicuous for respect for the Scriptures. Nobody understands profaneness better than they.—P. F.

‖ The clear shown bay of Dingle rises, on my soul, with springy freshness from this circumstance. Mrs. Gallagher made the use I intended of my poem:

ODE TO MRS. FLANAGAN.

Et peccare docentes Fallax historias monet:	By which, 'tis plain, she hopes to a surety, Soon to corrupt his natural purity; But he resists her arts and her flattery, Deaf and determined, just as a battery.*
Frustra; nam scopulis surdior Icari Voces audit, adhuc integer. At, tibi Ne vicinus Enipeus, Plus justo placeat, cave;	But there's a sergeant, one Patrick Hennessy, Keep away, Kitty, from all such men as he, Though he's so smart, that he's always employed, as
Quamvis non alius flectere equum sciens Æquè conspicitur, gramine Martio; Nec quisquam citus æquè Tusco denatat alveo.	Rough-rider to the old Marquis of Drogheda's,† Though there are few so brawny and big, my dear, Or far better at dancing a jig, my dear, Close down your windows when he comes capering,
Primâ nocte domum claude: neque in vias Sub cantu querulæ despice tibiæ: Et te sæpè vocanti Duram, difficilis mane.	Shut both your doors and your ears to his vapouring, Mind not the songs or sighs of this Hannibal, But, looking at him, cross as a Cannibal, Cry, "Come be off as light as a tailor, man, I will be true to my own dear sailor-man."

---

a rational piety and a manly patriotism should prompt a writer to excite those passions which nature has given us, and which tend to increase the population of the country. By smutty, is meant that I resemble Rembrandt in being dark, gloomy, and grand; it is a dear coming-round metaphorical expression, quite feet-on-the-fenderish, and reminds one of a poker in the fire, and a chimney corner.—LEIGH HUNT.

* Deaf as a battery, is not the proper phrase: it must have been put in *rythmia gratia*. I suggest the following:—

"But he's a deaf—as deaf as the postesses
To the design and the arts of his hostess's."
JOHN KEATS.

Postesses, in the Cockney tongue, signifies *Posts.*—P. F.

† The most noble Charles, Marquis of Drogheda, K. S. P. Colonel of the 18th hussars.—P. F.

Ode to Marshal Grouchy* on his Return.

I send another specimen of my deceased friend's poetry, and, mirabile dictu, it, as well as the former, bears a similitude to an Ode in Horace; indeed, I believe he wrote a set of parallel Carmina to the Horatian, and if Archdeacon Wrangham were to see them, I think he would give up for ever the idea of attempting to lay his versions before the public, for which reason I hope he never will see them.

I should say more, but that I am in a hurry, being called away to attend a coroner's inquest over the body of one Timothy Regan *alias* Tighe a Breeshtha, who was killed yesterday, fighting at a fair, in a feud, a bellum intestinum, between the Shanavests and Caravats.

PHILIP FORAGER.

DRUMMANIGILLIBEG, *August 6th*, 1820.

HOR. Od. 7. Lib. ii.	MSS. No. II.
Ad POMPEIUM.	To *Marshal Grouchy on his Return;* or,
Felicem ex infelici melitiâ reditum gratulatur.	*Congratulatory Address by Mons.* —.

1.

O saepe mecum tempus in ultimum	O WELCOME home, my marshal, my col-
Deducte, Bruto militiae duce,	league true and good,
Quis te redonavit Quiritem	When under brave Napoleon we dabbled
Dis patriis, Italoque coelo.	long in blood;
Pompei, meorum prime sodalium?	Who brought you back to Paris in Bour-
Cum quo morantem saepè diem mero	bon's royal days?
Fregi, coronatus nitentes	Was it Madame Bonaparte's man, our
Malobathro Syrio capillos.	own Monsieur de Cazes?†

---

* Count Emanuel Grouchy, a Marshal of the French empire, was born at Paris in 1766. Much trusted by Napoleon, particularly in the Hundred Days of 1815, his indecision at Waterloo prostrated the Emperor. With 35,000 men and 800 pieces of cannon under his command, he remained immovable in a position which could only be justified by the strict letter of his orders. It is a mooted point whether he intended to betray Napoleon's cause. But Napoleon believed him an imbecile, not a traitor. He was included in the special amnesty of 1819, and restored to his military rank on the accession of Louis Philippe. He died in 1847.—This "Ode" appeared in *Blackwood* in September, 1820.— M.

† Hodie Duc de Cazes, olim secretary to Madame Mere, the imperial mother of all the Bonapartes.— P. F.

ODE TO MARSHAL GROUCHY.

Tecum Philippos et celerem fugam
Sensi, relictâ non benè parmulâ;
Cum fracta virtus, et minaces
Turpe solum tetigere mento.

2.

With thee I robbed through Prussia,
through Portugal, and Spain;
With thee I marched to Russia, and
then — marched back again;
With thee I faced the red-coats awhile
at Waterloo;
And with thee I raised the war-song of
jolly* sauve qui peut.

3.

Sed me per hostes Mercurius celer
Denso paventem sustulit aëre:
Te rursus in bellum resorbens
Unda fretis tulit aestuosis.

I took the oaths to Louis, and now with
face of brass,
I bawl against the royalists all in the
Chambre Basse;
But you my lad were exiled, a mighty
cruel thing,
For you did nothing surely, but fight
against your king.

4.

Ergo obligatam redde Jovi dapem,
Longáque fessum militiâ latus
Depone sub lauru meâ, nec
Parce cadis tibi destinatis.

Then drink a health to th' Emperor, and
curse Sir Hudson Lowe;†
And decorate with stolen plate your
honest-earned chateau;
And merrily, my marshal, we shall the
goblet drain,
'Tis a chalice‡ that I robbed one day,
out of a church in Spain.

5.

Oblivioso levia Massico
Ciboria exple: funde capacibus

Fill, fill the bumper fairly, 'tis Chambertin,‖ you see,

* Jolly! Quoi? Jolly! Ma foi, voila une epithete assez mal appliquè.
— MARSHAL GROUCHY.

† Sir Hudson Lowe is a very bad man in not letting the Emperor escape.
LAS CASAS. He is a man of no soul. The world cannot decide whether
Bonaparte or Wellington is the greater general — I am sure the former is, without a second battle of Waterloo; and here we have a simple knight preventing
the solution of the question. He is an imbecile. I am sure he never had the
taste to read my Amyntas.— LEIGH HUNT.

‡ It was an instrument of superstition; and I, therefore, although a waterdrinker, approve of its being turned to any other use, just as I approved of the
enlightened revolutionists of France turning the superstitious bells of Paris into
cannon, although, on principle, a declared enemy of war.— SIR R. PHILIPPS.

‖ Bonaparte was fond of Chambertin. Teste TOM MOORE. I prefer whiskey.— P. F.

Unguenta de conchis. Quis udo
Deproperare apio coronas.
	The Emperor's favourite liquor, and
	    chaunt in pious glee,
	A song of Monsieur Parny's* Miladi
	    Morgan's bard,
	And curse the tasteless Bourbons who
	    won't his muse reward.

	6.

Curatve myrto ? quem Venus arbitrum
Dicet bibendi ? non ego saniûs
    Bacchabor Edonis: recepto
    Dulce mihi furere est amico.
	Then with our wigs all perfumed, and
	    our beavers cocked so fierce,
	We'll throw a main together, or troll
	    the amorous verse;
	And I'll get as drunk as Irishmen, as
	    Irishmen morbleu,
	After six-and-thirty tumblers† in drink-
	    ing healths to you.

---

* A pet poet of Lady Morgan's. Vide her France. I wonder what the medical Knight, her caro sposo, says, when he catches her reading " La Guerre des Dieux."— P. F.

† On this I must remark, that six-and-thirty tumblers is rather hard drinking. My friend Rice Hussey, swears only to six-and-twenty, though he owns he has heard he drank two-and-thirty, but could not with propriety give his oath to it, as he was somewhat disordered by the liquor. There is not a Frenchman in France would drink it: I will lay any wager on that. In fact, I back Ireland against the world. A few years ago, the Northumberland, a very pretty English militia regiment, commanded by Lord Loraine, who endeared himself wherever he went in Ireland, by his affable and social manners, arrived in the city of Cork. His Lordship gave a dinner to thirty officers of his regiment, who each drank his bottle. When the bill was called for, he observed to the waiter with a smile, that the English gentlemen could drink as well as the Irish. "Lord help your head, sir," said the waiter, " is that all you know about it ? Why, there's five gentlemen next room, who have drank one bottle more than the whole of yees, and don't you hear them bawling like five devils for the other cooper, ——— coming, gentlemen !"— P. F.— In Horace it is Edoni, not Irishmen ; but that is quite correct. The Irish are of Scythian descent, so were the Thracians.— Thos. Wood, M. D.

Semihoræ Biographicæ.—No. 1.*

WINIFRED JENKINS.

Leighton Buzzard, 6th July, 1820.

Mr. North,—Since the affront which the "Author of Waverley" put upon Captain Clutterbuck, touching the manner by which he obtained the papers on which The Monastery is founded, it has been hardly worth while to aver any thing relative to singular discoveries of literary documents. Suffice it then, that the *supellex necrologica*, which I herewith transmit to you, belonged to Q. Z. X., a deceased friend, who was a man of letters and industry. Among this immense mass of literary treasure, I do not find any one life thoroughly developed. Nevertheless, the subjoined specimen will demonstrate with what valuable accuracy he proceeded, and with what conscientiousness he admitted nothing into his collection which did not bear the stamp of authenticity. I am, learned sir, in the cause of letters, your brother and servant to command,

GILES MIDDLESTITCH.

MRS. WINIFRED CLINKER, ALIAS LLOYD, CI-DEVANT JENKINS.

SYNOPSIS. Winifred, born of David and Martha Jenkins, 3d of November, 1730, (day of St. Winifreda,) at Brambleton, Co. Monmouth—herded goats and knitted stockings till twelve—entered service of Mrs. Tabitha Bramble, and remained in it till her marriage—espoused Mr. Matthew Lloyd, commonly called Humphrey Clinker, parish-clerk of Brambleton—became a widow in 1797, died 1804, leaving two sons and three daughters—age on tombstone, 84.

DOCUMENTS. TYP. Adventures of Humphrey Clinker, 2 vols. London 1766.—Walk through Monmouthshire, by the Rev. R. Plodder, M. A. 1 vol. Bath. 1802.—MSS. Letters from Mrs. Clinker, Mr. Nichols, Mr. Kirby, Certificate of birth and burial, and epitaph, (quorum quicque exemplar penes me. Q. Z. X.)

---

* From *Blackwood* for September, 1820. This article was much praised, at the time, as a quiz on the solemn manner in which literary antiquarians make researches into the merest trifles of biographical facts.—M.

[Here follow mere transcripts from a well-known work, with which our facetious countryman, Dr. Smollett, long ago gratified, and still continues to gratify, every man, woman, and child, in his Majesty's dominions. We subjoin, however, our correspondent's note.]

I conceive that the autographs of the letters, which Smollett used in drawing up the biography of Mrs. Clinker's husband, are preserved among the "Bramble Papers," wherever they may now happen to be. When he edited them, they were in the possession of the Rev. Jonathan Dustwich, as appears by the preface. Now Smollett deserves thanks for having published them so faithfully, not correcting the spelling, as Ellis, Scott, and other injudicious editors have done. In fact, if this practice prevails, there will be no such thing as what may be called *idiosyncratic orthography*. The lamented Q. Z. X. would never alter a tittle when he transcribed a writing for publication.—G. M.

Extract from Plodder's Walk through Monmouthshire, pp. 121, 122.

[As the same objection of notoriety and popularity does by no means lie against this work, as against Smollet's, we give the extract, even though it is from a printed book.]

——"I descended a hill which afforded me a view of Brambleton-Hall on another eminence; it is now in the occupation of a Mr. Melford, but formerly belonged to squire Matthew Bramble. Leaving it on the right, I went to the village of Brambleton, and there met with a curiosity. This was a widow Clinker, a little shrivelled old woman, with more smartness about her than the general run of cottagers have. She turned out to be the identical Winifred Jenkins, whose part in the tour which goes under the name of the Adventures of Humphrey Clinker, is not the least amusing; and indeed, her topographical remarks therein inserted are by no means despicable, though couched in singular phraseology. I ascertained that her husband could not establish in the neighborhood his more ennobling name of Matthew Lloyd, so was fain to be called Clinker to his dying day, though he kept up a right to sign Matthew Lloyd on formal occasions, as it pointed out his alliance by blood, even if it were not by affinity, to the great folks at the Hall. The most edifying information I obtained from the old dame (who retained all the Abigail-propensity to be loquacious) was, that she found it more difficult, at her time of life, to walk to the Hall, which was on an ascent, than to return from it, which, by consequence, was on a down-hill road. She owned that she was in easy circumstances; and showed, with some pride, many articles of use and ornament, which Miss Lydia Melford gave her at the time of her marriage. I noticed an inlaid spinning wheel which had been kept in constant use, and which was one among these bridal presents; but the old lady evinced more satisfaction in parading before my eyes two or three trinkets of an antiquated shape, and of which the use is almost forgotten in the present day."

Letter from Mrs. Clinker to Q. Z. X.

Brambiltun, 19th Gully, 1799.

Sir,—I am groan very howld, and my mimmery is not so good as it have a bin. You asks me vare I vas born, and says you intend to cumpleat my bigrophagy, vich I hop you vill, if there is von belonging to me, and pleas to lit me know what sort of a think it is, and vether any boddy left it to me by lecksy in thur vill. As you minchin my burth, praps I should send a sortofagut afore I can receve it, vich I can git from Pasin Heavens for ayteen pins, thof I should be loth to throe away my munney for wot is not munney's wuth, so I shall wait for your ancer fust. As to your hinkwiries about my life, that is anuther mater, but Ile give you awl the settisfackshun as I can. I heird as how von mister Tubby Smallhat rit a print book all about my pore deer huzbeen, and I no as how he giv Molly Jones a nice inchey ankercher, spick and span new, all over rid flours on a yalow groun, to let him hav the litters as I rit ven I was travailing vith our howld master, mister matthu Brambil eskwire. Mister Smallit called it a *rummewnyrashun*, but we calls it a ankercher in Vales. I thot I ott to have had it, as I had all the trubbil of righting, but Molly maid the best of her market vile I vas avay, and vares the ankercher to this day a sundays. I vas burn and bread vare I lives, sins you vant to know; and I tented ninny gots vile I vas a yung think, til Mistress Tapifa Brambull tuck me to luck after her pulltree, and then I vaz Miss Lidcher Millfurt's one made; but ven I marred, I roes in the whirl for my pore deer Unfry Clinker, (thof his naim was, by rites, Mister Mathew Loyd,) was a sun of Esquewer Brambil, but not on the write side of the blenkit. The skwire was verry kind to him, and maid him clarck, and giv us the cottidge I am living in stil. My pore man dide of a cuff he got from a hevvy shore saven ears agun last micklemace, and I live upon an annaty which Mister Squeer Brampill left us, and I oanly spin a litil for pasttum and rackwryhessian. My sun Mathew, who is marred, manges our litil bit a land, and Jussuf is prentussed at Munmeth. Nin is mary'd, Pol izzent, but livs at the hall, and is lick to be huzkeeper; and Jenny is dearymeed at Sqiar Owen's farm, and the bayleaf lucks sweat upon her, so she will sun be pervaded for. I reckalex nothing more pertickler. So no more at present from your humble sarvant to commend,

WINIFRED CLINKER.

Posecribb. Pleas dont forgit to let me know vot the big ruffagee is that you say is to be finnicht for me, and it may cum by Jo Rice, who is always carrion partials to Abberjenny, and after its cum, I'le send you a jar of unicum mad by my one biz.

Extract of a Letter from John Nichols, Esq. F. A. S. Lond. Ed. and Perth.

* * * All that I can add to your store of information concerning W. Jenkins, relates to the shape of her monument alone, and this I derive from a contributor to the Gent. Mag. The curiosity of the tombstone is, that it is precisely after the same pattern as all the gravestones which have been generally used in Wales for the last two centuries, and differs in no respect whatever. This induced me to have an engraving made of it, which you will see in plate CCCLVI. of Gent. Mag. between a view of the broad-nibbed pen, which Sir Isaac Newton is supposed to have writ with, and a weapon found near an old farmhouse, and

which finally proved to be an ancient sacrificial cultrum, although it has been not more irreverently than absurdly stigmatized as a modern pig-knife. * * * * *

I am, your's, &c. J. N.

(I gather from the appearance of the above, that Q. Z. X. had written to Mr. N. on other points also of a similar nature, and so Mr. N. had probably satisfied him on many in the same letter, wherefore only a portion is here given, and the rest is distributed where the various parts tally with the subjects of inquiry.—G. M.)

Letter from Mr. R. S. Kirby, of London-House Yard, St. Paul's, Publisher of the Wonderful and Eccentric Museum.

London-Ho. Yard, 17 March, 1806.

SIR,—I can't say as how I know any thing about that there Mrs. Winifred Jenkins, *alias* Clinker, *alias* Lloyd, as you ask about; but suppose she was a swindler, as most of the women in my museum, who have *aliases* to their names, are no better than they should be. There is a life of the famous Henry Jenkins, who lived to be 169, (see vol. 5. p. 92,) and also a full and true account in vol. 3d, how that Mery Jenkins, of Warminster, slept day and night for a month. Now, if this Winifred is any kin to them, you are welcome to copy out any part of their lives —though, for doing so, it is only fair that you recommend my publication (the Wonderful and Eccentric Museum, in six vols. 8vo, and a 7th nearly ready) to any body likely to buy it. But indeed it is a work that recommends itself, for it not only gives lives and true reports of all the most astonishing and notorious characters living or dead, but authentic portraits of many; and indeed I do not scruple to say, that it is quite at the head of all the works in the *amazing line*. The Newgate Calendar sinks before it, and is, besides, a vulgar compilation; whereas, I admit nothing ungenteel. As for the pamphlets set forth by Mr. Thomas Tegg, of Cheapside—a word is enough, when I say, that he indulges a fiction, sir—*magnas est verity*—I can assure you, that his measurements of the Eynesbury giant, and of Lady Morgan, the least woman in the world, were most incorrectly stated: and his portrait of her ladyship was a mere fancy likeness; now mine is done by the same artist, who was universally allowed to have been so successful in Sir John Dinely, and Mr. Martin Van Butchell. It has just come into my head, that there is a paragraph in the Life of Dr. Katterfelto,* (see my 4th vol.,) which may perhaps relate to the Mrs. Jenkins you desire to know about. It states, that the Dr.'s deceptions were so marvellous, that people were often frightened out of their wits by them; and especially, it happened to one Miss Jenkins, that she fainted away, and remained in a swoon five minutes; and when she came to herself, she said, "Oh Dr. Flatterandkilltoo, you knows more than you should — shall I ever be married to Humphry?" taking him for a fortune teller, as it should seem. This is all I know: but if you should have any curious accounts of monsters, or of bigger or littler folks than common, or can let me into the right about the Sampford ghost, by shewing that it either was or was not a ghost that pinched Sally and beat Mr. Chave, or any such like, I should be glad to treat with you for it — but a gratis communication is what many gentlemen are in the habit of making to the Museum, and is thought more gentlemanlike. However, I am not unreasonable, nor above giving a proper consideration for any real original, extraordinary, and singularly surprising and incredible matters of fact, that are undoubtedly true. I am, Sir,

Your obedient humble servant,

R. S. K.

P. S. Please to pay the postage of your letters, unless they contain an order for some copies of the Museum.

Certificate of Birth and Decease of W. C.

Brambleton Co. Monmouth.
Baptisms. 12 Nov. 1730. Winifred, da. of David and Martha Jenkins.
Burials. 6 Dec. 1804. Winifred, Widow of Matthew Lloyd. Aged 84.
Truly extracted from the Registers, by me,

RICK EVANS, CURATE.

(* I presume that Dr. K. is the same person who is mentioned by a Mr. Wm. Cowper, in a copy of verses, called the Task, which was obligingly pointed out to me by a young gentleman, who hath a turn for poetry. He saith there is

————Katterfelto, with his hair on end,
At his own wonders wondering for his bread. — G. M,)

Inscription on her Tombstone in Brambleton Church-Yard.

Here lies Winifred,
The Wyfe of Humfry Clinker, who was
Clark of this Parrish. She
Dyed, 3 of December, 1804.

My dear Humphry Clinker, or rather, Matthew Lloyd — for that was your name — I am come again to you. We lived together many years, but you fell asleep first — But we shall wake at the same time, and rise from the dust.

Semihoræ Biographicæ.—No. 2.*

DICKEY GOSSIP.

Leighton Buzzard, 1st Nov. 1820.

DEAR NORTH,—My performance of posthumous justice to QZX., my late deceased and much deplored friend, has been somewhat interrupted by a short absence from the peaceful privacy I enjoy at Leighton Buzzard.

I am much grieved, however, to hear that the document, which purports to have come from Mr. Kirby, is apocryphal — and I fear some slur is thrown upon me, as if I were capable of knowingly sending you supposititious matter.† Since, Mr. Kirby has declared that he is not the author of the letter in question, (though I would that he had made an affidavit of it,) it shall be branded with the mark of apocryphal; and if he has a copy of the authentic letter which he probably sent QZX., and will transmit it to you, I make no doubt you will insert it in some supplementary manner, that the integrity of Mrs. Clinker's biography may be unimpaired.

This present *fasciculus* will be, I hope, as much approved as the former — I am, &c. GILES MIDDLESTITCH.

---

* From *Blackwood*, for December, 1820,

† Mr. Kirby, the London publisher of "Wonderful Characters," and other works, wrote to *Blackwood* seriously complaining that the letter, in his name, touching Winifred Jenkins, (Mrs. Humphry Clinker,) was likely to injure him in his business. Accordingly, Christopher North gravely apologized for the *jeu d'esprit.*—M.

MR. RICHARD GOSSIP, VULGARLY CALLED DICKY GOSSIP.

SYNOPSIS. Richard, illegitimate son of Margaret Gossip, chambermaid at the Salutation Tavern, born 1st April, 1735, his putative father was Jasper Quidnunc — ran on errands till ten years old — employed in a barber's shop in Seven Dials — in 1759, sets up trade as barber in the Barbican — marries Prudence Higgins, by whom he had one daughter, Tabitha, who survived him — find the access to news in London the cause of his neglecting his business — removes in 1791 to the village of Jadsby, where he officiated not only as shaver, but also as apothecary, carpenter, and dentist — died in 1801, aged 66.

DOCUMENTS. TYP. "My grandmother," by Prince Hoare, Esq. London. 8vo. 1806. Works of the City Poet, 2 vols. 1778. — MS. Journal of Philip Vapour, Esq, — An original authographic Bill and Note. — Letter from John Oldbuck Esq. — Register of birth, marriage, and burial. (penes me Q. Z. X.)

[My friend begins with all Mr. Gossip's speeches, and with the famous song, whose chorus ends with " Dicky Gossip is the man," from " My Grandmother," which is in the shape of a farce; although it cannot be doubted, that the real Dicky Gossip was the basis of the character there introduced. Unless, however, Mr. P. Hoare can assure us of the authenticity of the words, (and possibly some Boswell or Spence noted them down,) I shall be content to refer your readers to the printed work. The marrow of them is found in the synopsis.] G. M.

Odes by Q. Horatius Flaccus, and the City Poet of 1788.

AD THALIARCHUM.	TO DICKY GOSSIP.
Dum sævit hyems, voluptati indulgendum.	*While he thinks of little-tattle, not to forget his wiggery.*
VIDES, ut alta stet nive candidum Soracte, nec jam sustineant onus Silvæ laborantes, geluque Flumina constiterint acuto.	Do you see that stately cuxon, Which looks with all its whiteness, Like a bush o'erlaid with snow; And the curls which range below, Stand stiff in frosty brightness.
Dissolve frigus, ligna super foco Large reponens; atque benignius Deprome quadrimum Sabina, O Thaliarche, merum diota.	Come, melt some sweet pomatum — And, for powder do not stint us; Draw your irons from the stove; And, Dicky, quickly move, To make my old wig as portentous.
Quid sit futurum cras, fuge quærere; et Quem sors dierum cunque dabit, lucro	Don't ask of to-morrow's matters, Since them, nor you, nor I, know;

Appone; nec dulces amores	Mind your shop, my boy, nor spurn
Sperne puer, neque tu choreas.	From customers, to earn,
	For scraping their muzzles, their rhino.
Donec virenti canities abest	Show yourself a wise wig-maker,
Morosa. Nunc et campus, et areæ	For sure you've enough to handle,
Lenesque sub noctem susurri	As long as folks don't wear
Composita repetantur hora:	Their own untrimmed gray hair,
	Without heeding the whispers of scandal
Nunc et latentis proditor intimo	Yet ah, those ears so itching!
Gratus puellæ risus ab angulo,	My muse can not restrain 'em;
Pignusque dereptum lacertis	Should a laugh come from the street,
Aut digito male pertinaci.	Comb and razor you would quit,
	Nor longer could your fingers retain 'em.

I grieve to say, that I cannot find out who the city poet of London was in 1788. In former times, John Taylor, Elkaneh Settle, and Thomas Shadwell, acquitted themselves finely in that office. Nor can I learn that the place is filled up at present; the persons who occasionally come forward being voluntary, and not official performers. It is due to the young gentleman mentioned in No. 1. to say, that the discovery of the resemblance between the English and Latin ode is his; they are now printed, therefore, in juxtaposition, for the benefit of the curious, as indeed it is surprising, that two poets of such different ages should have hit on ideas so much alike. Q. Z. X.

An Extract from the Private Journal of the late Philip Vapour, Esq.

Tuesday—Low-spirited, cursed low—but not determined whether to shoot myself, drown, or go to Sir Matthew's. A fool of a fellow, who calls himself Dicky Gossip, came to shave me—never heard such a prater in my life; his tongue ran at such a rate, that I could get nothing from him but tattle. Souffrance did nothing but ejaculate *Quel babillard!* He put me in a passion, and I forgot my blue devils.

Thursday—To my infinite surprise, I found that my loquacious barber is the very person acting as my apothecary. The fellow, however, is amusing; and his boasts of being as much *au fait* in medicine as in shaving, are laughable enough, particularly as his gabble is unfailing, continuous, fluent upon every topic, and equally pertinent upon all, or rather impertinent.

Monday — Florella's trick has made me a happy fellow; but who should the carpenter be that fitted up the sliding pannel, which enabled her to appear as the picture of her grandmother, but my redoubted barber and apothecary Dicky Gossip! He has a fourth occupation; I wonder I did not want him in that department, as they say toothach is symptomatic of being in love — for the chattering rascal is a dentist also. Well may he sing, as Souffrance tells me he does—

> For this trade or that,
> They all come as pat as they can;
> For shaving and tooth-drawing,
> Bleeding, cabbaging, or sawing,
> Dicky Gossip, Dicky Gossip is the man.

AUTOGRAPHIC BILL AND NOTE.

The Worshipfull Mr. Alderman Pentweazle.

1787.   Dr. to R. Gossip.

		£	s	d
Jan. 4.	For a new tie wigg	8	8	0
Feb. 6.	Item for a powder puff	0	2	6
Mar. 17.	Item for a brown scratch	3	3	0
25,	Item for a quarter's shaving	0	10	6
		£12	4	0

WORSHIPFULL SIR,

I SHOU'DN'T have sent your worship's bill, only as you desired me, I thought your worship wou'd like to know, as how Captain Pursy, of the Train-bands, fell down in a fit just now, at Mr. Mudge's door — I can step up with the particklars in a minute, if your worship pleases. Also, Mrs. Morrison's marriage with Mr. Cruickshank's is broke off — some say that he trod upon her cat's tail, and others, that she has found out that he has another wife alive. If I can know for a sartainty, I will be with your worship in a minute. Your worship's old wigg is in pipes, and will be baked to-morrow. The day after next the address is to be carried up to the King, by the Common Council. I hope your worship will go—nobody's head shall be better or more handsomely dressed—and I am your worship's poor servant, to command, R. D. GOSSIP.

Letter from J. Oldbuck, Esq. to QZX.

Monkbarns, 7th July, 1806.

SIR,—I have applied to my barber, Jacob Caxon, according to your request, about the master of whom he learnt his notable art of torturing dead hair, and scraping chins, and bald pates. Not being acquainted with you, I do not venture to guess whether the information, which I have drained from his paucity of brains, will be looked upon as important—suum cuique. Caxon's mind has barely room for the entertainment of ideas arising from things present with him, and none hardly for those that are past. All he recollects is, that Dicky Gossip, who was his Magnus Apollo in the Barbican, in London, had a greater fondness for uttering news than for removing beards—that he was ambulatory rather than sedentary—and more inclined to pry into the secrets, under a wig, than to comb that useful appendage itself. The only specific fact pertaining to your hero, with which Jacob's memory seems charged, is, that Gossip once cut sheer through a gentleman's cheek, to his grinders, in shaving him, because he, the said Dicky, could not forbear watching the progress of a matrimonial dispute, in the opposite house; and, as it terminated in a leg of mutton being thrown out of the window by a vixen, before Dicky had completed his operation with the razor, so two catastrophes were simultaneous; the husband lost the promise of his dinner, and the *sharee* found, on rising from under Rd's hands, two fissures in his face, through which he might, if he pleased, put his dinner into his mouth. This noticeable fact "lies like a substance" upon Jacob's mind —and on jogging his memory three times—three times have we stumbled upon it, and upon nothing else. And now, if this is of use to you, learned sir, you are heartily welcome to it. Your apologies, for intruding inquiries upon a stranger, are unnecessary. The importance of what I can communicate, proves the propriety of your having made researches in this quarter. Doubtless, you cannot always get such an equivalent as the present, for your outlay in postage. If you ever publish your work, I shall have great curiosity to see it; but beg for time to deliberate, before I make myself responsible as a subscriber to it; I am not at all ambitious that my name should be addressed as authority for what I have here supplied you with.* With much respect for so pains-taking a man of letters as you are, for one who seems determined, not only to fish the great ocean of literature, but to catch the very sprats and shrimps in every creek of it,—I am, Sir, your obedient humble servant,

JONATHAN OLDBUCK.

P. S.—If you have any beggar's life in hand, I crave to recommend, as a most useful coadjutor, Mr. Adam or Edie Ochiltree, a gentleman of these parts, for he has made that branch of biography his particular study, and has devoted a considerable part of his life to it.†

* This suggestion of Mr. Oldbuck's modesty could not be complied with, as his communication would, in that case, fail of being sufficiently verified.—QZX.

† Press of matter prevents us from inserting the copies of the Parish Register Certificates, but they shall be forthcoming if any doubt arises.—C. N.

Semihoræ Biographicæ.—No. 3.*

AUTHOR OF WAVERLEY.

Leighton Buzzard, 28th December, 1820.

DEAR NORTH,—You must excuse me for occupying this third number by an inquiry exclusively my own. Do not suppose that I am wholly unjust to my deplored friend Q. Z. X. in this proceeding; for it is on a subject which he had much at heart; namely, the discovery of anonymous authors.

My present subject of research is the name of the person who has composed what are called The Scotch Novels. I know that divers conjectures have been put forth, but as none of them are satisfactory to me, I pass them by; and lest other conjectural critics should travel over ground, where I have sought in vain, I will first begin with discussing the claims of those persons of whom I had some suspicions, and also detail some of my reasons for excluding them. I flatter myself that I *burn*, (as children say at hide-and-seek, when they approach the person or thing concealed:) Yes, I do flatter myself that I *burn* in the conclusion of this paper. But first to my disappointments.

Now I had shrewd suspicions that it might be Mr. Maturin; and they were founded on these similar circumstances. Mr. M.'s "Women," and "Melmoth," are so far anonymous, as that they only allow in their title pages, that they are by The Author of "Bertram." "Ivanhoe," and "The Monastery" are in the same way declared to be by The Author of "Waverley." Moreover, the Tales of my Landlord bear the fabulous name of Jedediah Cleishbotham, as Editor; and Mr. M. the writer of "The Family of Montorio," walked forth heretofore, in the quaint disguise of Dennis Jasper Murphy. Surely these coincidences were wondrous! But alas! one author, in referring from book to book, drops the inquirer without betraying himself at the end of the chain; for if you trace the title-pages back from "The Abbot," to the earliest of the tribe, you will find no

* From *Blackwood* for January, 1821.—M.

more at last than "Waverley; or, 'Tis Sixty Years Since," and a preface full of *perhapses*. Perhaps the author may be a soldier or a sailor—perhaps a priest or a lawyer—an old man or a young one—a fine gentleman or a scrub—and it concludes nothing. Whereas, if we travel from "Melmoth" to "Pour et Contre," and thence to "Manuel," and so get, by regular stages to "Bertram," there we alight upon an explicit avowal that the Reverend Charles R. Maturin is the inditer thereof; and by logical consequence, of those divers and sundry aforenamed contributions to the stores of the reading public. As therefore Mr. M.'s concealment neither is, nor is meant to be, complete, I think this difference between him and the other writer so great, that I have reason to strike him off my list of competitors for the Waverley laurel.

Without all doubt, the author of "Waverley" can vary his manner, and so, at will, be grave or gay, lively or severe. Hence, I once thought to have found him in the person of Mr. Leigh Hunt; (whose name, by and by, is James Henry Leigh Hunt—I like to be accurate—vide his Juvenilia, in which there is also a demure portrait of him;) for he is described by his admirers as great in many species of authorship—great, as a political writer—great, as a poet—great, as a dissertator in prose, or story-teller—a sort of Hermes Trismegistus—in short, he may be reckoned *omni-scriptive* or *pangraphic*. Among other proofs, you may see an admirer's address to him, which he has printed, and it concludes thus:

"Wit, poet, prose-man, party-man, translator,
Hunt, your best title yet is Indicator."

But my particular suspicions of him originated in this: that the fourth number of his Indicator contained a story of " The Beau-Miser, and what happened to him at Brighton." This was written with such verisimilitude, as Mr. H. himself affirms, that some of his readers took it for a true circumstance, like those, I suppose, under the head of Police Intelligence in the Examiner newspaper. In the fifth number, therefore, to stop the spreading of this delusion, Mr. H. was obliged to give notice that it was purely his own fabrication. "We wish," says he, "to correct this mistake; and shall make a point hereafter, of so wording any think we write in the shape of a narrative, that a mere fiction shall not be confounded with our personal experience." What a proof of the *beau-natural* of the Beau-Miser! which, by the by, does not mean a *Wretched* Beau, but a Penurious one. Now I am sure it will be granted that the Scotch Novels have scenes which quite as much resemble every day life, as those in Mr. L. H.'s misleading narrative — ergo, there is presumptive proof that they may have been written by the same accurate painter of manners. Nevertheless, I am induced to withdraw Mr. H.'s claim; for, upon a comparison of styles, I find that of the Brighton incident, different from that in which the author of "Waverley" writes. The latter does not talk of a man " being twitched and writhed up;" nor of "a clipped-off lock of hair being glossy and *healthy!*" Nor do I find in the Scotch works, any instance of a stranger having given a gentleman, as he talked with him, "a thump on the shoulder, which made him jump" — nor of a *beau* having unconsciously walked about with an enormous coal-heaver's hat on his head, without finding out, even when he went a courting. All which decorate the said truth-like fable of Mr. H. So that, altogether, I dismiss Mr. J. H. L. Hunt from the imputation of having had any concern with " Waverley," and its associates.

Dr. Drake has tried his hand at a tale occasionally; and of late, in his " Winter Nights," he has given us his fireside story, called, " The Fate of the Bellardistons," and pretty enough it is. But, after all, I suspect that he is not the required author, as his taste in poetry differs so considerably from the Waverley wight, whose mottos, quotations, and small original pieces, betray that he adores the divine writers of the most palmy times of our literature, and at the same time possesses a keen relish for the best of those who now flourish. On the contrary, Dr. D. has, I fear, a palate easily tickled with very homely condiments — he is far gone as a lover of mediocrity in poetry. Witness the laud he gave to Cumberland's Calvary, and to Mason Good's Translation of Lucretius; and, from the living aspirants to poetic fame, he presents to notice, as bards of most excellent promise, Messrs. C. Neale, H. Neele, and J. Bird. No — Dr. Drake must be acquitted of having written the works in question.

I will not trouble you with my reasons for giving up my suspicions of Dr. Mavor, Mr. Pinkerton, Mr. Coxe, and some others, whose sole ground of resemblance, was in their fecundity, each, like the author of "Waverley," having sent at least a score volumes a-piece into the world.

A novel-reading lady friend of mine, recommended me to seek among the writers for Mr. Lane's Minerva Press; but I did it without profit; for there is this difference between the writings of the Scotch Novelist, and those of Miss Haynes, Miss Stanhope, Anne of Swansea, and Mr. Francis Lathom, that his run through many editions, while the public are well content with one edition of theirs. It is curious that some difficult lines in Milton may be explained by this latter circumstance. He says,

> "That two-handed engine at the door
> Stands ready to smite once, and smite no more."

The two-handed engine is evidently a printing-press; (say that of Minerva;) publishers do actually talk of striking off an impression; and every one knows, that to *strike* and to *smite* are synonymous, and the words *once and no more*, can only allude to a single edition of a book. So that by the practice of the Minerva Press, we get an elucidation, which we should have never found had our attention been restricted to such rapidly reprinted publications as those of the author of "Waverley."

My *critica vannus* having winnowed away those who are not the desired authors, I trust that I can now present him who is, and this is no less a personage than CHRISTOPHER NORTH, Esq. Editor of Blackwood's Magazine, &c. &c. &c.

Let me then advance to the proof of it. My grounds for thinking you the public benefactor in this particular, lie in these circumstances:— 1st. The author of "Waverley" chooses a sort of concealment; 2dly. He has great versatility in this style of composition; 3dly. He is well versed in the Scottish language; 4thly. He betrays a love of good cheer; 5thly. He is a Tory; and, 6thly. He cannot but be amassing wealth.

Now, is it not odd enough, that all these characteristics tally with the habit, tastes, and conditions of Squire North? Aut Erasmus, aut Diabolus—if you are not the author of "Waverley," the deuce is in it. But let me soberly show the parallelism under all the heads above stated.

1. You have no objection to play bopeep with the public; for we, who live at a distance, cannot forget, that for a long time you were only known to us, (if it can be called known,) as the Veiled Conductor. Just as a lamp of ground glass diffuses radiance, and yet suffers not any one to see the exact shape of the flame within; so, while the Veiled Conductor flourished, we saw that some one was edifying us, but his name and features we knew not; all that we were permitted to discern was that he was sensible and jocular; but this did not inform us whether his name was North or South; for you may recollect that acuteness and facetiousness have, in times past, been the property of persons bearing both these appellations. Dr. South was (saving your presence) as witty as you; — and the late Lord North was as ready at a repartee or a gibe, as even the great Edinburgh North of the present day. Now this hankering for the coy disguise of anonymity in you and in the Novelist, is very symptomatic of the identity of the two authors. For let us know in what degrees is the title of The Veiled Conductor a whit more explanatory than that of The Author of "Waverley?"

2. Let the different Tales be allowed to display as much versatility of genius as possible, yet they can hardly be pronounced to evince more than you possess; knowing, as we do, from your own confession, that most of the anonymous Articles in the Magazine are of your own writing. So that in this point, there is no bar to your being the author of whom we are in search; on the contrary, the likelihood is great and astounding.

3. The Novels demonstrate the writer's admirable acquaintance with the Scottish language. Now different references in your Magazine show that Dr. Jamieson's Etymological Dictionary is frequently at your elbow; and your occasional use of a word or two, proves your proficiency in that venerable tongue. Doubtless, you have possessed advantages for learning it, which do not fall to the lot of all; for I am told by a friend who has visited Edinburgh of late, that the use of that least corrupted dialect of the Anglo-Saxon, namely, the *gude braid Scots*, is not

even now wholly superseded by the more corrupted Teutonic, called English.

4. The author of "Waverley" enters cordially upon his descriptions of good cheer and merry-making. With what a smack of the lips did he report the decanting of the Baron of Bradwardine's claret; and with what kindred jollity does he accompany the carouse of the Black Knight, and the Clerk of Copmanhurst! Oh, Christopher! rheumatism doth not seem to have made thee less esurient or sitient, when the hospitality of Glasgow, or of other gormandizing and boozing places, is within thy reach. How cordial also is the *gout*, with which thou dost embody, in a durable record, thy prowess in mastication and deglutition! Can he, who with such unction composed and partook of the Glasgow punch, be other than he in whose gifted ear the claret of Tully Veolan gurgled so melodiously as it left the cobwebbed *magnum*? Can he to whom kidneys and kipper were so grateful, be other than the very same who records with such complacency the rapid despatch of Dandie Dinmont in the same hearty cause?

5. There is quite sunshiny evidence, that the great Novel-writer is a Tory. But what shall we say of Christopher North? Has he not grappled with the Edinburgh Reviewers—taken the very bull of Whiggism by the horns, so that roar as he will, he can no longer do mischief? Surely there was proof sufficient of high-minded Toryism in that hazardous but successful enterprise of yours. Well then, what else can we say, but that He who has instilled loyalty by the medium of fictitious narratives, and He who has wrought to the same good end in his own character as a political combatant, are two in semblance, but in reality *alter et idem*.

6. These unowned enchanting books, which I cannot help attributing to you, must have accumulated for their author quite a heap of gold. Now, is it not a strangely corroborative circumstance, that you confess that you are growing rich? The Magazine is referred to by you as the sole source of your wealth; but I fear you are like the lapwing which pretends to be most flurried and anxious about that place where her nest is *not*. Ah, Mr. North, is not your hyperbolical statement in No.

XLIII. of Mr. Blackwood's profits, a feint to withdraw our eyes from the real spot in which you have been reaping such a golden harvest? I apprehend that you are cater-cousin to the amusing hero of Shakspeare's Induction to the Taming of the Shrew, and are, as well as he — CHRISTOPHER SLY!

Well, I have done; and whether the author of "Waverley" be now *deterré* by these evidences, I leave (if you be not induced to confess) to impartial posterity to determine. Of one thing the present age may be assured, and this is, that I am, and ever shall continue to be, Yours very truly, &c.

GILES MIDDLESTITCH.

Drink Away!

1.

Come draw me six magnums of claret,
    Don't spare it,
But share it in bumpers around;
And take care that in each shining brimmer
    No glimmer
Of skimmering daylight be found.
Fill away! Fill away! Fill away!
  Fill bumpers to those that you love,
For we will be happy to day!
  As the gods are when drinking above,
Drink away! Drink away!*

2.

Give way to each thought of your fancies,
    That dances,
Or glances, or looks of the fair;
And beware that from fears of to-morrow
    You borrow
No sorrow, nor foretaste of care.
Drink away, drink away, drink away!
  For the honour of those you adore:
Come, charge! and drink fairly to-day,
  Though you swear you will never drink more.

3.

I last night, *cut*, and quite melancholy,
    Cried folly!
What's Polly to reel for her fame?
Yet I'll banish such hint till the morning,
    And scorning
Such warning to-night, do the same.
Drink away, drink away, drink away!
  'Twill banish blue devils and pain;
And to-night for my joys if I pay,
  Why, to-morrow I'll do it again.

---

* From *Blackwood* for April, 1824.—Sung at The Noctes.—M.

Drouthiness.*

I HAD a dream, which was not all-my-eye.
The deep wells were exhausted, and the pumps
Delivered nothing but a windy groan
To those who plied their handles; and the clouds
Hung like exsuccous sponges in the sky.
Morn came and went—and came and brought no rain,
And men forgot their hunger in the dread
Of utter failure of all drink—their chops
Were all athirst for something potable;
And they did swig, from hogsheads, brandy, wine,
Cider, brown-stout, and such like, meant to serve
For future merry-makings—cellars dim,
Were soon dismantled of the regular tiers,
Of bottles, which were piled within their binns;
Small beer was now held precious—yea, they gulp'd
Black treacle, daubing childish visages,
Gripe-giving vinegar, and sallad oil.
Nor were old phials, fill'd with doctor's stuff,
Things to be sneezed at now—they toss'd them off.
Happy were they who dwelt within the reach
Of the pot-houses, and their foaming taps.
Barrels were all a-broach—and hour by hour
The spigots ran—and then a hollow sound
Told that the casks were out—and the Red Cow,
The Cat and Bagpipes, or the Dragon Green,
Could serve no customers—their pots were void
The moods of men, in this unwatery,
Small-beerless time, were different. Some sat
Unbuttoning their waistcoats, while they frown'd,
Scarce knowing what they did; while hopeful, some
Button'd their breeches-pockets up, and smiled;
And servant lasses scurried to and fro,
With mops unwet, and buckets, wondering when
The puddles would be fill'd, that they might scrub
The household floors; but finding puddles none,
They deem'd their pattens would grow obsolete—
Things of forgotten ages. So they took

---

* This parody on Byron's impressive poem of "Darkness" appeared in *Blackwood* for December, 1821, and was given as if written by Blaise Fitztravesty, who dated from Ladle Court, near the Devil's Punch Bowl, Surrey.—M.

Their disappointed mops, and render'd them
Back to their dry receptacles, The birds
Forsook their papery leaves. The dairy cows
Went dry, and were not milk'd. Incessantly
Ducks quack'd, aye stumbling on with flabby feet,
Over the sun-baked mud, which should have felt
Pulpy beneath their bills; and eels did crawl
Out from what had been ponds, and needed not
The angler's baited hook, or wicker-pot,
To catch them now,— for they who baffled erst,
Through sliminess, man's grasp, were still indeed
Wriggling — but dusty, — they were skinn'd for food.
He who, by lucky chance, had wherewithal
To wet his whistle, took his drop apart,
And smack'd his lips alone; small love was left:
Folks had but then one thought, and that was drink,
Where to be had, and what? The want of it
Made most men cross, and eke most women too.
The patient lost their patience, and the sour
Grew still more crabbed, sharp-nosed, and shrill-voiced.
Even cats did scratch their maiden Mistresses,
Angry that milk forthcame not, — all, save one,
And he was faithful to the virgin dame
Who petted him;—but, be it not conceal'd,
The rumour ran that he his whiskers greased
From a pomatum-pot, and so he quell'd
The rage of thirst; himself sought naught to lap,
But, with a piteous and perpetual mew,
And a quick snivelling sneeze, sat bundled up,
And taking matters quietly — he lived.
The crowd forsook our village; only two
Of the parishioners still tarried there,
And they were enemies; they met beside
(One only stood before and one behind)
The empty settle of a public-house,
Where had been heap'd a mass of pots and mugs
For unavailing usage; they snatch'd up,
And, scraping, lick'd, with their pounced-parchment tongues,
The porter-pots a-dust; their eager eyes
Dived into gin-bottles, where gin was not,
Labell'd in mockery, — then they lifted up
Their eyes for one brief moment, but it was
To hang their heads more sillily, ashamed
Each of his futile quest; — but 'twas enough
For recognition, — each saw, and leer'd and grinn'd. —
Even at their mutual sheepishness they grinn'd,

DROUTHINESS.

Discovering how upon each foolish face
Shiness had written Quiz. The land was dry;
Day pass'd, defrauded of its moistest meals,
Breakfastless, milkless, tealess, soupless, punchless,
All things were dry, — a chaos grimed with dust.
Tubs washer-womanless, replete with chinks,
Stood in their warping tressels — suds were none;
And dirty linen lost all heart, and hope
Of due ablution — shirts were worn a month —
White pocket-handkerchiefs were quite abandon'd,
And so were nankin inexpressibles —
Yea, most things washable, — and Washing seem'd
To threaten that henceforth it must be named
Among lost arts. Water had fled the Earth,
And left no tears in people's eyes to weep
Its sad departure; — Drouthiness did reign
Queen over all — She was the universe!

A Ladleful from the Devil's Punch Bowl.*

Dear North,

As "Drouthiness" gave such superlative satisfaction, (that is, to myself,) I proceed in the course which Nature has at last pointed out to me. Questionless, I was born a poet, and yet I never found it out till lately. However, I shall spur on Pegasus the faster, to make him fetch up for lost time. I ride light weight, and do not expect that I shall blow him, even if I should push him rather smartly. To say the truth, I possess a spur, which makes him lift his legs nimbly again whenever he slackens. (Allegory apart, this means Walker's Rhyming Dictionary, but it is a profound secret.) As I mean to make you profit by my journeys, I send herewith the products of my two last rides, performed at a hand-gallop, in which I trust you will think that Peggy has bumpered but seldom. But here allow me to get off the great horse, and talk in a more pedestrian manner.

My first poem is a parody on Sir William Jones's spirited paraphrase of a fragment of Alcæus. His contains a palavar about Liberty, and Rights, and the Fiend Discretion, while mine alludes to the less disputable good of a hearty appetite and a dinner to satisfy it.

My second poem is a metrical advertisement of all Lord Byron's works; and for drawing it up, Mr. Murray ought, I am sure, to be grateful to me, for it will save him I know not what in paper and printing, as there is little doubt of its being got by heart by all those for whom he stitches up his announcements. I have secured this, by making my dedication so diffusive—it is to the reading public, that abstract *Helluo librorum*, to whom Mr. Coleridge has such an antipathy; but Mr. Murray has a fellow-feeling for the omnivorous monster, and supplies him with frequent supplies of papyrus, which is the fodder he delights in. Indeed, this pamphlet-perusing prosopopœia the reading public aforesaid seems to squat like the night-mare on the chest of the author of the Ancient Mariner and Kubla Khan; and I much wish that so powerful a somnoversifier would harrow up our souls

* From *Blackwood* for February, 1822.— M.

with some of the dreams, (all probably ready tagged with rhyme for the press,) which that incubus has occasioned.

You will observe that this copy of verses is wholly composed in double rhymes, a feat on which I pride myself, for they are sometimes monstrously hard to find. With one line, which I was determined not to alter, and to whose *finale* I could find nothing correspondent in the compass of the language, I was so vexed, that in an unversifying and unguarded moment I was all but tempted to jump headlong into the Devil's Punch Bowl, that huge circular abyss in my neighborhood—" and there an *end!*" But the catastrophe was prevented by a timely discovery of the required *ending*. A happy termination this; I may well call it so, both of the couplet (which now jingles most musically) and of my perplexity, which thus evanished without a dive of some fathoms downwards. In some cases, however, the will must be taken for the deed, I fear; but you will be pleased, according to the dictum of a sage critic, to crush the syllables, if they are refractory, and then they will fit much better. If my Lord B. should make you the channel of communication, in returning his grateful thanks on this occasion, let no time be lost in conveying them to yours, BLAISE FITZTRAVESTY.

Ladle Court, near the Devil's Punch Bowl.

Dedication

TO THE PHYSICIAN WHO PENNED
PEPTIC PRECEPTS,*
AND PRESCRIBED THOSE PILULAR PRODUCTIONS OF THE PESTLE,
PRÆNOMINATED
PERISTALIC PERSUADERS,
THIS PRETTY POEM IS PRESENTED
BY ITS PARENT.

A FESTAL ODE.

What constitutes a feast?
Not haunch of venison, of flavour true,
Fat, juicy, nicely drest;
Nor turtle calipash of verdant hue;

---

* Dr. W. Kitchener, author of "The Cook's Oracle."— M.

Not soup, in whose rich flood,
French cooks a thousand relishes infuse;
   Not fricassees well stewed,
Nor France's greater boast, high-famed ragouts;
   Not a sirloin of beef,
Crowning a dish in which rich gravy lies;
   Not turbot, ocean chief,
Which ruddy lobster-sauce accompanies,
   No — a good appetite,
And good digestion, turn into a feast
   Whate'er front-tooth can bite,
And grinders manducate, and palate taste.
   Be it homely bread and cheese,
Of which the ravenous carl tucks in some pounds;
   Or bacon smoked, where grease,
Five fingers thick, each stripe of lean surrounds;
   Be it onion, fiery root,
Whose rank effluvia draws unbidden tears;
   Potato, Erin's fruit,
With which the bogtrotter his stomach cheers;
   Be it cabbage, flabby leaf!
Which cross-legg'd tailors smack with liquorish chops;
   Or oatmeal porridge, chief,—
Undoubted chief of Scotland's rustic slops.
   Yet in these meals so plain,
Let but sharp appetite as guest attend,
   And napkin'd Aldermen
May grudge the goût with which the bits descend.
   This constitutes a feast,
To experience hunger and have wherewithal
   (Though it be not of the best)
To stop the void bread-basket's healthy call.

Lord Byron's Combolio.*

INTRODUCTION.

Reading public! whose hunger,
Thou egregious bookmonger,
Gets monthly large parcels
Of fresh sheets, for thy morsels;
And though publishers race, yet
Thou never art satiate
Of new poems, new histories,

---

* As his lordship imported this word from the East, it is but justice that he should have the benefit of it. In the Bride of Abydos, where it is used, he tells us it means the rosary which the Turks use. Here, of course, it is figuratively applied to the series of his poems, which are to be looked upon as the beads of this combolio, (what a mouthful the word is!) and they are beautifully strung upon the golden thread of my verses. Et ego in Arcadia! ahem.—B. F.

New dramas, new *Mysteries*,
New romances, new novels,
New voyages, new travels,
New tourifications,
New *post prandium* orations;*
New lives and new memoirs,
New guide-books, new grammars,
New systems of science,
(Some writ in defiance
Of the sense that's called common)
New endeavors to hum one,
Of old lies new editions,
Of old follies new visions,
New modes of abusing,
(Peep for these the Reviews in),
New revivals of scandal,
By some right or wrong handle;
In short, what is new, Sir,
Finds in thee a peruser.
Reader General! thou patron
Of many a squadron,
Who, with goose quills ink laden,
(Which their stands had best staid in,)
Lose available labour
In blurring white paper,—
To thee do I dedi-
cate, now this most edi-
fying sample of doggrel,
Which will sure catalogue well
The works now abundant,
Of an Author redundant:
And we do not disparage
The rolls of the Peerage
In saying, though they strive all
To discover a rival;
And be Horace Walpole
Stirr'd up with a tall pole,†
And his book's last edition
Put in due requisition :‡
Let the Lords not be hindered
From including their kindred,—
Yet they will not environ
Such a Poet as Byron.
Him, thou, Reading *Demus!*
Hast been pleased to make famous;
So take to thy favour
This industrious endeavour
To make out a list of
"The hanks, which his distaff
Has long time been untwining,
Of verses so genuine,
That renown they must e'en win.
Let some fame too o'erbubble
On his pate, who great trouble
(Behold it) hath taken
In this catalogue making.

THE ROSARY.

The first stretch of his powers
Was made in " The Hours"
'Clept " of Idlesse," that syren,
" By George Gordon Lord Byron."
No need of diviner,
To shew that " a Minor"
The book had compounded;
But to warn us, we found it
Printed under and over,
On the back on the cover,
On the title-page ominous,
And in prose prologomenous.
'Twas, in spite of the pother
Neither one thing nor t'other;

---

* Beware of mistaking,—no allusion here to *brandy*,—gin being the drink of our indigenous orators. Indeed, one of the speechifying Radicals averred in public, that " English gin," (sink the circumstance that he was a vender thereof,) " is as nutritive as mother's milk to an Englishman." Radical harangues are not generally specimens of *after-dinner* eloquence,—they are oftener *orationes impransæ*, or *ad prandium ad ipiscendum.*—B. F.

† *Tall* is surely synonymous with *long*, which is, I know, the epithet in commonest use in menageries, whence we borrow the metaphor.—B. F.

‡ His " Royal and noble authors," which Mr. Park lately edited.—B. F.

And though it was poorish,
It deserved not the flourish
Of that tomahawk cruel
In the saffron and cerule,
Which notch'd it and nick'd it;
In short those wits wicked
Had their sport with the lordling,
Whom they thought a soft bardling,
Too meek to retort it;
But they were not so sorted,
For his next was a stinger;
Master Frank found his finger
Had been burnt in the venture
With one, not a flincher
When his Pegasus skittish
Gave a fling at " Bards British."
 If the " Hours" failed in merit,
There was talent and spirit
In this nettle stuff'd satire;
And the blows, like the platter
Of hail, fell by dozens
On our splenetic cousins
Dun-Edin's Reviewers,
Those paddlers in sewers,
Where their mud-ammunition
(Hooting, hissing, derision,)
Is mix'd up for griming
All those who won't chime in
With jacobin shoutings,
And infidel doubtings.
 Then came doughty Childe Harold,
With whom the world quarrell'd,
Because this aspirant,
Though observant, enquirant,
Shrewd, keen, energetic,
Sublime, and pathetic —
Contriving to wedge in all,
In one word, original;
Yet betray'd the foot cloven,
Scepticism being inwoven
In his talk upon matters
Best left to his betters.
 How plain folks roll'd their gogglers!
How the learned prov'd bogglers!
At the name of the " Giaour."
For sure ne'er to that hour

Did four-fifths of the vowels
Congregate in the bowels
Of a syllable single;
Even yet how to mingle
Their sounds in one's muzzle,
Continues a puzzle.
But the fragments are clever,—
Surpassed has he never,
In his loftiest of stretches.
Two or three of the sketches.
 " The Bride of Abydos"
Next sprang up beside us;
From the first time I met her,
The Giaour pleased me better;
Although I must own it,
With reluctance upon it,
Since my preference showing,
O'er a lady so glowing,
Of a wretch with a white face,
Argues not much politeness.
 With a head rough as horse hair,
Heaves in sight now " The Corsair.
His Lordship here followed
The metre that's hallowed
By the poets, whose due, d'ye see,
Is no longer *sub judice*.
Ne'er could fail this fine story
To find fit auditory;
It holds one quite breathless
With interest; yet, nathless,
'Twould accord with my wishes,
If stops, 'stead of dashes,
Were put to the poem,
(How to do it I'd shew 'em;)
For, I'm sure, I was wearied,
Seeing comma and period
Smash'd,—as if punctuation
Were gone out of fashion.
 " An Ode," rather warty,
Came to Nap Buonaparte;
Wherein he was scolded
For not having folded
His cloak like a Roman;
And, indebted to no man,
Kick'd the bucket with glory,
And lived ever in story.

Then appear'd Senor "Lara,"
Which, at sight, one could swear a
Reappearance of Conrad.
The attempt though did honour add
To our author, clear sighted;
And ne'er hath he indited
With more perspicacity,
And psychologic sagacity.
 To each "Hebrew Melody,"
Alas! and Ah, well-a-day!
For most are but rudish,
And a scantling are goodish;
So let Messrs. Braham
And Nathan enjoy 'em.
 "The Siege," next, "of Corinth,"
Illustrates a war in th'
Morea;—but I dare say,
From perusal or hearsay,
Most now think on the munching
Of the dogs, and their "crunching,"
(On what, in his jargon,
Dr. Gall calls an organ,)
Stripping off the scalp, rot 'em!
"As ye peel figs in autumn."
 With Alp to the arena
Came the fair "Parisina."
That he should not have written,
On this subject forbidden,
Still sticks in my gizzard,
'Spite of "gruff General Izzard."
Who devoid of all mercy is
Tow'rds King Leigh and his verses;*
And because without panic,
That monarch Cockannic,
Rhymed lightly on incest,
Z., with fury intensest,
Pour'd out a full bottle†
Of wrath on his noddle;
But of Byron he's chary,
And lauds this same "Pari-

sine," as if it were shapen,
All the perils escaping.
 All we say of a "Monody"
Is, it issued forth on a day.
 After this, the "Third Canto
Of Childe Harold" was sent to
Find its fate with the nation;
And it gained approbation.
 "The Prisoner of Chillon"
Was sufficient to mill one;
So doleful,—so grievous,—
With nought to relieve us!
 Enter "Manfred;" a serious
Sort of white witch mysterious;
Of our genuine erratic
The first effort dramatic,
And so well in that province
He has never come off since.
 "Tasso's sad Lamentation"
Much requires condensation;
But 'tis plaintive and striking,
And suits with my liking.
 Not so the sarcastic
"Sketch on topics Domestic;"
As the matter has ended,
Least said's soonest mended.
 To Venice he hied him,
And that city supplied him
With the matter capricious
For his "Beppo" facetious;
A model, so please ye,
Of a style free and easy.
The story that's in it
Might be told in a minute;
But *par parenthèse* chatting,
On this thing and that thing,
Keeps the shuttlecock flying,
And attention from dying.
There are some I could mention,
Think the author's intention

---

* Lockhart under the signature "Z" lashed Hunt and the Cockney Poets.—M.

† *Bottle* is here used *aggravando* for *vial*, which is the old established wet-measure of wrath; but surely in these days when energy of language is so much in vogue, I shall find followers to adopt the more forcible expression. Z. gave full measure, whether it were bottle or vial.—B. F.

Was to sneer and disparage
The vow made in marriage;
But the sneer, as I take it,
Is 'gainst those folks who break it.
The lengthy " Fourth Canto
Of the Childe" makes us pant, oh!
It exceeds altogether
The three first in a tether;
But 'tis greatly applauded,
Yea, exceedingly lauded.
Now, though, without flattery,
It has powerful poetry,
Yet the world henceforth will know
Meo proprio periculo,
That, to my mind, the style of it
Is ambitiously elevate,
Too much in the fashion
Of a prize declamation;
Rather pompous and dullish,
Of *falsetto*, too, fullish;
As it don't wholly please me,
Of the subject I ease me.
   Thunders in now on horseback
" Mazeppa" the Cossack;
Though he was not a Hettman
In performing that feat, man,
And a wag, for his trouble,
Call'd him John Gilpin's double.
   With many an ill-omen,
'Neath no publisher's *nomen,**
(Proof that mischief was brewing)
Sneak'd forth, of " Don Juan"
Canto first, Canto second;
But here my Lord reckon'd,
His host unconsulted,—
Staunch admirers revolted,
And made a stern stricture
On the profligate picture;
E'en the wit could not save it

From being upbraided;
And, though read by the many,
No one champion'd Giovanni.
   " The Great Doge of Venice"
Little joy stirred within us;
And the purse of Old Drury
Was not burst, I assure ye,
With the weight of the treasure,
When, in spite of displeasure,
And legal injunction,
Abjuring compunction,
This play they enlisted,
And to act it persisted
Till 'twas thoroughly hiss'd at.
   The " Three Cantos" more recent
" Of Don Juan" are decent
Compared with the couple,
Of morals more supple,
Which first made us wonder.
But the three are much under
Their loose brethren in satire,
And in interesting matter;
Though they shew more decorum,
We could sooner snore o'er 'em.†
   Last came to assail us
Great " Sardanapalus,"
" The Two Foscari's History,"
And " Cain" in a " Mystery."
Had they staid in his pinnace
On the waters of Venice,
His fame had not suffer'd,
For though they discover'd
Some power in the terrible,
They were not all agreeable.
Cain's murderous fury
He had best, I assure ye,
Have left where he found it,
Nor essay'd to expound it;
For, howe'er he conceit it,

---

* Pray be careful to understand that *nomen* is set down here, and not *gnomon*, which would do just as well for the rhyme sake; but then it would not accord with the truth of things; for though *Don Juan* was not sold under any publisher's *name*, it was sold under the *nose* of many a one.— B. F.

† After all that has been said on Don Juan, what comes up to " Don Juan unread?" One of the pleasantest parodies that ever was written. — B. F.

We are bold to repeat it,
He's by no means a fit one
To play pranks Holy Writ on.
Milton's self, when he travell'd,
From the record was gravell'd,
In parts of his epic.
So abstain from the topic,
And with easy restriction
Seek the regions of fiction,
Extend thither your pinion,
For there lies your dominion.

L'Envoy.

Lo! in melody worthy
Of immortal Tom D'Urfey,
Have I chanted, my lyre on,
The doings of Byron.
And, as faithful recorder,
Chronological order
Have I kept. Now, as clincher,
I take heart, and will venture
To suggest to his Lordship
A proposal, (no hardship,)
Which he should not be sorry at —
Let him make me his Laureate.

Royal Visit to Ireland.

AUGUST XII., MDCCCXXI.*

I. THE KING'S LANDING.

PROEMIUM.

1.

The poet flabbergasted by ane strange apparition.

As I was sitting on the Shannon side,
　Lull'd by the sound of that majestic flood,
A horseman on a sudden I espied,
　Galloping by as quickly as he could;
I hail'd him, but he slacken'd not his pace,
　Still urging on his steed, a gallant gray,
Until he passed me, then he turned his face,
　Back towards his horse's tail, and thus did say,—
"I ride express with news to strike you dumb,
　Our monarch has arrived at last—King George the Fourth is come!"

2.

Which leaveth him in ane awkward doldrum, after the manner of W. Wordsworth, Esq.

He scarce had spoken, ere away he pass'd
　Out of my sight as rapid as a bird,
And left me there in much amazement cast,
　Looking, perhaps, in some degree absurd;
The noble river rolling calmly by,
　The horse, the hasty rider, all did seem,
Even to the vision of my outward eye,
　Like the thin shadowy figments of a dream;
I felt, in short, as Wordsworth did, when he
Chanced the leech gatherer on the moor all by himself to see.

3.

Shaketh it off, and marcheth homewards.

By the exertion of judicious thought,
　At last I from this mental trance awoke,
Marvelling much how in that lonely spot,
　Upon my eyes so strange a vision broke;
From the green bank immediately I went,
　And into Limerick's ancient city sped;

---

* In August, 1821, Ireland was "honoured" by a visit from George IV., and got drunk with joy, loyalty, and—whiskey-punch. The Royal Advent was duly commemorated in *Blackwood* at the time. Maginn's portion is here subjoined—M.

During my walk, with puzzled wonderment
  I thought on what the rapid horseman said;
And, as is commonly the case, when I
  Feel any way oppress'd in thought, it made me very dry.

4.

When I arrived in brick-built George's-street, *Turneth star-*
  Instinctively I there put forth my hand   *gazer.*
To where a bottle, stored with liquid sweet,
  Did all upon an oaken table stand;
Then turning up my little finger strait,
  I gazed like *Doctor Brinkley on the sky,
Whence heavenly thought I caught — pure and elate
  Of holy harpings of deep poesy;
And, ere a moment its brief flight could wing,
I threw the empty bottle down, to chant about the King.

ODE.

1.

A VERY glorious day this is indeed!   *He calleth up-*
  This is indeed a very glorious day!   *on Ireland to*
For now our gracious monarch will proceed   *rejoice in the*
  On Irish ground his royal foot to lay.   *fashion of a*
Rejoice, then, O my country, in a tide   *pot of porter.*
  Of buoyant, foaming, overflowing glee;
As swells the porter o'er the gallon's side,
  So let your joy swell up as jovially;
Shout, great and little people, all and some,
Our monarch has arrived at last — King George the Fourth has
  come!

2.

Come down, the mountains, bend your numbsculls low,   *Inviteth the*
  Ye little hills run capering to the shore,   *mountains to*
Now on your marrow bones, all in a row,   *ane saraband.*
  From all your caves a royal welcome roar.
Howth is already at the water-side,
  Such is that loyal mountain's duteous haste;
Come then to join him, come with giant stride,
  Come, I repeat, there's little time to waste;
In your best suits of green depart from home,
For now our monarch has arrived — King George the Fourth has
  come!

---

* Dr. John Brinkley, Astronomer Royal of Ireland, was one of the Professors in Trinity College, Dublin. He was born in 1760, and died in 1835. He was created Bishop of Cloyne in 1826. He was the discoverer, in 1814, of the parallax of the fixed stars. — M.

3.

Maketh of them ane catalogue most musical.

Down should despatch Morne's snowy-vested peaks,
  And Tipperary, ⁻Knocksbeogowna's hill,
  Kerry, the great Macgillycuddy's reeks,
    Cork, the Galtees, studded with many a still,
    Gallop from Wicklow, Sugarloaf the sweet!
    From Wexford, bloody Vinegar† the sour!
    Croagh‡ must be there, from whose conspicuous seat
      St. Patrick made the snakes from Ireland scour,—
    All, all should march, tramp off to beat of drum,
    For now our monarch has arrived—King George the Fourth has
      come!

4.

A word of advice to the rivers, in the style of Master Edmund Spenser, late of Kilcolman.

Rivers, dear rivers, in meandering roll,
  Move to your Sovereign merrily along;
  Ye whom the mighty minstrel of old Mole‖
    Has all embalmed in his enchanting song;
  Liffey shall be your spokesman, roaring forth
    A very neat Address from either Bull,§
  While all the rest of you, from south to north,
    Shall flow around in currents deep and full,
  Murmuring¶ beneath your periwigs of foam—
    "Our monarch has arrived at last—King George the Fourth has
      come!"

5.

Anent lakes.

Killarney sulkily remains behind,
  Thinking the King should come to wait on her;
  And if he wont, she swears with sturdy mind,

---

* Which, being interpreted, signifies, the hill of the fairy calf; there is many a story about it.—M. OD.

† Vinegar Hill, where a decisive battle was fought in 1798, with the rebels, who were totally defeated.—M. OD.

‡ Croagh-Patrick, in Mayo.—M. OD.

‖ Spenser, who dwelt beneath old father Mole,

  (Mole hight that mountain gray
  That walls the north side of Armulla vale.)
              Collin Clout's come home again.

He has catalogued our rivers in the Fairy Queen, B. 4. Cant. 2. St. 40-44.—M. OD.

§ In Dublin Bay are two sand banks, called the North and South Bulls. Not far from them is a village called Ring's-End which gives occasion to the facete to say, that you enter Dublin between two bulls and a blunder.—M. OD.

¶ Something Homeric—
          περὶ δὲ ῥόος Ὠκεανῖο
        Ἀφρῷ μορμύρων ῥέεν. Κ. Σ.—M. OD.

That not one step to visit him she'll stir.
But all the other loughs, where'er they be,
  From mighty Neagh,* the stone-begetting lake,
To Corrib, Swilly, Gara, Dearg, or Rea,
  Or Googaun-Barra,† when the Lee doth take
Its lovely course, join in the general hum —
"Our monarch has arrived at last — King George the Fourth has
    come!"

6.

O ye blest bogs,‡ true sons of Irish soil,   *Lealty of the bogs.*
  How can I e'er your loyal zeal express!
You have already risen, despising toil,
  And travell'd up, your Sovereign to address.
Clara has led the way, immortal bog,
  Now Killmalady follows in his train;
Allen himself must soon to join them jog
  From Geashil barony, with might and main,
In turfy thunders, shouting as they roam,
"Our Sovereign has arrived at last — King George the Fourth has
    come!"

7.

Ha! what's this woful thumping that I hear?   *Ane caution to the Giant's Causeway not to tread upon the learned weavers of Belfast.*
  Oh! 'tis the Giant's Causeway moving on,
Heavily pacing, with a solemn cheer,
  On clumsy hoofs of basalt octagon.
(Gigantic wanderer! lighter be your tramp,
  Or you may press our luckless cities down;
'Twould be a pity, if a single stamp
  Smash'd bright Belfast — sweet linen-vending town.)
Why have you travelled from your sea-beat dome?
"Because our monarch has arrived — King George the Fourth has
    come!"

8.

Last slopes in, sailing from the extremest south,   *Showing how Cape Clear becometh ane Marcus Tullius.*
  Gallant Cape Clear, a most tempestuous isle;
Certain am I, that when she opes her mouth
  She will harangue in oratoric style.

---

* Est aliud stagnum quod facit ligna durescere in lapides; homines autem findunt ligna, et postquam formaverunt in eo usque ad caput anni, et in capite anni lapis invenitur, et vocatur Loch-Each, ac (Lough Neagh.) See Mirab. Hib. — M. OD.

† *i. e.* The hermitage of St. Finbar, who lived there as a recluse. He was first, Bishop of Cork. It is a most beautiful and romantic lake, containing a pretty island. It is a great place of pilgrimage. — M. OD.

‡ Every body has heard of the movement of the Irish bogs. — M. OD.

So North, and South, and East, and West combine,
  *Ulster, and Connaught, Leinster, Munster, Meath,
To hail the King, who, first of all his line,
  Was ever seen old Ireland's sky beneath.
All shall exclaim, for none shall there be mum,
  " Our monarch has arrived at last — King George the Fourth has
    come!"

L'Envoy.

1.

<small>Mocke commendation on various folk.</small>

How living people joy, I shall not tell,
  Else I should make my song a mile in length;
Plebeian bards that theme may answer well,
  Chanting their lays with pertinacious strength:
They may describe how all, both man and beast,
  Have in the general glee respective shares;
How equal merriment pervades the breast
  Of sharks and lawyers — usses and Lord Mayors —
  Of whelps and dandies — orators and geese —
In short, of every living thing, all in their own degrees.

2.

<small>Where it is earnestly requested of the poets of Dublin, not to slay the King after the fashion of Ankerstroem or Ravillac.</small>

But ye, remorseless rhymesters, spare the King!
  Have some compassion on your own liege Lord!
Oh! it would be a most terrific thing
  Were he to death by Dublin poets bored.
See three sweet singers out of College bray,
  And all the aldermen have hired a bard,
The Castle, too, its ode, I ween, will pay,
  And the newspapers have their pens prepared.
Be silent, then, and mute, ye unpaid fry!
Let none attempt to greet the King, save such great bards as I.

---

* The five ancient kingdoms of Ireland. — M. OD.

II. A Welcome to His Majesty.*

Tune — Groves of Blarney.

Synoptical Analysis for the benefit of Young Persons studying this Song.

Stanza I. Welcome in general; in the following verses the specific excellencies of Ireland are stated. Stanza II. 1. National meat, and drink, and valour. Stanza III. 2. National riot in a superior style. Stanza IV. 3. National music. Stanza V. 4. National oratory. Stanza VI. 5. National gallantry. Stanzas VII. and VIII. National uproariousness. All these offered for the diversion of the King.

1.

You're welcome over, my royal rover,
  Coming in clover to Irish ground ;
You'll never spy land, like this our island,
  Lowland or Highland, up or down !
Our hills and mountains, our streams and fountains,
  Our towns and cities all so bright,
Our salt-sea harbours, our grass-green arbours,
  Our greasy larders will glad your sight.

2.

'Tis here you'll eat, too, the gay potato,
  Being a root to feed a king;
And you'll get frisky upon our whiskey,
  Which, were you dumb, would make you sing;
And you'll see dashers, and tearing slashers,
  Ready to face ould Beelzebub,
Or the devil's mother, or any other
  Person whom you'd desire to drub.

3.

Just say the word, and you'll see a riot
  Got up so quiet, and polite,
At any minute you'd please to wish it,
  Morning or evening, noon or night.
I'll lay a wager, no other nation
  Such recreation to you could show,
As us, all fighting with great good manners.
  Laying one another down so low.

4.

And as for music, 'tis you'll be suited
  With harp or bagpipe, which you please;

---

* This " Welcome" was published as by Richard Dowden (Richard) of Cork, who never wrote a line of poetry in his life ! — M

With woful melting, or merry lilting,
  Or jovial quilting your heart to raise.
Sweet Catalani won't entertain you
  With so much neatness of warbling tone,
As those gay swipers, or bold bagpipers,
  Chanting in splendour over their drone.

5.

Then there's our speaking, and bright speech-making,
  Which, when you hear, 'twill make you jump ;
When in its glory it comes before you,
  'Twould melt the heart of a cabbage stump
'Tis so met'phoric, and paregoric,
  As fine as Doric or Attic Greek,
'Twould make Mark Tully look very dully,
  Without a word left in his cheek.

6.

If any ladies, they should invade us,
  The darling creatures, in your *suite,
We'll so amuse them, and kindly use them,
  That in ould Ireland they'll take root.
Our amorous glances, modest advances,
  And smiling fancies, and all that,
Will so delight them, that they'll be crying,
  Were you to part them away from Pat.

7.

The mayors and sheriffs, in paunchy order,
  And the recorders will go down
To gay Dunleary, all for to cheer ye,
  And give you welcome to the town ;
But though their speeching it may be pleasing,
  All written out in comely paw,
'Twont be so hearty, as when all parties,
  With million voices roar Huzza !

8.

God bless your heart, sir, 'tis you will start, sir,
  At that conspicuous thundering shout,
When Ireland's nation, with acclamation,
  To hail their Sovereign will turn out.
England shall hear us, though 'tis not near us,
  And the Scotch coast shall echo ring,
When we, uproarious, joining in chorus,
  Shout to the winds, GOD SAVE THE KING !

---

* To be pronounced Hibernically — shoot. — R. D. R.

III. ODOHERTY'S IMPROMPTU.*

My landlady enter'd my parlour, and said,—
" Bless my stars, gallant Captain, not yet to your bed?
The kettle is drain'd, and the spirits are low,
Then creep to your hammock, Oh go, my love, go!
     Derry down, &c.

" Do look at your watch, sir, 'tis in your small pocket
'Tis three, and the candles are all burn'd to the socket:
Come move, my dear Captain, do take my advice,
Here's Jenny will pull off your boots in a trice.
     Derry down," &c.

Jenny pull'd off my boots, and I turn'd into bed,
But scarce had I yawn'd twice, and pillow'd my head,
When I dream'd a strange dream, and what to me befell,
I'll wager a crown you can't guess ere I tell.
     Derry down, &c.

Methought that to London, with sword at my side,
On my steed Salamanca in haste I did ride,
That I enter'd the Hall, 'mid a great trepidation,
And saw the whole fuss of the grand Coronation.
     Derry down, &c.

Our Monarch, the King, he was placed on the throne,
'Mid brilliants and gold that most splendidly shone;
And around were the brave and the wise of his court,
In peace to advise, and in war to support.
     Derry down, &c.

First Liverpool moved at his Sovereign's command;
Next Sidmouth stepp'd forth with his hat in his hand;
Then Canning peep'd round with the archness of Munden
And last, but not least, came the Marquis of London-†
     derry down, &c.

Then Wellington, hero of heroes, stepp'd forth;
Then brave Graham of Lynedoch, the cock of the north;

---

* This was published as an "Extempore Effusion, sung with great effect by Morgan Odoherty, Esq., on the evening of the 19th July, 1821,"—the day on which George IV. was crowned, in Westminster.—M.

† In 1821, Lord Liverpool was premier; Sidmouth, Home Secretary; Canning, Ex-Minister; Londonderry, (Castlereagh,) Foreign Secretary, Wellington, Master General of the Ordnance; Lynedock, Hopetown, and Anglesey, had won their laurels and coronets in the Peninsula and at Waterloo.—M.

Then Hopetoun he follow'd, but came not alone,
For Anglesey's leg likewise knelt at the throne.
     Derry down, &c.
But the King look'd around him, as fain to survey,
When the warlike departed, the wise of the day,
And he whisper'd the herald to summon in then
The legion of Blackwood, the brightest of men!
     Derry down, &c.
Oh noble the sight was, and noble should be
The strain, that proclaims, mighty legion, of thee!
The tongue of an angel the theme would require,
A standish of sunbeams, a goose quill of fire.
     Derry down, &c.
Like old Agamemnon, resplendent came forth,
In garment embroider'd, great Christopher North;
He knelt at the throne, and then turning his head,—
"These worthies are at the King's service," he said.
     Derry down, &c.
"Oh, Sire! though your will were as hard to attain,
As Gibraltar of old to the efforts of Spain,
The men who surround you will stand, and have stood,
To the last dearest drop of their ink and their blood.
     Derry down, &c.
"From the Land's End to far Johnny Groat's, if a man,
From Cornwall's rude boors to Mac Allister's clan,
Dare raise up his voice 'gainst the church or the state,
We have blisters by dozens to tickle his pate.
     Derry down, &c.
"We have Morris, the potent physician of Wales,
And Tickler, whose right-handed blow never fails,
And him, who from loyalty's path never wander'd,
Himself, *swate* Odoherty, knight of the standard."*
     Derry down, &c.
"We have sage Kempferhausen, the grave and serene;
And Eremus Marischall from far Aberdeen;
Hugh Mullion, the Grass-market merchant so sly,
With his brethren Malachi and Mordecai.†
     Derry down, &c.

---

* Lockhart published his "Peter's Letters to his Kinsfolk" under the sobriquet of Dr. Morris.—"Timothy Tickler," was the *nom de plume* of Mr. Syme, uncle of Professor Wilson, and a constant contributor to *Blackwood*.—Odoherty, as Ex-Ensign in the 99th, was 'yclept "the Standard-bearer," the colours of a regiment being always carried by the two junior ensigns.—M.

† Imaginary contributors to *Blackwood*.—M.

We have also James Hogg, the great shepherd Chaldean,
As sweetly who sings as Anacreon the Teian;
We have Delta, whose verses are as smooth are as silk;
With bold William Wastle, the laird of that ilk.*
                    Derry down &c.
" We have Dr. Pendragon, the D.D. from York,
Who sports in our ring his huge canvass of cork;
And General Izzard, the strong and the gruff,
Who despatches his foes with a kick and a cuff.†
                    Derry down, &c.
" We have Seward of Christchurch, with cap and with gown,
A prizeman, a wrangler, and clerk of renown;
And Buller of Brazen-nose, potent to seek
A blinker for fools, from the mines of the Greek.
                    Derry down, &c.
" Nicol Jarvie from Glasgow, the last, and the best
Of the race, who have worn a gold chain at their breast;
And Scott, Jamie Scott, Dr. Scott, a true blue,
Like the steel of his forceps as tough and as true.
                    Derry down, &c.
We have Cicero Dowden, who sports by the hour,
Of all the tongue-waggers the pink and the flower;
And Jennings the bold, who has challenged so long
All the nation for brisk soda-water, and song.
                    Derry down," &c.
Methought that the King look'd around him and smiled;
Every phantom of fear from his breast was exiled,
For he saw those whose might would the demagogue chain,
And would shield from disturbance the peace of his reign.
                    Derry down, &c.
But the best came the last, for with duke and with lord,
Methought that we feasted, and drank at the board.
Till a something the bliss of my sweet vision broke —
'Twas the watchman a-bawling, " 'Tis past ten o'clock."
                    Derry down, &c.
But before I conclude, may each man at his board
Be as glad as a King, and as drunk as a lord;
There's nothing so decent, and nothing so neat,
As, when rising is past, to sit down on our seat.
                    Derry down, &c.

---

* " Delta" was D. M. Moir, of Musselburg, an awful verse-spinner. " William Wastle" of that ilk was a fictitious character.— M.

† Dr. Pendragon had no existence, save in *Blackwood*, and Lockhart's acknowledged signature, in Maga was " Z."— M.

IV. Translation of the Royal "Adventus."*

1.

Muse! take up your joyful fiddle,
And twang it *pizzicato*,†
But don't attempt the folks to diddle,—
A fib I've nought to say to.

---

* These stanzas are a translation of a Latin poem, generally attributed to Maginn, (and even claimed for him by Mr. Kenealy, his erudite and generally accurate biographer,) but really written by Jeremiah Daniel Murphy, of Cork, who died January 5, 1824, aged eighteen years and a few months. Mr. Murphy spoke or wrote the Greek, Latin, French, Spanish, Portuguese, German, and Irish languages, with the utmost fluency and precision. His command over the Latin language was great. He was little more than 15, when he contributed the "Adventus in Hibernium Regis vera atque perfecta historia," which was thus prefaced:

JACOBUS CORCAGIENSIS CHRISTOPHORO SEPTENTRIONALI, S. D.

Quum in Magazinâ vestrâ pro mense Augusti, (charissime) Dowdeni cujusdam civis mei, satisque mihi noti versus legerem, quosdam ex iis pseudo-prophetico spiritu inspiratos (ut probavit eventus) statim sensi. Ne posteros igitur ea res fallat, sequentem *veram* adventûs Regis historiam ad te mittere decrevi. Poeta enim noster prophetavit dicens, Regem ad Dunlearium appulsurum esse, quod ne credant futura secula, obsecro ut sequentibus versibus locum in Magazinâ tuâ haud deneges.

Datum Corcagiæ, hâc die Octobris 10*mâ*, 1821.

Another of Mr. Murphy's Latin performances was a version of the old ballad of "The Rising of the North," not inferior to Maginn's rendition of "Chevy Chase." It was published in *Blackwood* for August, 1822, and commences thus:

   Listen, lively lordlings all,
    Lithe and listen unto me,
   And I will sing of a noble earle,
    The noblest earle in the North Countrie.

thus rendered,

   Auscultate, Domini,
   Audite me canentem
   Nobilissimum olim Comitem
   Sub Boreâ degentem.—M.

† The Plectrum is admitted to have been a sort of hook used by the ancients (who had not at that time learned the use of their fingers), for twanging their stringed instruments,—a mode of performance, called by our more accomplished violinists, "Playing *Pizzicato.*"—M. OD.

Where's the use of telling stories,
When you're to sing of so great glories,
As foreigners, both Whigs and Tories,
    May wonder and cry " Nay!" to.*

2.

The coming of so great a King
    Would need lore to tell on:
Madam! my tale's no common thing,
    It is one to think well on.
For mighty powers it sure requires,
The Dukes and Barons, Knights and Squires,
Their grand processions and attires,
    That graced that day, to dwell on.

3.

But fear won't further my design,
    Faint heart ne'er won fair lady,
And want of pluck's no crime of mine,
    So I'll describe this gay day.—
There is a village called Dunleary,
Where all did crowd from far and near; I
Ne'er saw the like—so loud and cheery,
    " God save the King!" they said aye.

4.

Thither came Justices of Quorum,
    To punish any rash one,
Who'd break the peace—and just before 'em
    I saw Lord Talbot dash on.—
The Corporation tried to wedge in
Bellies so huge you can't imagine!
Midst men, wives, tailors, in a rage, in
    Order to learn the fashion.

5.

The crowd was great! in number more
    Than sands upon the sea-shore!

---

* The first verse of the original runs thus:—

  Tolle lætas, Musa fides,
  Tange plectro citharam,
  Sed nil pange, quod non vides,
  Si mentiris, taceam.
  Quidnam opus est fallendi,
  Quum triumphi sint dicendi
  Peregrinis vix credendi
  Propter rerum gloriam?—M.

So much the folks their King adore,
    And love him without measure!
They came to see and know the worth
    Of George the Good, of George the Fourth.
The roads were cramm'd from south to north
    As full as they could be, sure.

6.

Och! ye can't read the Book of Fate
    While standing there so weary,
And thinking still, as it grows late,
    The King must sure be near ye.
That King, whose much-desired arrival,
Would give your wearied bones revival,
Has changed his mind! Off ye may drive all,
    He won't come to Dunleary.

7.

There is a harbour, Howth by name,
    That he'll for certain steam on;*
Stewart and Fate ye have to blame,
    For this which ye ne'er dream on.
But pleasure oft comes after pain,
You shall be christen'd o'er again;†
When he returns, he'll not disdain
    Your town his grace to beam on.

8.

But now the ships began to fly‡
    Like swallows through the sea, ma'am,
Or swim like fishes in the sky,
    As swift as swift could be, ma'am.
And as they came still nigh and nigher,
Hope made our hearts beat high and higher,
And all cried out aloud, "I spy her;
    That surely must be she, ma'am!"

---

* Another instance of modern improvements, is the use of steam. To think that it was reserved for modern times to find out the use of fingers and hot-water! The latter discovery has introduced, and is introducing, great changes in all the departments of mechanics — in language among the rest. On board a steamer, instead of saying "Up with the main-sail!" the cry is, "On with the steam!" In like manner, instead of "sailing on a point," we must say "*steaming.*"—M. OD.

† Dunleary was afterwards called Kingstown. George the Fourth stood sponser at the ceremony.—M. OD.

‡ *Volare Æquore* cannot be translated in *English*. In *Irish* it signifies *uti supra*.—M. OD.

9.

But Murraboo! This crowd of folks
  Will get a mighty take-in;
They might as well have worn their cloaks,
  Their blue coats are mistaken.*
Past them the fleet doth swiftly sail,
Their hopes and wishes can't prevail,
And born on wings of steam and gale,
  Howth they their rest will make in.

10.

Like hungry, disappointed Whigs,
  In vain for places praying;
Like starving, desperate, gambling prigs
  Losing each bet they're laying;
Like such, were all the doleful people —
Like them, the female sex did weep all,
When from their sight, they from the steeple
  Saw George their King astraying.

11.

About two hundred Irish lads,
  Were standing on Howth height, ma'am,
Whose heart sufficiently it glads,
  Far off to see the sight, ma'am,
Of all the frigates, yachts, and steamers,
And royal standards, flags, and streamers,
About the King — They were not dreamers
  That he'd be there that night, ma'am.

12.

But when they saw, that to their town,
  The Royal Navigator
Approach'd — And when all bearing down
  Came boat, sloop, ship, first-rater —
Lord! what a row the fellows raised!
And how his Majesty they praised!
The shout the very shores amazed!
  No King e'er caused a greater.

13.

At length with fav'ring steam and gale,†
  The Lightning safe did steer in;

---

* Blue coats were worn in honour of this Majesty's expected arrival.—
M. OD.

† I don't remember whether I meant *gnis* in the original, to signify "The

The crowd the Royal Ensign hail,—
Each bright eye bore a tear in
Token of joy! The foremost ranks
Slid down a gangway from the banks:
With silk they carpeted the planks—
THE KING HAS STEPT ON ERIN!*

14.

Could I write melodies like Moore,
Or ballads like Sir Walter,
Or any such great poet, sure
My strain should be no halter.
I'd sing a song without a blunder,
Should make posterity all wonder,
And George's praise should sound like thunder,
Before my voice should falter!

15.

But since poor I am not the least
Like them, a wight rhetorical,
My reader's precious time to waste
With Blarney a damn'd bore I call.
But yet I needn't hold my tongue,
I'll tell how round the King they hung,
Although this story be not snug
In language metaphorical.

16.

Our gracious King to all the crowd
His willing hand extended,

Lightning," which was formerly the name of the steam-packet, which brought the King, (now the Royal George the Fourth,) or the fire which boiled the water, which made the steam which made her go. The fact is, I was engaged at the time in the two occupations of writing about George the Fourth, and drinking his health; and my aunt tells me, I never can do two things clearly at once. I never chuse to alter what my muse inspired; and, therefore, to be safe, I have preserved both meanings in my translation.—M. OD.

> * Tandem Euri flatu et igne,
> (Ignis enim egerat)
> Stetit navis quæ insigne
> Regis boni tulerat;—
> Appulit;—nec mora—ferunt
> Ligna supra quæ straverunt
> Sericam—deposuerunt—
> TERRAM REX TETIGERAT!

And even the poorest Pat felt proud,
 So much he condescended.
And *willing hands* the pockets picking,
Gold watches grabbing, brass ones nicking,
Made no distinction more than the King,
 Lest folks should feel offended.

17.

Mounting the carriage steps with grace,
 " My friends," he cried, " I thank ye!"—
The coachman takes his reins and says,
 " My tits soon home shall spank ye."—
Than came the horsemen on with pride,
Some of them their own chargers ride,
While some paid half a crown a-side,
 And some had but a donkey.

18.

The crowd increased as they went on,
 Because their hearts were loyal;
They ran so fast their breath was gone,
 They scarce could speak for joy all.
But of their great politeness judge,
When they came to the Porter's Lodge,
They not one other step would budge,
 Because the grounds were royal.

19.*

But when the King cried " Come along,
 My friends, pray don't be frighted;"
No sooner said than all the throng
 Rush'd on to where he lighted.
Again at stepping on the ground,
He shook the hands of all around,
And made their hearts with joy rebound,
 When he with face delighted,

---

* 19.

Timidis tunc Georgius inquit:
" Heus! amici, pergite."
Portam populus relinquit
Statque coram Principe.—
E curriculo descendit,
Manus rursùm ad eos tendit,
Osque placidum ostendit,
Gratâ hæc aiens facie:

20.*

Exclaimed, "My soul is glad to day,
  My own dear Irish nation;
I love you more than I can say,
  So great my agitation.
I've loved you always — man and boy —
And here I'm come, and will employ,
To drink your health, without alloy,
  Of whiskey a libation."

21.

Thus said the King, and then the stair
  He royalty ascended.
God save the King! through all the air,
  With four times four was blended!
This being all I had to say,
About this memorable day,
Contentedly my pen I lay
  Down — for my tale is ended.

---

* 20.

"Chara mihi gens Hiberna!
Gaudium mentem agitat;
Cordis semper mei interna
Patria vestra flagitat. —
Senex — juvenis — amavi;
Ideo nunc vos visitavi. —
Mox — saluti quam optavi
Animus 'whisko' ebibat!"

21.

Dixit, — inque domum lætus
Ambulat nobiliter, —
Admiransque totus cætus
Plausibus prosequitur. —
Hic triumphus, hic adventus,
Hic gratissimus concentus
Verè scriptus est — contentus
Pennam pono. — Dicitur.

Who wrote "The Groves of Blarney"?

'Who,'—ask ye! No matter.—This tongue shall not tell,
   O'er the board of oblivion the name of the bard;
Nor shall it be utter'd, but with the proud spell,
   That sheds on the perish'd their only reward.

No, no! look abroad, Sir, the last of October;
   In the pages of Blackwood that name shall be writ,
For Christopher's self, be he tipsy or sober,
   Was not more than his match, in wine, wisdom, or wit.

Ye Dowdens and Jenningses, wits of Cork city,
   Though mighty the heroes that chime in your song,
Effervescing and eloquent—more is the pity
   Ye forget the great poet of Blarney so long.

I mean not the *second*, O'Fogarty hight,
   Who can speak for himself, from his own native Helicon*
I sing of an elder, in birth and in might,
   (Be it said with due deference,)—honest *Dick Millikin*.

Then fill up, to his mem'ry, a bumper, my boys,
   'Twill cheer his sad ghost, as it toddles along
Through Pluto's dark alleys, in search of the joys
   That were dear upon earth to this step-son of song.

And this be the rule of the banquet for aye,
   When the goblets all ring with "Och hone, Ullagone!
Remember this pledge, as a tribute to pay
   To the name of a minstrel so sweet, so unknown

---

* "Daniel O'Rourke, an Epic Poem, in six cantos," professing to be written by one Fogarty O'Fogarty, (attributed to Maginn, but really composed by his friend William Gosnell, of Cork,) had recently appeared in *Blackwood*. This tribute to the memory of the author of "The Groves of Blarney' was published in Maga in November, 1821.—M.

Specimens of a Free and Easy Translation,

In which HORACE *is done (for) into English, and adapted to the Taste of the Present Generation.**

PRELIMINARY LETTER.—*Private.*

DEAR NORTH,

I AM sorry to learn, by your last, that you have had such a severe twitch this time; keep warm in Welch flannel, live soberly, and no more desperate attempts with the Eau Medicinale d'Husson. It will be no farce, I assure you, if the gout fly bolt into your stomach, like a Congreve rocket into the ditto of a whale, and carry you off in the twinkling of a walking-stick. Then there would be wiping of eyes and blowing of noses; crape, weepers, and long cravats, throughout the land. Then there would be a breaking up of the glorious divan. Wastle would leave his High Street lodgings, and retire to his "airy citadel;" Morris would sell his shandrydan, and keep house at Aberystwith for life; Kempferhausen would pack up for Allemagne; Eremus would commence grinder to the embryo divines at Aberdeen; The Odontist would forswear poetry, take a large farm, and study Malthus on Population; Delta would take parson's orders; Paddy from Cork would fall into "a green and yellow melancholy," toss the remaining cantos of his epic to Beelzebub, and button his coat behind; Mullion would sell butter and eggs at his provision-warehouse, Grassmarket, and sedulously look forward to the provostship; while poor Odoherty (alas, poor Yorick!) would send his luggage to Dunleary harbour, and away to the fighting trade in South America.

Then would there be a trumpeting and tantararaing among the Whigs,—"Quassha ma boo! our masters are no more!" would be echoed by every lip among them; and then, but not till then, with some shadow of hope might they look forward to their holding the reins of government, though, after all, most of them, if they did not hold well by the mane, would fall off the

---

* From *Blackwood* for December, 1821.—M.

steed's back into the mire, they are such shocking bad riders; while the Radicals would press forward, and tread on their ribs in turn; Glasgow weavers would spin ropes to hang up whoever was obnoxious to them; Sheffield cutlers would grind razors to cut throats; and the Ribbonmen of Erin, and all "the ragged, royal race of Tara," would look forward to seats in the Cabinet. Then, indeed, would there be a complete revolution in Church and State; churchmen would be cut shorter by the head, the national debt washed out with a dishclout, and taxes abolished; and then, instead of election being fettered, and parliaments septennial, there would be universal suffrage, and no parliaments at all. Then would the Saturnian age return to bless the world; then would Lucifer hawk about his golden pippins, and find abundant sale for them; then would all property be common, and pickpockets left without a trade; while no person would have any thing to do—at least, any right to do any thing, except smoking his pipe, draining his mug, and snoring in his hammock.

My dear North, take care of the damp weather, and I warrant, that for many a long year to come, you shall keep death and the doctor at complete defiance—behold the cause of true freedom and loyalty prospering around you—and, were it not that you are a bachelor, rejoice in the caresses of your children's children.

From you, my revered friend, I shall descend to a humbler topic, "one of which," to use the words of Byron, "all are supposed to be fluent, and none agreeable—self."

1stly. With regard to health, I find myself as well as I wish all others to be. My sprained ancle is now quite convalescent, poor thing; and, by persevering in rubbing a tea-spoonful of opodeldoc upon it every morning, it will soon be as strong as a bedpost. I occasionally take a Seidlitz powder to keep my stomach in order; for, depend upon it, the stomach of a literary man is almost of as much consequence as his head. Talking of the top-piece, I have an occasional headach; that is to say, after being too late out at night; but which I effectually remove and rectify by a bottle of soda water—our friend Jennings' if possible; for it excels all others, as much as his poetry the common run of verses, and stands, in relation to every other compound of the kind, in the same degree of excellence and superiority, as Day and Martin's patent blacking to that made with soot, saliva, and small beer.

2dly. With respect to my intellectual pursuits. Pray, what makes you so earnest to learn what a retired and obscure man like me is about, and whose poor contributions to literature are but a drop in the bucket, compared with what you every day receive from the bright luminaries of the age? But I value your partiality as I ought; and, though I am to these as a farthing candle to a six-in-the-pound, you generously dip my wick in your own turpentine, to make it blaze brighter.

I blush scarlet, (God bless the army, and their coats of scarlet!) when I confess, on my knees (by the bye, there is no need of kneeling, when you cannot see me,) that I have been for some time notoriously idle. Salamanca is such a noble beast, that I could not resist taking him out to the hounds; (I have won the brush thrice) and then, partridges were so plenty, I said it would waste little powder and shot daily to fill and replenish my bag;—and then, there was sometimes cricket in the morning—and loo in the afternoon—and blows-out at night, and all that. *Horresco referens.* I have been shamefully idle; but I am determined to stick to it like rosin this winter; and, hang me if I do not astonish the natives; I shall make some of them gaze up to the clouds in wonder, and others to shake in their shoes. In the interim, I enclose specimens of a new, free, and easy translation—I should say, imitation, of Horace. I have got finished with the Odes, and am busy with the Satires, writing at the rate of four hundred lines a-day. Let me know, when convenient, what you think of them;—make a church and a mill of them afterwards;—give my best respects to Mr. Blackwood, when you see him; and believe me, while I have breath in my nostrils,

Your's devoutly,
Morgan Odoherty.

Dublin, *2d December*, 1821.

A FREE AND EASY TRANSLATION OF HORACE.

HORACE, BOOK FIRST.

ODE 1.

Ad Mæcenatem.

Maecenas, atavis edite regibus,
O et praesidium et dulce decus meum!

Sunt, quos curriculo pulverem Olympicum
Collegisse juvat metaque fervidis
Evitata rotis, palmaque nobilis
Terrarum dominos, evehit ad deos:

Hunc, si mobilium turba Quiritium
Certat tergeminis tollere honoribus:

Illum, si proprio condidit horreo
Quidquid de Libycis verritur areis.
Gaudentem patrios findere sarculo
Agros.

Attalicis conditionibus
Nunquam dimoveas, ut trabe Cypria
Myrtoum pavidus nauta secet mare.

To Christopher North, Esq.

HAIL! Christopher, my patron, dear,
Descended from your grandfather;
To thee, my bosom friend, I fly,
Brass buckler of Odoherty!
Some are, who all their hours consume
With well-train'd horse, and sweated
    groom,—
Who, if the Doncaster they gain,
Or, coming first, with lighten'd rein,
At the St. Leger, bear away
Elate the honors of the day,
Pull up their collars to their ears,
And think themselves amid the spheres.
Such art thou, Lambton, Kelburne, Pierse,
And more than I can name in verse.
Another tries, with furious speech,
The bottoms of the mob to reach;—
Here on the hustings stands Burdett,
With trope and start their zeal to whet;
While jackall Hobhouse, sure to tire on
Tracking alway the steps of Byron,
Stands at his arm, with words of nectar
Determined to out-hector Hector.—
Preston, with rosin on his beard,
Starts up, determined to be heard,
And swears destruction to the bones
Of those who will not hear Gale Jones:
While Leigh Hunt, in the Examiner,
About them tries to make a stir,
And says, (who doubts him?) men like
    these
Shame Tully and Demosthenes.—
A third, like Sir John Sinclair, tries
To hold the harrow to the skies;
And thinks there is no nobler work,
Than scattering manure with the fork,
Except (as Mr. Coke prefers,)
To catch the sheep, and ply the shears:
Although you'd give, in guineas round,
A plum, (*i.e.* one hundred thousand pound,)

Luctantem Icariis fluctibus Africum
Mercator metuens, otium et oppidi
Laudat rura sui : mox reficit rates
Quassas, indocilis pauperiem pati.

Est, qui nec veteris pocula Massici,
Nec partem solido demere de die,
Spernit

   nunc viridi membra sub arbuto
Stratus, nunc ad atquae lene caput sa-
  crae.

Multos castra juvant, et lituo tubae
Permixtus sonitus,

    bellaque, matribus
Detestata.

   Manet sub Jove frigido
Venator, tenerae conjugis immemor :
Seu visa est catulis cerva fidelibus,
Seu rupit teretes Marsus aper plagas.

You could not get these men, I know,
Aboard the Northern ships to go,—
Through frozen latitudes to stroll,
And see if ice surrounds the pole ;—
They wish success to Captain Parry,
But yet, at home would rather tarry.
In slippers red, before the fire,
With negus to his heart's desire.
The merchant sits ; he winks and snores,—
The north wind in the chimney roars :
Waking, he bawls aloud — " Od rot 'em,
" I fear my ships are at the bottom !—
" The crews are trifles to be sure,
" But then the cargos a'n't secure :
" 'Change will be changed for me to-mor-
  row,—
" Alack ! for poverty and sorrow !"
Men are — I know them — let that pass,
(Who crack a joke, and love a glass)
Whether, like Fulstaff, it be sack,
Champaigne, Old Hock, or Frontiniac,
Or Whiskey-punch, which, jovial dog,
Is true heart's-balsam to James Hogg ; —
Like Wordsworth, under pleasant trees,
Some take delight to catch the breeze ;
Or lie amid the pastoral mountains,
And listen to the bubbling fountains.
Many in camps delight to hear
The fife and bugle's music clear,
While hautboy sweet, and kettle-drum,
Upon the ear like thunder come.
Though youngsters love a battle hot,
Their anxious mothers love it not ;—
While in the fray a son remains out,
Some erring ball may knock his brains out.
O'er hedge and ditch, through field and
  thicket,
With buck-skin breeches, and red jacket,
On spanking steed the huntsman flies,
Led by the deep-mouth'd stag-hounds'
  cries :
Meanwhile his spouse, in lonely bed,
Laments that she was ever wed ;
And, toss'd on wedlock's stormy billow,
Like the M'Whirter, clasps her pillow,

Me doctarum hederae praemia frontium
Dis miscent superis;

           me gelidum nemus,
Nympharumque leves sum Satyris chori
Secernunt populo:

           si neque tibias
Euterpe cohibet, nec Polyhymnia
Lesboum refugit tendere barbiton.

Quod si me Lyricis vatibus inseris,
Sublimi feriam sidera vertice.

And sighs, while fondling it about,
"Thou art my only child, I doubt!"
— For me a laurel crown, like that
Used for a band to Southey's hat,
(Not such as Cockney Will abuses,
And Leigh Hunt for a night-cap uses,)
Would make me, amid wits, appear
A Samson, and a grenadier!
Then, many a nymph, with sparkling eye,
Would crowd around Odoherty;
Swift at the tune, which Lady Morgan
Would play upon the barrel organ;
MacCraws, and all my second cousins,
And light-heel'd blue-stockings by dozens
With nimble toe would touch the ground,
And form a choral ring around.—
Oh! that James Hogg, my chosen friend,
His glowing fancy would me lend,
His restless fancy, wandering still
By lonely mount, and fairy rill!
That Dr. Scott, with forceps stout,
Would draw my stumps of dullness out;
Exalt my heart o'er churlish earth,
And fill me with his fun and mirth;
Then, Anak-like, 'mid men I'd stray,
Men, that like mice would throng my way,
Rise high o'er all terrestrial jars,
And singe my poll against the stars.

ODE FIFTH, BOOK FIRST.

Ad Pyrrham.

Quis multa gracilis te puer in rosa
Perfusus liquidis urguet odoribus
  Grato, Pyrrha, sub antro?
  Cui flavam religas comam,

Simplex munditiis? heu! quoties fidem
Mutatosque deos flebit, et aspera
  Nigris aequora ventis
  Emirabitur insolens,

To Molly M'Whirter.

What Exquisite, tell me, besprinkled with civet,
  With bergamot, and l'huile antique a la rose,
Now presses thee, Molly, (I scarce can believe it,)
  To march to the Parson, and finish his woes?

For whom do you comb, brush, and fillet your tresses;—
  Whoever he be has not sorrows to seek;

Qui nunc te fruitur credulus aurea:
Qui semper vacuum, semper amabilem,
  Sperat, nescius aurae
    Fallacis! Miseri, quibus

Thou daily shalt bring him a peck of distresses;
  Then kick him, and kiss a new gallant next week.
He trusts that you'll love him, and doat on him ever,
  And thinks you a goddess reserved for himself;
But, Molly, there's too much red blood in your liver,
  And antlers shall soon grace the poor silly elf.

Intentata nites! Me, tabula sacer
Votiva paries indicat, uvida
  Suspendisse potenti
    Vestimenta maris deo.

To some Johnny Raw thou wilt shine like a planet,
  For lecturing Magnus has left thee behind;
And since I have escaped thee, (oh! blessings be on it,)
  I will hang up an old coat in St. Mary Wynd.

ODE NINTH, BOOK FIRST.

Ad Thaliarcham.

VIDES, ut alta stet nive candidum
Soracte, nec jam sustineant onus
  Silvae laborantes, geluque
    Flumina constiterint acuto.

Dissolve frigus, ligna super foco
Large reponens: atque benignius
  Deprome quadrimum Sabina,
    O Thaliarche! marum diota.

Permitte divis cetera; qui simul
Stravere ventos aequore fervido
  Depraeliantes, nec cupressi,
    Nec veteres agitantur orni.

Quid sit futurum cras, fuge quaerere, et,
Quem Fors dierum cumque dabit, lucro
  Appone; nec dulces amores
    Sperne puer, neque tu choreas,

To Dr. Scott.

LOOK out, and see old Arthur's Seat,
  Dress'd in a periwig of snow,
Cold sweeps the blast down Niddry Street,
  And through the Netherbow.

Sharp frost, begone! haste send the maid,
  With coals two shovels-full and more;
Fill up your rummers, why afraid,
  And bolt the parlour door.—

Leave all to Fortune, Dr. Scott,
  Though tempests growl amid the trees,
While we have rum-punch smoking hot,
  We sha'n't most likely freeze.

A fig about to-morrow's fare!
  A twenty thousand prize my buck,
(Nay, do not laugh,) may be my share,
  Wont that be rare good luck?

A FREE AND EASY TRANSLATION OF HORACE.   189

Donec virenti canities abest
Morosa. Nunc et campus, et areae,
Lenesque sub noctem susurri
    Composita repetantur hora:

Doctor, I'm sure you'll toast the fair;
    Shame to the tongue would say me nay;
You'll toast them, till the very hair
    Of your peruke turn grey.

St. Giles's spire with snow is white,
    And every roof seems overgrown;
Sharp winds that come, at fall of night,
    Down High Street closes moan;

Nunc et latentis proditor intimo
Gratus puellae risus ab angulo,
Pignusque dereptum lacertis,
    Aut digito male pertinaci.

There, battering police officers,
    Hark! how the mad jades curse and ban
While Polly cuffs some spoonie's ears,
    And cries, "Sir, I'm your man!"—

Remarks on Shelley's Adonais.*

Between thirty and forty years ago, the *Della Crusca* school was in great force. It poured out monthly, weekly, and daily, the whole fulness of its raptures and sorrows in verse, worthy of any "person of quality." It revelled in moonlight, and sighed with evening gales, lamented over plucked roses, and bid melodious farewells to the "last butterfly of the season." The taste prevailed for a time; the more rational part of the public, always a minority, laughed and were silent; the million were in raptures, and loud in their raptures. The reign of "sympathy" was come again,— poetry, innocent poetry, had at length found out its true language. Milton and Dryden, Pope and the whole ancestry of the English Muse, had strayed far from nature. They were a formal and stiff-skirted generation, and their fame was past and for ever. The trumpet of the morning paper, in which those "inventions rich" were first promulgated, found an echo in the more obscure fabrications of the day, and milliners' maids and city apprentices pined over the mutual melancholies of *Arley* and *Matilda*.

At length, the obtrusiveness of this tuneful nonsense grew insupportable; a man of a vigorous judgment shook off his indolence, and commenced the long series of his services to British literature, by sweeping away, at a brush of his pen, the whole light-winged, humming, and loving population. But in this world folly is immortal; one generation of absurdity swept away, another succeeds to its glories and its fate. The *Della Crusca* school has visited us again, but with some slight change of localities. Its verses now transpire at one time from the retreats of Cockney dalliance in the London suburbs; sometimes they visit us by fragments from Venice, and sometimes invade us by wainloads from Pisa. In point of subject and execution,

---

* I give this review of Shelley's Adonais, (an elegy on the death of John Keats, author of "Endymion,") as the earliest specimen I can present of the *slashing* order of criticism of which Maginn subsequently became so thorough a master. It appeared in *Blackwood* for December, 1821.— M.

there is but slight difference; both schools are "smitten with
nature, and nature's love," run riot in the intrigues of anemo-
nies, daisies and butter-cups, and rave of the "rivulets *proud*,
and the deep *blushing* stars." Of the individuals in both establishments, we are not quite qualified to speak, from the peculiar-
ity of their private habits; but poor Mrs. Robinson* and her
correspondents are foully belied, if their moral habits were not
to the full as pure as those of the Godwinian colony, that play
"the Bacchanal beside the Tuscan sea." But we must do the
defunct *Della Crusca* the justice to say, that they kept their private irregularities to themselves, and sought for no reprobate
popularity, by raising the banner to all the vicious of the community. They talked nonsense without measure, were simple
down to the lowest degree of silliness, and "babbled of green
fields" enough to make men sicken of summer, but they were
not daring enough to boast of impurity; there was no pestilent
hatred of every thing generous, true, and honourable; no desperate licentiousness in their romance; no daring and fiend-like
insult to feeling, moral ties, and Christian principle. They were
foolish and profligate, but they did not deliver themselves, with
the steady devotedness of an insensate and black ambition, to the
ruin of society.

We have now to speak of Mr. P. B. Shelley and his poem.
Here we must again advert to the *Della Crusca*. One of the
characteristics of those childish persons was, the restless interest
which they summoned the public to take in every thing belonging to their own triviality. If Mrs. Robinson's dog had a bad
night's repose, it was duly announced to the world; Mr. Merry's
accident in paring his nails solicited a similar sympathy;† the
falling off of Mrs. R.'s patch, at the last ball, or the stains on
Mr. M.'s full dress coat, from the dropping of a chandelier, came
before the earth with praise-worthy promptitude. All within

---

* Mrs. Robinson, the "Perdita" of that voluptuary George IV., was one of
the Della Crusca poetlings of the latter days of the 18th century, and wrote as
"Laura Maria." — M.

† Mr. Robert Merry, who died in America in 1798, was founder of the
Della Crusca school of poetry, and immortalized as such, by the satiric pen of
Gifford. — M.

their enchanted ring was perfection; but there the circle of light and darkness was drawn, and all beyond was delivered over to the empire of Dulness and Demogorgon. The New School are here the humble imitators of those original arbiters of human fame.

The present story is thus:—A *Mr. John Keats*, a young man who had left a decent calling for the melancholy trade of cockney-poetry, has lately died of a consumption, after having written two or three little books of verses, much neglected by the public. His vanity was probably wrung not less than his purse; for he had it upon the authority of the Cockney Homers and Virgils, that he might become a light to their region at a future time. But all this is not necessary to help a consumption to the death of a poor sedentary man, with an unhealthy aspect, and a mind harassed by the first troubles of versemaking. The New School, however, will have it that he was slaughtered by a criticism of the Quarterly Review.—" O flesh, how art thou fishified!"—There is even an aggravation in this cruelty of the Review—for it had taken three or four years to slay its victim, the deadly blow having been afflicted at least as long since. We are not now to defend a publication so well able to defend itself. But the fact is, that the Quarterly finding before it a work at once silly and presumptuous, full of the servile *slang* that Cockaigne dictates to its servitors, and the vulgar indecorums which that Grub Street Empire rejoiceth to applaud, told the truth of the volume, and recommended a change of manners and of masters to the scribbler. Keats wrote on; but he wrote *indecently*, probably in the indulgence of his social propensities. He selected from Boccacio, and, at the feet of the Italian Priapus, supplicated for fame and farthings.

"Both halves the winds dispersed in empty air."

Mr. P. B. Shelley having been the person appointed by the *Pisan* triumvirate to canonize the name of this apprentice, "nipt in the bud," as he fondly tells us, has accordingly produced an Elegy, in which he weeps "after the manner of Moschus for Bion." The canonizer is worthy of the saint.—"*Et tu, Vitula!*" —Locke says, that the most resolute liar cannot lie more than once in every three sentences. Folly is more engrossing; for we could prove, from the present Elegy, that it is possible to write two sentences of pure nonsense out of every three. A more faithful calculation would bring us to ninety-nine out of every hundred, or,—as the present consists of only fifty-five stanzas,— leaving about five readable lines in the entire. It thus commences:—

> "O weep for Adonais—he is dead!
> O, weep for Adonais! though our tears
> *Thaw not the frost* which binds so dear a head!
> And thou, sad hour! selected from all years
> *To mourn our loss,* rouse thy obscure compeers,
> *And teach them thine own sorrow, say with me*
> *Died* Adonais! till the *future does*
> *Forget the past.* His fate and fame shall be
> *An echo and a light!!!* unto eternity."

Now, of this unintelligible stuff the whole fifty-five stanzas are composed. Here an hour—a *dead* hour too—is to say that Mr. J. Keats died *along with it!* yet this hour has the heavy business on its hands of mourning the loss of its *fellow-defunct,* and of rousing all its *obscure compeers* to be taught its *own sorrow,* &c. Mr. Shelley and his tribe have been panegyrized in their turn for power of language; and the man of "Table-talk" swears by all the gods he owns, that he has a great command of words, to which the most eloquent effusions of the Fives Court are *occasionally* inferior. But any man may have the command of every word in the vocabulary, if he will fling them like pebbles from his sack; and even in the most fortuitous flinging, they will sometimes fall in pleasing though useless forms. The art of the modern *Della Cruscan* is thus to eject every epithet that he can conglomerate in his piracy through the Lexicon, and throw them out to settle as they will. He follows his own rhymes, and shapes his subject to the close of his measure. He is a glutton of all names of colours, and flowers, and smells, and tastes, and crowds his verse with scarlet, and blue, and yellow, and green; extracts tears from every thing, and makes moss and mud hold regular conversations with him. "A goose-pye talks,"—it does more, it thinks, and has its peculiar sensibilities,—it smiles and weeps, raves to the stars, and is a listener to the western wind, as fond as the author himself.

On these principles, a hundred or a hundred thousand verses might be made, equal to the best in Adonais, without taking the pen off the paper. The subject is indifferent to us, let it be the "Golden Age," or "Mother Goose,"—"Waterloo," or the "Wit of the Watchhouse,"—"Tom Thumb," or "Thistlewood." We will undertake to furnish the requisite supply of blue and crimson daisies and dandelions, not with the toilsome and tardy lutulence of the puling master of verbiage in question, but with a burst and torrent that will sweep away all his weedy trophies. For example — *Wontner*, the city marshal, a very decent person, who campaigns it once a year, from the Mansion-house to Blackfriars bridge, truncheoned and uniformed as becomes a man of his military habits, had the misfortune to fracture his leg on the last Lord Mayor's day. The subject is among the most unpromising. We will undertake it, however, (premising, that we have no idea of turning the accident of this respectable man into any degree of ridicule,)

O WEEP FOR ADONAIS, &C.

O weep for *Wontner*, for his leg is broke,
O weep for Wontner, though our pearly tear
Can never cure him. Dark and dimly broke
The thunder cloud o'er Paul's enamelled sphere,
When his black barb, with lion-like career,
Scattered the crowd. — Coquetting Mignionet,
Thou Hyacinth fond, thou Myrtle without fear,
Haughty Geranium, in your beaupots set,
Were then your soft and starry eyes unwet?

The pigeons saw it, and on silver wings
Hung in white flutterings, for they could not fly,
Hoar-headed Thames checked all his crystal springs,
Day closed above his pale, imperial eye,
The silken zephyrs breathed a vermeil sigh,
High Heavens! ye Hours! and thou Ura-ni-a!
Where were ye then? Reclining languidly
Upon some green Isle in the empurpled Sea,
Where laurel-wreathen spirits love eternally.

Come to my arms. &c.

We had intended to call attention by *italics* to the *picturesque* of these lines; but we leave their beauties to be ascertained by individual perspicacity; only requesting their marked admiration of the epithets *coquetting, fond, fearless,* and *haughty,* which all tastes will feel to have so immediate and inimitable an application to mignionet, hyacinths, myrtles, and geraniums. But *Percy Bysshe* has figured as a sentimentalist before, and we can quote largely without putting him to the blush by praise. What follows illustrates his power over the language of passion. In the *Cenci,* Beatrice is condemned to die for parricide,—a situation that, in a true poet, might awaken a noble succession of distressful thought. The mingling of remorse, natural affection, woman's horror at murder, and alternate melancholy and fear at the prospect of the grave, in Percy Bysshe works up only this frigid rant:—

> "—— How comes this hair undone?
> Its wandering strings must be what blind me so,
> And yet I *tied it fast!!*——
> *   *   *   *
> The sunshine on the floor is *black!* The air
> Is changed to vapours, such as the dead breathe
> In charnel pits! Poh! I am choak'd! There creeps
> A clinging, black, contaminating mist
> About me—'tis substantial, heavy, thick.
> I cannot pluck it from me, for it glues
> My fingers and my limbs to one another,
> And eats into my sinews, and dissolves
> My flesh to a pollution," &c. &c.

So much for the history of "Glue"—and so much easier is it to rake together the vulgar vocabulary of rottenness and reptilism, than to paint the workings of the mind. This raving is such as perhaps no excess of madness ever raved, except in the imagination of a Cockney, determined to be as mad as possible, and opulent in his recollections of the shambles.

In the same play, we have a specimen of his "art of description." He tells of a ravine—

> "And in its depths there is a mighty Rock,
> Which has, from unimaginable years,
> Sustain'd itself with *terror and with toil!*
> Over a gulph, and with *the agony*

> *With which it clings*, seems slowly coursing down;
> Even as a wretched soul, hour after hour,
> Clings to the mass of life, yet clinging *leans*,
> And leaning, makes *more dark* the dread abyss
> In which it fears to fall. Beneath this crag,
> *Huge as despair*, as if *in weariness*,
> The *melancholy* mountain *yawns* below," &c. &c.

And all this is done by a rock — What is to be thought of the *terror* of this novel sufferer — its *toil* — the *agony* with which so sensitive a personage clings to its paternal support, from *unimaginable* years? The magnitude of this *melancholy* and injured monster is happily measured by its being the *exact size of despair!* Soul becomes substantial, and *darkens* a *dread abyss*. Such are Cockney darings before "the Gods, and columns" that abhor mediocrity. And is it to this dreary nonsense that is to be attached the name of poetry? Yet on these two passages the whole lauding of his fellow-Cockneys has been lavished. But *Percy Bysshe* feels his hopelessness of poetic reputation, and therefore lifts himself on the stilts of blasphemy. He is the only verseman of the day, who has dared, in a Christian country, to work out for himself the character of direct ATHEISM! In his present poem, he talks with impious folly of "the *curious* wrath of man or GOD!" Of a

> "Branded and ensanguined brow,
> Which was like *Cain's* or CHRIST'S."

Offences like these naturally come before a more effective tribunal than that of criticism. We have heard it mentioned as the only apology for the predominant irreligion and nonsense of this person's works, that his understanding is unsettled. But in his Preface, there is none of the exuberance of insanity; there is a great deal of folly, and a great deal of bitterness, but nothing of the wildness of his poetic fustian. The Bombastes Furioso of these stanzas cools into sneering in the preface; and his language against the *death-dealing* Quarterly Review, which has made such havoc in the Empire of Cockaigne, is merely malignant, mean, and peevishly personal. We give a few stanzas of this performance, taken as they occur.

> "O weep for Adonais! He is dead!
> Weep, **melancholy** mother, wake and weep;

> Yet *wherefore?* quench within their burning bed
> Thy *fiery* tears, and let thy *loud* heart keep
> Like his, a mute and uncomplaining sleep,
> For he is gone, where all things wise and fair
> *Descend!* Oh dream not that the *amorous* deep
> Will yet restore him to the vital air.
> Death *feeds* on his *mute voice*, and *laughs* at our despair."

The seasons and a whole host of personages, ideal and otherwise, come to lament over *Adonais*. They act in the following manner:—

> "Grief made the young Spring *wild*, and she threw down
> Her kindling buds, as if the Autumn were,
> Or they dead leaves, since her delight is flown,
> For whom should she have wak'd the sullen year?
> To Phœbus was not Hyacinth so dear,
> Nor to himself Narcissus, as to both,
> Thou, Adonais; wan they stand, and sere,
> Amid the drooping comrades of their youth,
> With dew all turn'd to tears, odour to sighing ruth."

Here is left, those whom it may concern, the pleasantest perplexity, whether the lament for Mr. J. Keats is shared between Phœbus and Narcissus, or Summer and Autumn. It is useless to quote those absurdities any farther *en masse*, but there are flowers of poesy thickly spread through the work, which we rescue for the sake of any future Essayist on the Bathos.

Absurdity.

> The green lizard, and the golden snake,
> Like *unimprison'd* flowers out of their trance awake. An hour—

> Say, with me
> Died Adonais, *till the Future dares*
> *Forget the Past*—his fate and fame shall be
> An *echo* and a *light* to all eternity.

> Whose *tapers yet* burn there the night of Time,
> For which *Suns perish'd!*

> Echo,—pined away
> Into a *shadow* of all *sounds!*

> That mouth whence it was wont to draw the breath
> Which gave it strength to pierce the guarded wit!

> *Comfortless!*
> As *silent* lightning leaves the starless night.
>
> ———
>
> Live thou whose *infamy* is not thy *fame!*
>
> Thou *noteless* blot on a remembered name!
>
> We in mad trance *strike with our spirit's* knife,
> *Invulnerable nothings!*
>
> ———
>
> Where lofty thought
> Lifts a young heart above its mortal lair,
> And love, and life, contend in it — for what
> Shall be its earthly doom — The dead live there,
> And move, like *winds of light,* on dark and stormy air.
>
> ———
>
> Who mourns for Adonais — oh! come forth,
> Fond wretch! and know thyself and him aright,
> *Clasp* with thy *panting* soul the *pendulous Earth!*
>
> ———
>
> Dart thy spirit's light
> Beyond all worlds, until its *spacious might
> Satiate* the *void circumference!*
>
> ———
>
> Then sink
> Even to a point within our day and night,
> And keep thy heart *light,* lest it make *thee sink,*
> When *hope has kindled hope,* and *lured thee to the* brink.
>
> ———
>
> A light is past from *the revolving year;*
> *And man and women,* and what still is dear
> Attracts to crush, repels to make thee wither.
>
> ———
>
> That benediction, which th' *eclipsing curse*
> Of birth can quench not, that sustaining love,
> Which, through *the web of being blindly wove,*
> By *man, and beast, and earth, and air, and sea!*
> Burns bright or dim, as each are mirrors of
> The *fire* for which all *thirst.*

Death makes, as becomes him, a great figure in this " Lament" — but in rather curious operations. He is alternately a person, a thing, nothing, &c.

> He is, " The coming bulk of Death,"
> Then " Death feeds on the *mute voice.*"
> A clear sprite
> Reigns over Death —

      Kingly Death
Keeps his pale court.
      Spreads apace
The *shadow* of *white* Death.
      The damp Death
Quench'd its caress—
      Death
Blush'd to annihilation!
      Her distress
Roused Death. Death rose and smiled—
He lives, he wakes, 'tis Death is *dead!*

As this wild waste of words is altogether beyond our comprehension, we will proceed to the more gratifying office of giving a whole, unbroken specimen of the Poet's powers, exercised on a subject rather more within their sphere. The following Poem has been sent to us as written by Percy Bysshe, and we think it contains all the essence of his odoriferous, colorific, and daisy-enamoured style. The motto is from "*Adonais.*"

ELEGY ON MY TOMCAT.

"And others came—Desires and Adorations,
Wing'd Persunsions, and veil'd Destinies,
Splendours, and blooms, and glimmering Incantations
Of hopes and fears, and twilight Phantasies;
And Sorrow, with her family of Sighs;
And Pleasure, *blind* with tears, led by the *gleam*
Of her own *dying smile instead of eyes!*"

ELEGY.

Weep for my Tomcat! all ye Tabbies weep,
 For he is gone at last! Not dead alone,
In flowery beauty sleepeth he no sleep;
 Like that bewitching youth Endymion!
My love is dead, alas, as any stone,
 That by some violet-sided smiling river
Weepeth too fondly! He is dead and gone,
 And fair Aurora, o'er her young believer,
With fingers gloved with roses, doth make moan,
 And every bud its petal green doth sever,
And Phœbus sets in night for ever, and for ever!
And others come! ye Splendours! and ye Beauties!
 Ye Raptures! with your robes of pearl and blue;
Ye blushing Wonders! with your scarlet shoe-ties;
 Ye Horrors bold! with breasts of lily hue;
Ye Hope's stern flatterers! He would trust to you,
 Whene'er he saw you with your chesnut hair,

> Dropping sad daffodils; and rosepinks true!
>   Ye Passions proud! with lips of bright despair;
>   Ye Sympathies! with eyes like evening star,
>   When on the glowing east she rolls her crimson car.
>
> Oh, bard-like spirit! beautiful and swift!
>   Sweet lover of pale night; when Luna's lamp
> Shakes sapphire dew-drops through a cloudy rift;
>   Purple as woman's mouth, o'er ocean damp;
> Thy quivering rose-tinged tongue — thy stealing tramp;
>   The dazzling glory of thy gold-tinged tail;
> Thy whisker-waving lips, as o'er the swamp
>   Rises the meteor, when the year doth fail,
> Like beauty in decay, all, all are flat and stale."

This poem strikes us as an evidence of the improvement that an appropriate subject makes in a writer's style. It is incomparably less nonsensical, verbose, and inflated, than Adonais; while it retains all its knowledge of nature, vigour of colouring, and felicity of language. Adonais has been published by the author in Italy, the fitting soil for the poem, sent over to his honoured correspondents throughout the realm of Cockaigne, with a delightful mysteriousness worthy of the dignity of the subject and the writer.

First Notes of an Incipient Ballad-Metre-Monger.*

DEAR CHRISTOPHER,

I AM true to my new profession as a poet, but for the life of me I cannot find out what line I am most fitted for. At one time I think I have an epic genius, and am half tempted to take up the "Caledoniad," which Jonathan Oldbuck recommended to Mr. Lovel, and offered to decorate with notes — indeed, I have gone so far as to send a letter or two to that eminent antiquary, directed to Monkbarns, *via* Fairport, but I know not how it is, he is slow in replying; can they have miscarried? perhaps he is not so much bent upon the work as he was formerly. In other moments I believe myself to be rather possessed of a talent for lyrics; and whether this shall be cultivated by the composition of gratis birth-day and new-year odes, since the Laureate cuts off the court with an exercise of hexameters, or whether I shall tune my throat to something bacchanalian, under the title of Devil's Punch-Bowl Melodies, is yet undetermined. For blank verse I find I have a decided partiality — and as our bards measure it out to us at present, (five feet more or less in a verse, and those not always free from symptoms of lameness) it is the very "writing made easy" of all the poetic schools now going; but it by no means forms a "reading made easy" to the purchasers of their light labours. I call their labours light, because it is owing to the compositor in many instances that the poems assume the semblance of being verse at all. Let him, however, take care that the lines begin with capitals, and the world is good-natured enough to believe there is rhythm in them, if it could be but discovered.

My present attempt, as a ballad-writer, arises from a disappointment I experienced from that arrant jiltflirt Maga. A lithographic print from a very clever sketch stopt the veering weather-cock of my imagination, and you see it now points due north. The drawing I allude to is by a lady, who is more capable than I am of doing poetical justice by her pen to the handicrafts of her pencil. However, it has fallen to me to illustrate

* From *Blackwood* for July, 1822. — M.

this amusing production of hers, and I have not introduced a single extraneous character—all are to be seen in the graphic "Packing up;" and the only liberty I take with the puppets is, like Punch and Judy's master, to squeak for them, and make-believe that the conversation is theirs. My ballad is but the vestibule of the ball-room which I have as yet painted. Perhaps success will induce me to attempt to portray the inner regions. But I shall wait and see how the public receives my first essay, and listen to hear a similar eulogy which Goldsmith gave Tickell, namely, that there was a vein of ballad-thinking throughout his works. Should I hear any such decision, I shall march forward with a bold step, and, perhaps, purchase a fiddle or bagpipe, till when,—I am yours,

BLAISE FITZTRAVESTY.

PACKING UP AFTER AN ENGLISH COUNTRY BALL.

The clock has struck the midnight hour, and the chandeliers burn low,
And the final couple are dancing down on somewhat wearied toe;
Each belle now takes her partner's arm, who squires her to her seat,
And chaperoning matrons talk right solemnly of heat.

The gallery is clearing of the drowsy fiddlers twain;
And he who blew the clarionet, with all his might and main,
And he who made the tambourine ring and vibrate with his thumb,
Have oped their eyes and stopp'd their yawns, for their release is come.

The Ball at the Red Lion is, at last, then at an end;
All agree it has been a pleasant night, as down the stairs they wend;
And we'll descend along with them to see the ladies muffle
Their finery in hoods and shawls, and in cloaks of serge and duffle.

But oh! alas! and well-a-day! 'tis raining cats and dogs,
And men and maids have brought umbrellas, pattens, boots, and clogs;
And lest white satin shoes be soil'd, they supply some pairs of stouter,
And lanterns, lest their mistresses should flounder in the gutter.

The ladies rather wish, 'tis true, that the gentlemen were gone,
And had left them to pack up their duds, at leisure and alone;
But Captain Cartridge has engaged, and so has Ensign Sabre,
To guard the three Miss Johnsons home, and their ancient maiden neighbour.

So they're lolling on the table, waiting the damsels' hest,—
Yet though these beaux so welcome are, it still must be confess'd,
That Miss Amelia would prefer, while tugging her boot lace,
That the Captain who's short-sighted, should not raise his quizzing glass,

Come, little merry Mrs. Cushion is first and foremost ready,
And stands in act to issue forth on her clicking pattens steady,
With gown drawn through her pocket-holes, secure from dirt suburban,
And with a safe-guard handkerchief, enveloping her turban.

But see what's going on behind, where Emma Parkes is dressing!
Sure young John Leigh's attentions are most marvellously pressing;
With what an air of tenderness, he enshawls each ivory shoulder—
An offer sure will come of this, ere he is twelvemonths older!

At least so think the tabbies—and I see, Miss Prudence Herring,
(Who, with sister Grace, is cloak'd to the chin, so at leisure to be peering,)
Has had enough side-glances at this love-scene to instruct her
How to frame on it by inference, a gossip's superstructure.

But their tall prim niece is packing too, Miss Patience Prettyjohn,
Demurely settling her calash those towering plumes upon:
(Calashes are good things enough, when the weather's wet and muggy,
But they make a woman's head look like the head of an old buggy.)

"Well, sister Grace," says Prue, "thank Heaven! our niece takes after us;
You never find the men round her, making that odious fuss,
Whispering such stuff! No, she can tie her cloak without assistance,
For I've always told her—Patience dear! keep fellows at a distance.

"Uphold your dignity, my love! The boldest men, you see,—
The most presuming,—never take such liberties with me;
Once when a suitor knelt to me, imagine, if you can,
The air with which I waved my hand, and said, Begone, base Man!

' That was a moment—oh, my dear! I felt exalted so
In conscious virtue—Sister Grace! I've always preach'd, you know,
Thus to our niece, and she, good girl, is an attentive hearer;
Patience *does* keep the men in awe—observe, not one comes near her."

But hark! a strife—some silver pipes are pitch'd above the key,
Which maiden's meekness best befits, and lady's courtesy;
"'Tis mine," resounds in tones so shrill, we cannot call them polish'd,
And a bonnet seems to run the risk of being there demolish'd.

For Julia Graves has seized it, and hers it is, she swears,
And Mary Russell, chiding her, protests that is hers,
And o'er Miss Julia's shoulder she darts her hand to snatch it,
Who at arm's length holds the fragile prey, baffling her foe to catch it.

"Miss Russell, you have spoilt my sleeve, what can be your design?"
' I only mean to get, Miss Graves, what you have seiz'd of mine.'
"Yours, Ma'am?"—' Yes, Ma'am,—this very day I pinn'd that ribbon on it—
A very likely thing indeed I should not know my bonnet!'

"Pray, Ma'am, don't push so." ' Ma'am, you've pok'd your elbow in my eye.'
"That's your fault, Ma'am—I shan't let go." ' No, Ma'am, no more shall I—'

One should be more particular what company one's in,
For really, some folks now-a-days think stealing not a sin;
Things have walk'd off in the strangest way from routs and balls of late'—
"You'd best take care, Ma'am, what you say — My Pa's a magistrate."
'Well, Ma'am, and what's your Pa to me?'—Then comes a desperate tustle,
But the powers that guard meek innocence, keep watch for gentle Russell.

For up comes Betty Chambermaid — "Here, ladies! arn't this he?"
"What, that squabb'd thing? that's none of mine." 'That don't belong to me?'
Cry both at once — but — lights are brought — a second glance upon it,
And poor Miss Julia's spirits fall — 'tis sure enough *her* bonnet.

Miss Russell triumphs loudly, nor spares recrimination;
Her antagonist is cow'd beneath the deep humiliation,
And she whining says, "I'm sure I thought"—'Yes, Ma'am, I understand,
Having lost your own, you *thought* you'd take the best that came to hand.

Captain Cartridge has been enjoying this, and to the Ensign sware he
That if it came to fisticuffs, he'd bet on tart Miss Mary;
What a wreck of flowers and gauze had been the fruits of such contention!
But the fates were kind and stopt the fray by Betty's intervention.

While all this hubbub fills the room, Mrs. Moss heeds not the clash,
But shawl'd, fur-tippeted, and glov'd, and with head in huge calash,
She wants but one protection more to save her silks and satins,
And her little footboy's on his knees to mount her on her pattens.

Mind, Tommy, mind, 'tis a tender job — press gently, 'twill not suit
To handle with a clumsy paw an ancient lady's foot.
Oh! the matron twists, for the awkward chit has hit upon a corn,
Which has laugh'd her nostrum, ivy leaves and vinegar, to scorn.

A start is made — umbrellas flap and rustle as they spread,
And, the threshold past, the pattering rain beats on them overhead;
The bespattered beaux have hard ado to wield these bucklers light,
For while they guard the ladies left, the gusts assail their right.

The noise of pattens waxeth faint, as homeward-bound they travel,
Now clattering on the pavement-stones, now grinding in the gravel;
This dies — though ever and anon, the listening ear is roused,
By some front-door's slam betokening a party snugly housed.

The lanterns, which so brightly stream'd, have vanish'd one by one,
As a lane was turn'd, or a rat-tat-tat announced the journey done;
And a few were on a sudden quench'd by puffs of winds uproarious,
Envious of those "earth-treading stars" which made dark night so glorious.

But who encounter'd these mishaps — and who caught cold and fever —
And who drest well — and who drest badly spite of best endeavour —
And what new lights in love or hate, from the meeting we must borrow,
We shall learn at length when we call upon our partners fair to-morrow.

The Wine-Bibber's Glory—A New Song.*

Tune— The Jolly Miller.

> Quo me, Bacche, rapis tui
> Plenum?————
>   Dulce periculum est
> O Lenæe! sequi Deum
> Cingentem viridi tempora pampino.— Hor.

1.

If Horatius Flaccus made jolly old Bacchus
  So often his favourite theme;
If in him it was classic to praise his old Massic,
  And Falernian to gulp in a stream;
If Falstaff's vagaries, 'bout Sack and Canaries,
  Have pleased us again and again;
Shall we not make merry on Port, Claret, Sherry,
  Madeira, and sparkling Champagne?

2.

First Port, that potation, preferr'd by our nation
  To all the small drink of the French;
'Tis the best standing liquor, for layman or vicar,
  The army, the navy, the bench;
'Tis strong and substantial, believe me, no man shall
  Good Port from my dining-room send;
In your soup — after cheese — every way — it will please,
  But most tête-a-tête with a friend.

3.

Fair Sherry, Port's sister, for years they dismiss'd her,
  To the kitchen to flavour the jellies —
There long she was banish'd, and well-nigh had vanish'd
  To comfort the kitchen-maids' bellies —
Till his Majesty fixt, he thought Sherry when sixty
  Years old, like himself, quite the thing—
So I think it but proper, to fill a tip-topper
  Of Sherry to drink to the King.

4.

Though your delicate Claret by no means goes far, it
  Is famed for its exquisite flavour;
'Tis a nice provocation, to *wise* conversation,
  Queer blarney, or harmless palaver;

* From *Blackwood* for January, 1822.— M.

'Tis the bond of society — no inebriety
    Follows a swig of the Blue;
One may drink a whole ocean, nor e'er feel commotion,
    Or headache from Chateau Margoux.

5.

But though Claret is pleasant, to taste for the present,
    On the stomach it sometimes feel cold;
So to keep it all clever, and comfort your liver,
    Take a glass of Madeira that's old:
When 't has sail'd to the Indies, a cure for all wind 'tis,
    And colic 'twill put to the rout;
All doctors declare, a good glass of Madeira,
    The best of all things for the gout.

6.

Then Champagne! dear Champagne! ah! how gladly I drain a
    Whole bottle of Oeil de Perdrix;
To the eye of my charmer, to make my love warmer,
    If cool that love ever could be,
I could toast her for ever — But never, oh! never,
    Would I her dear name so profane;
So if e'er when I'm tipsy, it slips to my lips, I
    Wash it back to my heart with Champagne!

Translation of the Wine-Bibber's Glory.*

By Philips Potts, Esq., Holyhead.

****, but your Latin is not quite classical — somewhat raffish, my very good friend?

Transeat — it is good enough for an ungrateful world.

Then what a word " Portum" is! and " Claretum," still more abominable. Why, sir, it is worse and worse, as Lord Norbury said, when a witness confessed his name to be Shaughnessy O'Shaughnessy.

And how the devil was I to get better words? Was I to put in *Vinum Lusitanicum*, or *Burdigalense*, to the utter confusion of my line? As Ainsworth bids me, I have clapped in

* From *Blackwood* for February, 1822.— M.

TRANSLATION OF THE WINE-BIBBER'S GLORY.

Vinum Hispanicum for Sack, against my better judgment; but my complaisance was not to extend any farther. Hear, most asinine critic — hear, I say, what Horatius Flaccus himself sings, as interpreted to us by the melodious Phil. Francis, D.D.

> Shall I
> Be envied, if my little fund supply
> Its frugal wealth of words — since bards, who sung
> In ancient days, enrich'd their native tongue
> With large increase, &c.

Or, as I may say, paraphrasing what he writes a little before —

> If jolly Virgil coin'd a word, why not
> Extend the self-same privilege to Pot.

And here you may remark, that Pot is put for Potts, to assist the rhyme.

Hum! But your verses totter a little every now and then — so much the more in character for a drinking song; and you alter the tune — that of the original is the Jolly Miller. I have put one as harmonious — a most excellent tune — a most bass tune — and as thou singest basely, basely shalt thou sing it after dinner. Are all your objections answered?

I may as well say that they are; but——

But me no buts! — Shut thine ugly countenance, and listen to my song.

Potoris Gloria.

A LATIN MELODY.

To a Tune for itself, lately discovered in Herculaneum; being an Ancient Roman Air, — or, if not, quite as good.

Cum jollificatione boisterosa: *i. e.* with boisterous jollification.

Si Ho - ra - ti - o Flac - co de hi - la - ri Bac - cho mos
If Ho - ra - ti - us Flac - cus made jol - ly old Bacchus so

car - mi - na es - set can - ta - re, Si Mas - si - ca vi - na vo -
of - ten his fa - vourite theme, If in him it was clas - sic to

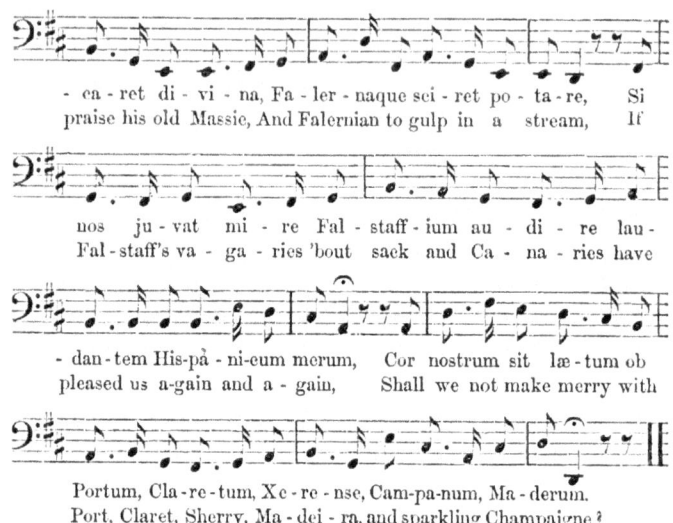

- ca - ret di - vi - na, Fa - ler - naque sci - ret po - ta - re, Si
praise his old Massic, And Falernian to gulp in a stream, If

nos ju - vat mi - re Fal - staff - ium au - di - re lau -
Fal - staff's va - ga - ries 'bout sack and Ca - na - ries have

- dan - tem His-pà - ni-cum merum, Cor nostrum sit læ - tum ob
pleased us a-gain and a - gain, Shall we not make merry with

Portum, Cla - re - tum, Xe - re - nse, Cam-pa-num, Ma - derum.
Port, Claret, Sherry, Ma - dei - ra, and sparkling Champaigne?

1.

Si Horatio Flacco de hilari Baccho
   Mos carmina esset cantare,
Si Massica vina vocaret divina,
   Falernaque sciret potare ;
Si nos juvat mirè Falstaffium audire
   Laudantem Hispanicum merum,
Cor nostrum sit lætum ob Portum, Claretum
   Xerense, Campanum, Maderum.

2.

Est Portum potatio quam Anglica natio
   *Vinis Galliæ prætulit lautis ; —
Sacerdote amatur — a laicis potatur,
   Consultis, militibus, nautis.
Si meum conclave hoc forte et suave
   Vitaverit, essem iniquus,
Post caseum — in jure — placebit securè —
   Præsertim cum adsit amicus.

3.

Huic quamvis cognatum, Xerense damnatum
   Gelata culinâ tingebat,

---

   * Vinis — lautis, Ang. *neat* Wines.

Vinum exul ibique diu coquo cuique
  Generosum liquorem praebebat.
Sed a rege putatum est valdè pergratum,
  Cùm (ut ipse) sit sexagenarium —
Largè ergo implendum, regique bibendum,
  Opinor est nunc necessarium.

4.

Claretum oh! quamvis haud forte (*deest nam vis
  Divino sapore notatur;
Hinc dulcia dicuntur — faceta nascuntur —
  Leniterque philosophizatur.
Socialis potatio! te haud fugit ratio
  Purpureo decoram colore!
Tui maximum mare liceret potare,
  Sine mentis frontisve dolore.

5.

Etsi verò in præsenti Claretum bibenti
  Videatur imprimis jucundum,
Citò tamen frigescat — quod ut statim decrescat,
  Vetus vinum Maderum adeundum.
Indos si navigârit, vento corpus levârit,
  Colicamque fugârit hoc merum.
Podâgrâ cruciato "Vinum optimum dato"
  Clamant medici docti "Maderum."

6.

Campanum! campanum! quo gaudio lagenam
  Ocelli perdricis sorberem!
Ad dominæ oculum exhauriam poculum
  Tali philtro si unquam egerem —
Propinarem divinam — sed peream si sinam
  Nomen carum ut sic profanetur,
Et si cum Bacchus urget, ad labia surgit —
  Campano ad cor revolvetur.

Explicit P. P. Id Feb. MDCCCXXI.

*** Our Gosport friend's Greek translation of the same song, beginning —

Ει Ορατιου Φλακκου περι θειου ιακχου
  πολλαι αγαθαι ωδαι μενωσιν.

is not good. We perceive, that like Platonist Taylor, he puts no accents to his Greek — we fear for the same reason.—C. N.

* Deest, one syllable. Vide Carey, p. 171.

A Running Commentary on the Ritter Bann.*

There is, we must say, a dirty spirit of rivalry afloat at present among the various periodicals, from which ours only, and Mr. Nichols', the two Gentleman's Magazines, are exempt. You never see the Quarterly praising the lucubrations of the Edinburgh — far less the Edinburgh extolling those of the Quarterly. Old Monthly and New Monthly are in cat-and-dog opposition. Sir Richard† exclaims that they have robbed him of his good name — while Tom Campbell is ready to go before his Lordship of Waithman to swear that that was an impossibility. There is, besides, a pair of Europeans boxing it out with most considerable pluck; and we are proud to perceive our good friend Letts of Cornhill bearing himself boldly in the fight. The Fancy Gazette disparages the labours of the illustrious Egan — and Pierce is equally savage on the elegancies of Jon Bee.‡ A swarm of twopennies gallops over the land ready to eat one another, so as, like the Irishman's rats in a cage, to leave only a single tail behind. We, out of this turmoil and scuffle, as if from a higher region, look down, calm and cool. Unprejudiced by influence, and uninfluenced by prejudice, we keep along the even tenor of our way. We dispute not, neither do we quarrel. If the golden wheels of our easy-going chariot, in its course, smooth sliding without stop, crush to atoms any person who is unlucky enough to come under their precious weight, it is no fault of ours. Let him blame destiny, and bring his action against the Parcæ.

So far are we from feeling any thing like hostility, spite, envy, hatred, malice, or uncharitableness, that we rejoice at the rare exhibition of talent whenever it occurs in a publication similar to ours. We do our utmost to support the cause of periodical literature in general. But for our disinterested exertions, the Ed-

---

* Among the very worst poems written by Thomas Campbell was a sort of ballad called "The Ritter Bann." It was too tempting to escape the notice of Maginn, who wrote this severe word-criticism on it, in *Blackwood* for April, 1824. — M.

† Sir Richard Phillips, publisher and editor of the *Monthly Magazine*. — M.

‡ Jon Bee, author of a Slang Dictionary, edited a sporting paper, in opposition to Pierce Egan's *Life in London*. — M.

inburgh Review would have been long since unheard of. For many years we perpetuated the existence of the old Scots Magazine, by mentioning it in our columns. Finding it, however, useless to persevere, we held our peace concerning it; it died, and a word from us again restored it to life and spirit, so that Jeffrey steals from it all his Spanish literature. We took notice of the Examiner long after every other decent person said a word about it. Our exertions on behalf of the Scotsman were so great, that the learned writers of that paper pray for us on their bended knees. But it would be quite useless, or rather impossible, for us to go over all our acts of kindness. We have, indeed, reaped the benefit, for never since the creation of the world was any Magazine so adored by every body as ours is. It is, indeed, carried at times to an absurd, nay, we must add, a blameable length, for we must exclaim with the old poet:—

"If to adore an idol is idolatry,
Sure to adore a book is bibliolatry."

An impiety to be avoided.

In pursuance of our generous system, we here beg leave to call the attention of our readers to a poem in the last New Monthly Magazine, written by the eminent editor of that celebrated periodical, and advertised, before its appearance, with the most liberal prodigality of puffing, in all the papers. Mr. Campbell is advantageously known to the readers of poetry, a very respectable body of young gentlemen and ladies, as the author of the Pleasures of Hope, Gertrude of Wyoming, Lochiel's Warning, O'Connor's Child, and other pleasant performances, which may be purchased at the encouraging price of three and sixpence sterling, at the stalls of the bibliopolists of High Holborn. But the poem which he has lately contributed to the pages of the New Monthly, outshines these compositions of his more crude and juvenile days.

———"Velut inter ignes
Luna minores."———

It is entitled the Ritter Bann, and we do not know how we can bestow a more acceptable compliment on our readers, than by analysing this elegant effusion.

What the words Ritter Bann mean, is not at once open to every capacity, and they have unfortunately given rise to the most indefensible puns and quizzes in the world. But we, who despise such things, by a due consultation of dictionaries, lexicons, onomasticons, word-books, vocabularies, and other similar treatises, discovered that Ritter, in the Teutonic tongue, as spoken in High Germany, signifies Rider, or Knight—Bann is merely a man's name, the hero being son of old —— Bann, Esq., of —— place, Glamorganshire. Why a Welsh knight should be called by a German title, we cannot immediately conjecture; but suppose it adopted from euphonious principles of melting melody. Let the reader say the words—Ritter Bann—Ritter Bann—Ritter Bann—to himself, with the assistance of a chime of good bells, such as those of Saint Pancras, Saint Mary Overy, Saint Sepulchre's, opposite Newgate, Saint Botolph's, Aldgate, Saint Clement Dane's, Saint Dunstan's, in Fleet Street, not to mention various provincial utterers of Bob Majors; and he must be struck with the fine rumbling clang, and sit down to drink his Burton at 3d. the nip, with increased satisfaction.

So far for the title. Listen now to the exordium.

> "The Ritter Bann from Hungary
> Came back, renown'd in arms,
> But scorning jousts of chivalry,
> And love and ladies' charms.
> While other knights held revelry, he
> Was wrapt"—

in what? Surtout? Roquelaure? Poodle Benjamin? bang-up? doblado? frock? wraprascal? No, no! What then? Sheet? blanket? quilt? coverlet? counterpane? No? What then? Why

> —"in thoughts of gloom,
> And in Vienna's hostelrie
> Slow paced his lonely room."

This is a very novel and original character in our now-a-days poetry.

> "There entered one whose face he knew,
> Whose voice, *he was aware*,
> He oft at mass had listen'd to,
> In the holy house of prayer."

Who is this fine fellow? Wait a moment and you will be told.

"'Twas the Abbot of Saint James's monks,
A *fresh* and fair old man."

Fresh no doubt, for you will soon learn he comes in good season.

"His reverend air arrested even
The gloomy Ritter Bann;
But seeing with him an ancient dame,
Come clad in Scotch attire,
The Ritter's colour went and came,
And loud he spoke in ire:
'Ha! nurse of her that was my *bane*—'"

Here Campbell's Scoticism has got the better of him. The lady of whom the Ritter speaks is his wife, who, in Caledonia's dialect, is said to be *bane* of a man's *bane;* but in English we always say *bone* of my *bone*. We hope Thomas the Rhymer will anglicise the phrase in the next edition.

"Name not her name to me,
I wish it blotted from my brain:
Art poor? take alms and flee!'"

A very neat and pretty turn-out as any old lady would wish of a summer's morning; but it won't do. For

"'Sir Knight,' the Abbot interposed,
'This case your ear demands!'
And the *crone cried*, with a *cross enclosed*
In both her trembling hands—"

Read that second last line again. "The Crone Cried with a Cross enClosed!" Oh! Pack: send the Razor Grinder. What do you say to that? We can only match it by one passage of Pantagruel. Lesquelles [the frozen words] ensemblement fondues, ouysmes hin, hin, hin, hin, his, ticque, torche, longue, bredelin, bredelac, frr, frrr, frrrr, bou, bou, bou, bou, bou, bou, bou, trace, trr, trr, trr, trrr, trrrr, trrrrr, on, on, on, on, ouououounon, goth, magoth. "And the Crone cried with a cross enclosed,"

"Remember each his sentence waits,
And he who would *rebut*!!
Sweet Mercy's suit, on him the gates
Of mercy shall be shut!"

The Abbot proceeds to give our friend Ritter some novel information.

> "You wedded, undispensed by church,
> Your cousin Jane in spring;"

Pretty colloquial style!

> "In autumn, when you went to search
> For churchmen's pardoning,
> Her house denounced your marriage-band,
> Betrothed her to De Grey;
> And the ring you put upon her—"

Her what? Finger, perhaps. No—

> ——"her hand
> Was wrench'd by force away."

Here commences a pleasant familiar prose narration. We like this manner of mixing prose with verse, as Mr. Stewart Rose has done in his translation of Boiardo. Campbell, in imitation, proceeds. "Then wept you, Jane, upon my neck, crying, 'Help me, Nurse, to flee to my Howell Bann's Glamorgan hills:'

> "But word arrived, ah me! you were not there;
> And 'twas their threat, by foul means or by fair,
> To-morrow morning was to set the seal on her despair."

"I had a son," says Nurse, after this little triplet, "a sea-boy, in a ship at Hartland bay: by his aid, from her cruel kin I bore my bird away. To Scotland, from the Devon's green myrtle shores, we fled; and the hand that sent the ravens to Elijah, gave us bread. She wrote you by my son; but he, from England, sent us word you had gone into some far country; in grief and gloom, he heard. For they that wronged you, to elude your wrath, defamed my child."—Whom she means here is not quite evident at first sight, for she had been just speaking of her son, for whom the Ritter, we opine, did not care a button, whether he was famed or defamed; but it will be all clear by and by.— "And you—ay, blush, sir, as you should,—believed and were beguiled." In which last sentence the old lady is waxing a little termagantish on our hands. She proceeds, however, in a minor key.

"To die but at your feet, she vowed to roam the world; and we would both have sped, and begged our bread; but so it might not be; for, when the snow-storm beat our roof, she bore a boy," —a queer effort of a snow-storm, *entre nous*—"Sir Bann, who

grew as fair your *likeness-proof* as child e'er grew like man." A
likeness-proof! Some engraver must have been talking to Tom
about proof-impressions of plates, and he, in the simplicity of his
bachelorship, must have imagined that there were proof-impressions too of children. Let us, however, permit Madame la Nou-
rice to proceed.—" 'Twas smiling on that babe one morn, while
heath bloomed on the moor, her beauty struck young Lord Kinghorn, as he hunted past our door. *She* shunned him; but *he*
raved of Jane, and roused *his* mother's pride; who came to us
in high disdain, and ' Where's the face,' she cried, ' has witched
my boy to wish for one so wretched for his wife ? Dost love thy
husband ? Know my son has sworn to seek his life.' "

Poetry breaks out here again in the following melodious
lines:
" Her anger sore dismayed us,
For our mite was wearing scant;
And, unless that dame would aid us,
There was none to *aid* our want.

" So I told her, weeping bitterly, what all our woes *had* been;
and, though she was a stern lady, the tear stood in her een.
And she housed us both, when cheerfully my child [that is not
her son, the cabin-boy, but her bird Jane,] to her had sworn,
that, even if made a widow, she would never wed Kinghorn.

" Here paused the Nurse;" and, indeed, we must say, a more
pathetic, or original story, or one more prettily or pithily told,
does not exist in the whole bounds of our language. The Nurse
mistook her talent when she commenced the trade of suckling
weans. She should have gone to the bar, where, in less than no
time, she would have been a pleader scarcely inferior to Counsellor Phillips himself.

After the oration of the Nurse, then began the Abbot, standing by—" Three months ago, a wounded man to our abbey
came to die."—A mighty absurd proceeding, in our opinion.
Had he come there to *live*, it would have been much more sensible.—" He heard me long with ghastly eyes," (rather an odd
mode of hearing,) " and hand obdurate clenched, speak of the
worm that never dies, and the fire that is not quench'd.

" At last, by what this scroll attests,
He left atonement brief,

> For years of anguish, to the breasts
> His guilt had wrung with grief.
> There lived,' he said, 'a fair young dame
> Beneath my *mother's* roof—
> I loved *her*' "—

Not his mother we hope.—

> ———" 'but against my flame
> Her purity was proof.
> I feign'd repentance—friendship pure;
> That mood she did not check,
> But let her husband's miniature
> Be copied from her neck.' "

Her husband's miniature in the days of jousts and chivalries! But great poets do not matter such trifles. We all remember how Shakspere introduces cannon into Hamlet. *Pergit Poeta.*

"As means to search him, my deceit took care to him was borne nought but his picture's counterfeit, and Jane's reported scorn. The treachery took: she waited *wild!* My slave came back, and did whate'er I wish'd: She clasped her child, and swoon'd; and all but died."

The pathos and poetry of this beautiful grammatical, and intelligible passage, is too much for us. We cannot go on without assistance. We shall, therefore, make a glass of rum grog, for we are writing this on a fine sunshiny morning. As we are on the subject of grog, we may as well give it as our opinion, that the young midshipman's method of making it, as recorded by the great Joseph, is by far the most commodious. Swallow we, therefore, first a glass of rum—our own drinking in Antigua—and then, baptizing it speedily by the affusion of a similar quantity of water, we take three jumps to mix the fluids in our stomach, and, so fortified, proceed with the contemplation of the Ritter Bann. We get on to a new jig tune—

> "I felt her tears
> For years and years,
> Quench not my flame, but STIR!"

> "The very hate
> I bore her mate,
> Increased my love for her.

"Fame told us of his glory: while joy flush'd the face of

Jane; and while she blessed his name, her smile struck fire into my brain, no fears could damp. I reached the camp, sought out its champion; and, if my broadsword (Andrew Ferrara would be a much more poetical word, Mr. Thomas) failed at last, 'twas long and well laid on. This wound's my meed—My name is Kinghorn—My foe is the Ritter Bann.

> "The water to his lips was borne,
> And we shrived the dying man.

He died not till you went to fight the Turks at Warradein; but I see my tale has changed, you pale.—The Abbot went for wine, and brought a little page, who poured it out and smiled."

How beautiful! and how natural at the same time!—" I see," says the old Abbot, who, we warrant, was a sound old toper, a fellow who rejoiced in the delightful music of the cork, "the curst stuff I have been talking to you has made you sick in your stomach, and you must take a glass of wine. What wine do you drink, Hock, Champagne, Sauterne, Dry Lisbon, Madeira, Black Strap, *Lachryma Christi?*—my own tipple is Rhenish. See here, I have some *Anno Domini*, God knows what. Pleasure of drinking your good health in the meantime."

"The stunn'd knight saw himself restored to childhood in his child, and stooped and caught him to his breast—laugh'd loud, and wept anon; and, with a shower of kisses, pressed the darling little one."

The conversation soon becomes sprightly. Nothing can be better than the colloquial tone of the dialogue.

"*Ritter Bann.* And where went Jane?

"*Old Snoozer.* To a nunnery, sir,—Look not again so pale:
—Kinghorn's old dame grew harsh to her.

"*Ritter Bann.* And has she taken the veil?

"*Old Snoozer.* Sit down, sir, I *bar* rash words.

"They sat all three, and the boy played with the Knight's broad star, as he kept him on his knee. 'Think ere you ask her dwelling-place,' the Abbot father said; 'time draws a veil o'er beauty's face, more deep than cloister'd shade: Grief may have made her what you can scarce love, perhaps, for life.'— 'Hush, Abbot,' cried the Ritter Bann, (on whom, by this time, the tipple had taken considerable effect,) 'or tell me where's my wife.'

What follows? Why

> "The priest UNDID! — (*Oh, Jupiter!*)
> Two doors that hid
> The inn's adjacent room;
> And there a lovely woman stood,
> Tears bathed her beauty's bloom.
> One moment may
> With bliss repay
> Unnumbered hours of pain;
> Such was the throb,
> And mutual sob,
> Of the Knight embracing Jane."

And such is Mr. Tom Campbell's poem of the Ritter Bann!!!

Need we add a word? Did any body ever see the like? What verse, what ideas, what language, what a story, what a name! Time was, that, when the brains were out, the man would die; but *on a change tout cela.* We consign Campbell's head to the notice of the Phrenologicals.

Let us sing a song. Strike up the bagpipes while we chaunt

The Writer Tam.

By T. Dromedary.

> The Writer Tam, from Hungryland,*
> Comes, famed for lays of arms,†
> And, writing chaunts of chivalry,
> The Cockney ladies charms.
> While other hands write Balaam, he,
> In editorial gloom,
> In Colburn's magazinary,
> Gives each his destined room.

---

* See Jack Wilke's Prophecy of Famine. A poem, as Tom himself observes, amusing to a Scotchman from its extravagance. To oblige him, therefore, the name is adopted here. — M. OD.

† The Mariners of England — the British Grenadiers — The Battle of the Baltic, &c. — M. OD.

Critique on Lord Byron.*

"Claudite jam rivos, pueri, sat prata biberunt."—VIRG.

So the Public at length is beginning to tire on
The torrent of poesy pour'd by Lord Byron !
Some guess'd this would happen : — the presage proved true.
Then now let us take a brief, rapid review
Of all, or at least of each principal topic,
Which serves as a theme for his muse misanthropic.
  First, note we the prelude, which sung by the Minor,
Gave promise of future strains, bolder and finer ;
Though the bitter Scotch critic loud raised his alarum,
And swore men and gods could not possibly bear 'em !†
To the fame of the bard *men* have given a shove —
Whate'er may be judged of his merits *above*.
Thus stung, did the youngster assail, we must own,
Some names which his fury had well let alone ;
As a colt, who a thistle beneath his tail feels,
At all things around madly launches his heels.
Yet blithely, though sharply, the young minstrel caroll'd,
To Reviewers and Bards, ere he croak'd with Childe Harold,
That wight, who, in endless Spenserian measure,
Roams through the wide world without object or pleasure ;
Till at last, we find out, with the pilgrim proceeding,
That we gain no great object nor pleasure in reading !
But, first, with what glee did all palates devour
The fragments, which bear the strange name of the Gaiour !
'Tis a tale full of pathos, and sweet is the verse : —
Would some pains in connecting have render'd it worse ?

---

* From *Blackwood* for April, 1822. — M.

† The Edinburgh reviewer, who vainly attempted to crush Lord Byron at the commencement of his poetical career, thus began his animadversions : " The poetry of this young Lord belongs to the class which neither men nor gods are said to permit. His effusions are spread over a dead flat, and can no more get above or below the level, than if they were so much stagnant water." Having made this estimate of the noble poet's powers, which, however justified by some of the Minor's Hours of Idleness, must preclude the Northern Seer from all pretension to the gift of second sight, he adds the following wholesome advice :—
  " Whatever success may have attended the peer's subsequent compositions, it might have been followed without any serious detriment to the public. We counsel him that he do forthwith abandon poetry, and turn his talents and opportunities to better account."— M. OD.

Then next was our caterer pleased to provide us
With an exquisite treat in the Bride of Abydos; —
Zuleika, so lovely — so simple — so tender —
Yet firm, — from her purpose no danger could bend her.
Sour critics may say, all this praise duly granting,
There seems in the plan probability wanting.
By what happy means could these lovers contrive,
With Giaffer's suspicions so warmly alive,
Of the Harem's strict bondage to lengthen the tether,
And so pleasantly take their amusements together?
Of Eastern seráis, though not versed in the fashions,
We've heard, in those climates, where boil all the passions,
No youth could approach, howe'er prudent they thought her,
The sacred retreat of his own father's daughter.—
Such objections are dull; — 'tis a pity to show 'em,
If adherance to fact would have spoil'd a good poem.

Now swift in his bark sails stout Conrad, the Corsair,
To surprise Seyd Pashà, with his three tails of horse-hair.
But the destinies order — unlucky mishap!
That Conrad, not Seyd, should be caught in the trap.
Those minds must be steel'd with an apathy rare,
Which mourn not Medora, nor sigh for Gulnare.
Medora, soft Queen of the Island of Thieves,
Whose heart, too susceptible, bursts as it grieves!
The woes of Gulnare, too — we feelingly share 'em —
The pride, though the cold passive slave of Seyd's harem: —
But touch'd by the robber, she mounts to the class
Of dames whose whole soul is inflammable gas.
Though caught was the Corsair, the fates had decreed
That this foe, though in chains, should be fatal to Seyd.
Ah! sensitive reader, 'tis hard to persuade ye,
That man could be cool to so kind a fair lady —
When we knew her warm heart, of his terrible fate full,
Risk'd all for his safety — 'twas somewhat ungrateful!
And since such great hazard she ran for his sake,
Could his fancy prefer writhing spik'd on a stake,
To giving — (but Poets are full of their fibs)
The savage Pasha a deep thrust in the ribs!
Such delicate scruples we prize at a high rate —
They seem rather squeamish, perhaps, in a pirate!

Quick vanishes Conrad: — bold rover, adieu!
But who is this Lara, that starts into view?
If Conrad thou art, as some people suppose,
Gloomy chief, thou'rt less qualmish with friends, and with foes!
If strong were the "stuff o' thy conscience," oh say
How was Ezzelin so snugly put out of the way?

We see, too, the spirit and warmth of Gulnare in
That feminine page, so attach'd and so daring;
And we shrewdly suspect that the small crimson spot
On her amazon forehead is nearly forgot.
'Tis true, when the Corsair old Seyd's palace saw burn,
The Queen of his harem had ringlets of auburn;—
That the page's are black contradicts not our guesses—
Since ladies sometimes change the hue of their tresses.*
  Then tack'd to this story, strange mixtures, are seen,
Those dullest of stanzas 'yclep'd Jacqueline.
Alas! for poor Rogers—'twas certainly hard
To be made, as a compliment, foil to a bard
Who needs no such foil—so unapt too to flatter!
'Twere better have borne the worst lash of his satire!
Yet of high-season'd praise he is sometimes the organ,
This Shelley can witness, and eke Lady Morgan.
Shall Rogers's name be inscribed in this set
Whose former bright laurels none wish to forget?
But Jacqueline sues for the garland in vain,
For Memory here brings us nothing but pain.
Can the laud be much relish'd by Gifford and Crabbe,
Which is shared by the crazy-brain'd muse of Queen Mab?
Would Dryden or Otway, or Congreve, or Pope,
Sweet Burns, or the Bard who delights us with Hope,
Be flatter'd to find they were join'd in this *melée*,
And placed cheek by jole with dame Morgan and Shelley?†

---

* The Poet in describing the faithful attendant on Count Lara, did not perhaps exactly recollect his former account of Gulnare's person—

  That form of eye so dark, and cheek so fair,
  And *auburn* waves of gemm'd and braided hair."

Dealers in fiction, both in verse and prose, require good memories. Whether this solution, or the suggestion in the text, best meets the difficulty, the sagacious reader will determine according to his fancy.—ED.

† The noble Baron, in his appendix to the Two Foscari, is pleased to call Lady Morgan's Italy "a fearless and excellent work." The world in general will be more ready to subscribe to the first than the last half of the panegyric. In the same place he tells us that he "highly admires Mr. Shelley's poetry, in common with all those who are not blinded by baseness and bigotry." It might be wrong to advise readers to have recourse to Mr. Shelley's works and judge for themselves. Those who desire to see specimens, and to compare Lord B.'s opinion with that of other critics, will do well to consult the Quarterly Review, in which work may also be seen some useful remarks on the fearless Lady Morgan's literary labours.

  A few of the poets of former and the present times are here noticed as hav-

Next scowls the fell wizard, hight Manfred the bold,
Who broods over sins which wont bear to be told.
'Tis a drama repulsive, but still it has force.—
How well does he paint the sharp pangs of remorse!
That quill which seems pluck'd from the wing of a raven,
Gives a touch almost worthy the poet of Avon.
 Are the pictures from fancy?—fictitious or real?
Surely Satan himself is the bard's *beau ideal!**
Yet 'tis strange that each image that glides through his lanthorn
From Juan, whose joy is on husbands to plant horn,
Who views with delight tears of damsels deluded,—†
To the wretch who hates all things, himself too included,—
All in some striking feature each other resemble,
As in Hamlet, or Rolla, we still saw John Kemble.
If the draughts smack of nature, we care not a straw
Where he finds the dark model he chooses to draw.
Of smaller effusions I pass over loads—
The Family Sketch—Hebrew Melodies—Odes;—
Sad Tasso's Lament—soft occasional Verses—
And levell'd at Elgin stern Pallas's curses;‡
Mazeppa's long race, that intrepid rough-rider,—
And adieus to a Lady, whose Lord can't abide her.
Within two blue paste-boards what contraries meet—
The fragrant, the fetid, the bitter, the sweet:—

---

ing the good fortune to receive honourable mention from Lord B.; a glory they enjoy in common with the Hibernian Lady-errant, and the poetico-metaphysical maniac. David long ago designated the atheist as a fool; it is more charitable to consider him as a madman.—M OD.

* Mr. Southey has conferred the appellation of "the Satanic School" on a certain class of poets. The idea is as obvious as that of calling Venice the "Rome of the Ocean."—Let the worthy Laureat, however, have undisputed claim to the original invention.—M. OD.

† Mrs. Joanna Baillie has illustrated different passions by a tragedy and a comedy on each subject. Lord Byron has also thus drawn a double representation of human depravity. In these, Don Juan performs the part of first Buffo, whilst Manfred leads those who are invested with the serious buskin.—M. OD.

‡ Much abuse has been lavished on Lord Elgin for having sent to this country the spoils of the Parthenon. If this celebrated temple could have remained in security, the removal of its ornaments might have been called a sort of sacrilege. But it is well known that a Turk, who wants to white-wash his house, makes no scruple of destroying the finest remains of ancient art for that ignoble purpose. Was it not, therefore, better to place these precious relics under the protection of Britain, where they will be admired and appreciated, than to let them remain in the power of barbarians, who might speedily reduce them to dust in a lime-kiln?—M. OD.

Like a garden neglected these fences enclose
The violet, the nettle, the nightshade, the rose.

But amongst these sarcastic and amorous sallies,
Who marks not that effort of impotent malice,
Aim'd at worth placed on high — nay, the most lofty station,
Whose strongest, best guard, is the love of a nation.
Far wide from its mark flew the shaft from the string,
Recoils on the archer, but wounds not the King: —
He smiles at such censures when libellers pen 'em —
For Truth bids defiance to Calumny's venom,
We know 'tis the nature of vipers to bite all —
But shall Byron be preacher of duties marital?

Now to poems we turn of a different nature,
Where harangues Faliero, the Doge, and the traitor.
The Doge may be prosy: — but seldom we've seen a *
Fair Lady more docile than meek Angiolina.
Yet to move us her griefs don't so likely appear, as
The woes the starved Poet has made Belvidera's.
I'm far from asserting we're tempted to laugh here; —
But the Doge must be own'd not quite equal to Jaffier.
These ancient impressions the fancy still tarries on,
When forced with old Otway to make a comparison.
Oh! best, tuneful Peer, shone your genius dramatic
Ere your Muse set her foot on those isles Adriatic!
Let her shun the Rialto, and halls of St. Mark,
Contented with Manfred to rove in the dark.

On the banks of Euphrates you better regale us,
With the feasts and the frolics of Sardanapalus.
Philosophic gourmand! — jolly, libertine sage!
Only Pleasure's soft warfare determined to wage,
With goblet in hand, and his head crown'd with roses,
He teaches that death everlasting repose is.

---

* The ending of the first line of this and the following couplet is designed as an humble imitation of the manner in which Lord B. sometimes closes his lines in serious, as well as ludicrous poetry, in blank verse, as well as in rhyme. In compositions of humour it may be allowable to disjoin words at pleasure, and finish a verse with a most feeble termination; but the license granted to Beppo or Don Juan would be thought unreasonable in works of a graver character. Whoever takes the trouble of examining Sardanapalus, the Foscari, and the Mystery of Cain, will find that the lines are very differently constructed from the practice of the best preceding writers. The Italian poets may have adopted some such mode in their stanzas; but the following this example will not improve the majestic *inceding* step of the English Muse, as exemplified by Shakespere and Milton.— M. OD.

The tenet may fairly belong to the story;
But here we perceive that 'tis preach'd *con amore*.
This volatile heart Grecian Myrrha could fix,
Though he laughs at her creed about Pluto and Styx.
His love she returns when his virtues she conn'd over,
And was true, e'en to death, when she found him so fond of her
But the sot whom his subjects had rated at zero,
Bravely fights, and then dies in a blaze like a hero!

You can next (for stage magic you're ne'er at a loss) carry
Your friends back to Venice, and show them the Foscari.
To these luckless isles we're transported again!
Lo! a youth harshly judged by the Council of Ten,
Most wilfully rushes on horrible tortures,
Lest in some foreign clime he should take up his quarters!
His hatred invincible tow'rds all the men is,
But he doats with strange love on the mere mud of Venice.
For the Doge—there is no known example will suit us;
His phlegm patriotic out-Brutuses Brutus.
In his chair, whilst the rack's wrenching torments are done,
He watches the pangs of his innocent son.
His nerves such a spectacle tolerate well;
Yet he dies by the shock, when the sound of a bell,
On a sudden, to Venice announces the doom,
That another mock-sovereign reigns in his room.

Now last, though not least, let us glance at the fable
Your Lordship has raised on the murther of Abel.
But chiefly that wonderful flight let us trace,
Which Lucifer wings through the regions of space;
Where with speed swift as thought with his pupil he runs,
Threading all the bright maze of the planets and suns;
And lectures the while all these objects they're viewing,
Like a tutor abroad, who leads out a young Bruin.
Thus, Satan exhibits pre-Adamite spectres,
And lays down his maxims there free from objectors.
How we turn with disgust, as we listen'd with pain,
From the vile metaphysics he whispers to Cain!*

---

* The demon's insinuations, tending directly to an object the reverse of that which Pope aims at in his Essay on Man, the present being evidently designed to make man doubt the benevolence and goodness of his Maker, might justify harsher terms than are here employed. Instead of vile metaphysics, they might have been termed horrible blasphemies. Let not the noble author shelter himself under the example of Milton. The author of Paradise Lost displays want of taste in making the Almighty argue like "a school divine," as the artists of the Roman Catholic Church have done in representing him under the form of an old man with a long beard; but neither the poet nor the painter

Fit talk for the fiend and the fratricide felon, —
But this is a subject too hateful to dwell on ; —
A lash light as mine, grave offences can trounce ill —
Then here let me end with a short word of counsel : —
'Twould be wrong, noble Bard, Oh ! permit me to tell ye,
To establish a league with Leigh Hunt and Bysshe Shelley ;*
Already your readers have swallow'd too much,
Like Amboyna's swollen victims when drench'd by the Dutch.†
The world cries, in chorus, 'tis certainly time
To close up your flood-gates of blank verse and rhyme.
Hold ! Hold ! — By the public thus sated and cramm'd,
Lest your lays, like yourself, stand a chance to be d——d !

---

intended to commit an irreverend insult. Milton's devils talk and act sufficiently in character, but they are kept within decent bounds. Belial himself, however qualified " to make the worse appear the better reason," is not suffered by the poet to practise his arts on the readers of his divine epic.—M. OD.

* This alludes to a rumour in the newspapers of an intended triple alliance between these three personages, for the amusement and edification of mankind. — M. OD. [The result was " The Liberal."— M.]

† The Island of Amboyna, one of the Moluccas, was formerly occupied jointly by the English and Dutch. In the year 1622, the Hollanders feeling the superiority of their numbers, which was about three to two in their favour, conceived the design of making themselves masters of the whole island. For this purpose they pretended to have discovered a plot contrived by the English for their expulsion. Many of the English settlers were accordingly arrested and exposed to torture, in order to enforce a confession. Amongst the methods employed, was the extraordinary one here alluded to. The accused was fastened to a seat, in an upright posture, with a piece of canvass fixed round his neck, extended above the head in the form of a cup. Water being repeatedly poured into this receptacle, it was necessary to swallow the liquid to avoid suffocation. Under this infliction, the bodies of the sufferers were said to be distended to double their ordinary size. — M. OD.

Modern English Ballads.*

[* * * * The Ensign was evidently much affected on the defeat of his countryman. It was remarked, that some days after the event, he went to bed bare-footed, and rose fasting. But on the occasion of Spring's triumphant entry, he was peculiarly dejected, and refused to look at it, which called forth the following ballad. It will be often imitated by modern poets, both in Spain and Germany.

> Pon te a tancard de brounstout, dexa la suipa de strongsuig
> Melancholico Odorti, veras al galopin Tomspring, &c.

It bears a great resemblance to the bridal of Andalla, in Lockhart's Spanish Ballads; and the succeeding one on poor Thurtell may more remotely, remind the sentimental reader of his "Lament for Celin."]

No. 1.—Spring's Return.

Rise up, rise up, my Morgan, lay the foaming tankard down,
Rise up, come to the window, and gaze with all the town.
From gay shin-bone and cleaver hard the marrowy notes are flowing,
And the Jew's-harp's twang sings out slap-bang, 'twixt the cow-horn's lordly
    blowing;
And greasy caps from butchers' heads are tossing everywhere,
And the bunch of fives of England's knight wags proudly in the air.
Rise up, rise up, my Morgan, lay the foaming tankard down,
Rise up, come to the window, and gaze with all the town.

Arise, arise, my Morgan, I see Tom Winter's mug,
He bends him to the Fancy coves with a nod so smart and smug;
Through all the land of great Cockaigne, or Thames's lordly river,
Shook champion's fist more stout than his, more knock-me-downish never.
Yon Belcher twisted round his neck of azure, mix'd with white,
I guess was tied upon the stakes the morning of the fight.

---

* These National Ballads appeared in *Blackwood* for January, 1824.— Spring's victory over Langan, celebrated in this parody on one of Lockhart's Spanish Ballads, very suitably may follow the Idyll on his battle with Neat of Bristol. Jack Langan, an Irishman, eventually became a publican in Liverpool, realized a fortune there, distinguished himself by subscribing to the O'Connell Rent, and died, some twelve years ago, in a Lunatic Asylum.—M.

Rise up, rise up, my Morgan, lay the foaming tankard down,
Rise up, come to the window, and gaze with all the town.

What aileth thee, my Morgan? what makes thine eyes look down?
Why stay you from the window far, nor gaze with all the town?
I've heard thee swear in hexameter, and sure you swore the truth,
That Thomas Spring was quite the king of the first-beshaking youth.
Now with a Peer he rideth here, and Lord Deerhurst's horses go*
Beneath old England's champion, to the tune of Yo, heave ho!
Then rise, oh rise, my Morgan, lay the foaming tankard down,
You may here through the window-sash come gaze with all the town.

The Irish Ensign rose not up, nor laid his tankard down,
Nor came he to the window to gaze with all the town;
But though his lip dwelt on the pot, in vain his gullet tried,
He could not, at a single draught, empty the tankard wide.
About a pint and a half he drank before the noise grew nigh,
When the last half-pint received a tear slow dropping from his eye.
No, no, he sighs, bid me not rise, nor lay my tankard down,
To gaze on Thomas Winter with all the gazing town.

Why rise ye not, my Morgan, nor lay your tankard down?
Why gaze ye not, my Morgan, with all the gazing town?
Hear, hear the cheering, how it swells, and how the people cry,
He stops at Cribb's, the ex-champion's shop;—why sit you still, oh! why?
"At Cribb's good shop let Tom Spring stop, in him shall I discover
The black-eyed youth that beat the lad who cross'd the water over?
I will not rise with weary eyes, nor lay my tankard down,
To gaze on Langan's conqueror, with all the gazing town."

No. 2.—The Lament for Thurtell.†

A LOUD Lament is heard in town — a voice of sad complaining —
The sorrow Whig is high and big, and there is no restraining.
The great Lord Mayor, in civic chair, weeps thick as skeins of cotton,
And wipes his eyes with huckaback, sold by his own begotten.
Alas, says he, thy thread of life is snapt by sheers of Clothor
And a winding sheet, a yard-yard-wide, enwraps thee, O, my brother!

---

* The late Earl of Coventry, (the Lord Deerhurst of 1823,) had the honor of driving Spring, in his four-in-hand, to the battle-field. He backed him heavily and won on him largely.—M.

† Thurtell, son of an Alderman of Norwich, executed for the murder, in the winter of 1823, of William Weare, a gambler, near Gill's Lane Cottage, Hertfordshire. He was an unmitigated ruffian, with heart and nerves of iron.—M.

Howl, buff and blue! of that dear crew, whose brows the patriot myrtle
Shades for Harmodius Thistlewood! Howl, howl for Whig Jack Thurtell!

The doves and rooks who meet at Brooks',* sob loudly, fast, and faster,
And shake in skin as rattlingly as they ere shook the castor.
O, by the box of Charley Fox, and by his unpaid wagers,
Shame 'tis, they swear, for hangman cocks to hang our truest stagers ;
What if he cut the fellow's throat in fashion debonnaire, sir,
'Tis only like our own Whig case, a bit the worse for *wear*, sir ;
What if, after swallowing brains and blood, he ate pork chops like turtle,
Sure, don't *we* swallow anything ? Alas ! for Whig Jack Thurtell !

Lord Byron, gentleman is he, who writes for good Don Juan,
Huzzaed when my Lord Castlereagh achieved his life's undoing.†
No Tory bard, that we have heard, so savage was or silly,
As to crow o'er cut-throat Whitbread Sam, or cut-throat Sam Romilly.‡
We laugh at them — they sighs with us — we hate them sow and farrow —
Yet now their groans will fly from them as thick as flights of arrow,
Which Mr. Gray, in ode would say, through the dark air do hurtle, —
Moaning in concert with ourselves — Alas ! for Whig Jack Thurtell !

---

* Brooks' is a Club in London which used to be peculiarly Whig, when there were only two political parties (Whig and Tory) in England.—M.

† In "The Liberal," (the quarterly periodical established, at Pisa, in 1822, by Lord Byron, in conjunction with Leigh Hunt,) appeared three epigrams, totally unworthy of the Author of Childe Harold, whether as a poet or a man. The Marquis of Londonderry, (better known as the Lord Castlereagh who virtually carried the parchment Union between Ireland and Great Britain,) was Foreign Secretary of England from 1812 until 1822, when he committed suicide. On this person, and his fate, it pleased Lord Byron to be facetious. The last, and least offensive of his epigrams on this suicide ran thus :

"So *He* has cut his throat at last !— He ! Who ?
The man who cut his country's long ago."

The rhyme, reason, and delicate feeling of such a couplet are on a par.—M.

‡ Samuel Whitbread, for many years a member of Parliament and head of the great porter brewery in Chiswell-Street, London, was a leading member of the Whig party, and, as such conducted the impeachment of Lord Melville in 1805. He died by his own hand in 1815.—Sir Samuel Romilly, who for many years was the leading Chancery lawyer in England, was Solicitor General during the brief administration of Mr. Fox, in 1806, and eminently distinguished himself by his constant efforts to revise and mitigate the criminal code. He was a Whig in politics. In 1818, he perished by suicide.—It is true, as Maginn states, that neither the Tory press nor the Tory party exhibited any joy on the death of Whitbread or Romilly. On the contrary, they expressed, and no doubt felt, great sorrow at their untimely death.—M.

He was a Whig—a true, true Whig—all property he hated
In funds or land, in purse or hand,—tithed, salaried, or estated.
When he saw a fob, he itch'd to rob, the genuine whiggish feeling ;
No matter what kind was the job, fraud, larceny, cheating, stealing.
Were he a peer our proud career he'd rule in mansion upper,
In the Lower House, behind him Brougham would amble on the crupper,
Like Bennet Grey, or Scarlett J.* he'd wield the poleaxe curtal
(My rhymes are out) 'gainst Ministers! Alas! for Whig Jack Thurtell!

* Grey Bennett and Sir James Scarlett (afterwards Lord Abinger, and Chief Baron of the Exchequer,) were leading members of the Whig opposition in 1824.—M.

Moore-ish Melodies.*

1.—THE LAST LAMP OF THE ALLEY.

The last lamp of the alley
  Is burning alone!
All its brilliant companions
  Are shivered and gone.
No lamp of her kindred,
  No burner is nigh,
To rival her glimmer,
  Or light to supply.

I'll not leave thee, thou lone one!
  To vanish in smoke;
As the bright ones are shattered,
  Thou too shalt be broke:
Thus kindly I scatter
  Thy globe o'er the street;
Where the watch in his rambles
  Thy fragments shall meet.

Then home will I stagger,
  As well as I may;
By the light of my nose sure
  I'll find out the way.
When thy blaze is extinguished,
  Thy brilliancy gone,
Oh! my beak shall illumine
  The alley alone.

2.—'TIS THE LAST GLASS OF CLARET.

'Tis the last glass of Claret,
  Left sparkling alone,
All its rosy companions
  Are *clean'd out* and gone.
No wine of her kindred,
  No Red Port is nigh,
To reflect back her blushes,
  And gladden my eye.

---

* These appeared in the *Literary Gazette* for 1820, 1821, and 1822.—M.

I'll not leave thee, thou lone one,
  This desert to crown:
As the bowls are all empty,
  Thou too shalt float down.
Thus kindly I drink up
  Each drop of pure red,
And fling the bright goblet
  Clean over my head.

So soon may dame Fortune
  Fling me o'er her head,
When I quit brimming glasses,
  And bundle to bed.
When Champaigne is exhausted,
  And Burgundy's gone,
Who would leave even Claret,
  To perish alone.

3.—RICH AND RARE.

Rich and rare was the chain he wore,
And a long white wand in his hand he bore;
But oh! his paunch strutted far beyond
His bright gold chain, and his snow-white wand.

"Oh, Alderman, dost thou not fear to go,
Where the turtle shall smoke, and the Burgundy flow?
Are the doctors so sparing of lancet and pill,
Not to physic or bleed thee for this night's swill?"

"Good ma'am," said he, "I feel no alarm;
Nor turtle nor Burgundy does me a harm;
For though of your doctors I've had a score,
I but love good eating and drinking the more."

On he went—and his purple nose
Soon over dish, platter, and bottle glows:
And long may he stuff, who thus defied
Lancet, pill, bolus, and potion beside.

4.—TOM STOKES LIVED ONCE.

"Young Love."

Tom Stokes liv'd once in a garret high
  Where fogs were breathing,
  And smoke was wreathing

Her curls to give the cerulean sky,
Which high up above Tom's head did lie:
    His red cheeks flourish'd,
    For *Sam Swipes* nourish'd
Their bloom full oft with *Whitbread's* showers.
    But debts, tho' *borish*, must be paid,
And Bailiffs a'nt *bam'd* for many hours.

Ah! that the *Nabman's* evil eyes
    Should ever come hither,
    Such cheeks to wither!
The fat soon, soon, began to die,
And *Tom* fell sick as the blades drew nigh.
    They came one morning,
    Ere *Stokes* had warning,
And rapp'd at the door where the wild spark lay.
'Oh, ho!' says Tom, 'Is it you?' good bye.—
So he pack'd up his awls, and he trudg'd away.

5.—BILLINGSGATE MUSIC.*

Hark! Billingsgate music
    Melts o'er the sea,
Falling light from some alehouse,
    Where Kerry men be;
And fishwomen's voices
    Roar over the deep,
And waken around us
    The billows from sleep.

Our potatoe boat gently
    Wades over the wave,
While they call one another
    Rogue, baggage, and knave!
We listen — we listen —
    How happy are we,
To hear the sweet music
    Of beauteous Tralee!

---

* This is scarcely a Moore-ish *chanson.*—M.

6.—TO A BOTTLE OF OLD PORT.

1.

When he, who adores thee, has left but the dregs
  Of such famous old stingo behind,
Oh! say will he bluster or weep; no, ifegs!
  He'll seek for some more of the kind.
He'll laugh, and though doctors perhaps may condemn,
  Thy tide shall efface the decree,
For many can witness, though subject to phlegm,
  He has always been faithful to thee!

2.

With thee were the dreams of his earliest love,
  Every rap in his pocket was thine,
And his very last prayer, every morning, by Jove,
  Was to finish the evening in wine.
How blest are the tipplers whose heads can outlive
  The effects of four bottles of thee,
But the next dearest blessing that heaven can give,
  Is to stagger home muzzy from three!

7.—TO THE FINISH I WENT.

1.

To the Finish I went, when the moon it was shining,
  The jug round the table moved jovially on;
I staid 'till the moon the next morn was declining—
  The jug still was there, but the punch was all gone!
And such are the joys that your brandy will promise,
  (And often these joys at the finish I've known)
Every copper it makes in the evening ebb from us,
  And leaves us next day with a headache alone!

2.

Ne'er tell me of puns or of laughter adorning
  Our revels, that last till the close of the night,
Give me back the hard cash that I left in the morning,
  For clouds dim my eye, and my pocket is light.
O! who's there who welcomes that moment's returning,
  When daylight must throw a new light on his frame—
When his stomach is sick, and his liver is burning,
  His eyes, shot with blood, and his brow in a flame!

Anecdotes and Facetiæ.*

A LATE member for Trinity College, Dublin, found himself seated one day at a large dinner, given by one of the senior fellows of that university, near a young man to whom he had not been introduced. They, however, soon entered into conversation; and the M. P. was quite delighted by the colloquial powers and great information of his neighbour. He took an early opportunity of asking his host the name of the young gentleman. "I thought you knew him," was the reply. "It is ——— the new Fellow." (It is to be remarked, that the Fellows of Trinity College, Dublin, vote for members of Parliament, and are generally very influential in elections.) "Ah!" said the member, "is that the case? I really felt an *attraction* for him." "I do no doubt it," replied Dr. Kyle; "it must be an *elective attraction.*"

AT the Irish bar, Ninian Mahaffy, Esq. is as much above the middle size, as Mr. Collis is below it. (Mr. Mahaffy, in Curran's life time, was Deputy to Sir Jonah Barrington, Judge of the Admiralty in Ireland, and whenever he presided there, Curran used to say, that Court was very fitly called, the *high* Court of Admiralty.) When Lord Redesdale was Lord Chancellor in Ireland, Messrs. Mahaffy and Collis happened to be retained in the same case a short time after his Lordship's elevation, and before he was acquainted personally with the Irish bar. Mr. Collis was opening the motion, when Lord R. observed; "Mr. Collis, when a barrister addresses the court, he must stand." "I am standing on the bench, my Lord," said Collis. "I beg a thousand pardons," replied his Lordship, somewhat confused; "sit down, Mr. Mahaffy." "I am sitting, my Lord," was the reply to the confounded Chancellor.

ON this occasion, the following epigram, (attributed, as every pun in Ireland, good or bad is, to Lord Norbury, but really the

* From the *Literary Gazette* for 1820, 1821, and 1822. — M.

production of a barrister then eminent, but now retired from the bar) was composed.

> Mahaffy and Collis, ill paired in a case,
> Representatives true of the rattling size ace;
> To the heights of the law, though I hope you will rise
> You will never be judges, I'm sure of *assize*.

The motto of the city of Cork arms is, " Statio *benefida* carinis," altered from the *malefida* of Virgil; and most deservedly, with regard to the harbour of Cork. The city arms are of course commonly adopted for signs to houses of entertainment. But the ingenuity of a sign-painter has, by a happy blunder, made the motto quite appropriate for an eating-house, over which his graphic pencil has displayed the arms. He has exhibited it, " Statio benefida *carnis*," (omitting the central i,) which may be translated, " An excellent place for meat."

The following anecdote of General Ross, the incendiary of Washington, has never we believed appeared in print. He was educated in Trinity College, Dublin, during the Provostship of Hutchinson, who was pretty generally disliked in College, and accused of keeping it in a perpetual ferment of electioneering and other intrigues. In carrying on these, he frequently made use of the assistance of his son's tutor, Adair, (afterwards Dr. Adair, master of a highly respectable classical school in Fermoy, who has been some years dead) and he of course shared the unpopularity of his employer. Ross and he had a particular quarrel, and the future general revenged himself on his antagonist, by caricaturing him (for which art he had a peculiar talent) in the act of bestowing a salutation on a very unseemly part of the provost's person, with the motto of "tenacem *præpositi* virum." He pasted it on the College gate, and it nearly procured him the honours of an expulsion.

Puns on names are so easy to make, and so hard to be comprehended, except on the spot where they are vented, that it is seldom worth while to write them. Perhaps this may pass. A member of parliament who was paying his addresses to a lady of the name of Weekes, had gone up to town to attend his parliamentary duty, and returned in a very short time. On its being remarked that he had not delayed long in the metropolis, it was replied, that he had business to attend to at home, from which he could not be long absent. "True," said a person, "Mr. ——— can be absent for days, but it is quite impossible he should be so for *Weeks*."

Miss Edgeworth has written a most witty essay on Irish Bulls, in which she is very eager to defend our honest neighbours across the channel from the imputation of bull-making. She herself however appears to have fallen into the practice, which is very contagious, in the following passage of her life of her father— we know not whether in jest or earnest. She tells us (Edgeworth's Memoirs, vol. 2, p. 355), "The last letter poor Johnson ever wrote, or I should rather say, dictated, was to my father; it was in his nephew's handwriting, and gives the following account of his death." Dr. Johnson, it was said, believed in ghosts; but we think it still harder to believe that his namesake wrote or even dictated a letter, containing an account of his own death.

ANOTHER.—The translator of Madam de Laroche Jacquelin's Memoirs, has caused that noble lady to make a very fair bull, without, we presume, any co-operation on her part. The memoirs are dedicated to the children, and the translator makes her use the following sentence, in addressing them: "I feel a mournful pleasure in recounting to you the life and *death* of your *parents* and friends." This admirable blunder, which makes a mother tell her children of the death of their parents, must arise from ignorance of the meaning of the French word *parens* —relations.

AMONG the apologies received by the Lord Chancellor from Peers praying to be excused attendance on the Queen's trial, the Morning Chronicle seriously states one urging a very sufficient reason, namely, "The Bishop of Cloyne, dead!" Thus we see that the fact of posthumous correspondence does not rest only on Miss Edgeworth's authority.

FRUIT AND TIMBER.—In the Commercial Dictionary for Ireland, Scotland, &c. lately published (which by the way is a most ridiculously incorrect work) under the head Dungarvon, is the following paragraph. "It [Dungarvon] was formerly noted for its export of fruit and timber to Dublin; but the trade has lately declined, and in its place has sprung up a considerable export of corn, butter, and provision, to the ports of the English Channel," p. 191. Fruit and timber! Somebody must have been laughing at the unfortunate compiler, for the export of Dungarvon, designated by this splendid title, was literally no more than *potatoes and brooms*. The joke is quite proverbial in the South of Ireland; and it seems hardly possible even far a bogman to have been humbugged by it.

AN IRISH TRIBUTE TO GENERAL VALLENCEY.—The General was regarded by some of the *Milesians* of Ireland with enthusiastic affection, for his exertions in the cause of the ancient literature and history of that country. Many odd proofs were given of this feeling. Among the rest, the veteran used to tell with the utmost good humour, that a Kerry gentleman waited on him in Killarney with a knife of antique fashion, which he presented him with these words: "General, this knife has been in my family one hundred and fifty years, during which time it had only three blades and two handles; and though it is a family relic, it is perfectly at your service, for the zale you have shown in the cause of ould Ireland. I got the last blade in yesterday, and the last handle a month ago, that I might give you this rale antiquity as perfect as possible."

BARON SMITH'S RIDDLE.—Some men of the greatest talents have taken delight in composing or endeavouring to unravel riddles. Dean Swift is a case in point. Sir William Smith, the learned Irish Baron of the Exchequer, at one time spent two days and nights in considering the answer to this conundrum: Why is an egg underdone, like an egg overdone? He would not suffer any one to give him the answer, which he at last discovered. It is a tolerable pun enough. Because they are both *hardly* done.

IRISH BANKS.—There has been sad havock among the southern banks of Ireland within these few months, and of course their failures have furnished very constant topics of conversation, with respect to their presumed solvency. A dispute arose about the comparative merits of the banks of Cork and Clonmell, in one of these conversations. "I own," said one of the company, "I prefer Clonmell to Cork. In the former, the banks are always on the *Sure* side, and in the latter, as constantly on the *Lee* side." The Suir and Lee are the rivers on which these towns stand.

A HEBREW PUN, FOR THE BENEFIT OF HEBRAISTS ONLY.— A Jew not long since failed for a considerable sum, and a meeting of his creditors was of course called. On examining his accounts one of these gentlemen expressed his apprehensions that the bankrupt would be very defective. "Indeed," said a brother Israelite, "I am sorry to agree with you; he will be a defective in *Pe nun*" (pay none).

PUN PROSODIAL.—The facetious Jeremy Keller, one of the oldest and most respectable members of the Irish bar, was once rallied, by a brother barrister, for not prefixing an O to his name. O'Keller, Jeremiah O'Keller! "Why," said he, "the very sound would give you a claim to *undoubted* antiquity of family." "Nay," replied Mr. Keller, "I agree with old Alvany, *O datur ambiguis.*"

A BULL FROM ENGLAND.—In the eighteenth number of the Imperial Magazine, published in the town of Liverpool, we have the following passage in a paper on 'Ancient Manners and Customs of the English.' "*The nuns* of St. Mary Kingston, in Wilts, were often seen coming forth into the Nymph Hay, with their rocks and wheels to spin, sometimes to the number of seventy;

all of whom *were not nuns*, but young girls sent there for education." So the nuns of St. Mary's were *not* nuns, according to this Imperial bull-breeder.

A BULL FROM IRELAND.—A gentleman in a provincial city of Ireland, who had been for a couple of weeks employed on valuation juries, was summoned on the petty jury for the assizes, which unluckily for him commenced on the day the valuations had concluded. He was a good deal vexed at this new intrusion on his time, and in his indignation exclaimed, "Why then, is not this too bad! I am here put on this curst jury, after having been on juries a *fortnight this week*."

A CONSIDERATE MAN.—A basket woman coming out of a market-place in a town in Ireland, loaded with a basket full of provisions, met a very parsimonious gentleman, who observed that she was rather heavily laden. "Ah! God bless you, sir," answered she, "you were always a considerate man, *you* never break poor women's backs by loading them with your joints of meat."

THE late Sir Boyle Roche, in Ireland, was usually set down as the author of all description of bulls in his time; and he really used to make a great many. He however vented some tolerable witticisms, and in fact, it was pretty generally suspected that the bulls were very often designedly made, to amuse his companions in the Irish House of Commons. One of his puns is perhaps worth preserving. It was argued in his presence, whether Dante or Milton was the superior poet. "I think," said he, "Horace, a very competent judge of poetry, has decided against Dante long ago." "Horace!" said one of the disputants, expecting a new bull; "when could Horace say any thing about Dante?" "Don't you recollect," replied Sir Boyle, "that he asserts most roundly *Dante minor?* Ep. I. xvi. 22."

DR. WADE, agricultural professor to the Dublin Society, sometimes lectures his class in the fields, among the productions on which he is lecturing. As he was thus employed one day, treating on potatoes in the beds themselves, he took occasion to speak in favour of this practice. "Why, doctor," said one of his auditors, "I think you are very right to lecture here by the side of the beds; for you know the faculty always recommend students to attend *clinical lectures.*"

ANECDOTES OF CURRAN.

IN Phillips's life of Curran, we have a vast deal in that gentleman's peculiar style, about the great uneasiness, and the tender feelings of his hero, concerning his domestic circumstances. There is much fustian of the same kind in O'Regan's Memoirs of Curran; but I am very much inclined to think that no such sorrows existed. In Ireland it is very generally believed that Mrs. Curran was an extremely injured woman, and her family, a highly respectable one, received her with open arms after the verdict obtained against her supposed paramour. Many ugly stories are current with respect to the evidence adduced on that trial; and Curran was so anxious to hinder the proceedings on it from obtaining publicity, that he had notices served on all the newspapers of Dublin, enjoining them not to publish it; and accordingly it never was given to the public.

The reason that inclines me to think that he never felt very severely on his matrimonial misfortune is the great levity with which he was frequently in the habit of speaking about it. A couple of coarse jests on the subject have come to my knowledge; for the accuracy of the first of which I can positively vouch, and the second I have on tolerably good authority.

HE was a fine musician, and had frequently concerts in his house in Dublin. At one of these, a young barrister at Cork, a distinguished amateur, bore a part. After the concert had concluded, Curran went up to him and said, "Well, H. what do you think of that? Do you not think it at least as good as any of your Cork concerts?" "Why," replied his friend, "it was very fine; but in Cork we can procure military music much more readily than you can in Dublin: the want of it was very discernible in your concert; for instance," said he, repeating a passage, "would not the French horn have made a great improvement there?" "Well, H." said Curran, laughing, "you are the first who has complained of the *want of horns* in my house."

ON another occasion, he and the late Sir Richard Musgrave, the historian of the Rebellion in Ireland, whose lady's frailties were numerous and notorious, met at the house of a common friend. They were decidedly hostile in politics to each other, and had even proceeded to personal altercations. On being summoned up-stairs to the dining-room, they happened to arrive at the foot of the stairs together, and, as is usual on such occasions, when enemies meet, their behaviour was ceremoniously polite. Weary at length of alternately conceding the *pas*, Sir Richard, assuming an air of familiarity, took him by the arm, and said, "Well, well, let us settle the matter by walking up together." "Pardon me, Sir Richard," replied Curran, "that is impossible; *our antlers would entangle!*" He that could jest thus, could not feel deeply.

I HAVE heard also, that on the day of the trial in which his wife's character was involved, he appeared in an obscure corner of the court, where however he could be seen by the opposing lawyer, and there diverted himself with putting him out during his speech, by erecting his fore-fingers over his ears, making faces and performing various droll gesticulations, for which he had a peculiar talent. Whether this be true or not, I cannot say; but it is commonly believed; and I am sure that could he hear half the eloquence bestowed on his woes by Phillips, he would laugh outright in his face. That he had not a very high opinion of his biographer, the following anecdote will evince:—He came into Phillips's room one day while he was writing, and inquired what he was about. "I am writing a speech, sir," was the reply; "and I can tell you that I intend to give your friend, Mr. Grattan, a rating in it." "Never mind it, Charley," said Curran, "never mind it; it would only be a child throwing a stone at the leg of a colossus."

Curran's talent were of the very first order, but they were too often sadly misapplied; and the stern moralist would find much to censure, both in his public and his private life: but he was a highly fascinating man in conversation. His wit, his drollery, his eloquence, his pathos, were all irresistible. The only defect in him in this respect was a love of acting, which made his wit often degenerate into mere buffoonery, and his pathos into canting and overstrained sentiment. It must have been in some of these latter moods that his biographers observed his sensibility; but there never was any thing real in it. It was often put on even to convey ill natured remarks; and as this straggling notice (which has far outstripped the bounds I at first intended), has been little than a vehicle of jests, I shall conclude by giving another, connected with this splenetic tenderness of heart. At a supper party in Brighton, I believe, he began to lament the desolation of his old age: he was a solitary unfortunate old man, he said, who had not even a child he could call his own. *His son was sitting at table with him at the very time.* This observation created much disgust in the company; and a young barrister who was present, in relating it afterwards to an elder brother of the profession, added, with much vehemence, " By G— if *my* father had said so in my presence, I would have forgotten all filial reverence, and knocked him down." "Ay," said the senior, "that would certainly prove you were not a *natural* son."

Irish Counties.—During the rebellion of 1798, Ireland was subject to the severe discipline of military law, and sentries were placed in every important situation, with the strictest orders not to let any person pass after nine o'clock at night without a knowledge of the proper pass-word. The Comte de Clermont, a French emigrant residing in Dublin, had unluckily staid out one night beyond the prescribed hour, and on endeavouring to get into the castle, where he slept, was stopped of course by the sentry, who was inexorable. "Oh, sare," said the angry Frenchman, "you must let me in; *je suis*—I am the Comte de Clermont." "A county Clare man!" replied the soldier— "devil a bit of me would care if you were a county Kerry man, or even come out of the heart of Tipperary like myself: clear my post," continued he, repelling the count, " or you will never see the county Clare in your days again."

PROVINCE OF THE CHIMÆRA.—A student, from the south of Ireland, in the university of Dublin, who was unfortunately, at the same time, so idle as to stand in need of continual prompting at examinations, and so deaf as to be almost incapable of benefiting by it, was once asked by his examiner, "What was the Chimæra?" He instantly cocked his ear to catch a whisper from his neighbour, who, vexed at seeing him so ignorant, said, rather impatiently, "Why, 'tis a monster, man!" The deaf scholar taking the prompt imperfectly, cried out with the utmost confidence, "The chimæra, sir, why sure every body knows he is a *Munster-man!*"

THE RULING PASSION STRONG IN DEATH.—All through Ireland, the ceremonial of wakes and funerals is most punctually attended to, and it requires some *sçavoir faire* to carry through the arrangement in a masterly manner. A great adept at the business, who had been the prime manager at all the wakes in the neighbourhood for many years, was at last called away from the death-beds of his friends to his own. Shortly before he died, he gave minute directions to his people, as to the mode of waking him in proper style. "Recollect," says he, "to put three candles at the head of the bed, after you lay me out, and two at the foot, and one on each side. Mind now, and put a plate with the salt on it just a-top of my breast. And, do you hear, have plenty of tobacco, and pipes enough. And remember to make the punch strong. And—but what the devil is the use of talking to you; sure, I know, you'll be sure to botch it, as I won't be there myself."

A WINDOW tax collector in Ireland, a man of convivial habits, was pressing a friend of his after dinner to fill his glass. "I have filled," said the other. "Ay," replied the taxman, "but not full." "Well," said his friend, "you are too strict in your office; cannot even a *sky-light* escape you?"

BON MOT OF MR. PLUNKETT.—In 1818, when Mr. Plunkett and Mr. Croker, of the Admiralty, were candidates at the general election (the latter being the government candidate) for the representation of the College, Dublin, a gentleman asked Mr. P. whether Mr. Reagh, one of the fellows of the College, would vote for him:—"He will," replied Mr. P.; "If he did not, he would be *a Castle* Reagh."

THE late Dr. Hudson, of Dublin, having acquired a large fortune as a *Dentist*, built a very beautiful and expensive house of hewn stone adjoining Mr. Curran's demesne, near Rathfarnham, the front of which was ornamented with a handsome portico in the Doric order. From the close friendship that subsisted so long between these gentlemen, it may be supposed they spent together almost every moment they could spare from professional pursuits, many of which were, of course, engaged in inspecting the workmen employed at this building. On one of these occasions, while watching the progress of the portico, Mr. Curran turned to his friend, and said, "Well, Med! though *I* have always admired the chaste simplicity of the Doric order, I wonder YOU could have preferred *any* to the TUSK-an, which has such strong claims on your gratitude."

IT was on this same occasion, that Dr. H. having congratulated Mr. Curran on the felicity of his pun, the latter exclaimed, "Oh! if I were PUNISHED for every PUN-I-SHED."——To which Dr. Hudson replied, "If you were, Jack, you'd not be left a PUNY-SHED to hold your PUNNISH-HEAD."

The Route.*

"Send for a chair — it blows so hard — I can't bear windy weather;
Now, you and I in one sedan can go quite well together,"
Said Mrs. Frump, while folding tight her shawl around each shoulder,
She took the lean and wither'd arm of sweet Miss Nancy Holder.

This Mistress Frump and Nancy dear were old maids stiff and stupid,
Who long had been shot proof against the darts of cunning Cupid;
So now, good souls, they both were off to Lady Betty Randle,
To have a little shilling whist, and talk a deal of scandal.

The chair it came, and in they went, together sideways sitting,
As closely pack'd as all the threads they just before were knitting.
In minutes three they safe arrived, the double knock foretelling
The fast approach of these two dames to Lady Randle's dwelling.

Forthwith the bawling footman shewed up stairs Miss Nancy Holder,
And Mrs. Frump; while stared Miss Young, and Mrs. Young the older.
"Dear Lady Randle, how d'ye do? I am very glad to see you,"
Quoth Mrs. Frump. Miss Sugarfist cried, "Dear Miss Nan, how be you?"

"Miss Charlotte, I am quite rejoiced to have the boundless pleasure
Of shaking hands, my love, you're looking charming beyond measure;
That roseate bloom upon your cheek outvies the soft carnation."
"O lawk! Miss Ann, you fluster me with such great admiration."

Now, Mr. Sugarfist had been in tea and figs a dealer,
Which was the cause Miss Sugarfist, his child, was not genteeler;
He, having made a fortune large, and trade no more admiring,
Sold all his stock, and cut the shop and business, by retiring.

Yet still he dealt — that is, the cards, for he to whisk was partial;
His partner now, a soldier bold, was gallant Major Martial,
Who oft had seen much service hard, round Brentford, Kew, and Ryegate,
And e'en that very day had march'd from Paddington to Highgate.

By Mr. Sugarfist there sat, of turtle feasts a giver,
A Nabob, who came home with gold, but not an inch of liver;
His partner was no less a man than portly Parson Sable;
Which, if you reckon right, you'll find just makes up one whist table.

But next to these, a noisy set of talking Dames were playing
At guinea Loo, and now and then a temper vile betraying.
Miss Winter, Mrs. Crookedlegs, Miss Glum, and Mrs. Hearty,
With hump-back'd Lady Spindleshanks, exactly made the party.

---

* From *Blackwood* for October, 1822.— M.

Upon the sofa, Mrs. Frump, dear soul! had squatted down to
Some shilling whist, with Mrs. Prim, and lo! a foreign Count, too!
Who, as Dame Fortune will'd it, soon became her partner chosen;
While Mr. Prim, congenial man! sat opposite Miss Frozen.

Around the room, in various parts, some motley groups were seated:
In one place, Captain Splinter bold, with grape (not shot) juice heated,
Made desp'rate work with Sophy Blaze, who swore he meant to kill her;
For, in the warmth of love, he grasp'd her hand just like a tiller.

Then, in the room adjacent, young Miss Randle and Miss Parking,
To *treat* the company, began through two duets sky-larking.
When Mr. Simple ask'd Miss Quiz, " In what key are they playing?"
" 'Tis what you are, — A flat," she said, a sneering smile betraying.

Now up and down the ivory keys the Misses twain kept flying.
As if to make as great a din as could be they were trying.
This o'er, the kind Miss Symphony, with lungs indeed appalling,
Sat down before the harpsichord, and had a bout at squalling.

While all these things were going on, Miss Holder, in a corner,
Had fix'd upon a school girl, Miss Honoria Julia Horner,
Who'd *just begun to be come out;* so Nancy, by explaining
The histories of the folks around, Miss H. was entertaining.

" Look there! d'ye see? that's General Bomb, just come from Gibraltar;
'Tis rumour'd he will lead next week Miss Simper to the altar:
He's sixty-five, and she sixteen, — a pretty match this, truly!
No doubt, in time his brow will be with antlers cover'd duly.

" There goes Miss Flirt, who fancies she is able to discover
In every man she dances with a true and ardent lover.
And here comes Mrs. Paroquet, a widow young and wealthy,
Who's waiting just to catch some peer, old, gouty, and unhealthy.

" That kind of man with whiskers large, and hair that's rather sandy,
A stiff cravat, gold chain and glass, is what they call a Dandy.
Those ladies standing by the door, and making such wry faces,
Because they've lost twelve points at cards, are call'd the faded Graces.

" The youngest's *only* fifty-eight, the second sixty-seven;
The oldest, who is seventy-six, ought now to be in——heaven.
Folks say they once were pretty girls, but would be always flirting;
A thing, my dear, the hopes of being nicely married hurting.

" Now, goodness me! as I'm alive! there's little Fanny Sawyer
Engaged in earnest chat with Mr. Honesty, the lawyer.
If that turns out to be a match, I'm sure 'twill be a wonder.
But only look at Mrs. Bounce with one-arm'd Colonel Thunder.

"Well, how some people can!—but see, the card parties are breaking,
And yonder there's dear Mrs. Frump of tipsey-cake partaking."
So here Miss Holder's eloquence at once was put an end to,
At sight of delicacies, which she ever was a friend to.

Now Champagne bottles, knives and forks, plates, glasses, scandal, chatter,
With laughter interspersed, began to make a glorious clatter.
"Dear Colonel, pray be good enough to help me to a custard"—
"A little lobster, if you please"—"I'll thank you for the mustard.

"Miss Holder, won't you take a seat?"—"What shall I have the pleasure,
Miss Sugarfist, of giving you?"—"Why, when you be at leisure,
I'll take some raisins, if you please."—"That savours of the Grocer,"
Miss Clackitt whispered Mr. Prim, "her dad was one, you know, sir."

Now Mr. Prim, alas! poor man! was very absent, making
Sometimes great blunders, which would after set his heart an aching:
Thus sage Miss Clackitt's shrewd remark to him was quite a poser,
Yet, just for answering's sake, he roar'd out, "Yes, her dad's a grocer!"

On which Miss Charlotte's cheeks, poor thing, became as red as scarlet,
And pouting like a sulky child, she sobb'd out, "O the varlet!"
But he, the cause of her dismay, stood looking blank and foolish;
While Dandy Bubble said, "Why, Prim, upon my soul! 'twas coolish."

Now other noises swell'd the roar: Good gracious! what's the matter?
"O never mind, 'tis Sophy Blaze, again the Captain's at her:—
I wonder if these rattling romps will end in ought like marriage!"—
"Lord Random's Stanhope stops the way"—"Count Marasquino's carriage."

Then rose among the female tribe a strife of silk and satins,
Miss Holder's chair's announced, and Mrs. Bubble's maid and pattens.
In groups the company paired off; some chairing it, some walking,
But all fatigued with doing nought, save playing cards and talking.

As home our brace of old maids went, each passing watchman's warning,
Proclaim'd, "Past two;" said Mrs. Frump, "Dear me, 'tis Sunday morning!
Well, who'd have thought it! what a shame! now is it not, Miss Nancy?
I wish we'd come away before."   (She told a lie, I fancy.)

But here to this my beauteous strain, at length I must say, Amen,
And bid adieu to Lords and Counts, to Ladies gay, and gay Men;
And much I hope, although these things sometimes should not be slighted,
When next her Ladyship's "at home," I may not be invited.

A Happy New-Year.*

1.

Hark! hark! the sharp voice of Old Christopher North
Rings out from Edina, the gem of the Forth:
The year twenty-three like a vapour has past,
And he's nearer by one twelvemonth more to his last.
He dreads not that day — for he trusts he has stood,
Though too freakish at times, yet in all by the good;
So he watches the march of Old Time without fear,
And wishes you, darlings, a Happy New-Year.

2.

He greets you, because the dear bond of our love
Is flourishing proudly all others above;
Her sons still as manly, her daughters as true —
[He speaks of the many, and mourns for the few —]
That she still is the realm of the wise and the free,
Of the Victors of Europe, the Lords of the Sea —
And gratitude dims his old eyes with a tear,
While he wishes you, darlings, a Happy New-Year.

3.

His heart sings with joy, while all round him he sees
Her citizens prosper, her cities increase, —
Her taxes diminish, — her revenues rise, —
Her credit spring up, as her oaks to the skies, —
Her coasts full of commerce, — her purses of gold, —
Her granary with corn, and with cattle her fold.
He prays that for aye such may be her career,
And wishes you, darlings, a Happy New-Year.

4.

He is proud to see Monarchs bend low, cap in hand,
To ask aid from her merchants, plain men of our land,
To see them their millions so readily fling,
And book down as debtor an Emperor or King:
That a nod from her head, or a word from her mouth,
Shakes the World, Old and New, from the North to the South;
That her purse rules in peace, as in war did her spear,
And he wishes you, darlings, a Happy New-Year.

---

* From *Blackwood* for January, 1824. — It is given as addressed "To the True Men of the Land, from Christopher North." — M.

5.

Laugh, fiddle, and song, ring out gay in the town,
And the glad tally-ho cheers the dale and the down;
The rich man his claret can jollily quaff,
And the happier poor man o'er brown stout may laugh;
And the demagogue ruffian no longer can gull
With Jacobin slang, for John's belly is full;
And 'tis only when hungry that slang he will hear—
So, Kit wishes you, darlings, a Happy New-Year.

6.

He rejoices to see every engine at work,
From the steamer immense, to the sweet knife and fork;
The weaver at loom, and the smith at his forge;
And all loyal and steady, and true to King George.
Whigs, therefore, avaunt! there's no chance now for ye—
We forget they exist in the general glee;
He begs you won't let them diminish your cheer,
So he wishes you, darlings, a Happy New-Year.

7.

There's the King, bless his heart, long is likely to live,
And the Duke at the head of the army to thrive;
There's Wellington extant, who badger'd the Gaul,
And Eldon still sitting in Westminster-Hall.
There's Scott writing prose—and there's—who writing verse?
Why, no one; but, hang it, think never the worse.
Sure, there's Christopher North writes your Magazine here,
And wishes you, darlings, a Happy New-Year.

8.

In the midst of this wealth, of this national pride—
Of our honour, our glories, spread far, far, and wide,
While proudly we traverse the sea and the sod,
Let us never forget for a moment our GOD!
It was he raised us up, and, remember, his frown,
If we swerve from his cause, would as soon cast us down;
But that so we shall swerve shall Old Kit never fear,
And he wishes you, darlings, a Happy New-Year.

Henderson the Historian.*

UNCHANGED amidst the petty mutabilities of rank and station, I still claim it, as my peculiar privilege, to review all books allied in any way whatever to the two great sister sciences of eating and drinking. Blackwood's Magazine is the place, and mine is the pen. *imprimis*, ϰαι ἐξοχω, and *par excellence*, consecrated to the discussion of all such delightful themes. Let the Quarterly rejoice in the noble art of boiling down into a portable essence, the diffusive lucubrations of all voyagers by land or sea: let old Blue and Yellow keep unpoached the jungles and juggleries of political economy: let The Writer Tam glorify himself in Jem Smith's quaint little ditties, and his brother's quaint little criticisms on the *minora moralia* of Harley Street, and Gower Street: let the London flourish on the misty dreams of the opium eater, and lay down the law unquestioned as to the drinking up both of eisel and laudanum: sacred to the quackeries of the quack-doctors, be the pungent pages of the Scalpel: let John Bull vibrate his horns *ad libitum*, among the merciful bowels of Mr. Zachariah Macaulay: and let the Examiner be great as of old, in the reign of second-rate players, and fifth-rate painters. Let each man buckle his own belt, according to the adage, and that in his own way: but let me unbuckle mine, and luxuriate in the dear, the dainty, the delicate, paradisaical department of deipnosophism.—Above the rest, let THE BOTTLE, and all that pertains to it, be my proper concern. Here indeed I am great. If Barrow, as being himself a practised traveller, is fitted more than any other of our tribe for discussing the vagaries of the Parrys, the Vauxes, the Basil Halls, the Fanny Wrights, the Edward Daniel Clarkes, and the John Rae Wilsons† of our time—Surely

---

* These remarks on "The History of Ancient and Modern Wines," were published in *Blackwood* for July, 1824. The vinous historian was Dr. Henderson, of Aberdeen.— M.

† Sir John Barrow, Secretary of the Admiralty from 1804 to 1845, was himself a great traveller, the voluminous author of travels and biographies, and critic-general, in the Quarterly Review, of works of that class. He died in 1848.— Sir Edward Parry, the Arctic voyager, is yet alive and in office in London.— Mr. Vaux wrote "A Year's Residence in America," which gave satis-

I have at least as unquestionable a title for predominating over all that is connected with the circumvolutions of the decanters. It is recorded by Athenæus, that Darius, *the great Darius*, commanded them to inscribe upon his tombstone these memorable, and even sublime words: "ΗΔΥΝΑΜΗΝ ΚΑΙ ΟΙΝΟΝ ΠΙΝΕΙΝ ΠΟΛΥΝ ΚΑΙ ΤΟΥΤΟΝ ΦΕΡΕΙΝ ΚΑΛΩΣ:" which signify, being interpreted: "Here lies Darius the King, who drank three bottles every day, and never had a headach in his life." I flatter myself that my epitaph might tell a similar story, without any impeachment of its veracity.

The volume now in my eye, then, belongs in an especial manner to my province. At first, on perceiving it to be a bulky quarto, you may be inclined to hesitate as to this; but when you put on your spectacles, and discover that the title is "The History of Wines, Ancient and Modern," your scruples will evanish as easily as do the cobwebs of a Jeffrey beneath the besom of a Tickler. Turn over these costly pages, and feast your eyes with the delicious vignettes, that ever and anon glance out from between the leaves, like the ruby clusters of Bacchus himself, glowing amidst the foliage of some tall marriageable elm, or stately poplar; pause upon these exquisite gems; contemplate the rosy god in each and and all of these five thousand attitudes: worship him where, frantic and furious, he tosses the thyrsus amidst the agitated arms of his congregated Mænades: adore him where, proudly seated upon the rich skins of the monsters whom he subdued, he pours out the foaming cup of wine and wisdom before the eyes of savage men, whom the very scent of the ethereal stuff hath already half civilized: envy him, where beneath the thick shadow of his own glorious plant, he with one hand twines the ivy wreath around the ivory brows of Ariadne, and with the other approximates the dew of divinity to the lips of beauty. Feast, revel, riot in the elegance of the unrivalled

faction to no one. — Basil Hall, in 1824, had written only his Voyage to Corea and the Loo-Choo Island, and Extracts from a Journal on the Coasts of Chili, Peru, and Mexico. He died in 1844. — Fanny Wright, after having long been a resident in the United States, died in 1853. — Dr. Clarke's Travels in Europe and Asia, between 1794 and 1802, were very popular in their day. He died in 1821. — William Rae Wilson, known by his "Travels in the Holy Land," and other works, died in 1849. — M.

cameos, and when you have saturated your eye with forms that might create a thirst beneath the ribs of gout, and draw three corks out of one bottle—then, O Christopher! and not till then, will you be in a fit condition for understanding the profound feelings of respect, and grateful attachment, with which it is now my agreeable duty to introduce to your acquaintance, and that of "my public," the learnedly luxurious Dissertations of my friend, and jolly little compotator, Dr. Alexander Henderson.

The Doctor is, *absque omni dubio*, the first historian of our age. He unites in his single person the most admirable qualifications of all the other masters in this great branch of literature, who now lend lustre to the European hemisphere—the extensive erudition of a Ranken—the noble self-reliance and audacious virtue of a Brodie—the elegant style of a Sismondi—and the practical sense of an Egan. In many respects, to be sure, the superiority he displays may be referred to the immense superiority and unapproachable merits of the theme he has chosen. The history of the Cellar of Burgundy is a matter of infinitely more improving nature than that of the House of the same name: a thousand will take profound interest in a dissertation upon the sack and hippocras of the middle ages, for one that will bother his head with the small Italian republics of the same era: We would rather have luminous notions touching the precise nature of the liquor which Sir John Falstaff quaffed, than the secret intrigues which brought Charles the First to the scaffold: and, great as is our respect for Mr. Langan, there is still another claret which possesses claims upon our sympathies, far, far above that which has of late flowed so copiously from his potatoe-trap.[*]
This work, in a word, is fitted to interest and delight, not one class of students, but all. The classical scholar will here find the best of all commentaries on the most delightful passages of those delightful writers, whom he is accustomed to turn over with a daily and a nightly hand: he will speculate upon the flavour that a Nestor loved, and sit in erudite judgment over the *benmost* binns of a Nero. The English antiquarian will enjoy the flood of light that streams upon the joyous pages of Ben Johnson: *verdea* will no longer puzzle the Giffords, nor *Peter-*

[*] John Langan, the Irish pugilist.—M.

sameen be a stumbling-block to the Nareses.* The man of science will analyse the effervescence of Sheeraz; the Physician will hear the masterly defence of Claret against the charge of goutification, and return humanized to the exercises of his calling: the ecclesiastical historian will mourn with Dr. Henderson over the injuries done to the Medoc and the Cote d'or by the suppression of the monastic establishments of France: the lover of light reading will find the charms of romance united with the truth and dignity of history: The saint will have no lack of sighing, as he glances his grave eye over the records of human debauchery, and at the same time, he may, in passing, pick up a hint or two that will be of use at the next dinner of the African Association: The conscious wine-merchant will read and tremble: and every good fellow, from George the Fourth down to Michael Angelo the Second,† will read and rejoice.

It was in England only, and perhaps in this age of England, that a work of this complete and satisfactory description could have been prepared. We produce no wines, and we are the great consumers of all the best wines of the globe. We are free from the violent prejudices, therefore, which induce the man of the Marne to turn up his nose at the flask of him of the Loire, and *vice versa*. We look down as from a higher and a calmer region, upon all the noisy controversies about the rival claims of the Lyonnais and the Bordelais, the Mayne and the Rheingau. We can do equal justice to the sweets of Malaga and Rousillon, and despise the narrow-minded bigotry which sets up either Madeira or Sherry at the expense of the other's ancestral stimulancy.

In former days, indeed, we partook, however absurdly, in the paltry prejudices which we now spurn with our heels. Time was when we were all for the Cypress—time was also when we were all for the Xeres grape—time was when little or nothing would go down with us but Hockamore—and time was when even Rhedycina's learned bowers resounded to strains not simply laudative of Oporto, but vituperative and vilipensive of Bourdeaux.

* The Pedro-Ximenes is the name of the best Malaga grape.—M. OD.
† Michael Angelo Taylor, M. P. for Durham, who kept open table, during the Parliamentary session, for his Whig associates.—M.

We have outlived these follies. We are now completely of the liberal school of winebibbing: our grandsire's dumpy black bottle of sherry leaves the vicinity of the oven, and stands in friendly juxta-position with the long-necker of five year old *demi-mousseux*, and the doubly-iced juice of Schloss-Johannisberg that has been buried in the cave of caves ever since the great era of The Reformation. The native of the Alto-Douro is contented to precede him of Gironne, as some sturdy pioneer trudges in proud solemnity before the march of a battalion of Voltigeurs. The *coup-de milieu* of Constantia or Frontignac forms an agreeable link between the Sillery, which has washed down the venison, and the Hock, which is to add pungency to the partridge-pie. We take Chambertin to the omelet, and Sauterne to the tart. In a word, we do justice to the boundless munificence of nature, and see no more harm in imbibing white wine and red wine, dry wine and sweet wine, still wine and sparkling wine, during the same repast, than we would in doing homage within the same fortnight to the ripe luxuries of a Ronzi de Begnis, the airy graces of a Mercandotti, the vigorous charms of a Vestris, and the meek modest radiance of a Maria Tree.[*] This speaks the spirit of the same unfettered age that can love a Virgil as well as worship a Homer; that places the bust of a Dante beside that of a Milton; that binds the laurel on a Hogg — without robbing the brows of a Hesiod — and thirsts for Lord Byron's autobiography without offering to sacrifice for its purchase, either the veracities of a Rock, or the decencies of a Faublas.

On a work such as Blackwood, calculated for extensive and popular circulation, it would ill become an individual like myself to obtrude much matter of a recondite and obscure order, or adapted to the intellectual taste of particular classes of readers only. Allow me, therefore, to pass lightly over the dissertations with which this volume opens, touching the various vintages of the nations of antiquity. In truth, even the genius and erudi-

[*] Ronzi de Begnis, a distinguished vocalist, Mercandotti, a graceful Spanish *danseuse*, who married Mr. Hughes Ball — commonly called "Golden Ball," from his wealth; Eliza Bartolozzi, better known as Madame Vestris, once a lively actress and extremely ill-conducted woman; Maria Tree, (sister of Ellen Tree,) a charming English singer, who left the stage to marry Mr. Bradshaw, afterwards M. P. for Canterbury. — M.

tion of a Henderson have been able to scatter but an imperfect ray over subjects, mantled, as these are, with the shades of a long night of nearly two thousand years' duration. It is still, we must admit, dubious whether the wine that Telemachus drew out of the cellars of his royal father partook more of the nature of port or of sherry. The Homeric epithet of *Black* may mean either the deep hue inalienable from the juice of the purple grape or the fine grave tinge merely which wines that are called *white* acquire, in consequence of being kept for several lustres, whether in glass bottles, according to the modern custom, or in earthern jars, after the manner of the heroic ages. That Nestor, however, drank, during the battle with which the 13th book of the Iliad opens, wine both of a red and of a strong sort, is indisputable. The epithets of αιθοψ and ιουθος are used together in the same line, and their significancy is clear and obvious to the most German capacity. Dido, again, when she gave her first grand dinner to the Trojan prince, appears to have sported something near akin to champagne.

"IMPIGER hausit
SPUMANTEM pateram."

The epithet *impiger* is admirably chosen, since the act is that of swallowing sparkling, or right *mousseux* wine—for a *spumans patera* can hardly be supposed to mean in the mouth of a writer so chaste as Virgil, any thing short of that. He would not have talked of that as *foaming*, which, in point of fact, merely *creamed;* and while the rapidity of quaffing a cup of *foaming* champagne cannot be too great, since the vinous principle of that wine evaporates in a great measure with the effervescence of the gas it embodies, a poet of Virgil's delicate taste would have been careful not to represent Bitias as tumbling down his throat, in that hasty and furious method, a glass of burgundy, or claret, or indeed of any other wine whatever. On the contrary, he would no doubt have pictured this "officer and gentleman" as sucking down his liquor in a quiet, decorous, leisurely, and respectful style, suffering his lips to remain as long as possible in contact with the rim, which had just been honoured by the touch of the imperial beauty. And, indeed, when I look at the passage again, nothing can be more admirable than the strict

cohesion and propriety of all the terms, applied either to what
the Queen, or to what her guest, does.

> "Hic regina gravem gemmis auroque poposcit
> Implevitque mero pateram ....
> Primaque, libato, summo tenus attigit ore —
> Tum Bitiæ dedit increpitans: ille impiger hausit
> Spumantem pateram — et pleno se proluit auro."

Observe the politeness of her Majesty. She merely touched
the cup with the extreme edge of her charming lip; not that
she would not have liked abundantly to take a deeper share, but
that she knew very well her friend would not get the article in
its utmost perfection, unless he caught the foam in its boiling
moments — *summo tenus attigit ore* — and then how does she
hand it to the Trojan? — Why *increpitans* to be sure; in other
words, saying, "Now's your time, my lord — be quick — don't
bother with drinking healths, but off with it — off with it like a
man." This is the true meaning of the *increpitans*. Upon the
impiger we have already commented — and what can be better
than the fine, full close — so satisfactory, so complete, so perfect
— *pleno se proluit auro*. He turned up the cup with so alert a
little finger, that some of the generous foam ran down his beard
— *se proluit*. As to the exact sense of *pleno auro*, I really cannot speak in a decisive style. Does it mean the full golden cup?
or does it rather point to the wine itself — the liquid gold? — the
rich amber-coloured nectar? If this last be the truth of the
the case, then Dido's champagne was not of the Ay sort, which
is almost colourless, but right Sillery, the hue of which is very
nearly the same with that of gold in its virgin state — or perhaps
Vin de la Marechale, which generally has even a deeper tone.
Pink champagne it certainly could not have been, since, whatever might have been the case at a subsequent period of the
entertainment, it is impossible that a lady who had just sat down
should mistake the brightness of the *rosé* for the transparency
and indeed pellucidity of the *doré*.

N. B. — Many people read the works of the classics merely
for the words, the language, the poetry, the eloquence and so
forth. This is highly absurd. Lessons of practical sense and
real wisdom are lurking in every page, if one would but look for

them. And here, for example, the Virgilian narrative of the Carthaginian banquet affords an excellent hint to many worthy persons, who, I hope, will attend to the thing, now that I have fairly pointed it out. Champagne should always be given in a large, a very large glass. Pateræ are out of date, but ale-glasses, or at least tumblers, are to be found in every establishment; and he who gives champagne in a thimble, betrays the soul of a tailor.

But let us get on : I hate the chat of those *beaux-esprits*, who dare to cast out insinuations against the wines that bedewed the lips of the Anacreons and the Horaces. They mixed sea-water with their wine in making it, says one : They put honey in it, cries another : They drank it sorely diluted, grumbles a third : It tasted of pitch and rosin, mutters a fourth. I despise this. When we shall have reared buildings equal to the Parthenon or the Coliseum : when we shall have written poems as sublime as the Iliad, and as elegant as the Pervigilium Veneris : when our statuaries rival the Phidiases and Praxitileses : our historians, the Tacituses and Thucidideses ; our philosophers, the Platos and Aristotles,—(Aristotle, by the way, wrote a History of Wines, which has unfortunately perished, and I heartily wish all his metaphysics had gone instead ;)—when our orators, shall rival the Ciceros and Demostheneses of antiquity, then, and not till then, shall we be entitled to imagine the palates of those great men were less refined than our own. Can any man presume to dream, that Falernian was not every bit as good as Sherry ?—Only think of that picture which Horace has given us of human beatification—

" Seu te in remoto gramine per dies
Festos reclinatum bearis
Interiore notâ Falerni !"——

Do you not see him before you ?—Spread out at full length upon the *remote* herbage, far away from the din of cities, flinging all the hum of men and things a thousand leagues behind him, he devotes not the night, not the afternoon, but the day, the whole of the blessed festival day, to the employment of *making himself happy*—what English circumbendibus can do justice to the nervous and pregnant conciseness of the word *bearis?* — with a flask of Falernian from the deepest recesses of his cellar! — *Interiore notâ Falerni!* and *bearis!* — What words are these? Was this a man that did not possess the right use of his tongue, lips, and larynx? Was this a man upon whom you could have passed off a bottle of vin ordinaire, or mere *tischwein*, as the genuine liquor of Beaune or Rudesheim? No, no; you may depend upon it these people were up to the whole concern just as much as the very best of us. — Think of but these glorious lines of old Hermippus —

> Εστι δε τις οινος ον δη Σαπριαν καλεουσιν
> Ὀυ και απο στοματος, σταμνων ὑπανοιγνυμένων,
> Ὀζει ιων, ὀζει δε ῥοδων, ὀζει δε ὑακινθε
> Ὀσμη θεσπεσιη, κατα παν δ' εχει ὑψιφερες δω,
> Αμβροσια και Νεκταρ ὁμε.

Could any modern extol the divine ethereal aromatic odour of Tokay, or, what in my private opinion is a better thing, Southside's own old Lafitte, in any terms more exquisite than this hoary toper consecrates to his Saprian? What a fine obscurity! — a mingled undefinable perfume "a *heavenly odour* of violets, and hyacinths, and roses, fills, immediately on the opening of the vessel, the whole of the lofty chamber" — ὑψιφερες δω — climbs in one moment to the rafters, and confers the character of Elysium upon the atmosphere — "ambrosia and nectar both together!" Nothing can be finer! Or turn to Seneca, himself, the philosopher, and hear him talking about the preference that ought to be given to a youth of grave disposition over one conspicuous for his gaiety and all-pleasing manners, and illustrating this by the remarks that "wine which tastes hard when new, becomes delightful by age, while that which pleases in the wood never proves of durable excellence."* Could Mr. Albert Cay or Mr. Samuel Anderson† talk in a more knowing vein upon this subject than the tutor of Nero the Matricide? No — meo periculo, answer *no!* These folks drank their champagne when it was young, and their sherry when it was old, just as we do — they quaffed their Rozan, Sir, from the tap, and bottled their Chateau Margoux in magnum bonums.

* Epist. 36.
† Cay and Anderson, eminent wine-merchants in Edinburgh thirty years ago. — M.

The wines of these glorious days having, it is but too apparent, followed the fate of the poetry, rhetoric, sculpture, and architecture of those who consumed them in commendable quantity, and with blameless *gusto*—the semi-barbarous possessors of the European soil were constrained to make the best of it they could. They gradually, as the Scotch philosophers say, *would* improve in the manufacture; and, by the time of Charlemagne, and our own immortal Alfred, it appears not unlikely that a considerable portion of really excellent wines existed in the Western hemisphere. The monks were the great promoters of the science:—Successively spreading themselves from Italy to the remotest regions of Europe, these sacred swarms carried with them, wherever they went, the relish which their juvenile lips had imbibed for something stronger than mead, and more tasty than beer. Wherever the plant would grow, it was reared beneath their fatherly hands, and to them, as Dr. Henderson has most convincingly manifested, the primest vineyards of the Bordelais, the Lyonnais, and the Rhinegau, owe their origin. Unsanctified fingers, it is, alas! true, now gather the roseate clusters of THE HERMITAGE, yet the name still speaks—*stat nominis umbra*—and the memory of the Sçavants of the Cloister lingers in like manner in *Clos-Vogeot*, *Clos*-du-Tart, *Clos* St. Jean, *Clos* Morjot, and all the other compounds of that interesting family. —The Bacchus of modern mythology ought uniformly to sport the cucullus,

"And I do think that I could drink
With him that wears a hood."

I have already hinted, that the taste of our own ancestors, in regard to wine, underwent many and very remarkable mutations: and this is precisely one of the subjects which my jolly little Aberdonian M.D. has treated in a most felicitous manner.

Claret became the standing liquor at the Restoration, and continued so until the abominable Methuen treaty gave those shameful advantages to the Portuguese growers, by which their pockets are to this hour enriched, and our stomachs crucified. Since the peace, however, a visible increase in the consumption of French wine has taken place; and it may at this day be safely stated, that the man, generally speaking, who sported *good* port in

1812, sports good claret in 1824. Still a fine field remains for the patriotic exertions of Canning, Huskisson, and Robinson. And if any body, out of a shovel-hat, drinks port habitually in 1834, these statesmen will have done less for their native land than I at present auspicate, from the known liberality, good taste, &c. &c. &c. by which they are, one and all of them, so egregiously distinguished. Let no filthy, dirty notions of conciliation condemn much longer the guts of the middle orders — the real strength of the nation — to be deluged diurnally with the hot and corrosive liquor of Portugal — the produce of grapes grown by slaves and corrupted by knaves — while, by a slight alteration of the British code, every rector, vicar, and smallish-landed proprietor in England, might easily be enabled to paint his nose of a more delicate ruby, by cultivating an affectionate and familiar intimacy with the blood of the Bordelais.

But enough of all this. It is a truly distressing thing to me, and I am sure every right-feeling mind will go along with me in what I say, to observe the awful ignorance which most men make manifest whenever the different branches of oinological science happen to be tabled in the common course of Christian conversation. I speak of men in other respects estimable. I allow the full meed of applause to their virtues, personal, domestic, civic, and political; — but is it, or is it not, the fact, that they scarcely seem to be aware of the difference between Lafitte and Latour? — while, as for being in a condition to distinguish Johannisberg from Steinwein, or Hockheimer from Rudesheimer — the very idea of it is ridiculous. I earnestly recommend to those who are sensible of their own culpable deficiencies in these branches of information, or rather indeed I should say, of common education, to remain no longer in their present Cimmerianism; and the plan I would humbly propose for their adoption is a very simple one. Buy this work of Dr. Henderson's, and do not read through, but drink through it. Make it your business, after coming to the page at which he commences his discussion of the wines now in daily use among the well-bred classes of the community, — make it your business to taste, deliberately and carefully, at least one genuine sample of each wine the doctor mentions. Go through a regular course of claret and burgundy in particular. Lay the foundations of a real thorough-knowledge of the Rhine-wines. Make yourself intimately acquainted with the different flavours of the dry wines of Dauphiny and the sweet wines of Languedoc. Get home some genuine unadulterated Alto Douro, and compare that diligently and closely with the stuff which they sell you under the name of port. Compare the real Sercial which has been at China, with the ordinary *truck* or *barter Madeira*, and let the everyday *Sherry* be brought into immediate contact with the genuine *vino catholico* of Xeres. Study this with unremitting attention and sedulity for a few years, and depend upon it, that, at the end of your apprenticeship, you will look back with feelings, not of contempt merely, but of horror and disgust, upon the state in which you have so long suffered many of your noblest powers and faculties to slumber, or at least to doze.

I cannot sufficiently expatiate upon the absolute necessity of this in the course of a periodical paper, such as the present. Let it be impressed upon your minds—let it be instilled into your children—that he who drinks beer, ought to understand beer, and that he who quaffs the generous juice of the grape, ought to be skilled in its various qualities and properties. That man is despicable who, pretending to sport *vin de Bourdeaux*, gives you, under the absurd denomination of claret, a base mixture of what may be called Medoc smallbeer, and Palus, and Stum wine, and Alicant, and Benicarlo, and perhaps Hermitage, if not brandy—*poison*, for which he pays, it is probable, three shillings a-bottle more than he would do if he placed upon his board in its stead the genuine uncontaminated liquid ruby of the Bordelais. I want words to express my contempt for him whose highly powdered and white-waistcoated butler puts down *vin de Fimes*, that is to say, the worst white Champagne, stained with elderberries and cream of tartar, when the call is for Clos St. Thiery, or Ay—wines tinged with the roseate hues of sunset by the direct influence of Phœbus. If you cannot afford claret, give port; if you cannot afford port, give beer—The only indispensable rules are two in number: Give the article you profess to give, genuine, pure, and excellent;

and give it freely, liberally, in full overflowing abundance and profusion.

Farewell, for the present, to the great historian of Wine. I seriously, and to the exclusion of all puffery and balaam, consider his book as an honour to him — to Aberdeen, which nursed his youth — to Edinburgh, which gave him his well-merited degree — and to London, which has enjoyed the countenance of his manhood — and as a great gift to the public at large, destined, I fondly hope, to profit widely and deeply by the diffusion of his udious labours. Two centuries ago, Lord Bacon declared that a good history of wine was among the grand desiderata of literature: Such it has ever since continued to be; but proud and consolatory is the reflection, that we are the contemporaries of a Henderson, and that such it can never again be esteemed, unless, indeed, some awful world-shaking revolution shall peradventure pass once more over the races of mankind, and bury the bright and buoyant splendours of Champagne, the balmy glutinous mellow glories of Burgundy, the elastic never-cloying luxury of Claret, the pungent blessedness of Hock, and the rich racy smack of the mother of Sherry, beneath the same dark and impenetrable shades which now invest the favourite beverages of the *prima virorum*.

"The Massic, Setine, and renowned Falerne."

It will strike every one as odd, that I should have gone through an article of this length without once alluding to the very existence of — PUNCH. Reader, the fault is not Dr. Henderson's — no, nor is it mine. The fact is, that punch-drinking and wine-drinking are two entirely different sciences, and that while, in regard to the latter, Dr. Henderson has written a book, and I a review of it in Blackwood, it seems by no manner of means improbable that, as touching the other, we may be destined to exchange these rôles — I to compose the history of that most imperial of all fluids,* and he, if it so pleases him, to comment upon my labours in the pages of

"My Grandmother's review — the British."

---

* Maginn's history of Whiskey-punch — "the most imperial of all fluids" — never went farther than this announcement. — M.

My work will probably be rather a shorter one than the Doctor's. Say what we will about the other arts and sciences, it must at least be admitted that there are three things whereon, and appropriately, the moderns do most illustriously vaunt themselves, and whereof the godlike men of Old were utterly ignorant and inexperienced. I allude to gunpowder, the press, and the punchbowl, the three best and most efficient instruments, in so far as my limited faculties enable me to form an opinion, for the destruction of the three worst and most disgusting of our annoyances in this sublunary sphere—I mean Duns—Whigs—and Blue Devils: Wishing to which trio every thing that is their due, and every thing that is stomachic, invigorative, stimulant, and delightful to yourself, I remain, dear Mr. North, your humble and obliged servant, and affectionate friend,

M. ODOHERTY.

Eltrive Lake, July 4th, 1824.

Parody on Wordsworth.*

My heart leaps up when I behold
　A bailiff in the street:
'Twas so since from one first I ran;
'Twas so even in the Isle of Man;
'Twill be so even in Newgate's hold,
　Or in the Fleet!
A trap is hateful to a man!
And my whole course in life shall be
Bent against them in just antipathy!

---

* This, given as an Extract from " Poems of the Apprehension," appeared in the *Literary Gazette.*—M.

A Traveller's Week.*

DOVER.

MONDAY.— Roused out of a dreary dose — the fruits of last night's surfeit of tough mutton and brandy port — by the waiter, with the intelligence that the Steam-boat was *just* going off.— Started from bed, in an agony of nervous hurry — Put a *posse* of porters, waiters, and chambermaids, in requisition to bundle me off. — Rushed down to the pier, with the whole clan at my heels, and every eye in the town turned on my flight — reached the shore *time enough* to see the packet under easy sail. — Paid half the passage for a boat to take me five hundred yards, and was at last trundled on board unshaved and half-dressed, "unanointed and unaneled," to cool my *pores* in a raw, foggy breeze.

The deck crowded with spruce Londoners and their *ladies*, feathered and flounced for a water-party.——Chagrined to the soul, and attempting to get rid of my discomfort by contempt of the whole set. Took out my pencil, and attempted a caricature — sketched an alderman and a half-pay officer in strong dispute on the National debt — fine contrast of figure, pursy pride, and meagre pertinacity; fat, contented ignorance, and ignorance neither the one nor the other — turtle beside ration soup. The Prior and the Laybrother in the Duenna; Lambert and Romeo's seller of mandragora. — Weather delightful. — Sea smooth as my lady's mirror. — Wondered that I had not been bred to the navy. — Began to think of a course of voyages for the next dozen years. — Undetermined whether to commence with the east or the west, Botany Bay or Buenos-Ayres, China or Chili — determined on China as the longest voyage. Reprobated the folly of looking for the north-west passage, as tending to shorten the indulgence of living on shipboard. — Waited half an hour for passengers — Cursed, in the fervour of my delight,

* This Sketch which was published in *Blackwood*, for September, 1823, is chiefly noticeable for its rapidity of incident, concentration of expression, and constant interweaving of personal and political allusions into the mere narrative.—M.

the wretched habit of lingering till the last moment—and resolved in future to rise with the sun.—Dover Castle magnificent—tints of time, silvery lights, verdurous clothing; heard a Cockney compare it to an old woman wrapped up in a rug. Cast a look at the fellow that ought to have annihilated him. The Castle certainly not unlike an old woman, after all. Resumed my caricature, and put the Cockney into the group.

* * * * * *

Completely at sea—the Castle sinking—a breeze—pearly fringe in the surge—groans from below, with frequent calls for the steward. Determined *not* to be sick. Saw several of the dead and wounded brought up for fresh air, and several of the living suddenly plunged into the cabin.—Those detestable steam-vessels roll worse than a sailing boat—they *bore* the surge instead of sliding over it—a heavy sea—postponed my caricature—doubted whether a peculiar native configuration of stomach, a something differing from that of a being born to live on land, as much as webbed feet are from human toes, a sort of amphibious or fishy interior, is not to be found on dissection in every "able seaman."

Surrounded by sufferers drooping over the sides of the vessel like fowls in a coop—endeavoured to hum a song of Dibdin's—confounded nonsense, a sea song under *any* circumstances—as well dance quadrilles in an hospital—dare not look at the deck, nor at the sky, nor at the water. Determined to go to China by land—more variety of scenery, Tartary, the *Great Wall*, &c.—shun *Euxines* and *Caspians*—and wait till *Wolgas* and *Dniepers* were frozen over.—A merciless brute ordered his lunch close at my side—ham, brandy, and biscuit—a meal for Alecto, Megæra, and Tisiphone—How the devil can any body think of eating or enjoyment on board a packet? The ship tossing and jumping from side to side like an unbroke horse—desperately sick—torture—red-hot grappling irons—cantharides-soup, &c.

DIEPPE.

THE port in sight—windmills sprawling like gigantic spiders—churchspires with saints impaled upon their tops—yellow roofs spreading below them, ragged and dingy, like a gipsy's encampment—all squalidness, stench, and clamour.

Flung up on the pier, roped into an enclosure like negroes at market—to prevent intercourse with the native smugglers. Surrounded and surveyed in all our abomination by all the loungers of the place, in full dress and high merriment—marched under the yoke to the Custom-house to be searched for lace, veils, ribbons, &c.—A battle with a virago to prevent my valise from being clawed away under pretence of porterage.—The Custom-house—the whole party passed deliberately under the seculra arm—every cranny of my costume keenly probed by a veteran official, who must have been bred a thief. Surprise expressed at my pocket-handkerchief—which was handed up to the *Chef de Douane*, to ascertain its use—a family arrested for having a pair of salt-spoons in their baggage—supposed a cover for conspiracy—nothing of the kind having been seen in France before—passports demanded—mine forgotten in my hurry at Dover—ordered under *surveillance*—marched to a hotel by a gendarme—the crowd honouring me with an escort—and the appellations of " *Traitre! —Monstre! —Coquin-Anglais,*" &c.

Too sick to dress—determined on seclusion and books for the day—looked over the bill of fare—a bill of mortality—bile and indigestion under a hundred shapes—puzzled with vapid superfluity—left the choice to the waiter—fell into a dose, with my elbows on the table—roused by the coming in of dinner—felt stiff, cold, benumbed from head to foot—the solitary lord of a dozen dishes, that might have been so many compilations of boiled cats and ass skin—no appetite—the soup hot water and horse-beans—the fowl tough, rancid, and impregnable—the parsley and butter hemlock and oil—the tarts lard, saw-dust, and blackberries—the parmesan granite and sand-stone—the fruits green and griping—the wine last year's vinegar.—" Bah! *La cuisine Française.*"—Went to bed—bed and blankets a bale of horse-hair, covered with sheep-skin—lay down in submission to my fate, and prepared for suffocation.—Arrival of the Paris diligence—every quadruped and biped in the house and the street in sudden commotion—sleep impossible—sprang out of bed on the stone-floor—chilled as if I had jumped into a cold bath — shivering from head to foot — slunk into bed again, and tried to recover my dose. — The diligence going off — another uproar of dogs, waiters, chambermaids, donkeys, passengers clamouring for drams and great-coats, &c. — The diligence moving off with the heave and rattle of an earthquake — Feverish and restless — incapable of sleep; and fretting myself still more by the miserable old-woman tricks for alluring it — counting a thousand, humming some air hackneyed by boarding-schools and barrel-organs — recounting the signs of the inns — repeating one of Sir J.'s stories,* &c. — Morning — the sun rising — frowsy as a Frenchwoman before breakfast — dropped into a dose — haunted by recollections of the voyage — sea-sickness, Custom-house officers, Cockneys, and conger-eels, rushing round my defenceless head in full cry, mouthing, and moving on wings, fins, and claws — "Griffons dire." — Wake late in the day — hot, cold, comfortless, irritable in every pore — attempted to scold the waiter for breakfast in his own tongue — miserable work — the man obsequious; but frequently adjourning outside the door to laugh. — Called for the newspapers — French too small — contains nothing — English, a huge hotch-potch, a mass of heavy absurdities — politics and pomade; reviewing and robbery; Parliamentary debates and Doctor Solomon;† — jokes from Joe Millar; and wit, honesty, and patriotism, from the Whigs — Threw it away in disgust — Liberty of the press — liberty of nonsense! The size of an English newspaper, like the size of St. Luke's, a monstrous libel on the common sense of the nation.

Overhauled my valise — my best suit utterly undone — saturated with sea-water, that has dyed the "blue one red," and more or less incarnadined every inch of my wardrobe — Sent for a scourer, tailor, laundress, &c. — all lingering till I lost the fragment that remained of the day, and all coming together — inhuman confusion of tongues — headach — sent for a doctor — was visited by a spruce practitioner in Brutus' head, a rose-

* Sir James Macintosh.—M.
† Inventor of a quack medicine called: "Solomon's Balm of Gilead." It was *eau de vie*, neatly sweetened and spiced — a dram in disguise, in fact — and the Doctor realized a large fortune by its sale.—M.

coloured coat, a pair of white gloves, and smelling all over of
jonquille, attar, and other sickening and overpowering essences
— gave myself up to be drenched with raisin ptisannes and
rhubarb soup — prohibited to eat or drink — called for a book
— one brought after vexatious delay, and the exhaustion of all
my French in the entreaty — that one the French Calendar for
the year, containing the titles of the reigning family at full
length, with their ancestry from Pharamond — Dragged over its
pages — wondered what folly could induce a man of any brains
to quit his fireside for foreign noise, solitude, dirt, and discomfort. — Roused by a thunder of the Cathedral bells, followed by
all the minor *cloches* of the town, — hoped that there was a general insurrection, or general conflagration, — thrust my head out
of the window — those cursed casements, that one can scarcely
open, and can never shut; — the night bitter as a blast from an
ice-house — a spout over my head suddenly let loose, and playing away like a fountain, — a dozen lights twinkling down the
street — lamps in a sepulchre — whips cracking, dogs baying,
postilions *sacre-dieuing*. His Serene Highness — die *Furst* —
of some German village, was entering the gates of this fortunate
town, and was coming to honour this still more fortunate hotel
with his presence. — I determined to quit my lodgings by daybreak.

TUESDAY. — Winter in all "its virgin fancies;" wind, cold,
fog, and rain — Chained to the house — A fete — The bells dis-
charging regular volleys throughout the day — All the waiters
occupied, either in attending his Serene Highness, or in looking
at those who did — The hope of breakfast consequently "a hope
deferred" — At length succeeded in tearing down my bell-cord
— No resource but to roar from the stairs, in the midst of a rush
of moist, penetrating air, that might have turned a mill — Fortunate enough, when in the extremity of famine, to rouse the
attention of one of the subordinate monsters of the kitchen, a
"fat, foolish scullion," directly transferred from Mr. Shandy's
scullery — My breakfast administered by this naked-legged
Hebe, a moving heap of rags and repulsion of every kind. —
Weather thickening — called for my bill — astonished by its ex-
action — resolved the sooner to escape its authors — sallied out

plunged, in a state of desperation, into the storm that seemed
to come from all points of the compass at once, a regular *typhoon*
—Succeeded at length in forcing an entrance into a *logement
meuble*, a dreary, disconsolate receptacle; but no other resource
—My baggage conveyed piecemeal, from the sudden avidity of
the whole household of the hotel to serve me—had every grin-
ning and grimacing soul of them to get rid of by a separate *dou-
ceur*, in consequence—shut them all out at length, and myself
in—Ordered a fire; wood incombustible—laboured at the bellows myself for an hour or two, with no other effect than that
of blistering my hands and embittering my remorse at having
left the land of coal-fires and comfort.—Night—Asked for a book
—But one in the house—The French Calendar!—Wished, in
the spirit of vexation and Nero, that all the copies had been in
that one, that I might have flung it into the fire. Read it over,
notwithstanding, through mere weariness—beginning at the end
for the sake of novelty.—Poked, blew, and fretted till bed-
time.—Resolved never to get up again, *till* I returned to England. *Bulls* the natural language of eloquent minds under
strong circumstances.

Wednesday.—Woke before dawn—Weather decidedly fixed
—a July winter; made up my mind for silence and sufferance.
The market opening within a yard of my window—a rolling
of carts from day-break, succeeded by a perpetual explosion of
voices, fierce with all the barbarous dialects of Normandy. A
Basbreton, with the throat of a speaking trumpet, opening shop
under my nose, and hailing for custom.

Spent the day in revolving from window to window—looking
for the sun among clouds thick as "the blanket of the dark;"
playing with a kitten that honoured me with a visit; reading
the *non*-entity of a French paper; practising at push-pin—Invented a new and infallible *push*. Measuring the dimensions of
the chamber from side to side, end to end, circularly, diagonally
—with diligent feet—Taking up the French Calendar!!—
nothing new any longer discoverable.—Ringing a dozen times
for the English papers, letters, &c.; at last informed that it was
not post-day. Went through the whole of the wretched re-
sources for the aimgeance—abandoned all hope. Saw the mar-

ket-place even deserted — missed its noise, and wished for its mob back again.

Probing every cupboard in the room — found an old flute — overjoyed — commenced regular practice — the instrument cracked from stem to stern — toiled away, however, and completed "God save the King," at the expense of nearly blowing out my lungs. — Conscious that this pleasure could not be continued but with the certainty of sudden death, sat down exhausted — fell asleep in my chair — awoke, after a long and wretched interval, crushed and chilled all over — the lamp gone out, the fire gone out, the waiters gone to bed — the principle of life extinct around me. — Crept to my couch, and shivered into morn.

THURSDAY. — A burst of sunshine. All the world in the streets. Engulphed in a whirlpool of English — all telling me and each other that it *was* sunshine. A multitude of nondescripts, half Bond-Street, and half Whitechapel — *Mulier formosa superne in atrum — desinens*, &c., flooding every street, and rolling down the refuse of London, like the stream of a *Cloaca maxima* to the sea-shore.

The Pier! the favourite place of display — a narrow neck of rough stone, infested by the low-water smells, fragments of crabs, cray-fish, and usual nameless and horrible *exuviæ* of a French town.

The male loungers affecting the combined air of the East and West — the slang of the city with the dress of May Fair. The women, attired loose as Venus rising from the waters, and compensating for the display of their persons by their deformity. Sick of the eternal sound of the English *patois*, — followed a French nymphlike form, in close conversation with an old Chevalier de St. Louis — spurred into full speed to get a view of her face — walked myself out of breath, and succeeded. Saw the jaws of my old Parisian friend, the Marchioness of Passetemps, a *septuagenaire*, who introduced me to the Chevalier, her *son!* Determined to trust the physiognomy of a French woman's *back* no more.

Roused from my contemplations by a dash of rain. — The whole promenade put to the rout on the instant, French and English — rushing back, horse, foot, and artillery, draggled and bedevilled, to their lodgings.—Cursed La Belle France, and engaged my place in the first steam-packet that was to boil away from this land of disappointment and deluge.

Friday.—Mail arrived.—A letter from my wife, telling me that London was basking in serenity and the perpetual sun; that the whole family had caught the typhus, and that I must not return till farther orders. No letter from my banker—despondingly shook the half-dozen sovereigns lingering in my purse, and thought of the alternative of flight or famine. Went to the library—all the newspapers engaged ten deep—Lord E. reading three at a time—Sir J. with one under his arm, and the other in his paw—Alderman S. grasping the only remaining one—commenting on it as he stumbled from paragraph to paragraph, and at last hitching in a desertation on the new loan. —Mixed in an expectant group.—Bewildered with the jargon of coffee-house politicians, all contradictory, and all commonplace—the ministry strong—the ministry weak—Lord Grey retiring to La Trappe, under a vow of taciturnity for life—his head already half shaved.—Lord Holland forbidden the use of pen, ink, and paper—War certain—war impossible—Captain Guyon a goose, Captain Guyon a hero;—frowned on by Croker, and supposed to have gone to Chili;—kissed by Croker on both cheeks, and dancing a *fandango* at Almack's.—Tired to death, and retreating to the door for fresh air, and a cessation of tongues.

Still haunted by the echo, and overhearing the nonsense, quilted in such patches and fragments as these—" Nothing more about the King of Spain—A poor devil of a pickpocket dragged about and ducked within an inch of his life by a rascally mob of—Placemen and Pensioners crying out—Candle-ends and cheese-parings, the ruin of official honesty, and—Lord George gone to Portugal, to fight the French, with a d—d bad poem as ever was printed by—Murray—the family name of the great Lord Mansfield, and—The man with the nose, who broods somewhere about—Hampstead, a favourite haunt of the Cockney rhymesters—Petty larceny rogues, stealing lines from laundresses, and hazarding their—Sheep's brains, ten pounds of fat each, fit to be swallowed—only by a Hottentot—Embassador to the Pope, as great a novelty as — Plunkett's conscience pitted against his place. — No fight whatever, after all! a miserable draw — The tight Irish lad — Humbug and hodge podge — Old and dry as my grandmother, not a word of sense, nor a grain of honesty in the whole compilation of — The Common Council. — Why, what the deuce more can men do? they — Eat the best turtle and drink the best claret at any — Cathedral in the kingdom — Crowded with — The most magnificent old wigs, gowns, bands of broomsticks, and other remnants of — The Levee — a gathering of — Antiquated pictures, black as Beelzebub with varnish, and beyond all vamping; no character in their countenances, nor — Anywhere else, the absurdity might have passed; but to burst out with a song of that kind at the — Bishop of London's table, full of dignitaries, grave as — George Selvyn, Joe Millar, and Jack Bannister, and Monsieur Alexandre, dressed up as dowagers in — The Queen's business, the most generous and striking display of — English boobyism, blindness, and gullibility, since the — Birth of Whiggery — an *Incubus* generated in a Scotch garret, and then transmitted at the — Instigation of the devil, and without having the fear of God before — The Edinburgh Review, a great — Molehill, my dear sir, and nothing but a molehill; — a blind — Borough, rotten to the core — the receptacle of — Every species of vermin killed by — Quarterly instalments, paid under the head of — Gifford, Southey, and Co., a younger firm, but sure as — Any team of asses from Mount Jura to — Mount Charles, a showy young — Lord *Seven's the Main;* certain to win — just bought the — Hotel, most fashionable situation in the metropolis — To be fitted up in the handsomest style for the accommodation of ladies whose situation requires a temporary retirement — And the Duchess of R——d* — decidedly the most showy figure at Almack's, a brilliant, blooming — Maiden-ray of the largest dimensions, that would turn the — Peristaltic region of — Alderman Curtis, that fine, jovial, old — Turtle, cooing like — Lord and Lady Westmeath,† and — Several other married persons of distinction at

* Duchess of Rutland, — who had been a beauty. — M.
† This noble pair had just commenced the law-quarrel which is not yet finished. — M.

this moment in — Doctors' Commons — a perpetual — Libel on
English decency and the connubial — Tie of Lord Ellenborough's cravat a — Phenomenon of the first magnitude, and unequalled by anything but — Lord Petersham's whiskers; remarkable for — Specimens of red hair turned blue by the use
of the Macassar oil and — Bishop Magee's conciliatory charge
to the Papists; a splendid, powerful, and original — Contrivance
for tearing up pavements, and converting them into missiles for
the annoyance of — Coach-panes and window-glass of the ordinary size shivered as by the explosion of — Bitter ballads sung
out of tune by breechless mendicants at the — Irish Viceregal
dinner, a formal affair, in which etiquette supplied the place
of hospitality, and Attorney-Generals and Court-Chaplains, are
reckoned for gentlemen with other — Curiosities too numerous
to mention; all for sale without reserve — A portrait of the
Vice-Chancellor, as a Newmarket jockey at full speed — The
Master of the Rolls lying on his back, and making his bread
fast asleep — A dinner at Brooks' a close representation of the
— Beggars' Opera, a mischievous display of impudence, insolence, and roguery, triumphant — Law, a name perfectly unsuited to the authors of Marriage Acts, and similar anomalies
of the human — Calves'head hashes, that are carried about on
— Two legs and upright, a preposterous contradiction of that
law of nature, which ordained that all the species should run on
four paws at — Madam Catalani, more tempting than ever, fat,
fair, and forty; her countenance noble, her voice delicious as the
pipe of — Charles Wynne, turning tail on the Opposition, for
the good of — Himself and family, just arrived in Downing
Street, after a long tour on — Welsh goats followed by a *mob*
with leeks in their hats, and their hands full of — India bonds
never fallen so low before in — Whitehall market — a show of
decidedly the best fed carcases ever — Killed by Napoleon in
his numerous battles with the — Cabinet Council, distracted by
— Variety of foreign tunes — Spanish marches — Turkish retreats — Russian storm-hymns — French and German snuffs —
confounded things that make an honest man's head ache, — Give
me Irish Blackguard, *alias* Prince's Mixture, sprinkled over
with a little — Harvey sauce, and be hanged to it — Essence of

fungus and earth-worms, duckweed and dandelions, pestilent as a—Speech of the Newcastle Patriot, a compound of radical—Gin and ditch-water, drinkable by none but Cyprians of the lowest brutality, as besotted and riotous as—the Hatton-Garden Orator, or the—Reverend William Bengo Collyer, the Duke of Sussex's chaplain, *Tria juncta in uno.*—Puffing, piety, and pharmacy—Impossible—Calumny," &c. &c. &c.

After dinner, went to the theatre—not a place to be had—a discovery which I made only *after* feeing the box-keeper. Had the pleasure of observing the first three acts through a chink in the door.—The lobby, round and behind me, promenaded as lobbies usually are—An incessant chatter of puppies and their *chere amies*—talking on the silliest possible subjects, in the silliest possible way—The *Decens Venus*, the only absentee of the family—The door burst back, to let out a fainting lady, followed by a stream of heated, feverish, human vapour, deadly as the Simoon.

A battle to succeed to her place—my efforts crowned by conquest, and the loss of half my coat—Fairly seated—Black-hole of Calcutta—play, Macbeth, Frenchified by Ducis, and played, *comme il plaisait a la Vierge*—Herod out-Heroded—Macbeth murdered as thoroughly and as early as Duncan—Banquo doubling the old king; and Lady Macbeth bewitching us as Hecate.—Song, scenery, and acting, worthy of each other, and of an English barn—the company a *pendant* to the malefactors of Sadlers' Wells and the Surrey theatre.—Hurried out before the catastrophe.—Resolved never to repeat the experiment, *quamdiu vixere*, &c.

SATURDAY.—Startled by the roar of cannon—another fete, the St. Louis—the whole population in a bustle, singing, scampering, and screaming.

Drums in every quarter rattling to the parade in the Market-place—under my window too—in the proportion of four drums to three men—the *batterie* incessant and intolerable—Closed up my casements—hung towels and tablecloths against every aperture—*All* in vain—unluckily my ears still unplugged—no cotton.—

The air ringing with a new thunder of horse-volunteers, gensdarmes, civic authorities, &c., trumpeted, drummed, and *bel-*

led, to High Mass—Discharge of cannon—merciless shouts of fellows with the lungs of buffaloes in full roar.—Resolved on instant escape, and went to obtain my passport.—Every soul abroad—the office closed.

Induced in an evil hour to take a ticket for the ball, under pompous promises that it was to be the *ne plus ultra* of taste, novelty, and magnificence, *tout a fait Français*, &c.

Considered my ways and means for killing the intermediate time.—Had the choice of the *French Calendar*, or a promenade on the pier—variety of wretchedness—Went to the pier—assailed by harbour-smells of every formidable kind—a compound of tar, smoke, dead dogs, and fish-women—the tide coming in, and duly returning the ejections of the town to the shore.

Lingered on the pier—exacerbated by the infinite vapidity of the gabble called conversation round me—Weather talk—the history of last night's rubber—history of the morning—bathe—mutual and solemn assurances, fortified by an appeal to the bystanders, that the tide was coming in, &c.—Every soul round me English—faces whose familiarity haunted me—yet whom I could not possible have seen anywhere but behind band-boxes and counters—the Eastern sperme of *La nation boutiquiere*.

To get rid of them and *ennui*, walked to the waterside, with a faint determination to bathe, for the *first* time. The wind coming at intervals in hot gusts, the water looking surly, and gathering in short angry waves.—Put down my name as a candidate for a bathing-machine—the fiftieth in succession!

Lingered about the shore—gazing like a philosopher on fragments of seaweed, making matter of contemplation out of an untenanted oyster-shell, and diligently inspecting the washing of a poodle by a chambermaid, &c.

Tired of waiting for the machine,—which had a dozen cargoes of girls, matrons, and elderly gentlemen, drawn up rank and file beside it, waiting for the ablution, or the drowning, of the groups stowed within,—tore off my clothes in a fit of desperation, and rushed in "naked, to every blast of scowling Heaven."
—Met by a surge ten feet in advance of the rest, that seemed expressly delegated to carry me out to sea.—My resolution greatly shocked by this unexpected attention;—pondered a

minute or two, half way, immersed like a mermaid—but "returning were as tedious as go on."—Saw the eyes of the whole beach upon me—and rushed "*en avant.*"

A rolling sea—the sky suddenly as black as my hat.— Looked to the shore—men, women, children, and machines, in full gallop to shelter—Tide coming in like a mill race—lifted off my feet—swimming for my life—Thoughts of conger-eels a hundred feet long, swordfish, sharks, &c.—A porpoise lifting up his fishy face at my elbow—Roaring surge—My will unmade—Thought of a Coroner's inquest—Clarence's dream, &c.

Tost on the shore on the back of a mountain of water— bruised, battered, and half-suffocated—not a soul within hail— A remote view of a few stragglers that looked like pilots speculating on a wreck—The sea following from rock to rock, staunch as a blood-hound.

Searching for my clothes—my whole wardrobe hopelessly missing—probably stolen—Pondering on the pleasant contingency of making my entry into the town like a negro, or a plucked fowl—Tide rushing on, with a hideously desolate howl of the wind—Rocks slippery, the higher the ascent, scarped and perpendicular as a wall.

A gleam of joy at seeing my coat scooped out of the crevice of the rock where I had left it, as I ignorantly thought, above the reach of ocean, and sailing towards me—Grasped it like an old friend—flung it over my shoulders, and made my escape— My breeches, shoes, watch, and purse, of course, left to be fished for on the fall of the tide.

Rapid movement towards home—in the midst of the titter of girls, and the execration of matrons, and other "Dii majorum gentium," vehement against what they looked on as my *voluntary* exposure.

As I passed the principal hotel, betted on by a knot of picktooth puppies, who would have it that I was walking for a wager.—The way through the Market-place consequently cleared for me,—and I the universal object of ridicule, surprise, and reprobation, till I rushed within the door of my lodging.

Wearied to death—sick—dirty, and disheartened, flung myself into my bed, and rehearsed in my sleep the whole *spectacle* of the day.

Roused by my landlady, who had found my ticket for the ball on my table.—Informed that it was midnight, and that I had no time to lose—Angry at being disturbed—yet afraid to undergo the work of my sleep again—pondered—cast my eyes on a new suit sent home that evening by the "Tailleur plus magnifique," of the world and Dieppe.—Ought to go to the ball,—it was the first and last opportunity of seeing the true glory of France.—Ought to go to sleep—tired, feverish, and spiritless. —Ought to go to the ball to revive my spirits, and shew the fools and puppies of the place, that I was neither mad nor merry in my morning's promenade.—Sprang out of bed.

At the ball-room door, met half the company coming out— Had to force the breach through a host of insolents, in the shape of footmen, gensdarmes, police-officers, and mendicants.

Breasted my way up-stairs through a descending current of bonnetted, shawled, surtouted, swaddled, nondescript figures, that had once been quadrillers, card-players, pretty women, and prettier men.

My entrance made good at last, the company reduced to a scattering of a couple of dozens, unhappy reliques of the rout, uncouthly toiling down a dance, or loitering along the benches, yawning at each other, in pale despondency; the gentlemen drained to the last civil speech, and the ladies consuming the dregs of the orgeat and lemonade.—Every soul English, bronzed up in turbans that might have frightened the Grand Turk; bedizened in tawdry costumes, imported along with themselves, and made more burlesque by an attempt to ingraft them with French alterations. The young women universally lath, plaster, and chalk; the old ones, London porter, and prize-beef,—absolute Bluebeards.

Tottered home.—My landlady fast asleep;—and defying all the usual expedients of breaking a pane in her bed-chamber— tearing out her bell by the roots—Hallooing till I was hoarse— Every soul in the street poking their night-caps out of the windows, and reviling the *coquin Anglais*—Landlady still unshaken.

Taken up by the gensdarmes for disturbing the neighbourhood, amid surrounding cries of "*Eh, ah! Bah, hah!*" "*Sacre!*" "*Bien fait, bonhomme.*" *Au cachot!*—A sudden population of thieves and *filles de nuit* starting, as if out of the ground, to attend me to the door of my new lodging.—Locked into the *cachot* for the night.

Sunday.—In the Cachot.—The sous-prefect having gone to his country-seat—Unspeakable vexation—Thinking of liberty, and England.

Monday.—The affair explained—Let loose—bounded like a lunatic home—Flung my trunk upon the neck of the first *garçon* I met, and hurried down to the steam-boat.—Boat to move in a quarter of an hour; felt for my watch—clean gone. —A family-repeater that I would not have lost for the whole bourgeoise of Dieppe.—In my vexation, called the town a nest of thieves and knaves.

Called upon by a Frenchman at my side for an explanation of my words—Tried it—He could not comprehend *my* French —Gallic ass—A mob gathered—Cards given—to meet in half an hour.—The steam-boat under way, *I* remaining to be stabbed or shot—My baggage *on board!*

The challenge getting wind.—Bored with inquiries and observations—how it happened?—who it was?—whether with sword or pistols?—whether on the cliffs or in the coffee-room? —a promise that whatever *might* happen, my remains should be taken *care of*.—Congratulations on the extinction of the *Droit d'Aubaine*, &c.

Went to the ground.—No Frenchman forthcoming—Lingered in the neighbourhood till dinner time.

At the tavern, had my cotelette served up by a face that I half recognized—my morning challenger—the head waiter!— Saw a sneer on the fellow's countenance, and kicked him into the street—Indignantly left my dinner untouched, and walked down to the pier, to embark immediately.

No vessel going off—Lounged about till dusk—hungry and chill—Hired an open boat at ten times the price of the packet.

All night at sea—Heavy swell—Not knowing where we were—the Azores, the Bay of Biscay, or Brighton—In distress —Sick to death—the men mutinous, lazy, and despairing.

Picked up by a steam-boat going to Dieppe, with a promise of being discharged into the first homeward vessel.

Letter from a Washerwoman.*

Puddleditch-Corner, Islington, January 30, 1823.

Worshipful Sur,

I'm a lone widder woman, left with five fatherless children to purvide for in a wicked world, where simple folks is shure to be putt upon, as ive larnt to my sorrow; but i'm not one to sit down content, if there's la or gustice to be had above ground. My good man used to say, rest his sole, Patience, you've a sperrit, says he, and so i have, thank God, for what shuld a pore lone widder do without in such a world as this where honnor goes afore honesty. Well, sur, how i comes to rite you these few lines, is this. You must know i'm a washer-woman, an' lives at Islington, and takes in loddgers; but I ant come to that yet; only i must say summut about it, by way of beginnin to let you know how i've got a new loddger; for i takes in single gentlemen; an' i was telling of he, what oudacious treetment id met with from they; he, i would say, the other was as bad as he, as hockipied my apartments last, how i was flammed over tho' i mid a known fine words buttered no passenips, to give em trust, an' let em turn evry thing topsy turvy, so long as it sarved their turn to stay, and then they takes French leave, an' walks off, without paying so much as a brass farden, and what's warse, wi' Nance; but i ant come to that yet. Only, sir, the long and the short's this; i was gust telling of these here purceedins to my new loddger, and how they'd a sarved me, an habsconded,

---

* For the first eight or nine years of *Blackwood*, Hunt, Hazlitt, and Keats, as the head of what was called "The Cockney School of Poetry and Criticisms" were perpetually assailed in its pages. This Letter from a Washerwoman was one of the few contributions, in that line, from Maginn's pen. There is no wit and little humour, even in the best specimens in bad spelling. Winifred Jenkins may be endured and even laaghed at, as one of the earliest in that field of *pseudo* illiteration. "Yellowplush" and "Jeames" fall far beneath. So did Maginn's Washerwoman. But the article is fairly entitled to a place in this collection, as showing to what follies of composition a clever man could descend, and also on account of the parodies on Leigh Hunt's early mannerisms, and love of "Mars, Bacchus, Apollo, Vivorum," with which it concludes. — M.

as the gustice called it, and left nothing to pay my rent, an' all the power o' mischif they'd a done me, with all their outlandish heethen fancies, but a room full of dryd weeds, peeble stones, cracked chalk images, an' bits of crumpled paper, all over blots, an' ritin stuff that no Crisetcun can make head nor tale on. Well, i was a tellin of all my misfortins to Mr. Perkins, who seems a civil, pretty behaved sort of a gentleman, only he's allways att his books and his pen, an' at first i was rather huffed, for he sniggered and sniggered, but it want att me, only at them graceless chapps i was telling about, an' att last he says, says he, when I told him how Gustice Dosy could get me no redress nor cumpinsashun, i tell you what Mrs Lilywhite says he, tell your story to the larned Kristophur North, an maybe hel gif you cumfurt an' cumpinsashun besides. Att first I thot how he was a hummin me, tho he's a grave godly lookin gentleman, not much given to vain talkin an' gestin; butt at last i found he was in downrite earnest, an' thatt you was a friend of his, a sort of a Scotch gustice, an' rites a book every month, an' mite maybe take up the cawse of hingured hinnocence, as we said to the late Queen of blessed memory,[*] and put in mi pittiful story to shame their parjury willains, an' mite moreover make me a hansome present into the bargain, an' he promissd if id rite a letter, hed send it safe to you, and so worshippfull sir, tho' i never heard youre name before i makes bold to tell you how i've been put upon.

Well, sur, you must know then my name is Patience Lilywhite, an' i'm a washerwoman, an' lives att Islington,.at Puddleditch corner, a pretty rural spott, where i letts loddgins to single gentlemen as wants a little country hair and quiett, after the noise an' smoke of Lunnon. Well, sir, the 20th of last July was twelvemouth, i minds the day peticklar, bein that ater the crownashun day,[†] comes a thin spindle shanked gentleman to look at my loddgins, bein, as he said, ordered into the country for change of hair, and shure enuff he looked as yoller as a kite's foot. The rooms seemed to please him mitily, and well they mought; two prettier, pleasanter, more convenienter, a king

[*] Caroline of Brunswick.—M.
[†] George IV. was crowned on July 19, 1821.—M.

need'nt covet, for the parlour winder looks out into our garden, thats very private an' rural, for 'tis parted off by a ditch an' an elder hedge from the backs of the sope manifacktory, an' Mr. Bullock's slawtur-house, so there bent no unpleasant hop-jacks ner it, an't overlookd by nobody. An' the parlor was just fresh painted very illigent, sky-blue in the pannells with yollor moldins; an' the corner cupbord was chock full of illigant chaney, an' id a just bought a spick an' span new gappan tea-tray, an' a spontious hurn, whereof he took peticklar notice, an' axed how much it constrained; and when i told him two gallons, that seemed to settle his mind at once, an' he agreed with me at haff a ginnee a week, little enough of all conshince; but he said how he was a very quiett body, an' shuld give but little trubbel, so i was agreeabel to take him in.—Well, rivrend sir, he comed shure enuff the very next eveenin off wun of the stages, an' brought all his luggadge in his hand, witch was no more than a smaal porkmanky, an' an ould earthen ware crate wi sum chalk himmiges.

He had nothin for supper, but some tea an' bread-and-butter, an' sett up haff the nite, rummadgin about the rooms, an' stickin up they himmiges as comed in the crate, an' sum books, an' bitts of broken stones, an' craked shells, out of the porkmanky, witch was crammed three parts full of sich rubbish, instead of good holland shurts an' warin apparel. Well, i seed there woodnt be many gobbs for me, in my way; but the gentleman seemed quiett an' civill, an' spoke verry goodnatured to the childern, an' i rather bepitteed him, for he seemd in a pore weak way.

Next day, about aternoon, a frind cawled in to see him, a shamblin sort of a chapp, with grate thick lipps, an' littel piggs eyes, an' a puffy unholesum lookin face, as yoller as tother; but he spoke verry soft an' civil too, an' took peticklar notice of Nance, as was mi eldest, an' just turned fifteen. Well, this here wun, i cant never mind his name, for they calld him bi too att wunce, seemed verry thik with my loddger, Mr. Pennyfeather, an' hardly missd a day cummin to see him, to mi sorrow; for i do think 'twas he put sich wild vagarys into tother's head, an' pswaided him at last to run off in mi dett, like a shabbroon as

he was. Youd niver beleeve me, wurshippfull sur, if i was to
tell you haff the goins on of they two rapscallions, an' watt
wurk they maid in mi pore littel garden, an' with mi Nance, but
i ant cum to that yet; the moore foole i, not to cutt em short in
there heethenish doins; but sum how they comed over me wi
thur fine hard words and palaverin spitches, tho i beleeve, o mi
conshince, twant nothing ater all butt a pack of nonsenciccle
jabber. So, sur, you must no, they gott mi leeve to halter or
transmoggrify our bitt of garden, that was a sweet spott they
said, only they wanted to lay it out classy cully. Tho, for my
part, i thot twas classed out rigglar enuff, wi beds of cabbadges
an' iniuns, an' sich like sensibel stuff. To work they fell, an'
routed out all they pore innocent things; an' watt do you think
they sett in the room of em? As im an honest woman, if yule
beleeve me, worshippfull sur, nothing but a pack o rubbitch i
woodnt a piled in mi faggit stakk. Wun blessed day they cums
home loded lik jack asses, wi grate bundels of long scragglin
green bows off the chesnut an' lime trees, an' never beleeve me,
if they didnt stick them up an end all about the garden, in the
room of mi fine guseberri bushes, the rite hairy sort, thatt theyd
grubbd up bi the roots, the moore fowl i to lett em. But they
wanted to convert it into a grove, they sedd. Lord bless ye,
gemmen, says i, why them sticks 'll all be dead in a weak; butt
they only nidged their heads, as mutch as to say, i spose weel
be off bi that time. An so when they bows was stuck about
like pee-sticks, they brings a parsel of daysys, nothin but common field daysys, an' primroses, an' gilty cupps, and sich like
trumpery, guodd for nothin weeds, and sets em in all amongst
tothers; an' wenn thatt was done to their minds, whatt maggots
shuld bite next, butt they falls to wurk, nocking up of our ould
piggsty. So then, thinks i, they be gott about some good att
last; for, to be shure, theyre goin to mend itt upp tidy, an'
prapps make mee a present of a fattin pigg, or a pritty littel
chany sow. But no sich things was in their noddels, gud sur.

Furst of all they piled up a sort of a mount, with peat an'
bricks, an' rubbitch, an' rite upon top on it, they setts about
bildin up o the piggsty, as i thot; so says i, "Lawk, gemmen,
how shall wee ever clamber up there wi the piggs vittels; an'

LETTER FROM A WASHERWOMAN. 283

watt for shuld ye perch un upp so hy, pore dumb beestesses."
So they seemd quite huffed. A piggsty, says they. Why,
woman—Mi names Lilywhite, says i.—So, says they, Mrs.
Lilywhite, were recktin a tempel to Pollar.— *Pollards* they must
meen, thinks i, for thatts piggs vittels; so they be goin to by
me one ater all, only they thinks to sprize me : so i wont take
no more notiss. But thatt was all mi innocence. They no more
thot of bildin up mi sty, than i didd of bildin the tempel of Geruz-
leum. Well, they cobbled upp a sort of a queer lookin fore
cornerd shed, and coverd it over wi a round bitt of oil cloth,
paneted wi yoller stripes, all round from the middel, for all the
world like a sunflower ; an' then they made a kind of paath upp
the mount, wi broken briks an' oyster shells, stikin out here an'
thare, to look like rokks, they sedd : an' ater thatt, they stuck
it full of grene lawrel bows, by the same token that Mr. Deppity
Doughnut, of Wellintun Willa, thretened to persecute em for
tarin down all his lawrel heddges. But they didnt care for la
nor gosple, not they.

An next there was a grand confab atwixt em, about makin of
a fowntane ; for witch there didn't seem, to mi thinkin, no manner of need, when there was a good pump, with beautiffull soft
water, not ten steps from our own dore. But a fowntane they
must have ; nothin else would serve em : so they take an' diggs
out the ditch up to the bottum of thatt new fangled mount, an'
damms upp the water, that was nothin but sope sudds an' kennel
stuff ater all, an' then setts it a running thro' a cows horn, as
they beggd of the buttchur, trickel, trickel, trickel over some
pebbel stons an' bitts of broken bottels as theyd strewd along
the bottom of the drain. Then, to sea how they rubbd there
hans, an' chuckeld an' capurd about wen they seed the dirty
water com spurtin out.

For mi part i begun to think they was craasy, butt my yung
wuns likd the sport well enuff, for 'twas summut in thur one
way. Well, then, they seemd to think 'twas all parfict, an 'two
or three more chapps of there one sort comd in, an' they all lade
thur hedds togethur, an' setteld to have a feest at the diddica-
shun of the Tempel, as they cawld it. Most of whatt they
tawkd was Greek to me ; but i prikkd up mi years wen i hurd

of a feest. Mortall pore livin theyd kept since id had to do for em. Mi loddger most times rambbeld away, lord nos were, wen he shuld hav bin enjoyin hisself in my comfurtabel parlor, over a good beef stake or a pork chopp, an' a pott of porter, wereby a body mite a gott sum smaal mattur now an then, in an onest way, for wuns toilin and moilin; butt itts mi belief, he fedd like the varment and the Frinch, upon froggs an' tods, an' ditch sallat. Howsumdever, wen tother cumd, as he did most aternoons, they two stowd in a mortal site of tea an' bread-an'-buttur. Oshuns an' oshuns of tea didd they sett an' swil, to be shure, till i sedd to owr Nance, says i, for sartain theyl go droppsicul.

Well, when i hurd em tawk of a feest, i makes bold to putt in mi ore. "An," says i, "there's sum butifull ducks just fatt in owr coup, and noo grin pees is cum in;" but lawk, they cutt me short in a giffy. "Ducks!" says Mr. Pennyfeather; an' then he runned on sich a pak of stuff, as i could't mak hedd nor tale on, only thatt there was to be no vittels bot, but Nektur an' Hambrowsy, two things i'd never hurd on, only i found out afterwards, them names wus Greak for tea, an' butter an' bread. Furst of awl, they sett about kristenin awl there fine wurks. But sich names they sett em, it's amost a shame for a Krisetcun to tell agen; for they sedd how the mownt was to be cawld Hellycome. Lawk, sur, sich blasphemy wickedness; and the fowntane was Hagganipper. Wat that ment i culdn't tell for sartin, only i nod well enuff 'twas no gud; so i told mi yung uns, if ever i ketched em sayin sich awfull wurds, i'd hang em up hyer than ever bakon was hung.

Then there was a deel of gabberin about Pollar an' Pollar, whoever he was, for i found out bi them 'twas a man's name, no sponsibel parson im sure, summut of a Jack Ketch, most lik, for they tawked about his halter; an' sum sedd that was upon Mownt Parnassus, an' how he oft to bide there; butt att last they agreed he shuld be had down too Hellycome; and then they fixed how that there commicle place a top of the Mownt was to be the Tempel of the Mooses. O Gemminnes! if i didn't think upon thatt, thatt they wer a goin to lugg over thatt ere grate beest as is showed in Lunnon, an' hoist em up for a site to the Islington fokes, att so mutch a hedd; but i culdn't abide the thot on it; so says i, awl in a flurry an' a combustion, "Lord's sake, gemmin!" says i, "wat be ye goin about? you mite as well go for to cram a cow in a coffee-pott, as thatt ere rampagus wild beest upp in thatt poppett-show place." Upon thatt they showted, an' fleerd, an' geerd att me, an' sedd how Mooses was yung ladys, an' how they was goin to hackd a play, and how my Nance, an' Sal, an' littel Hannermarier shuld pessonify the Mooses; only, as there was nine, neether more nor less, there must be six othur gurls to hact the tothers, an' them they soon pickd out. Then mi littel billy begun fur to cry, an' ax why he midn't be a Moose too, as well as the rest, for he was a cute littel feller, an' always foremost when there was anny thing to be larnd; but they passyfide him, and sedd, he shuld be Cubit, an' stan by Nance's side wi' a flambo, an' she was to be cawld Hairy-toe—a fritefull name to my thinking—wun of they Misses—Mooses, i wood say; an' Buttchur Bullocks wench was to be Polly summut, i forget wat; "but howsumdever," says i, "that av gott more of a Krisetcun sound with it, an' the gurls raal name is Mary." I forgets the rest of they heethenish names, fit for none but Turks and Hottenpots; butt there was a fine to do, wen evry thing was gott in order, as they cawled it. 'Twas rare funn to the gurls, and to awl the naburs too, for the mattur of that; and they broke down awl my butifull hedge, wi' clamberrin over to get a peep at the show.

There was owr Nance stuk upp, who butt she, more fool i to wink att sich doins, dressed out, nott in her Sunday gownd an' spenser, and beever hatt an' fethers, thatt she used to be so proud on; butt rolled up for awl the wurld lik a corps in a wite tabel cloth, skiverd together, as if there was no pins to be had, over wun sholder; an' awl mi cabbidge roses, wat i used to save for dryin, an' for to sell for popery's an' sich lik, wus pulld, an' plukkd, and stringd lik a rope of inions round her hedd, instead of a decent cap and top nott. Then they borried Tim Whippy's fiddle for she to hold, tho i told em sheed never larnd a toone; an' little Billy was strippt amost nakid, qwite nakid they wanted im, butt thatt i wasn't to be hargufied into; an' they put a lited link in his hand, an' stuk him up close bi Nance; an' awl the tother wenches wus figgerd up much the same, lik hidols an' himages, more than Kriseteun craturs; and then they strikes out all of a hurry, as how he wi' the two names as comd every day to see my loddger, should hackt Pollar. So they pulls off his shoos and stockins, pure and ragged they was; an' for the matter of thatt, they wanted to do the same bi the girls; but no — "D'ye think," says i, "mi hoffspring shall tramp about, barefoot, like begger-wenches?" Butt they off wi hisn howsumdeever, and strippt down his nekcloth an' shirt collar, and tyed wun of mi aperns round his neck, an' figured his head up wi lawrel bows, till he looked for all the wurld like a Jack in the Greene, only not haff so funny; and then they gave him hold of the ould base vial that theyd got the lone of from our parish clark, Old Mumps, — more sheame he to lend un, for to mi mind 'twas heethen sakerlidge. Well, then, the rest sett up sich a showt, and begun dancin an singin lik propper beddlamites, an' skreechin owt, "Hail, Pollar! Gloryows Pollar! Hail! Hail!"

Lord gif me patience to think o sich hardend wikkedness as cawlin down hail in the very middle of hay harvest, and the deppitys cropps a carryin; but they owd he a gruddge about thretteniu to take the law on em. Then the feest was to begin. "Sich a feest," i says; an' the Mooses was to sarve em wi necktur, meenin nothin else, your honor, then a power o wishy-washy tea thatt was made in owr grate hurn; an' wen i was a going to fetteh owt the best chany cups an' saasurs wi the goold rims, for i liks to see every thing hansom, they axed me if so be i hadn't a got anny antik vessells; an' afor i culd puzzel owt the meenin o that, they goes an' rummages owt sum owld crackd butterbotes, an' squatt bottles, an' empty oil flaskks, an' for wat wuld yur worshipp think? — why to drink tea owt on, ass i'm a livin woman, an' mi name's Patience; becawse, they sedd, the heethen Turks, that mi best cupps an' saasurs wasn't classycull. I don't know what ware that is — not i; but i'll tak mi Bibel othe, mi chany was the best Darby sheer. Well, they swiggd an' sung, an' sung an' swiggd, till he as hacktod Pollar turned ass sik ass a dogg, for hed a bin sukkin out of an oil flaskk, sarvd im rite too; an' i wishd the tother hadd bin ass badd, for turnin up their noses at my best chany. But wurse than thatt was brewin, for owr Bill an' the gurls hadd gott to rompps, an' stuffin of bred an' butter, an' the link as sarved for Cubit's flambo, sett fire to Nance's tabel-cloth, an' she in her frite rund up agen Pollar, so his apern ketched all in a blaaze, an' he tares it off, an' flares it away into the middel of the garden, where mi linnens was hangin on the lines, an' afore you culd say Jack Robbison, it was awl in a conflarashun.

Thatt ever i shuld liv to sea sich ruinn brot upon my honest cawlin, bi sich a pakk of ——; but that wern't the wurst. Well, Nance unskiverd the tabel-cloth sumhow, an' rund away in her flannel dicky. But sum of the other wenches raggs took fire, an' then fine fuzion there was. They put it owt among em, howsomdever, butt not afore the tempel pigoty, i says, ketched awl of a flame, an' the owld rotten postesses blaazed owt lik tutchwood, an' the oil cloth top blowed off rite agen the faggit pile, an' sett fire to thatt too. There was a kettel of fish. I speckted to sea house an' awl burnt to the ground, an awl Islington too, for wat wun culd tell; but the naburs cumb porin in, an' the hengins was brot owt; an' att last, bi the marcy of Heeven, the flames was got under, butt nott till i'd bin dammadged and hinjured, pownds an' pownds.

Well, honnurabel sur, mayhap you taks it for sartain thatt they rantipate chapps as maid awl the misschiff, lended a hand to get it under, for the best amens they culd mak. No sich a thing, yur wurshipp. They sneekt off att the first owtcry, lik cowwardly currs, with there tales betwene there leggs; an' from that ower to thisn—O, worshippfull sur, that such proffelgate villains shuld walk this blessed erth!—i've niver sett eyes upon a muther's sunn of em; an' ass if it wern't enuff to diddel me owt of haff mi subbstance, an' leeve me a ruinated undun widder. they ticed away mi Nance along wi em, tho for the matter o thatt, no feer butt watt she was willin enuff, for they'd turnd her poor foolish hedd among them; an' wun of owr naburs seed her thatt same blissed aternoon, purch'd up, who but she, from top o wun o the Lunnon stages between Pollar an' Mr. Pennyfeather.

So there's the long an' the shortt of mi true story, an' a pittyfull wun it is surely, thof i niver shuld a thot of ritin it to yur worshipp, but for Mr. Perkinses pswasions, an' the considderashuns

he putt into mi hedd; an wun thing that maid me more timmersome abowt trubbelling yur honour, is, thatt it awl happnd so long aggo, an' thatt i heers them parjury willains is gon beyond sees, butt Mr. Perkins says how they be playin off their owld pranks there; and thatt there's no place so far off butt wat yur wurshipps book getts there; an' that mi story oft to be deserted in it, if 'twas only for the porposs of putting pore hinnocent parsons like miself upon their offensive agen the hartfull magnations of them divels in scarlett. Moore over, he devises me to send you they scrapps of writin, ass they left to pay mi rent. To my thinkin, they bant worth rappin up a varden rushlite wi; butt he says, heve gott his reesons for giffin me this device; so i've a pickkd owt the best on em, an' bad they be, not a hole sheat among em. So, hoppin yore wurship will scuse awll fawts, an' tak mi pittyfull case into considderashun, no more at present from   Your wurshipps misfortunate an' obleegin sarvant,
PATIENCE LILYWHITE.

FRAGMENTS.

* * * * * * * *

I NEVER saw a more delightful spot! —
One might have lain there, when the days were hot,
Hours and hours — hark'ning to the sweet singers
Up in the leaves — twiddling one's thumbs and fingers —
Watching the sun-beams in that quiet scenery,
Spangling about the jaunty greenery,
And the small flies and gnats —— that sort called midges,
Bite one confoundedly, raising long ridges
Upon one's skin. —— Oh! it were sweet, most sweet,
As I before said, in the summer heat,
To lie there sprawling flat upon one's back,
Dozing and dreaming of one's —— Zounds! what's that? —
Pshaw! a cockchafers — what was I saying? —
Oh; that would be delicious, thus a laying,
To dream of   * * * * * * * * *

* * * * * * * * *

They were not married by a mutt'ring priest,
With superstitious rites, and senseless words,
Out-snuffled from an old worm-eaten book
In a dark corner (railed off like a sheep-pen,)
Of an old house, that fools do call *a Church!*

Their altar was the flowery lap of earth —
The starry empyreum their vast temple —
Their book, each other's eyes —— and Love himself,
Parson, and Clerk, and Father to the bride! —
Holy espousals! whereat wept with joy
The spirit of the Universe. — In sooth
There was a sort of drizzling rain that day,
For I remember (having left at home
My parapluie, a name than *umbrella*
Far more expressive,) that I stood for shelter
Under an entry not twelve paces off,
(It *might* be ten,) from sheriff Waithman's shop,
For half an hour or more, and there I mused,
(Mine eyes upon the running kennel fixed,
That hurried on a het'rogenous mass
To th' common-sewer, its dark reservoir,)
I mused upon the running stream of *life*.

But that's not much to th' purpose — I was telling
Of those most pure espousals. — Innocent pair!
Ye were not shackled by the vulgar chains
About the yielding mind of credulous youth,
Wound by the nurse and priest, — *your* energies,
Your unsophisticated impulses,
Taught ye to soar above their " settled rules
Of Vice and Virtue."— Fairest creature! He
Whom the world called thy husband, was in truth
Unworthy of thee. — A dull plodding wretch!
With whose ignoble nature, *thy free spirit*
Held no communion. — 'Twas well done, fair creature!
T' assert the independence of a mind
Created — generated I would say —
Free as " that chartered libertine, the air."
Joy to thy chosen partner! — blest exchange!
Work of mysterious sympathy! that drew
Your kindred souls by   *   *   *   *   *   *

           *   *   *   *   *   *   *
Come, and you'll find the muffins hot,
And fragrant tea in the tea-pot,
And she, you know, with the taper fingers,
Shall pour it out for you — Wherefore lingers
My friend so long? where can he be?
Didn't he promise he'd come to tea?
Ah! there's his knock — the very cat knows 'tis —
Now we'll be snug and toast our noses,
Now we   *   *   *   *   *   *   *   *

* * * * * * * * *

There fled the noblest spirit!—the most pure,
Most sublimated essence that e'er dwelt
In earthly tabernacle. Gone thou art,
Exhaled, dissolved, diffused, commingled now
Into and *with* the all-absorbing frame
Of Nature the great mother. Ev'n in life,
While still pent up in flesh and skin, and bones,
My thoughts and feelings like electric flame
Shot through the solid mass, towards their source,
And blended with the general elements,
When thy young star o'er life's horizon hung
Far from its zenith yet, low lagging clouds
(Vapours of earth) obscured its heav'n-born rays—
Dull fogs of prejudice and superstition,
And vulgar decencies begirt thee round;
And thou didst wear awhile th' unholy bonds
Of "holy matrimony!"—and didst vail
Awhile thy lofty spirit to the cheat.—
But reason came—and firm philosophy,
And mild philanthropy, and pointed out
The shame it was—the crying, crushing shame,
To curb within a little paltry pale
The love that over *all* created things
Should be diffusive as the atmosphere.
Then did thy boundless tenderness expand
Over all space—all animated things,
And things inanimate. Thou hadst a heart,
A ready tear for *all*—The dying whale,
Stranded and gasping—ripped up for his blubber,
By Man, the tyrant—The small sucking pig
Slain for his riot—The down-trampled flower,
Crushed by his cruel foot—*All*, each and *all*
Shared in thy boundless sympathies, and then—
(Sublime perfection of perfected *love*)
Then didst thou spurn the whimp'ring wailing thing
That dared to call *thee* "husband," and to claim,
As her just right, support and love from *thee*,—
Then didst thou * * * * * * *

* * * * * * * *

Pretty little playful Patty
Daddy's darling! fubsy fatty!
Come and kiss me, come and sip,
Little bee upon my lip—
Come, and bring the pretty ship,

Little brother Johnny made ye,
Come, ye little cunning jade ye,
Come and see what I've got here,
In my pocket, pretty dear!
What! and won't ye come no higher?

Want to go to aunt Marier?
Want to go to *   *   *   *

*   *   *   *   *   *

Oh! lay me when I die
   Hard by
That little babbling brook, where you
   and I
Have sat, and sauntered many a sum-
   mer's day,

Scenting the sweet soft hay;
There let me lay,
For there young mincing May
Comes first with mouth so meek,
And pale peach-coloured cheek,
And little naked feet,
That go pit pat,
   And all that,
Tripping among the sweet
   Daisies and violets,
And pale primroses;
   And there she comes and sits
A tying up of posies
Fit for immortal noses
To sniff unto, and there
With silky swaling pair,
And iv'ry hands that wring it,
And to the zephyrs fling it,

Up from that babbling brook
The little Naiad's look,
Heaving up round white shoulders,
That dazzle all beholders,
And then so graceful glide they,
Some crablike (sidling) sideway;
Then on the bank I mention,
Like turtles at Ascension,
In heaps they're all a laying,
And then with pretty playing,
One, like a frightened otter,
Flopps down into the water;
The rest they flounce in a'ter —
Then some, with pea-green blushes,
Hide in amongst the rushes,
And one lies shamming sleep,
And one squeaks out "bo peep!"
And one raised head doth peer
Out with a laughing leer;
And then pops up another;
Another and another;
Then they pretend to smother,
A titt'ring talk coquettish,
Then with affected wonder,
   And feigned frowns so pettish,
Like ducks they dive down under,
Then through the gurgling water,
To look and see *   *   *   *   *

The Night Walker.*

'Midnight! yet not a nose, from Tower Hill to Piccadilly, snored!'

In a crowded and highly cultivated state of society, like that of London, the race of exertion against time is incessant. Take a distant village, although a populous one, (as in Devonshire or Cornwall,) and even discord, during the hours of darkness, is found forgetting herself in rest. The last alehouse closes before the clock strikes ten, sending the very scapegraces of the hamlet, in summer, to bed by daylight; no lady would choose, after curfew hour, (even by beating her husband,) to disturb her neighbours; and, unless some tailor happens to be behindhand with a wedding pair of small clothes; or some housewife prolongs the washing-day, and gives an extra hour to her lace caps; or unless the village be a Post-stage, where the "first-turn-boy" must sleep in his spurs; or where, the mail changing horses, some one sits up to give the guard his glass of rum, no movable probably like a lighted candle is known to such a community from eleven o'clock on the Saturday night to six o'clock on the Monday morning. In London, however, the course of affairs is widely different. As the broad glare of gas drives darkness even from our alleys, so multitudinous avocations keep rest for ever from our streets. By an arrangement the opposite to that of Queen Penelope, it is during the night that the work of regeneration in our great capital goes on; it is by night that the great reservoirs which feed London and Westminster, repair the vast expenditure which they make during the day. As the wants of twelve hundred thousand persons are not ministered to with a wet finger, this operation of replenishment does not proceed in silence. Its action is best observable (as regards the season) towards the end of spring; when, the town being at the fullest, the markets are most abundantly supplied. Then, every succeeding hour of the four-and-twenty, brings its peculiar business to be performed, and sets its peculiar agents into motion.

Between half past eleven and twelve o'clock at night, the sev-

* From *Blackwood* for November, 1823.—M.

eral theatres of the metropolis discharge themselves of their loads; and at that hour it is (unless the House of Commons happens to sit late) that the last *flush* of pa engers is seen in the streets of London. The forth-rushing multitudes of Covent-Garden and Drury-Lane pass westward, in divisions, by King Street and Leicesterfields — eastward, by Catherine Street, the Strand, and Temple Bar; they are crossed at the points of Blackfriars, and St. Martin's Lane, by the Middlesex-dwelling visitors of Astley's and the Circus, and may be distinguished from the chance travellers (pedestrians) of the same direction, by their quick step, hilarious mood, and, still more, by that style of *shouldering* in which Englishmen, when they walk in a body, always indulge towards the single-handed. About this time, too, the hackney horses put their best feet (where there is a choice) foremost; knowing of old, that, whence comes one lash, there as easily come two. The less public and more peaceful districts of town are next flattered for some twenty minutes by the loud knocks of coachmen, occasionally commuted into "touches of the bell," for the sake of "the lodgers," or "the children," or, sometimes, "the old lady opposite." And before the stroke of midnight, in these comparatively pacific regions, the tom-cats and the watchmen reign with undisputed sway.

In the greater thoroughfares of London, however, and especially about Fleet Street and the Strand, the tumult of evening does not subside so easily. From twelve, by Paul's clock, until after two in the morning, the Gates of the Temple, and the nooks under St. Dunstan's Church; the corners of Bell Yard, Star Court, and Chancery Lane; the doors of the Rainbow, the Cock, and the other minor coffee-houses of Fleet Street, are beset by habitual idlers, or late-stirring "professional people," — members of spouting-clubs, and second-rate actors, — barristers without law, and medical students guiltless of physic; besides these, there flourish a set of City "choice spirits," who can't get so far west as "Pedley's Oyster-rooms," or "The Saloon," in Piccadilly, but must take their "lark" (moving homewards) between the Adelphi Theatre and Whitechapel; and now-and-then, perhaps, some grocer of Farringdon falls *(vino gravidus)* into the irregularity of a "set-to," and pays thirty shillings, "making-up" money, to his Jew-antagonist at St. Bride's Watchhouse, to save a *jobation*, at Guildhall, from the sitting Alderman, next day.

This is the very "witching time," *par excellence*, of night,

"When graves yield up their dead!"

(because resurrection-men will have it so), when lamps are "rifled at," and sots pushed out of public-houses; and when the sober wayfarer starts, ever and anon, at that prolonged Hilly-oh-ho-ho! — that bellow, as it were, *crescendo*, — peculiar, I think, to the throats of the English, which frightens watchmen into their hutches, and quiet citizens into the kennel. This whoop by the way prolonged, which invites MANKIND, as it were, to clear the way, is, with us, a pure national, and not a local, characteristic. Both high and low affect the practice; both "good men" and bullies. We have it at Oxford and at Cambridge, where the gownsmen, if opposed, strip, and buff to their work like stout "forty minutes" fellows; and again in London, where your flustered haberdasher, after defying perhaps a whole street, at last provokes somebody to thrash him, and is beat without a blow in his defence.

By two o'clock, however, the riotous get pretty well disposed of; some snug and flea-bitten, in their own personal garrets; more (and still fleabitten) in the compters of the police. The wickets of the night-houses, after this, open only to known customers; and the flying pieman ceases his call. The pickpockets, linked with the refuse of another pestilence of the town, are seen sauntering lazily towards their lurking places, in gangs of five and six together. And when these last stragglers of darkness have swept over the *pavé*, the *debris* of the evening may be considered as cleared off; and, except an occasional crash of oyster-shells cast *(maugre* Angelo Taylor) from some lobster-shop, or the sharp rattle of a late billiard ball echoing from the rooms over Mrs. Salmon's, silence, or something like it, obtains for some brief minutes, while the idlers of night give place to the dark-working men of business.

The earliest disturbers of London, until within these few years, were the market gardeners; who rolled lazily through the suburbs, about three, with their filled-up carts and waggons; —

some "well to do," and pompous, parading their four high-fed horses apiece; others, poor (and modest,) drawing with a single quadruped, and he, God wot, looking as though stray cabbage leaves were his holiday-fare,—that is, supposing (what is not supposable) that such a thing as a holiday ever happened to him;—all the *spring* vehicles, however, top-heavy with baskets of raspberries, strawberries, and currants; and followed by heavier machines bearing gooseberries, or frame potatoes; the cauliflowers, pease, and such more ponderous and plebeian esculents, having creaked into town (as they might) in the course of the preceding evening.

But two or three mild winters, of late, in succession, have brought a new article of foreign trade into England. Ice, for the use of the confectioners, comes now to us all the way from Norway; where a gentleman, we understand, is making arrangements to send over even snow, at a far cheaper rate than it can afford to fall in this country;—so that frost, in fact, (as regards Great Britain and Ireland,) may consider itself discharged from further attendance; and, with the help of a few more devices in the way of commercial arrangement, and perhaps a new improvement or two as to the application of steam, it shall go hard but we will, shortly, turn the seasons out of doors altogether. And this imported ice (jealous of sunshine) is foremost in our streets now of mornings, moving along, in huge cart-loads, from the below-bridge wharfs; and looking, as it lies in bulk, like so much conglutinated Epsom salts.

Meantime, the river, above bridge, is not suffered to lie idle; but the fruits of Putney and Fulham walk upon the shoulders of porters, from Hungerford and the Adelphi stairs, to the great mart of vegetable matter, Covent Garden. And upon this spot (Covent Garden) which circumstances seem to have erected into a sort of museum for all the varied *staple* of a crowded capital city;—to which all the patron friends of all the ills that scourge mankind, seem to have rushed, with one consent, day and night, to hold divan;—where Luxury roams gorgeous through her long range of lighted taverns, and brims the bowl with wine, which Discord waits to dash with blood;—where hunger, squalor, nakedness, and disease, dance, antic, round our NATIONAL

Monuments of national wealth and superfluity;—where vices too hideous to be contemplated in detail, assert their royalty over us, alike, in every class, and every condition;—blazing, in transient lustre, amid the splendid hotels of the Piazza; starving, in rags, (yet scarce more abject,) amongst the horrid fastnesses of Bedford Court!—Upon this spot, where all things monstrous are crowded and jumbled together;—where the sounds seem all confused, and the sights all anomalous;—where the wild laugh of revelry, and the low moan of suffering; the subdued whisper of entreaty, and the hoarse bark of execration, mingle, and mix, and blend, and half neutralize each other;—upon this spot, Covent Garden,—jovial Covent Garden,—the darling haunt alike of folly and of wit,—the great mart of all London for oranges, outcasts, and old clothes,—where the jokes are mostly good,—where the cookery is always excellent,—where the claret is commonly the best in England; and the morality never failingly the worst;—on this spot, one continued uproar of labour or dissipation, has endured, without intermission, for nearly a century gone by; and here, so long as London shall keep her holding as a city, silence, probably, by night or day, shall never find a resting place.

But we will tear ourselves from Covent Garden, even in "the sweet" (as Falstaff calls it) "of the night;" for we must take a peep at the other points of *provisional* concentration about town. We must look towards Cockspur Street, where the hay collects itself, in such quantities, that nothing but the stomach of a horse could ever hope to make away with it. And we must cross, too, into Smithfield, where herds of cattle keep coming in all night; and where it is amazing how anybody can get a wink of sleep, for the barking of the dogs, and the bellowing of the bulls, and, louder than all, the swearing of the drovers,—against whom, Heaven, Richard Martin, strengthen thine arm! Smithfield, however, to be seen to advantage, should be taken, from its eastern bearing, through the fogs of a November morning; when the lights, in the west quadrangle, at "The Ram," "The Goat," and "The Bull's Head," shew like beacons (though they shine but dimly) amid the total darkness on all sides of them; and when, looking at the hubbub of traffic which roars through the outward street, against the deep, unheeding silence that reigns within the houses, a man might fancy he witnessed the rush of an invading army, or division, into a town which the inhabitants had, the night before, abandoned. Then pick your way round, (for there is no venturing to cross,) and peep through the steaming window-panes into the parlour of an inn, where graziers and salesmen, in their fantastic, "auld world" dresses — flop-hatted, and top-coated — booted, and waist-be-girt — knee-capped, twenty handkerchiefed, mud-be-splashed, and spurred — snore, or smoke, in arm-chairs; and, between whiles, drive bargains for thousands. Mark the huge bulk of these men; — their bluff-bearing, and English countenances. Hark to their deep voices, strange dialects, and uncouth expression. Then take their attendant demons — the badged drovers — each his goad and cord in hand; and with garb so pieced together, patched, and tattered, that it might pass for the costume of any age; being like the costume of none. Catch the style of the old-fashioned building before you, — with its latticed windows and pent-house roof. Take the low ceiling of the sitting apartment, and the huge sea-coal fire that glows in it. Take the figures of the farmers within doors, and of the drovers hovering without, — of the gaitered, smock-frocked hostlers, carriers, and carmen, — of the ragged, patient, waiting ponies — and the still more ragged and patient sheep-dogs — the most faithful, intelligent, and ill-used beings of their species; — take these objects amid the darkness of the hour, and the exaggeration of the fog; and then, with a little natural romance, and a lively recollection of Shakspere, you may (almost) fancy yourself thrown back into the glorious rudeness of the thirteenth century, arriving from a recent robbery, (ah! those indeed were days) rich with the spoils of "whoreson caterpillars;" and calling for a light to walk between tavern and tavern!

But the sober clearness of a summer's morning is no nurse for these wild fancies. It shews all objects too plainly and distinctly for picturesque effect; the true secret of which, lies in never exhibiting anything *fully*, but in shewing just enough to excite the imagination, and in then leaving it room enough to act. — So we will turn back from Smithfield, just in the cold grey light of daybreak, and cross Holborn to Chancery-Lane, where the kennels by this time are overflowing; and rogues, with scoops, are watering the roads; that is, "making the *dust* one *mud !*" Now watchmen congregate round posts for a little sober conversation; old women make to their respective standings with hot saloop and bread and butter; and presently the light hung caravans of the fishmongers—built at first in imitation of the hearses, and now re-imitated into Paddington stage-coaches— begin to jingle along at a trot, by Thames Street, towards Billingsgate.

As the last stars fade in the horizon, and the sun coquets with the church spires, new actors, in sundry shapes, appear upon the scene. Milkwomen, in droves, clank along with their (to be filled) pails. The poorer fish-dealers, on their own heads, undertake the "care of *souls.*" Chimney sweepers shuffle on, straining out a feeble cry. And parties walk home (rather chilly) from Vauxhall, flaunting in satin shoes, silk stockings, and ostrich feathers; stared at now and then by some gaping, slip-shod baker, who fetches spring water from the pump to cool his *sponge*, and looks like the statue in Don Juan, or a sack of flour truant from the kneading trough; or hooted by some lost thing, all mad, and pale, and ghastly—some *creation* of gin, and carmine, and soiled muslin—which shews by daylight, as a being of other time and place,—an apparition—a prodigy—a denizen of some forbidden sphere,—a foul lamp, thickly glimmering out its dregs, which the sun's light, by some accident, has omitted to extinguish.

Five o'clock, and the world looks as if stretching itself to awake. Coal-waggons and drays start forth upon "long turns;" their country intent denoted by the truss of hay placed above the load. Butchers step sturdily towards Islington or Smithfield. Anglers, children of hope! stride fieldwards with baskets on their backs. And Holborn and Snow Hill are crowded with pony-carts—(since the Chancellor of the Exchequer rides nothing under fourteen hands)—bearing butter, cheese, poultry, sucking-pork, and eggs, from Newgate market to the distant parishes of Mary-le-bone and Pancras.

Six! and 'prentices begin to rub their eyes and curse their

indentures. Maid-servants at "the Piccadilly end" of the town, are not bound to stir just yet; but Russell Square and its dependencies set their spider killers in motion betimes; for courts of law and counting-houses both sit at nine o'clock; and an advocate in practice of ten thousand a-year, must step into his carriage at five-and-thirty minutes past eight in the morning.

And now the different shops begin to open themselves for action. Our friend the baker is first, for he has been up all night, and he is to cool his loaves at the open windows as he draws them from the oven. Next comes the pastry cook,—lotting his remnant of cheese-cake,—selling yesterday's dainties at half-price to-day; and still making money (as it is said) by the dealing. Then coaches, splashed and dirty, come labouring into town; and coaches, fresh and clean, drive out; and, by this time, the mercers and jewellers set their portal wide, in favour of sweeping, sprinkling, and window cleaning; for the show glasses (and here again sigh our friends the apprentices) must be emptied all, and polished, and refurnished, before breakfast.

The clock strikes eight; and the night walker must be seen no more. Hurry, and bustle, and breakfast, are on foot. The milkman cries in haste, and yet can scarce make his rounds fast enough. Maids with clean aprons (and sometimes with clean plates) step forth, key in hand, for the morning's modicum of fresh butter; and hot rolls (walk as you will) run over you at every corner. By nine, the clerks have got down to their offices —the attorneys have opened their bags; and the judges are on their benches,—and the business of the *day* in London may now be said to have begun; which varies, from hour to hour, as strangely as the business of the night; and (to the curious observer) presents even a more ample field for speculation.

Song of the Sea.*

"Woe to us when we lose the watery wall!"—Timothy Tickler.

If e'er that dreadful hour should come — but God avert the day!
When England's glorious flag must bend, and yield old Ocean's sway;
When foreign ships shall o'er that deep, where she is empress, lord;
When the cross of red from boltsprit-head is hewn by foreign sword;
When foreign foot her quarter-deck with proud stride treads along;
When her peaceful ships meet haughty check from hail of foreign tongue;—
One prayer, one only prayer, is mine, that, ere is seen that sigh,
Ere there be warning of that woe, I may be whelm'd in night.

If ever other prince than ours wield sceptre o'er that main,
Where Howard, Blake, and Frobisher, the Armada smote of Spain;
Where Blake, in Cromwell's iron sway, swept tempest-like the seas,
From North to South, from East to West, resistless as the breeze;
Where Russell bent great Louis' power, which bent before to none,
And crush'd his arm of naval strength, and dimm'd his Rising Sun —
One prayer, one only prayer is mine — that, ere is seen that sight,
Ere there be warning of that woe, I may be whelm'd in night!

If ever other keel than ours triumphant plough that brine,
Where Rodney met the Count De Grasse, and broke the Frenchman's line,
Where Howe, upon the first of June, met the Jacobins in fight,
And with Old England's loud huzzas broke down their godless might;
Where Jervis at St. Vincent's fell'd the Spaniards' lofty tiers,
Where Duncan won at Camperdown, and Exmouth at Algiers —
One prayer, one only prayer, is mine — that, ere is seen that sight,
Ere there be warning of that woe, I may be whelm'd in night!

But oh! what agony it were, when we should think on thee,
The flower of all the Admirals that ever trod the sea!
I shall not name thy honoured name — but if the white-cliff'd Isle
Which rear'd the Lion of the deep, the Hero of the Nile,
Him who, 'neath Copenhagen's self, o'erthrew the faithless Dane,
Who died at glorious Trafalgar, o'er-vanquished France and Spain,
Should yield her power, one prayer is mine — that, ere is seen that sight,
Ere there be warning of that woe, I may be whelm'd in night!

---

* This spirited lyric, "occasioned by seeing, in the *Quarterly Review* and *Blackwood's Magazine*, some gloomy anticipations of the effects of the change in the Navigation Code," was published in *Blackwood* for September, 1823 — M.

New Horatian Readings.*

"Sir,—You know, of course, the many charges against the unfaithfulness of translators, and against their frequent destruction of all the force, power, tenderness, sublimity, wit, &c., of the original; but I have never seen yet any satisfactory project proposed, by which the powers of the translator and original author could be both fairly represented in one book. True it is that you may print the original in one page and the translation in the opposite, but this is a poor mechanical bookbinding expedient. Dean Swift, you may remember, on getting a translation of Horace thus arranged, very quietly tore out the English part, and declared that he could safely say that half the book was good, and was much obliged to the compiler for giving him so easy a method of separating the worthy from the unworthy. But a project which I have devised will save the translator from such wicked waggery, while it will do as well to show off the original.

"I have begun on Horace, he being a jocose and handy author, and I send you a specimen of my labours.

"You will perceive that my plan is to give lines alternately English and Latin, the former my own, the latter from my friend Flaccus. We are both thus fairly represented, just as in divided counties a Whig and Tory member are returned to satisfy both parties without giving trouble. If the public approve, I shall publish a translation of all the odes in this style; and if the public be a person of any taste, I am sure of general approbation. Meanwhile, Sir, believe me to be

"Your most obediant servant,
"Dionysius Duggan."

"P. S.—Mind to pronounce my Latin lines with Latin accents, not Anglically. Thus, do not say,

Apros in ob-stántes plágas

Aprós in ób-stantés plagás

---

* From the *Literary Gazette*. — M.

SECOND EPODE OF HORACE DONE IN A NEW STYLE.

Blest man! who far from busy hum,
Ut prisca gens mortalium,
Whistles his team afield with glee
Solutus omni fœnore:
He lives in peace, from battles free,
Neq' horret iratûm mare;
And shuns the forum, and the gay
Potentiorum limina.
Therefore to vines of purple gloss
Alta maritat populos,
Or pruning off the boughs unfit
Feliciores inserit;
Or in a distant vale at ease
Prospectat errantes greges;
Or honey into jars conveys,
Aut tondet infirmas oves.
When his head decked with apples sweet
Autumnus agris extulit
At plucking pears he's quite *au-fait*
Certant, et uvam purpuræ.
Some for priapus, for thee some
Sylvane, tutor finium!
Beneath an oak 'tis sweet to be
Mod' in tenaci gramine:
The streamlet winds in flowing maze;
Queruntur in sylvis aves;
The fount in dulcet murmur plays
Somnos quod invitet leves.
But when the winter comes (and that
Imbres nivesque comparat)
With dogs he forces oft to pass
Apros in obstantes plagas;
Or spreads his nets so thick and close,
Turdis edacibus dolos;
Or hares, or cranes, from far away
Jucunda captat præmia:
The wooer love's unhappy stir
Hæc inter obliviscitur.
His wife can manage without loss
Domum et parvos liberos;

(Suppose her Sabine, or the dry
Pernicis uxor Appuli.)
Who piles the sacred hearthstone high
Lassi sub adventûm viri.
And from his ewes, penned lest they stray,
Distenta siccet ubera;
And this year's wine disposed to get
Dapes inemptas apparet.
Oysters to me no joys supply,
Magisve rhombus, aut scari.
(If when the east winds boisterous be
Hyems ad hoc vertat mare)
Your Turkey pout is not to us,
Non attagen Ionicus,
So sweet as what we pick at home
Oliva ramis arborum;
Or sorrel, which the meads supply,
Malvæ salubres corpori—
Or lamb, slain at a festal show,
Vel hædus ereptus lupo.
Feasting, 'tis sweet the creature's dumb,
Videre prop'rantés domum,
Or oxen with the ploughshare go,
Collo trahente languido;
And all the slaves stretched out at ease,
Circum renidentes Lares.
Alphius the usurer, babbled thus,
Jam jam futurus rusticus,
Called in his cash on th' Ides—but he
Quærit Calendis ponere.

First Love.*

I SHALL never forget the first time I ever drank rum-punch after having been smoking cigars. Dates, says De Quincy, may be forgotten—epochs never. That formed an epoch in *my* existence;

> "And the last trace of feeling with life shall depart,
> Ere the smack of that moment shall pass from my heart."

Let me recall it to my memory, with all its attendant circumstances, and while my soul broods over the delicious recollection, forget the present day, with its temporary miseries, and shut out from its views the follies, the frivolities, the wickedness, the baseness, the ingratitude of the world.

It happened, that though, like most men who, in my day, were reared in Trinity College, *juxta* Dublin, I had been tolerably well initiated into the theory and practice of compotation, I had never much taken to its greatest adjunct, smoking. I do not think that the Trinity men (Dublin) smoke—it certainly, as long as I remember that seminary, of which I cannot think with affection, never was a fashion there. Particular pipemen, and solitary cigarers, no doubt, always existed, but just as you now and then see a pig-tail (I do not allude to tobacco) dangling behind an elderly gentleman, or hear a shoe creak under the foot of a decent man. Smoking, in short, was the exception—non-smoking the rule. But the men of my time drank hard, though, as youths always do, unscientifically. I therefore, as the rest, drank, and did not smoke.

I was about twenty when I left the University, and went down to live with my father in a pretty seaport town. Here I mixed a good deal in boating-parties, and other such excursions with sea-faring men, and from them, after much persuasion on their parts, I learned to smoke. My first preceptors preferred the pipe. I shall not here enter into the controversy which has

* From *Blackwood* for August, 1826.—M.

so long agitated the world, concerning the superiority of pipe or cigar. I am tired of controversies.

"I am weary of hunting, and fain would lie down."

For the same reason, I pass all mention of the too celebrated, though in reality minor dispute, concerning the length of the pipe, which cost my friend Captain O'Shaughnessy his life. Though he died as became a man of honour and a gentleman, it may be permitted to a friend to avert his eyes from the melancholy cause which deprived the world of a true philosopher and a brave soldier.

I think I must have persevered in the pipe-system for nine months, when an accident (it is needless to encumber my narrative by detailing what it was) threw me in the way of Cornet Roger Silverthorne, of the 13th Light Dragoons, and Silverthorne Hall in the palatinate of Durham. This eminent and estimable young man—

> "O flos juvenum,
> Spes læta patris,
> Non certa tuæ
> Data res patriæ!
> Non mansuris
> Ornate bonis,
> Ostentatus,
> Raptusque simul,
> Solstitialis
> Velut herba soletǃ"

> "Flower of our youth, glad hope of thy fond sire,
> To whose bright course thy country looked in vain,
> Deck'd with proud gifts not destined to remain,
> But shown and snatched away—as, 'neath the fire
> Of tropic summers, plants bloom bright, and soon expire."——

Forgive these tears. I own it is folly—but nature will sometimes have her way in spite of all our philosophy. This eminent and estimable young man was perhaps the most persevering cigar-smoker that ever existed. If peerages were distributing, he should be Count Segar, instead of the gentleman who now holds that honourable title. He generally smoked five dozen a-day. You never saw him without one in his mouth; and as the voluminous smoke curled in picturesque wreathes from under his manly mustachio, while he luminously descanted on the various natures, uses, and proprieties of the several preparations of tobacco, he was one of the few men of whom you would decidedly say, that he was born *ex fumo dare lucem.* I never shall hear the like again: those eloquent lips are mute, and the brain that dictated the thought, and the tongue that clothed it in utterance, have mouldered into clay. His fate was singular. He died of indigestion, from having eaten four pounds and a half of tripe for a wager. Others, however, maintain that he was choked in the operation. I never could penetrate through the veil which thus hangs over his mysterious death. I, however, incline to the latter hypothesis; for my respected and lamented friend, I am sure, could have digested anything. The question, after all, is of little moment. He is dead — and I remain!

> "Sweet Roger,
> I thought I should have deck'd thy bridal bed,
> And not have strewed thy tomb!"

After some controversy, perhaps too obstinately persevered in on my part, the Cornet converted me to cigars. I have said already, that I do not wish to unsettle any man's opinions, and therefore will let those who prefer the pipe, prefer it. I smoked pretty strenuously with him, and after he had been ordered away to Flanders, continued the practice. I moistened always, as is the custom of my country — where scarcely any other spirit is ever used — with whiskey. Of that spirit let no one for a moment imagine that I am about to say anything but what is laudatory. If I did so, I were as ungrateful as unwise — but it is *not* the spirit to smoke with. I say this emphatically, because I know it to be the case. I am little inclined to dogmatize, but when once I have formed an opinion after careful examination, I uphold it with that firmness which a just regard for one's own character and the interest of truth and honour demand.

Shortly after Silverthorne's departure, business took me to Dublin. Fatal, though delicious visit! On what trifles our fate hangs! I had finished my business, and taken my seat on the outside of the coach to return home, when, as we waited outside the post-office in Sackville-street, I heard a sweet voice say

—I hear it yet tingling in my ears, though fifteen years have elapsed—I heard a sweet voice——

I cannot go on. I must lay down the pen——

Excuse this gust of passion—it shall be the last. I heard a sweet though rather loud voice say, "Put the little portmanteau into the boot, and take care to tie the two bandboxes tight on the top, covering them from the rain. You can put the big trunk where you like, and I'll take the cloth bag and two brown paper parcels into the coach—good bye, Judy. I'll write from Ballinafad, as soon as I see the old buck." I looked down, and my doom was sealed—I was in love—

"Dead shepherd, now I found thy saw of might—
He never loved, who loved not at first sight!"

That insidious passion had entered my bosom for the first time. Is there any one who has not experienced it? If there be, I may envy his freedom from disturbance, but I pity the callousness of heart, and the distortion of feeling, for which he is indebted to it.

Cecilia—shall I say, *my* Cecilia—was hasty in her movements, and rejecting the proffered aid of the guard, she stepped unassisted toward the coach. Her foot slipped in the attempt, and she fell on the flagging. I was smoking on the top when I saw this cruel accident, and without a moment's thought, flung from my jaw as fine a Havannah as ever saw the Moro, leaped on the ground and raised her. She was not hurt, but considerably agitated. She thanked me with hasty accents, and looked on me with a glance, which ever still is——but I have promised to repress my feelings.

The coach was full inside, and besides I had lived pretty close to my last tenpenny in Dublin, so that even if there had been a place vacant, I could not have taken it. She parted us about daybreak, but I was unfortunate in not being able to see her. In fact the agitation of my spirits was such that I had been obliged to drink fourteen glasses of whiskey and water during the night, which had in some measure got in my head, for, as will happen when friends are parting, I had indulged a little after dinner with some few acquaintance with whom I chopped in Exchequer-street—and the guard seeing me inclined to be topheavy, had laid me down in the well behind the coachman, where I was unluckily snoring when Cecilia left the coach. She asked for me, to thank me for my assistance, but on seeing how the land lay, they told me that she said in her own kind manner,

"Poor devil—he is flustered with drink—let him snooze it off." Sweet girl!

When I awoke and found her gone I was frantic. I had lost every clue to her. We were twenty miles away from the place she parted the coach before I roused, and the coachman informed me that a gentleman with a led horse was waiting for her, with whom she immediately galloped away—he forgot—insensible brute that he was—in what direction. A new agony seized my mind—the gentleman! WAS SHE MARRIED? My brain was wild. I had no way of satisfying myself, for the accursed mail-coach clerk had entered her name in the waybill in such a hand as to puzzle Beelzebub himself, were he the prince of decypherers, and the only letter I could make out was the first, which proved him to be as abominable in his ideas of spelling as in his writing—for her name, as I afterwards knew, was Crimeen, and the ruffian, regardless of all possible principles of orthography, had commenced it with a Q.

When I got home I concealed my unfortunate passion as well as I could, but what can escape the eye of a parent? About nine days had elapsed before my father noticed my loss of appetite and my silence, but at last he could not bear to pass it by. "Boy," said he, taking me affectionately by the hand, "something is ailing you." "Nothing, sir," said I, "indeed." "Ah!" said my father, "do not think to deceive me that way. There's your fifth tumbler lying before you this half hour, and you're scarce quarter through it yet. I've noticed the same this last week, and except on the day Lord Bullaboo dined with us, when it behoved you to make an exertion, you have not finished any one blessed day seven tumblers. Don't think, my boy, that your father is not minding your happiness. You arn't in love, are you?" The goodness of the old gentleman was not to be withstood, and I confessed the fact, and told him all about it. "Never mind it," said he, "it looks the devil to you just now; but when you come to my time of life, you won't think much about such little accidents as meeting a girl at a coachdoor. So, go travel in God's name, and drive this nonsense out of your skull; travelling, besides, opens the mind and polishes the manner. So, go to my cousin Gusty in Bristol, he lives out towards Lamplighter's Hall, and let me tell you, few soap-boilers from this to himself, and that's no small step, can beat him."

Good, venerable man, with what pleasure I record your honoured words! He gave me letters of change and introduction, adding his blessing and a gallon of whiskey, which, as he well observed, could not be got for love or money in England. I had no objection to the change of scene, and soon established my quarters at my cousin Gusty's. Gusty was a good fellow, hoggish in his manners like the Bristolians, but a strenuous supporter of Church and State. We dined punctually at one, and, except on melting days, which he was obliged to mind, smoked through the evening. So passed a fortnight, but at the end of that time I had occasion to go to Clifton to play a game of skittles with a Jamaica Captain for a dozen of rum, and as I went along, just as I entered the North Crescent, whom should I see but Cecilia!

Skittles were at once knocked out of my head. She was alone, and I ventured to join her. Our mail-coach adventure afforded a common topic of conversation, which soon grew animated. We talked of everything, and as I coaxed her towards Wardham Downs, I had established her arm under mine. At last we came on that eminence which exhibits the most beautiful and varied prospect of that delightful tract. It was summer, about three o'clock of a lovely June evening. Every sight and sound about us was such as to dispose the soul to tender emotions. Never did Cecilia look more lovely than when I persuaded her to rest herself by sitting down on one of the grassy points overlooking the descent below. What I said to her I cannot write, the first words of love are not to be profaned by exposure to the gaze of the world. Our thoughts were pure—pure as the cloudless sky overhanging the

lovely landscape, in the midst of which we sat forgetful even of
its beauties, wholly absorbed in the consideration of one another.
I had whispered, and she had heard without reply, what is never
whispered a second time.

We might have been half an hour together, it was but a
moment to my thought, when she recollected that she had left her
aunt waiting for her in a butcher's shop where she was buying
— how minutely love makes us recollect the merest trifles — buying a leg of pork, with a couple of pounds of sausages. I pressed her hand to my lips, and we returned to Clifton. Delightful day! Were my life prolonged to the day allotted to Methu-
selah, I never could forget a particle of what happened upon
thee! It is *the* bright spot in the waste of my memory.

When we parted, I put my hand mechanically and mourn-
fully into my waistcoat pocket, and found that I had forgotten
my cigar case. Love had so completely taken possession of my
soul, that I knew not what I was doing, and, by mere instinct,
walked into a tobacconist's shop, which, such was the absence
of my mind, I was about to leave without paying for the cigars,
until the tobacconist rather energetically reminded me of my
insouciance. Captain Snickersnee and his skittles were quite
out of my head, and I went across to a low-browed public house,
where a portrait of Lord Nelson, more spirited in conception,
than exact in likeness, or studied in composition, shone glitter-
ing in one-armed majesty in the evening sun. The room I went
into — why need I conceal that it was the tap-room? — was filled with the miscellaneous population of Bristol — men in general more noted for their candour than any other particularity in
their manners. But I heeded them not. I was as much alone
as if I was in the deserts of Tadmor, where the ruins of Pal-
myra tower towards the sky, or moulder upon the ground, filling
the awe-struck traveller with melancholy musing on the insta-
bility of things. I lighted my cigar by the assistance of the pipe
of a man sitting next me, who I have some reason to believe,
but I shall not be positive, was a tailor. I puffed away — soft
were my thoughts, delectable my visions. Every curl of smoke
contained the countenance of my Cecilia — every twinkle from
each surrounding pipe beamed upon me as if it was one of her

celestial eyes. I had forgotten where I was, when the waiter came to me, and jogging my elbow, said, "Thee musn't lumber the room, if thee'll not drink zummat." In general, I have remarked, that the language of these persons is seldom marked by the refinements of elegance, and that perhaps you might travel from one end of the country to the other without finding a waiter at a public-house who combines the terseness of Addison with the magniloquence of Johnson!

I replied to this rude man mildly, yet I think with sufficient dignity. "What have you in the house?" "Every thing," said he. In this the man's bad faith was evident, for, on scrutinizing the subject, I found that he had nothing but gin, a liquor I ever detested, and rum. "Rum, then," said I with a sigh, resigning myself to my fate, for I anticipated, in my ignorance, that I would dislike it.

My mouth was full of the cigar-smoke—full, ay, full as my heart was of my Cecilia. Divine girl! when I think upon thy perfections, on thy charms, on the manner in which thou wert lost to me, by that fatal and mysterious circle of events, never to be anticipated—never to be repeated—But I'll think no more. There is a point of human endurance, beyond which it cannot go. Let me proceed. I was saturated with smoke, when, in the wildness of the delirium of my love, I did not perceive the water bottle standing by the *bottom* of rum, and swallowed the spirit, unalloyed, unmoistened, undiluted, uninjured. It permeated my whole mouth—it filled it with a species of solidity that seemed altogether to have destroyed the liquid character of the spirits; I felt it melting into my palate, my tongue, my fauces, my gums. It was an intense gush, a simple, original, indivisible idea of delight. It rose to my brain, as the vapour of the tedded meadow rises to the sky in the balminess of morning. It descended to the sole of my foot as the sky sends back that delicious vapour in the shape of the dews of evening. It was a joy to be felt once, and no more. I never felt it again. It was

"Odour fled
As soon as sfied;
'Twas morning's wingéd dream,
'Twas a light that never shall shine again
On life's dull stream!"

I have tried it over and over, and it will not do. I smoke my cigar still in the evening, and frequently moisten with a quart or so of rum, naked, in grog, in punch, in flip — every way that can be thought of, but it will not return. That feeling of intense and transporting delight is over.

Days of my youth! when every thing was innocence and peace — when my sorrows were light, and my joys unsophisticated — when I saw a glory in the sky, and a power on the earth which I shall never see again — how delightful, yet how sad is your recollection! Here's, then, to the days gone by — to the memory of my first love and my first libation of rum over a cigar! Some young heart is now going the same round as I was then — revelling in delights which he fondly fancies are to last for ever — anticipating joys which never are destined to exist. Light be his heart, buoyant his spirits — I shall not break in on his dreams by the croaking of experience.

Farewell again, Cecilia! I never saw her after that day — in the evening she left Bristol with her aunt's butler — they were married three days after by the blacksmith at Gretna, and she is now, I understand, the mother of fourteen children, keeping, with her third husband, the sign of the Cat and Bagpipes somewhere about the Dock of Liverpool. I never could muster up courage to enter the house. The very sound of her voice saying, "Eightpence, sir," in reply to my question of what I had to pay, would inevitably overcome my feelings.

I was born to be unhappy — but I shall not intrude my sorrows on a thoughtless world!

The Crabstick.*

Air — The Green Immortal Shamrock.

Through Britain's isle as Hymen strayed
  Upon his ambling pony,
With Buller sage, in wig arrayed,
  To act as cicerone,
To them full many a spouse forlorn
  Complained of guineas squandered,
Of visage torn and breeches worn,
  And thus his godship pondered —
Oh, the Crabstick! the green immortal Crabstick!
    I'll ensure
    A lasting cure
In Russia's native Crabstick!

With magic wand he struck the earth,
  And straight his conjuration
Gave that same wholesome sapling birth,
  The husband's consolation;
Dispense, quoth he, thou legal man,
  This new-discover'd treasure,
And let thy thumb's capacious span
  Henceforward fix its measure.
Oh, the Crabstick! the green immortal Crabstick!
    Long essay'd
    On jilt and jade
Be Buller's magic Crabstick!

The olive branch, Minerva's boon,
  Betokens peace and quiet,
But 'tis sage Hymen's gift alone
  Can quell domestic riot;
For 'tis a maxim long maintain'd
  By doctors and logicians,
That peace is most securely gain'd
  By armed politicians.
Oh, the Crabstick! the green immortal Crabstick!
    Its vigorous shoot
    Quells all dispute,
The wonder-working Crabstick!

---

* From *Blackwood* for November, 1824. — M.

In idleness and youthful hours,
  When graver thoughts seem stupid,
Men fly to rose and myrtle bowers
  To worship tiny Cupid;
But spliced for life, and wiser grown,
  Dog-sick of sighs and rhyming,
They haunt the crab-tree bower alone,
  The leafy shrine of Hymen.
Oh, the Crabstick! the green immortal Crabstick!
  Love bestows
  The useless rose,
But Hymen gives the Crabstick!*

Sonnet.†

I stood upon St. Peter's battlement,
  And my eye wander'd o'er Imperial Rome,
  And I thought sadly on the fatal doom
'Neath which her ancient palaces had bent;
Of temple and tower outrageously uprent,
  Or mouldered into dust by slow decay:
Of halls where godlike Cæsar once bore sway,
Or glorious Tully fulmin'd eloquent!
  So shall all earthly fade! what wonder then,
  If Time can make such all-unsparing wreck,
If neither genius, art, nor skill of men,
  Can e'en pretend his felon-hand to check,
That this old coat, I've worn these three years past,
Should on each elbow want a patch at last?

---

* The hero of this song was Sir Francis Buller, an English Judge, and not the myth yclept "Buller of Brazenose." Sir Francis, who was so eminently henpecked at home that he never dared call his soul his own, stated, while presiding at Stafford Assizes, that, by the law of the land, a man might correct his wife with a stick "not thicker than his thumb." The incensed ladies of Stafford incontinently signed and sent in a round-robin, asking the learned judge to favour them with the dimension of *his* thumb. — M.

† From the *Literary Gazette.* — M.

Panegyric on Colonel Pride.*

"Then clear the weeds from off his grave,
And we shall chaunt a passing stave,
In honour of that hero brave."

At Nonsuch lies buried Sir Thomas Pride, the Republican Colonel, and hither have I come to gaze upon his tomb. Bold of heart, strong of hand, zealous of purpose, true in courage, daring in council, unflinching in execution, a better soldier or a firmer partisan never belted on a buff coat. His parentage could not be boasted of, for he was a foundling, abandoned in a church porch—which Lord Pembroke assigns, in his will, as a reason for wishing to be buried any where else. I was a lord, says the Earl, and cannot bear the notion of being laid where Colonel Pride was born. Nor could much panegyric be wasted upon the elegancies or refinement of his education, for he was originally a drayman. These things matter but little. The best blood, as they call it, may give life, as we see every day, to the meanest of mankind; and there is many a doctor of divinity of my acquaintance, to whom half the draymen of London are superior in intellect and honesty. Take them as a class, and no person of the slightest observation of mankind will compare them (I mean the draymen) in understanding and ability, with the young gentlemen who are senior wranglers, or first-class men, or authors of prize poems, or crack contributors to the periodicals, or writers of fashionable novels, or compilers of essays upon political economy, or chairmen of select committees. Heaven forefend that I should so disparage the honest and beer-bibbing wearers of the flapped hat!

Be that as it may, Pride performed his business well—he did the work of the Lord not negligently. From the beginning of the Civil War to the end, he was ever at his post, and there steady to his duty. Glad, then, am I to find that his bones were not disturbed; for though that would indeed have been nothing to him, it is to men of heart a grief that dishonour—or

* From *Blackwood* for December, 1829.—M.

what the world calls dishonour—should be offered to those whom we respect. It was ordered that the bodies of Oliver, Bradshaw, and Pride, should be exhumed and gibbeted; and this order was executed as far as regarded the first two, but Pride having married a niece of Monk's, his connexion with the Restorer obtained for him the grace that his remains should be unmolested. As for Bradshaw, as he was only a lawyer, it was little matter, indeed, what was done with his carrion; but I have been ever sorry that Charles the Second, for whom I have a high respect, (for many reasons, principally for his having robbed the Exchange,) should have been so far mistaken as to think that, in thus treating Oliver, he was degrading the bones of a hero, and not degrading himself. It was not worthy of the wit or the gentleman—and Charles was both—aye, and a brave fellow too, when need was. I have a hankering kindness after Old Rowley, the pot-companion of Rochester, and the patron of Tom D'Urfey.

Here then, Tom Pride, I dedicate a half-hour's thought to you! Many were his dashing actions, but that by which he is most remembered, and most worthy of being remembered, is his famous purgation of the House of Commons. Honoured and glorified be his name as long as history lasts, for such an action! Here was a set of scoundrels, sent by the people of England to do a great and important duty, not only neglecting to do it, but actually doing the contrary. To them was intrusted the guardianship of the religion of England, and they abandoned it to its enemies—to them was committed the protection of the liberties of England, and they were endeavouring, by clubbing and caballing, to make themselves perpetual petty despots under a greater despot. As for the men themselves, it was well said by one of their own order, that on no other principle than that of their election, could there be gathered together, from the four corners of the earth, a crew of such contemptible blockheads—a knot of wretches (I speak of the members of the Long Parliament) so personally stained with every blot of disgrace and infamy. As Oliver afterwards told them in the best, the most eloquent, the most serviceable and most seasonable speech ever spoken in their house, they were a set of sharpers, lewd livers, gamesters, hypocrites, knaves, jobbers, and poltroons. Translated into the fashionable language of the present day, and made applicable to our manners, in his speech would have been enumerated as the component parts of parliament, Stock Exchange swindlers, fashionable intriguers with Mr. A's and Mrs. B's, conniving wittols, beggarly rascals kept by actresses, political economists, confederates with Jews, and uncomplaining martyrs of the horsewhip. That any such persons could be found in the present House of Commons, is an impossibility; but history bears us out, that there have been Houses of Commons in which they might be discovered without the aid of a lantern.

These fellows had the insolence to think, that it was by them and by their exertions the cause had prospered; whereas they had been always a clog upon it. Things would have gone much better had the idle babble of their ignorant debates been totally suppressed. Their great speakers were at best but stringers-together of good-for-nothing words in tinkling cadence, devoid of sense, at the sound of which, particularly if it was tagged and jagged with scraps of schoolboy Latin, extracted from a book of accidence, the flap-eared boobies around would set up a shout of joy. Their great philosophers were fellows, who, having perhaps been apothecaries' boys, or cotton twisters, or distinguished "men" at college, or red-tape tyers in public offices, or correspondents of the diurnals, were filled with ignorance or upstart vanity, or inhaled stupidity, and who dealt forth cant maxims, either nauseous for being truisms or commonplaces, or mischievous for being utterly false in theory and ruinous in application. Was it wonderful, then, that the country rejoiced when Colonel Pride kicked them out—that there was a jubilee of exultation at each individual kick, with which each individual scoundrel was saluted on the most honourable part of his person, the only part employed in getting rid of corruption—and that the pumpings, and buffetings, and thrustings into damp dungeons, and the other indignities so justly and so liberally showered upon them, should have been considered from one end of the realm to the other as the most righteous visitation ever inflicted since the days of Sennacherib of Assyria. It must have been a delightful sight—one worth giving up ten years of life to have witnessed: and it is a matter of regret, in one sense, that there is no very immediate prospect of our being gratified with a repetition of such a scene. Our present House is so admirable that nothing like it could justly occur, and it would be unfair that we should expect that our taste should be indulged at the expense of justice. Yet imagination will sometimes draw pictures of things in themselves unreasonable, and never destined to occur. Methinks I see a starved vagabond belonging to the Treasury, a miserable, gaunt, intoothed, half-penny-a-day ghowl, who looks as if he had eaten nothing but his words— methinks I see that fellow scudding before the wind in all the shabby agonies of dirty terror, and long for an opportunity of joining in the calcitration with all the power of the arms of Man —videlicit, three legs. And sometimes fancy will body forth a similar ejection of a Home Secretary; but as that office is uniformly filled by men of great personal honour, unimpeachable political integrity, uniform consistency of principle, and all other qualities which command respect, I scout the idea as fast as it is formed. I dreamt, however, one night, that somebody said his only objection to such a proceeding was, that he would not like to contaminate his boot-toe-point with the contact; but that was only the absurdity of a dream.

A good precedent is never thrown away. Although we do not want Pride's Purge at present, a day may come when it will be useful to act upon it. I can conceive that a hundred years hence, when a supple and servile Parliament, having bent itself before the mandates of a military protector, having done his business up to a certain point, and promoted the objects of his ambition as far as they had it in their power, may be properly turned off by their iron-handed master—their use to him being past—amid the universal exultation of mankind. The fact that it has been already done, and been attended with such beneficial effects, will be a cheering precedent. I hope that when the hour arrives, if it ever should arrive, the Cromwell of the day will refine upon Colonel Pride's practice; for to act otherwise, would be to reverse the order of the great march of mind. I think, then, that he would afford a most gratifying spectacle to the populace, if, after the culprits were collared and handcuffed, he ordered them to be whipped forthwith, from the door of Saint Stephen's Chapel to the statue at Charing Cross, and back again. How pleasing it would be to behold, for instance, the herring-gutted frame of some west-country apostate, flagrant from the nine-tailed lash inflicted by the unsparing arm of a sixteen-stone drummer, originally educated in the West Indies as help to an overseer! With what an agreeable cadence the hollow howling of his sepulchral voice would fall upon the auricular drums of the amused assembly! How zummerzet, as Shakspere says, squeak *rats* beneath the *cat* —

"Like softest music to attending ears."

It is charming to be reminded of beautiful passages of romantic poetry in the midst of the jangling politics of the Roundheads. Romeo and Juliet! Delicious tale of love!——But I digress; and must go back to recommend his Highness to recreate the the crowd periodically, by exposing the purged-outs in the pillory, specially revived for their use, in the presence of a good-humoured congregation, too much pleased by the sight to indulge in any rancorous feelings, and therefore contenting themselves with pelting the culprits with nothing harder than congenial nastiness. It has ever been accounted good policy to supply the public with innocent recreations—to procure for them objects of laughter in all lawful ways—and therefore, I think, Woodfall is never sufficiently to be commended for having set the example of publishing the debates of the Houses of Parliament.

Why do I think of these things? What brings these dark visions of the future before my mental optics? It must be the impress produced upon me by the grave of Sir Thomas Pride, for assuredly there is nothing in present circumstances to suggest such ideas. If I turn my eyes from the tomb of the stern expurgator to look on the state of affairs around, is not every thing calculated to inspire, not such ferocious fancies—such fierce phantasmata of the halter and the lash—but, on the contrary, thoughts soft as down, and odorous as balm? Look round, and all is happiness. In Spitalfields, the weaver, no longer tormented with the tedious and unmanly shuffling of his shuttle, roams in liberty through the streets, accompanied by his wife and children, who, disdaining to be indebted to the base mechanical labours of the mason or the carpenter, prefer the gorgeous and star-spangled canopy of the glorious firmament itself, as curtain to their bed. In Barnsley and Manchester, in Congleton and Sheffield, a similar repose from toil prevails, and their gallant youth, despising their former servile avocations, are training themselves to the blood-stirring trade of arms, or take lessons in eloquence and politics from the honeyed lips of a Flanagan or a Peter Hoey. A spirit of jocularity has seized on the ribbonmen of Coventry, and they divert themselves with facetious processions of master-manufacturers mounted on donkeys, with their faces to the tail, and liberally supplying them with the produce of the soil, applied to their persons and countenances, if not with much delicacy, yet with hearty good-will and plentiful abundance. Elsewhere the same pleasantry of disposition leads them to make ribbons, not of their silk, but their masters, and to rip out the intestinal canals of obnoxious non-employers by the surgical instrumentality of a bill-hook. The ship-owners, disdaining to extort money from the merchant, carry freights for prices which will not pay the breakfasts of their sailors—the iron-master is so good as to work for the benefit of the public, at a loss of a pound a-ton—the woolstapler clothes as many of the people as still cling to the ancient prejudices of being clothed, at prices less than those which he promises to the farmer for his wool. The farmer himself, no more fatigued by following the profitless plough, sits at ease in a house unencumbered with furniture, and cheers himself, not with the stupifying extract of malt, but the pure and unadulterated fluid of the crystal spring —while in town, the merchant and trader are continually reminded of the propriety of dealing in ready-money transactions only, by the regular refusal of discount, and the unlimited protesting of their bills. True it is, that the customs and excise fall off—less moneys are paid in those obnoxious branches of revenue—but then, to compensate for that, the great domestic tax of the poor-laws is hourly increasing. Literature and morals are also on the rise. It is not only the illustrious order of the Gentlemen of the Press, a body of men unknown in the days of Alfred, and never employed, as Sharon Turner informs me, in reporting the useful debates of the Wittenagemot, who now contribute to the newspapers—for never does a week elapse without some fifty or sixty tradesmen of London supplying one paragraph a-piece to a paper published on Tuesdays and Fridays, under the name of the London Gazette, the editor of which, Mr. Gregson, is paid the moderate sum of £2000 a-year for his industrious and original labours; and morality is so protected, that of our three great theatres, which Mr. Prynne (one of the members ejected by Colonel Pride) proved long ago to be vomitories of vice, where the women deserve to be eaten by dogs—because, like Jezabel, they paint their faces—one is shut up, or dependent upon pauper subscriptions, and the other two are obliged to send, one to France, and the other to America,* for managers, no native being found sufficiently depraved to embark in such a business. It is needless to swell the catalogue of our joys. As Sir Christopher Wren's epitaph phrases it, *Si Monumentum* quæris—CIRCUMSPICE.

Of the Administration under which this flood of happiness has flowed upon us, what can be said?

Πως δ' αρ' σ' υμνησω παντως ενυμνον εοντα;

Is there a virtue under heaven with which it is not endowed? Purity of life, integrity of conduct, knowledge of equity, practice of piety, political consistency, cleanness of hand, singleness of purpose, dignity of personal fame, all these characterize those gifted individuals. How admirably each is qualified for his place! The Duke is first financier, on the strength of being a Field Marshal—the Chancellor of the Exchequer has studied for his office, by keeping up a correspondence with penniless Tipperary justices on the affairs of Eliogurty or Borris-o'-kane—the Chancellor is fitted for the woolsack by never having held an equity brief in his life—the Privy Seal is a Major-General, distinguished for having been second in a duel to a runaway Whig, who was at once Scotchman and attorney.† Lord

---

* Monsieur Laporte and Mr. Stephen Price.—M.

† The persons here referred to, members of the Wellington Cabinet, were "the Duke," Mr. Goulburn, ex-Secretary for Ireland, and then Chancellor of the Exchequer, Lord Lyndhurst, who succeeded Eldon as Chancellor, and the Earl of Rosslyn, who had been second to James Stuart, in his duel with Sir Alexander Boswell.—M.

Aberdeen's foreign politics were learnt in an illustrious assembly, where the History of Whittington and his Cat is discussed, and admirable dissertatations on old chamber-pots are poured into ears sesquipedal. Sir George Murray was taught the politics of our colonies in mess-rooms in Spain; and the destinies of India are aptly intrusted to Lord Ellenborough, because, like Samson, his glory lies in his locks. Of Mr. Peel what need I speak? Is not his praise to be gathered from the voice of Oxford and Sir Manasseh?* And why need I open my lips about the rest, seeing that their excessive modesty has always been so great, that nothing is known of their merits or abilities, except the simple but convincing fact of their being ministers? God knows why!

Happy people! favoured land! Farewell, then, Thomas Pride! Light be stones upon your bosom; and when the necessity arises for kicking out a parliament, may we have many a man ready to imitate your example!

* In 1829, when the University of Oxford refused to re-elect Peel, for his concession of the Catholic Claims, he was returned for the pocket-borough of Westbury, the property of Sir Manasseh Lopez. — M.

The Equality of the Sexes.*

My dearest Madam,

Allow me to return my warmest acknowledgments of the honour done me by your admirable letter on the comparative merits of the two sexes. May I hope that our opinions and sentiments, differing in words, may be found, ultimately, to coincide in spirit? You know my devotion to that side of the question to which you belong, and which you adorn and dignify equally by the charms of your mind, and your person. You maintain that women are equal, in all things, to men, and that any apparent inferiority on their parts must be attributed wholly to the institutions of society. Even in bodily powers you are unwilling to acknowledge defeat; and certainly, my dearest madam, you have argued the topic with the most captivating, the most fascinating eloquence and ingenuity. You refer, in the first place, to the inferior animals, arguing, my dearest madam, by analogy. Look, you say—look at Newmarket—there you behold mares running neck and neck with horses, gaining king's plates, and cups, and stakes of all sorts against them in spite of their noses, and occasionally leaving them at the distance-post. You then bid me consider the canine species, and I will find the grey-hound, and pointer, and terrier, and bull-bitch, equal, if not superior to the dog, in sagacity, fleetness, fierceness, and ferocity. You then fly with me to the interior of Africa, and, showing me in one cave a lioness, and in another a tigress, with their respective kittens, you ask me if the ladies are not as formidable as the lords of the desert? Turn your gaze sunwards, you next exclaim, guided by that lofty yell, and you may discern the female eagle returning from distant isles to her eyrie on the inland cliff, with a lamb, or possible a child, in her talons. Could her mate do more? You then beautifully describe the Amazons—and will you still obstinately adhere, you ask me, to the unphilosophical belief in the physical inferiority

* From *Blackwood* for August, 1826, as a "Letter to Mrs. M."—M.

of our sex to yours, seeing that, independently of other arguments, it militates against the whole analogy of nature?

My dearest madam, I acknowledge that the argument in favour of your sex, drawn from the inferior animals, is a very powerful one, perhaps unanswerable. Yet I believe that Childers, and Eclipse, and High-Flyer, and Sir Peter, and Filho da Puta, and Smolensko, and Dragon, were all horses, not mares; and for their performances I respectfully refer you to the racing calendar. Had the two first been mares, or had they been beaten by mares, I should most cheerfully have acknowledged, not only the equality, but the superiority, of your sex, and given in my palinode.

The lioness and the tigress are both on your side, and I should be sorry to say a single word against such arguments. May I be permitted, however, to hint, that it is in fierceness and ferocity, more, perhaps, than in strength, that they excel the male, and in fierceness and ferocity, awakened in defence of their young. In these qualities, I grant, your sex do greatly excel ours, especially when nursing; and at such seasons, in justice and candour, we must allow to you the flattering similitude to the lioness and the tigress. I also admit the force of the analogical argument in your favour, from birds of prey.

Passing from corporeal to mental powers, you ask, why a woman should not make, for example, a good Bishop? Why, really, my dearest madam, I humbly confess that I do not, at this moment, see any reason why you yourself should not be elevated to the Bench; and sure I am that, in lawn sleeves, you would be the very beauty of holiness. You have Pope Joan in your favour; and although I do not know of any instance of a lady of your years having become a spiritual Peer, yet time flies, and you may expect that honour when you become an old woman.

You then demand, why a lady of good natural and acquired parts, may not be a General, or a Judge? and *a fortiori*, anything else! Now, my dear madam, such has been the power of your eloquence and ingenuity, that they have completely nonplussed me — nor have I any thing in the shape of argument to rebut your irresistible logic. I therefore fling myself on a fact

—one single fact,—expecting an answer to it in your next
letter.

Suppose, my dearest madam, for a single moment, a Bishop,
or a Judge, or a General, in the family-way. How could her
ladyship visit her diocese? Or would it be safe to deliver her
charge? To be sure, it might be her ladyship's custom to visit
her diocese but once in three years,—nor are we to suppose
that she is always *enceinte*. But the chance is greatly in favour
of her being so—nor do I think that old maids would make by
any manner of means good bishops. I presume, my dearest
madam, that you would not doom the bishops of the church of
England to Catholic celibacy. Such a law is foreign, I well
know, to your disposition; and to say nothing of its gross and
glaring violation of the laws of nature herself, would it, in such
a case, be at all efficacious?

I think, my dearest madam, that I hear you reply,—" I would
elevate no female to the Bench till she was past child-bearing."
What, would you let modest merit pine unrewarded through
youth, and confer dignity only on effete old-age? The system,
my dearest madam, would not work well—and we should have
neither Kayes nor Blomfields.*

The same objection applies with tenfold force to a female
Judge. Suppose, my dearest madam, that you yourself were
Lady Chancellor. Of the wisdom, and integrity, and promptitude of your decisions there could not be the slightest doubt,
except in the minds perhaps of a Brougham, a Williams, or a
Denman. But although you could have no qualms of conscience
—yet might you frequently have qualms of another kind,
that would disturb or delay judgment. While the Court ought
to be sitting, you might be lying in; and while, in the character
of Chancellor, you ought to have been delivering a decision, in
your character of Lady, why, my dearest madam, you might
have yourself been delivered of a fine thumping boy.

Finally, suppose Lord Wellington to have been a female.
He might have possessed the same coup-d'œil, the same decision, the same fortitude, and the same resolution, on all occasions
to conquer or die. But there are times when ladies in the family-

* Drs. Kaye and Blomfield, Bishops of Lincoln and London.—M.

way (and we may safely take it for granted, that had Lord Wellington been a female she would generally have been in that interesting situation) are not to be depended on, nor can they depend upon themselves; and what if the Generalissima had been taken in labour during the battle of Waterloo? Why, such an interruption would have been nearly as bad as when his Lordship was superseded by Sir J. Burrard during the battle of Vimiera.

Now, my dearest madam, pray do let me have by return of post an answer to this great leading fact of the case. Nature seems to me to have intended women to be — mothers of families. *That* you yourself, my respected and highly-valued friend, are in an eminent degree.—So, kindest love to Mr. M. and all the children (fourteen); not forgetting that pretty puzzling pair, Thomas and Thomasine, the twins.

I have the honour to be,
My dearest Madam,
With the highest consideration,
Your affectionate friend,
JASPER SUSSEX.

Letters from the Dead to the Living.—No. 1.

BARRETTIANA.*

Contained in a Letter from Hades.

Dublin, 6th January, 1822.

CHRISTOPHER NORTH, ESQ.

DEAR SIR,—Agreeably to your request, I send you a few Notes, elucidative of the letter you have received from the Reverend the Ghost of Dr. Barrett. I return its letter therewith.

Yours, &c. &c., T. C.

Hades,

MISTHER NORTH,—The raisin I don't putt the day o' the month, is because there's no sitch thing here; but, as wan Southey says, in wan o' his prose works, "*time is not here, nor days, nor months, nor years,—an everlasting now.*" And the raisen I write to ye at all is, because it's a great shame that you putt sitch a piddlin' notice o' my death in your obituary. "*At Dublin, at an advanced period of life, Dr. John Barrett, Vice-Provost of Trinity College in that city.*" Why, the Freeman says as much for a namesake o' mine that wasn't the Vice-Provost. "*On the 27th ult. John Barrett, Esq. of Carrigboy, county Cork.*" Me, that was your correspondent, an' wrote you the Haibrew poem on the death of Sir Daniel Donnelly,[1] that Hincks translated, and putt your Magazine into the Fellowship coorse; as you yourself acknowledge, in the 27th line of the 1st

---

* Dr. John Barrett, Vice-Provost of Trinity College, Dublin, some of whose peculiarities and personalities are exhibited in these "Letters from the Dead to the Living," was at once erudite and ignorant—extremely wealthy and meanly parsimonious. He died, November 15, 1821, at a ripe age, leaving a vast accumulation of property, disposed of in a will which was eventually broken down on litigation. The original notes to these Letters are indicated by figures.—M.

[1] *Sir* is a College designation for an A. B. The Christian name is always omitted. The ghostly Doctor was not aware of the impropriety of such an omission out of College. Sir Daniel Donnelly never graduated in Trinity College.—[The poem will be found on page 70 of the present volume.—M.]

column of the 193d page of your Number for November, 1820. Now I send by opportunity the followin' aphorisms and anecdotes o' myself. The Weird Sisthers often come here, out o' kindness, to see William Shakespeare, because he tuck an' putt[2] them into his play of Macbeth, which no other author ever done. They're goin' back to Scotland, an' promised to take an' dhrop my paper into your letther-box in Prence's Sthreet.* An' as I'm not given to writin' English for magazines, but only the Haibrew, maybe ye won't, all o' ye, undherstand what I say; but has wan T. C., a correspondent o' yours, an' discreet graduate, that wrote them purty Spanish ballads,† [be the by, he's too fond o' luggin in his localities.] He got seven best marks at scholarships; but I only gave him a third[3] best, because he said, that αττηοι came from αττηςι and wance, at Haibrew examination, he gave הלב as a root, instead o' בלב; but they called him rabbi in College for all that, because he used to get the head præmium in Haibrew. He'll putt glosses to it if ye will. An' as to people sayin' that I didn't know how to spake English right, it's all folly; for I didn't spake bad English because I knew no betther, [for how could that be when I was the Vice-Provost,] but because it was only to Catty, an' Benson, an' the other porthers, that I had a right to spake English, an' they undherstud the bad betther nor the good. An' I always spell as its pronounced;[4] and that's the way all languages should be wrote. An' if the fellows didn't like me English, why didn't

---

[2] "Took and put." A favourite phrase of the Doctor's; originating, no doubt, from his long habit of *taking* the money, and *putting* it into the funds. "Put," in the Doctor's mouth, always rhymed to "cut."

[3] By a privilege conceded of old to the natives of Ireland, the different degrees of answering at examination for Scholarship are marked, not by *good*, *middle*, and *bad* marks, but by *best*, *middle*, and *bad* marks. There are three gradations of *middle* and *bad*, and, therefore, of *best* also;—1st BEST, 2d BEST, 3d BEST.

[4] And, naturally enough, he pronounced foreign languages as he found them spelt. Thus, he would tell you, that claret came from Bour-de-aux on the Ga-ron-ne, sounding every letter. But half the merit of the anecdotes about the Doctor is lost, by our not being able to print his face and voice.

* *Blackwood* was then published at 17 Prence's Street, Edinburgh.— M.

† It happened that "the purty Spanish ballads" were written, not by Maginn but by Lockhart. — M.

they spake Latin, seein' that, by the statutes, they are bound so to do. An' as for the chap that tuck an' putt me notice into Carrick's paper,[5] you may just tell him, that it would be fitther for him to mind his own business, an' not to be bitin' a cherry about me want o' punctuation, an' sitch things as don't consarn him. An' now I'm done.

THE LATE JOHN BARRETT,
that was the Vice-Provost.

P. S. — It wasn't fair o' you to putt upon me in this way, an' lave me to write my own obituary. It's thrue enough what Virgil says about the occupations o' the dead. Catty an' I's here as fresh as ever.

To MISTHER NORTH, *that keeps the Magazine in Prence's Sthreet. By favour o' the Weird Sisthers.*

No. I.

There's a chap in Nassau Sthreet, that prents caricatures, an' he wance[6] had the impidence to make one o' me that was librarian an' Vice-Provost; and Doctor ***** tould me of it at commons, an' I said to him, *Docther* *****, *I wich you was dead.*

No. II.

Another time I sent Catty for a hayperth [liars an' calumniathors say it was a farthinsworth] o' milk, an' poor Catty fell on the way, an' brok her mug an' leg; an' I tuck grate care o' poor Catty, an' became her college woman[7] myself, [but the mug was too far gone] and when she was brought home, I said, *Aye, Catty, but where's the haypenny.*

---

[5] The notice alluded to runs as follows, and was affixed to the College gate some time before the King's visit to Ireland: —

"The Library will close from the ** to the ** inst: for the purpose of cleaning
JOHN BARRETT."

The want of punctuation essentially altering the meaning, it was copied into a morning paper. "It's nonsense," said the Vice, now a ghost; "if I'm clane, I don't want to be claned; an' if I'm dirty, the library can't clane me."

[6] "Wance," *once.* From the root "wan," *one.* Do not *see*, but *hear* the late Vice-Provost PASSIM.

[7] The female servants in College are called *College-women.* Ugliness, age, and *honesty*, are the requisite qualifications.

No. III.

I wish the fellows would mind the statutes, an' spake Latn, an' not be mindin' other people's English. Wan mornin' I said to the chapel porther, *Is the two rowl-keepers come?* an' I overheard wan o' the fellows behind me say to another, *Isn't it sthrange to hear a man of education spake English so?* an' the other fellow that was behind me, said to the fellow that spoke before [that was the former fellow behind me] *Oh, he's the Vice-Provost, an' he's come to hendher[8] English from bein' spoken.*

No. IV.

I hate that Docther ****. He was always humbuggin' me at commons.

No. V.

I was wan day crossin' the coorts, goin' to the boord, an' I hard somebody say *Sweep, sweep!* an' I found him out, an' brought him before the boord, an' the blagard[9] said, that he was only a few days in the butthery[10] books, and didn't mane me. *That's a lie,* says I; *you must have meant me, Sarrah, for there was no other sweep in the coorts but me.*

No. VI.

I'm like St. Paul, I've gone through a gradle[11] o' perils,—I was wance gagged when I slep facein[12] College Green, by some young scapegraces, that got in through the window at night, an' stopt me mouth for fear I'd discover on them—I was wance plotted against to be murthered for my money—I was wance near bein pysoned by fairy mushrooms; an' now I'll tell you something worse. One day I had the tankard o' October[13] lifted to me mouth to take a drink, [because I was dhry] an' some

---

[8] "Hendher," *kinder.*

[9] "Blagard," *blackguard.*

[10] "Butthery," *buttery.* The buttery-books are those in which the names of the students, &c. are enrolled, and the fines registered.

[11] "Gradle," *great deal.*

[12] "Slep facein," *slept opposite to.*

[13] October is a sort of malt drink used in college. The Doctor was, it appears, near realizing the words of the old song:—

"*And dies in October.*"

young blagard plopped a potato from the end of the hall into the tankard undher my nose, an' wetted me, an' I called out to the fellow next me, *O Docther ****** I'm dhrownded.*

No. VII.[14]

They say I've a great memory, an' I'll tell ye the raisin why. At commons wan Sathurday [the porther had just brought in the October and the manshit[15]] They were talkin about the number o' men that was saved in the boat in Bligh's voyage, an' wan said wan thing, an tother said tother thing, an' they said to me, Docther Barrett, how many men was saved in the boat at Bligh's voyage, an I tould them the number, and tould them the names of all the men.

No. VIII.

There was a chap from Mullinahone[16] in Tipparary [he's gone to the Hottentots to be a missionary, an' T. C. calls him Bishop o' Caffraria.] They used to say he was mad, because he never learned anything in college but Irish, which was not taught there, an' didn't mind his scholarships [but now there's talk about learnin' it at the boord, an' wan of the fellows tuck lessons from Paddy Lynch[17] before he died, that he might be the professor]. An' he thrust his head into the[18] doore of the librarian's

[14] If the vice-provost were in the humour, he might tell stories innumerable of his prodigious memory. He knew the local station of every book in the great library of Trinity College. He remembered in general the particular page on which any fact was to be found, and as to dates, names, numbers, &c. his memory was inexhaustible. Ask him about a book, and you would instantly be answered, It is in the compartment Aa — on the seventh shelf — and the eighteenth book, or the nineteenth book — I don't remember which — it is the eighteenth book surely — on that shelf.

[15] "Manshit," *manchet*. The senior of the hall has a right to an additional roll and a draught of October every Saturday. The Doctor never failed to exact these dues.

[16] A notorious village. The meaning of it in Irish is rather indelicate for your pages: — how shall I say it? the ——, *the sitting part of the mill*. The inhabitants are a sort of Savoyards, always travelling *round the world for sport*. "Wherever," say the Mullinahonese, "you see three men together, you may be sure that one of them is a Mullinahone man."

[17] Now, the *ex*-paddy Lynch. A man of considerable learning, who held a situation in the Record-Tower, Dublin Castle, for many years before his death.

[18] "Doore," rhymes to "poor."

room where I was sitn an' burst out o' a laughin. *Who are you?* says I. *Beg your pardon, Sir,* says he, *I didn't know you was here* — *But that's no raisin,* says I, *that you should laugh at the rice-provost* — *I assure you, Sir,* says he, *I'm not laughin at you* — *O that may be very thrue,* says I, *but that's no raisin that you should laugh at the rice-provost* — *Upon my honour, Sir,* says he, *it's not you I'm laughing at* — *O, I dont doubt a word you say,* says I, *but that's no raisin that you should laugh at the rice-provost.*

No. IX.

They say I used to curse and swear, and I'll prove to you that I never did, but only putt little appales to heaven into my sayins, for every one of which I have Scripture. Read the followin, and then you'll see. Sir ***** [19] rapped at my doore in 1798. — *Who's there?* says I, — *It's I,* says he. — *And who are you?* says I. *****, says he, — *O! Sir ******,* says I, an' I opened the doore an came out; — and then, says I, *How are you, Sir ******?* *Now I know what you're come for, and by G—*[20] *I wont do it. You're goin to the country, and you want to get your things out at the gate.*[21] *By G—, I wont do it. — You must go to your tuther.*[22] — *You don't know at all what I want,* says he, — *an' it's not that* — *It's not that,* says I, — *O, ho! an' what is it that you do want?* — *Why,* says he, *if you'd given me time, I'd have tould you what I wanted.* — *O, ho!* says I, *go on.* — *Why,* says he, *I've some friends to coffee this evening, and I wish to give the ladies a walk in the Fellows' Garden, and I'm come to request the loan of your kay.* — *O! I can't do it* — *I can't do it,* says I. — *O! well,* says he, *it's no matther, I'll go elsewhere, I wish you'd let me spake at first,* and he was goin' off. — *D*******n to you,* says I, *what a hurry you're in, can't you sit down, an' I'll tell you the raisin why.* — *Do you see, when I be*-

---

[19] Here, and elsewhere, the names were given in full. I have taken the liberty of removing them.

[20] However innocent the Doctor may have considered his "little appales," I have thought it better to mollify them by a letter or two, wherever they occur.

[21] Without an order signed by a Fellow, no student is allowed to pass his furniture through the College gate.

[22] "Tuther," — *tutor.*

came a fellow I tuck my oath that I'd never lend the kay of the
Nassau Sthreet gate, and do you see me Sir *********, I'll shew
you it. The kay of the Nassau Sthreet gate, and the kay of
the gate laiden into the coorts is sawthred[23] together, and if I
lend you the kay of the gate laidin into the coorts, I must lend
you the kay of the Nassau Sthreet gate. All the time I was spaik-
en he was thryin[24] to get away, till I said, Sure, Sir *********
I'd do any thing to oblige you:— And now, wouldn't this do, if
I'd send Catty over with you to unlock the gate, and couldn't you
putt a stone against the gate, that the ladies and you needn't be
locked in all night in the Fellows' Garden, Sir *********.

No. X.

Its a foolish thing and extravagant, that sellin' by auction by
inch o'candle,— can't the buyers cut for it, as they do for præ-
miums in college, or thry the *Sortes Virgilianæ*. An' I'll tell
you two anecdotes, to shew you the value of an inch o' candle
— and this is the first:— Before that same Sir ******** became
Sir *********, he was sent wan evening, about dusk, to me by
his uncle, Docther *********, who lived at some distance in the
city that time. At this time the blagards used to be puttin
squibs and other misdemeanours into my letther box, an' I used
to be very cautious about openin the doore. And when I hard
the knock, I said, *Who's there?*— *It's I*, says he.— *Who are
you?* says I.— *I've a note from* Docther *********, says he.—
O ho! says I, an' I opened the doore, an walked out into the
coort to identify him. *You've a note from* Docther *********?
says I. So I brought him in. *Well — an' are you in College?*
says I.— *Yes*, says he.— *An' is* Docther ********* *in his house
in ———— Street now?* says I.— *Yes*, says he.— *Well, let us see
this note from* Docther *********, says I. I tuck an' read the
note. *Well, do you see me now?* says I; *do you sit down there,
an'* I pointed to a chair be the doore; *an' don't stir from that;
I have to go to the top o' the house to look for the book which
Docther ********* wants.* I went to the top o' the house, an'
brought down the book; an' then says I, *I'm not sure that this
is the book that* Docther ********* *wants, for, d'ye see, it's*

[23] "Sawthred,"— *soldered.* [24] "Thryin,"— *trying.*

a'most dark. But I'll tell you what you'll do — do you take it to Docther *********, and if it's not the book he wants, bring it back to me, an' I'll light a candle, an' get you the right wan.

No. XI.

Wan evenin ****** the fellow came to me in the dusk, an' says I to him, *Sit there near the window, for a candle's out o' the question.*

No. XII

F***** the fellow made a gradle o' money, and lived abroad for some years in the city, an' came home to die in the College. An' when he was dead I asked how much he left[25] to the College; an' they tould me, *Not a penny.*— *The d———d rascal*, says I, *the place where he was enabled to make so much money.*

No. XIII.

M**** the fellow, him who is now the bishop,* came to me wan day about bisnis, and I opened me desk to get him some papers he wanted. An' it was at the time when guineas was goin', an' I had a hundred of 'em in the desk, tied up in a string. An' by some accident I pulled the string, as I was takin' out the papers, an' all the guineas went rowlin on the floor.[26] So I jumped upon M. an' says I, M— M— for God's sake don't stir —don't take any of 'em—stay where you are like an honest man, until I pick 'em up. So he was huffed; but wasn't I right? How did I know what the devil might put in his head? Shure enough I picked up only ninety-nine, and says I, oh! now M. give it to me. He was very high about it; and says I, maybe its under your foot. Well, he lifted up his right foot, an' it wasn't there; an' he lifted up his left foot, an' it wasn't there, an' I never saw it from that day to this. Maybe it went into a hole, and maybe it didn't.

---

[25] This story comes with a peculiar bad grace from our ghost. The Doctor died worth nearly £100,000, but, except a few legacies, left all to charity. As he specified no charitable institution, the will will be litigated. One legacy was bequeathed under this express condition — that the legatee should give up all connection with *Peg the Nailer.*

[26] "Floor" also rhymes with poor.

* Dr. William Magee, Bishop of Cork, and afterwards Archbishop of Dublin, author of the great work on The Atonement.— M.

No. XIV.

They tell lies about me never stirrin' out of college. I was at the Bank often and often; an' I was as far as Kerry on a college law shoot. I saw many wonderful things on my thravels, which I wrote down when I came back. At Rathcool I got out of the coach, and I saw a fine bird walkin outside the doore of the public house; an' I asked the oslur—him who was mindin' the horses—Pray, sir, what fine animal is that? an' says he, scratchin' his head, Plase your reverence *we* calls him a turkey cock. An' I afterwards looked at a picther[27] of wan in a book, an' I found the osler was right.

No. XV.

When I was senior lekchurer[28] I gave the senior lekchurer's dinners as grand as they were ever given; and they cost me a power of money; an' the people never could dhrink all the wine I used to buy; so that many bottles of claret and port and other wines were left to me; an' I used to ask white-haired ***** him who is now chairman of the county of ***** to come to me often in the evenings, for he was a youth I liked. When I intended to give him wan of the bottles of claret, I'd say ***** come an' *sit* with me this evenin' an' he'd always come; for he was a good youth, an' I'd give him wan bottle, which is enough, an' I'd take wan myself. When I didn't intend to give him any, I'd say, ***** come an' *talk* with me this evenin'; an' he'd always say he was engaged. It was quare[29] he was never engaged on the nights he was to get the wine.

No. XVI.

They used to print stories about me, and they'd make out that every second word I'd say would be, *do you see me now?* That's a lie. I used to say it sometimes, but not often; and what harm is it, if I did? An' they used to say that when I was wance examinin' for a fellowship, I began my examination

---

[27] "Picther," picture.
[28] "Lekchurer," lecturer. This officer gives official dinners; and the Doctor is not gasconading when he praises his. They were really splendid.
[29] "Quare," queer.

by sayin' Domine *****, *Videsne me nunc*—but that's the biggest lie of all.

An' there's the sort of an obituary you ought to have made for me.—J. B.

Letters from the Dead to the Living.—No. 2.

CATTIANA.

To Christopher North, Esq. &c. &c. &c.

DEAR SIR,

AGREEABLY to your request, I have exerted myself to procure some particulars of the early life and education of your new subterranean correspondent—Catty.* I regret that the result has not been so satisfactory as I could have wished. The upshot of my inquiries has been simply the ascertaining of these three facts,—that her father was a tinker of repute, her mother a fishwoman, and that she herself, (after being carefully instructed in the several dialects employed by members of these itinerant professions, to which her parents belonged,) was very near undertaking the occupation of bar-maid in a public-house, until, in lucky hour, she determined on entering College; where, having gone through a regular course of attendance on undergraduates, bachelors, masters, and fellows, she was at length advanced to the honour of waiting on the Vice-Provost, in which service she died.

But why the blazes don't you print all the articles I sent you last years? I suppose you've mislaid them—or lit your pipe with them at Ambrose's—or singed a goose with them—or papered a closet with them, (as Dr. Smith did with his Gaelic Poems)—or—or———. By the ———, if I thought so, I'd off to Edinburgh with my shillelagh in a jiffy, and run a tilt against your types and metal rules, that would set your

* Catty was the ancient and ugly college-servant—commonly called the *gyp*—of Dr. Barrett.—M.

press-gang aghast — compositors, devils, and all! Don Quixote among the puppets, or Ariosto among the pots, was nothing to it.

However, hang it, I can't think you'd play me such a scurvy trick; but we contributors, you know, are sometimes a little uneasy, you know, lest our articles, you know, should be re...je... je...(hang it, the ink's so thick, and the pen so bad, that I can't get the word out—) je...je...je...jected, you know.

However, if my suspicions be, after all, well-grounded—mind your eye—that's all. T. C.

Dublin, Trinity College, 3d August, 1822.

P. S.—You needn't be sending to me to write notes to any more of your *Barrettiana* or *Cattiana,* until you print my articles first; for, bad fortune to me, if I'll be a cat's paw to you any longer.

2[1] *misther blacwud*[2]

heydays[3]

MISTHER BLACWUD

IM[4] catty[5] the owld enshint[6] catty hur[7] that bruck[8] the mug an lost the hepeny[9] ther was annuther catty that sarved the docther afther i dyed the blagard he left her loshins[10] o mummy

---

[1] 2: "to;" *passim.*

[2] *misther blacwud:* "MR. BLACKWOOD"—*magnum et venerabile nomen* and fit *vivo dare nomen*—"to give name to a river!" We have two rivers Black*water* in Ireland. If I had interest in any of the romantic parishes, through which either of them meanders as it flows, I would procure an act of vestry to have its name changed into that of Black*wood*. The RIVER BLACKWOOD!! Mercy on me—what pilgrimages we'd make to it! what punch we'd mingle from its tide!

[3] *heydays:* "Hades."

[4] *im:* "I'm"—"I am."

[5] *catty:* "Catty." This "pillar of the state" wants a *capital.*

[6] *enshint:* "ancient."

[7] *hur:* "her"—in English "she."

[8] *bruck:* "broke."

[9] *hepeny:* "halfpenny."

[10] *loshins:* "lashings." A word in the Hibernian language, equivalent to the Irish ZO TOP—Anglo Irish "gillore," and English "thousands" or "enough." On a late pedestrian excursion to the hill of Howth, my companions and I being in search of water to slake our thirst (say rather to mix our grog,) inquired of a gossoon [*garçon*] whether there were any water in the neighbourhood—"O yes!" replied he, "there's *loshins* above there."

an[11] shee never had look or grease[12] sense[13] till shee scalded the guts out o herself dhrinkin[14] in sarvin the docther hear thers a Grate collidg hear for awl the wurld like thrinity collidg onely docther kile aynt[15] provust but docther swathe in purge[16] thuther day says i 2 me[17] owld mather the docther sur says i[18] im livin with ye hear says i sense ye dyed says i an ye havnt gave me says i so mutch as a Thrawnieen[19] o Wages says i an i havnt a screed[20] 2 me back bad scrand[21] 2 ye says he for a goast[22] o a collidg wumman where id i get munny now says he havnt the[23] it awl on the erth abuv says he barrin[24] sum[25] of it thats in the canal[26] says he didnt the says he spind awl the good in the Nayshin[27] on bony[28] says he furst says he an then conjur up the bank noats that was the goasts o the owld Ginnees the melted

---

[11] *an:* "and;" *passim.*

[12] *look or grease:* "luck or grace;" a common Hibernicism.

[13] *sense:* "since."

[14] Said to be fact. The Doctor bequeathed a handsome sum to Catherine II. On the payment of the first instalment, she became so intoxicated (with whisky, not joy,) that she did not long survive her master. Catò (accented on the last syllable) is in the *fishwomanish* dialect, used for Catty, or Catherine. In his latter days, when the Doctor was disposed to be facetious, and to quote Cicero, he always spoke of the original Catty as his *Catò Major*, and called himself "King of *the Catti.*" The late Dr. * * * * * *, more distinguished for the number than the excellence of his puns, used to translate the *Docte Cati* of Horace—"the Doctor's Catty," pronouncing *Docte Docter*, according to the usage of Cockaigne.

[15] *aynt:* "a'n't"—"am not;" but used throughout Ireland for "is not."

[16] *swathe in purge!!!* I'm really at a loss here. Perhaps Caterina means Swedenburg. His doctrine of the existence of manufactories, schools, &c., in the other world, favours my supposition.

[17] *me:* "my;" *passim.*

[18] The continued reiteration of *says I*, is a common Hibernicism.

[19] *Thrawnieen.* An Irish diminutive, meaning a "trifle."

[20] *screed:* "rag."

[21] *scrand:* "*datur ambignis;*" ALVARY. It seems to mean "luck."

[22] *goast:* "ghost."

[23] *the:* "they;" *passim.*

[24] *barrin:* "barring"—"except."

[25] *sum:* "some."

[26] The Doctor lost a power on the failure of one of the Canal Companies.

[27] *Nayshin:* "nation."

[28] *bony:* "Bonaparte."

down an yoosed[29] 2 pass hear says he an lave us without a circle-eating Mediam[30] says he but ill tell ye says he what youll[31] doo says he ill giv ye haf a Duzzen o hang neck dose[32] o meself says he an yull take an putt them says he in 2 misther blacwuds Mag o sin[33] says he an dont rite 2 misther grease stuffer noth[34] says he bekays[35] the tell me hees only a Fantim[36] like ourselves catty but 2 misther blacwud himself says he an its ten to 1 says he but hell giv ye sumthin Hausim for em says he for says he he dusnt matther givn a 2 an six penny or maybe four tens[37] says he for an Arti—Arti—now as I hop 2 dye a singer[38] i cant rekillect what the dother cawld it twosnt an artichoak but an arti sum udder vegitibl o now i have it as shure as pays[39] an artikail thats i sup pos skotch kail for the say misther blacwud

[29] *yoosed:* "used."

[30] *a circle-eating Mediam!!!* "a circulating medium." The English translation of *Ranunculum sceleratus*, (a deleterious species of crow-foot,) — "celery-leaved crow-foot" — was nothing to this. Whether the Hedes could eat circles or no, it is certain that Dr. B. could never swallow a conic section. It is an authenticated fact — that, although he committed to memory the entire of Hamilton's work on the subject, he did not understand one demonstration from beginning to end.

[31] *youll:* "you'll" — "you will."

[32] *hang neck dose!!!* "anecdotes."

[33] *Mag o sin!!!* "magazine."

[34] I write in red ink to signify how I blush for the audacious — the unorthographical Catty! *grease-stuffer north;* "CHRISTOPHER NORTH!" The least we can do, by way of atonement, is to print his name in the largest capitals we can command.

[35] *bekays:* "because;" more correctly mis-spelt — "becase."

[36] *Fantim:* "phantom."

[37] *tens:* "tenpenny pieces." You don't know what they are in Scotland. Happy Jehus of the British mail-coaches! you are not put off with a ten instead of a thirteen, [12d. English is 13d. Irish.] Happy mail-coach travellers in the green isle of my nativity! your tenpennies suffice for the protection of your shillings!

[38] *dye a singer!!!* "die a sinner."

[39] *as sure as pays:* "as sure as pease." A common phrase throughout Ireland to imply metaphysical certainty. As to the origin of it — "*nec scio, nec curo*" — as one of the best classical scholars that Ireland has ever produced replied, when on the fellowship bench, to the following question: — "Who was the mother of Æneas's nurse?" I give it in English, because I don't know how to write bad Latin.

I cannot resist this opportunity of recording a ludicrous orthographical mis-

that yure a heelander[40] an wares pettycoats an the Bearer is misther pollock[41] he awlways spinds haf a yeer on the erth an haf a yeer hear an if yull jest giv him the munny or an ordure[42] on the bank hell no[43] what 2 doo with it giv me luv 2 bensin[44] an jerry[45] and misther mc allisther[46]

No. I.

I cut them them all wan day at commons, sainiors and juniors. It was in Asthrnomy. 'Who is the Man in the Moon,' says I, 'an where do ye find him?' An some said wan thing, an some said another thing, an nobody said the right thing. So I ansered the question meself; 'Why,' says I, 'he's a play be Settle,[o] an ye'll find him in the College Library if ye choose to look for him; an, if ye don't, Bensin ill[1] find him for ye.' So I settled em: ha ha ha!

No. II.

I was as good a saint as Saint Senanus, an Saint Kevin.[2] I didnt like to have women botherin me, an stravaguin[3] through

take, which I met with some years since on a tomb-stone, in a cemetery at Glendalough, county of Wicklow. *Requiescat in pace* was rendered — "May he rest in *pease!*"

[40] *heelander:* "highlander."

[41] *pollock:* Not Pollock, late of ******** Square, nor Pollock of ********* Street, but Pollux. See Lempriere's Classical Dictionary.

[42] *ordure:* "order." "Decency, Catty honey."

[43] *hell no:* "he'll know."

[44] *bensin:* "Benson." The premier porter of the library. One who will give his opinion on any question in politics, or of any book in the collection. "What news, Benson?" inquired I one morning. "Nothing but a little from *Parnambucka* [Pernambuco]," replied he. Another morning I was curious and indecorous enough to peep over his shoulder, in order to ascertain what book he was reading. It was "*The Life of Mr. Thomas Firmin, citizen of London.*"

[45] *jerry:* "Jerry." A badge-man. One of the "lords of the creation," as he was once facetiously termed.

[46] *misther mc allisther:* "Mr. M'Allister." The mace-bearer [ὁ ϰορυνήτης] and head-porter of the University. I am happy to have this opportunity of printing his name in capitals.

[o] *be:* "by."

[1] *ill:* "will."

[2] See Moore's Irish Melodies.

[3] *sthravaguin:* "stravaguing" — "strolling." Derived probably by pleo-

the library. Doether * * * * * [him that says Noah's ark is still in bein⁴] brought a whole bilen⁵ o them wan day into the librarian's room to me, an I was afeared, an began thinkin o Joseph an Potipher's wife: an I couldnt get out o the door, because it was chuck full o them, an I couldnt get out o the window, because Id break me neck: so I turned me back to them, the way⁶ they mightnt see me face, an thrust my head [face an all] into the safe,⁷ an called Bensin. 'Bensin,' says I, 'stand here close by me: an when theyre gone take an tell me, that I may take me head out o the safe again, Bensin.'

No. III.

They were always pestherin me about my memory, says the provost to me wan day.—'Doether Barrett,' says he, 'yere alway braggin o your memory: tell me who was Lord Mayor in the year 1739?' 'How should I know,' says I, 'who was Lord Mayor in the year 1739?' 'Well,' says he, 'who was Junior Altherman?' 'An how should I know who was Junior Altherman?' says I. 'Can't ye ask me somethin in me own way,' says I, 'an I'll anser ye?' 'Well, then,' says he, 'who was Bursar?' 'Why,' says I, 'it must be Hughes, for he was expelled that year be owld Baldwin, for callin him a rascal.'⁸

No. IV.

'You've only anserd me wan word in Greek, * * * * * * *,' says I, one day I was examinin him, 'and that's ἐπεί—an' do ye know the raisin why?—because ye didn't know e'er an other.'

nasm, from "straying." Thus "gallivant" from "gallant."—LOBSKI—passim.

⁴ *bein*: "being."

⁵ *bilen*: "boiling;" synonymous to "kit"—"crowd."

⁶ Many expressions considered essentially vulgar in Ireland, as used exclusively by the lower orders, are really correct and figurative forms still existing in the Irish language. The phrase "the way," as here employed, means "in order that." Instance are, I believe, to be found in the Irish Bible, of this application of the term.

⁷ A little recess in the wall of the librarian's room.

⁸ What will not potations of Lethe effect? The doctor, never known to trip during his lifetime, is here guilty of a gross inaccuracy. Most respectable testimony could be adduced in support of the assertion—that the word employed, so far from being "rascal," was simply—"*scoundrel*."

No. V.

I wans towld the fellows a story at Commons about an Indian custom, an a great many years afther they raped it up[9] to me again.' 'Do ye know where ye found the story ye towld[10] us wanst about the Indian custom?' says they. 'Why wouldn't I?' says I. 'And where did ye find it?' says they. So I towlt them that I found it in wan o' the volumes o' Churchill's Voyages, six pages from the end. 'An do ye recollect,' says they, wurkin[11] at me still, 'when you towld it to us?' 'In one thousand seven hundred and ninety-three,' says I.

No. VI.

In the owld Muses,[12] that was also used for a ball-court, they used to bob their heads again[12] the arches and partitions at night, because it was dark. So we tuck an locked the Muses up every night, and then they rised to commit misdemeanours about the palace outside, just as Lord Byron says the Italians does about a pillar at Ravenna, so that in a new sense—*olue runt manè Camœnœ.* So the board thought it best to take an put up a lamp in the Muses, and I thought it a very good plan, but liable to objections: so when it came to my turn to spake, I said—that it would be very well to putt up the lamp, but that it should be *taken down at night, for fear the lads id break it.*

---

[9] *raped* [*reaped*] *it up:* "referred to it"—"recalled it."
[10] *towld:* "told."
[11] *wurkin:* "working."
[12] An appurtenance to the University—situated behind the kitchen and dedicated to *post-culinary* purposes. It derives its name from an edifice—similar and similarly posited—of more ancient date, which contained *nine* stalls or recesses, separated from each other by wooden partitions. The increased diffusion of learning throughout the island cannot be better attested than by the circumstance—that it was found necessary, on re-edifying the building, to double the number of recesses. As the designation "Muses" seemed likely to be entailed upon the new structure, some noble-hearted youths—burning to protect their country from the impending imputation of a *bull*—resolved to adopt a new one, and accordingly dubbed it "The Fellows," (the number of the Junior Fellows being just eighteen.) In vain! Despite of loyalty, and gratitude, and fashion itself, Dunleary is Dunleary still—despite of patriotism, and decency, and common sense, "The Muses" are still "The Muses."

The Last Words of Charles Edwards, Esq.*

CHAPTER I.

I AM, or, more properly speaking, I have been, a man of pleasure. I am now forty years, less some few months, of age; and I shall depart this life at twelve o'clock to-night. About that hour it is that I propose to shoot myself through the head. Let this letter be evidence that I do the act advisedly. I should be sorry to have that resolution confounded with madness, which is founded upon the coolest and maturest consideration. Men are coxcombs even in death; and I will not affect to disguise my weakness. I would not forfeit the glory of triumphing over broken-spirited drunkards and half-crazy opium-chewers—of being able to die grateful for the joys I have experienced, and

---

* This striking paper, which appeared in *Blackwood* for October, 1823, was introduced by Maginn, in his usual manner of mystification, by the following epistle to the renowned Christopher North:—

"DEAR NORTH,—I shall be obliged by your sinking scruples, and giving a place in your next Number to the enclosed paper, entitled, 'The Last Words of Charles Edwards, Esq.' The production will of itself sufficiently explain who the writer *was*. I knew him in the Peninsula as a dashing fellow; and, notwithstanding all he says, he was a great favourite with his mess. Bad as he was, he did not want some good points: he was not a scoundrel to the core. He is gone! May the history of his errors do good to one young and unhardened sinner! I think it may well be expected to do good to hundreds of them.

"Some people will say you act wrongly in giving publicity to such a record. Don't mind this—it is mere cant. The paper is a transcript—I have no doubt a faithful one, of the feelings of a man who had strong passions himself, who understood human passion, who understood the world, and who lived miserably, and died most miserably, because he could not, or would not, understand himself; and therefore derived no benefits from his acute perceptions as to others. Is not this a lesson? I think it is not only a lesson, but a lesson of lessons; and I request you to print the thing as it stands.

"I received the paper from an old friend of mine, who at one time served in the same troop with Edwards. The packet was left at his house on Christmas night, 1822. He was from home at the time, and did not reach London until a week had elapsed. The hand-writing was disguised, but he recognized it notwithstanding; and the newspapers of the day sufficiently confirmed the import.—Yours truly, "MORGAN ODOHERTY."

of disdaining to calumniate pleasures after they have ceased to be within my reach. I do assure you, Mr. ********, that I should wait personally upon you with this epistle; but that I think the mere reasonableness of my suicide must carry conviction with it of my sanity; but that I trust to lay before you such facts, and such arguments, as shall approve me not only justifiable, but most philosophic, in destroying myself. Hear what I have done; weigh what I mean to do; and judge if I deserve the name of madman.

I was born of a family rather ancient than rich; and inherited, with something like the handsome person of my father, his disposition to expend money rather than to acquire it. To my own recollection, at eighteen, I was of a determined temper, rather than of a violent one; ardent in the prosecution of objects, rather than sudden to undertake them; not very hasty either in love or in quarrel. I had faculty enough to write bad verses,—not industry enough to write anything else; and an aptitude for billiards and horse-riding to a miracle.

Now I desire to have this considered not as a *confession*, but as a statement. As I plead guilty to no fault, I make a declaration, not an acknowledgment. I am not lamenting anything that is past. If I had to begin again to-morrow, I would begin again in the same way. I should vary my course perhaps something, with the advantage of my present experience; but, take it in the main, and it would be the race that I have run already.

At eighteen, with an education, as Lord Foppington has it, "rather at large;" for (like Swift's captain of horse) my tutors were the last people who expected any good of me,—at eighteen, it became necessary for me to think of a profession. My first attempt in life was in the navy. I was anxious to *go*, and cared very little whither; and a school-boy midshipman of my acquaintance cajoled me into a Mediterranean voyage, by promises of prize-money, and descriptions of Plymouth harbour.

If I were to speak from my feeling at the present moment, I should say, that the life of a sailor has its charms. I am bankrupt in appetite, as well as in estate; if I have nothing left to enjoy, I have little capacity left for enjoyment; and I now know how to appreciate that exuberance of spirit with which a man dashes into dissipation on shore, after six weeks restraint from it at sea. But I know also that these are the feelings of situation, and of circumstance. The past seems delightful, where no hope lives for the future. I am cherishing most fondly the recollection of those sensations which are now the most completely lost to me for ever. But it is the act of the moment which forms the index to the true impression. A ship of war may seem abstract liberty to him who pines in the dungeons of the inquisition. But confinement, monotony, coarse society, and personal privation;—the simple fact is worth all the argument;—after a cruise of two months, I quitted the navy for ever.

Charmed almost as much with my change of society as with my change of dress, I quitted the sea-service, and entered a regiment of light dragoons; and, for two years from the time of my joining the army, I led the life which lads commonly lead in the outset of a military career. And even to the occurrences of those two years, rude and unintellectual as they were, my memory still clings with pleasure and with regret. Toys, then, however trifling, pleased; the most refined enjoyments could have done no more. Is there a man living, past thirty, who does not sometimes give a sigh to those days of delicious inexperience and imperception, when the heart could rest content with the mere gratification of the senses; when the intimacies of the dinner-table passed current for friendship; when the woman who smiled on all, was to all, nevertheless, charming; and when life, so long as health and money lasted, was one uninterrupted course of impulse and intoxication?

It was my fate, however, to continue but a short time a mere follower of opera *figurantes*, and imbiber of strong potations. Just before I was one-and-twenty, a woman eight years older than myself in great measure fixed my destiny, and entirely formed my character.

Boys who run riot commonly attach themselves, I think, to married women. Wives, where by ill fortune they incline to irregularity, are more understanding, and more accessible, than girls; and hope is your only food for an incipient passion. Many a woman becomes an object of desire, when there seems to be a probability of success; upon whom, but for such fore-knowledge or suspicion, we should not perhaps bestow a thought.

Louisa Salvini was eight-and-twenty years of age; a Sicilian by birth; full of the climate of her country. Hers was the Spanish or Italian style of beauty;—small rather as to figure, yet of exquisite proportion. She had a shape which, but to behold, was passion;—a carriage, such as nothing but the pride of her own loveliness could have suggested;—her eyes! their glance of encouragement was fascination!—her lips confused the sense to look upon them;—and her voice!—If there be (passing attraction either of face or form) one charm about a woman more irresistible than every other, it is that soft—that mild, sweet, liquid tone, which sooths even in offending, and when it asks, commands; which shakes conviction with its weakest word, and can make falsehood (ay, though known for such) so sweet, that we regard the truth with loathing. Oh heaven! I have hearkened to the delicious accents of such a voice, till, had my soul's hope been asked from me, it would have been surrendered without a struggle!—To-night, at midnight, I shall hear such a voice for the last time! I shall hear it while I gaze upon features of loveliness; while my soul is lulled with music, and when my brain is hot with wine; and the mere melody of that voice will go farther to raise the delirium I look for than * *

* * * * * *

But enough of this now. My tale should be of that which was. Let that which shall come hereafter give some other historian material.

My acquaintance with Louisa Salvini was of her seeking rather than of mine. Accident threw me, under favourable circumstances, in her way; but it so happened that, at the moment, I did not perceive I had excited her attention. The manner of our subsequent introduction was whimsical. I was not a man (at twenty) to decline an adventure blindfold; a well-played-upon old lady carried me, as a visitor, to Salvini's house; and my fate was decided from the first moment that I entered it.

Gracious Heaven! when I reflect that the woman of whom I speak;—whom I recollect one of the loveliest creatures that nature ever formed;—whose smile I have watched, for its mere beauty, even in the absence of passion;—at whose feet I have sat for hour after hour, intoxicating myself with that flattery which is the only flattery true manhood can endure!—When I reflect that this woman, at the moment while I write, is a withered—blasted—aged creature of fifty!—Madness—annihilation—is refuge from such a thought. I met her, scarce a month since, after an absence of years. Those eyes, which once discoursed with every rising emotion, retained still something of their original brightness, but it now only added horror to their expression. That hand, which I had pressed for hours in mine, was now grown bony, shrunken, and discoloured. Her once cloudless complexion *reeked* with paint, through which the black furrow of time shewed but more deep and ghastly. Her lips— *Oh!* they were the same lips which —— The voice too;— more dreadful than all! That voice which had once been sweetest music to my soul;—that voice which memory still is sounding in my ears;—that voice which I had loved—had worshipped;—that voice was gone;—it was no more;—and what remained was harsh,—tremulous,—broken,—discordant! —And this is the woman whom I so adored? It is she, and she is unconscious of change!—and I shall be—must be—the thing that she now is! Hold, brain!—The blow of this night saves me from such a fate!

My love for Louisa Salvini endured two years without satiety. An attachment of equal duration has never befallen me since. But at the time to which I refer, all circumstances were in my favour. I was glowing with all the fervour of youth, and with all the vigour of unwasted constitution. My mistress's beauty delighted my senses; her avowed preference gratified my vanity; she was charming to me, (love apart) taken merely as a companion; and what conduced still farther to the keeping alive our passion, she was not (being another's) constantly in my presence.

Contentment, however, is not the lot of man. Give a Mahometan his paradise; and in six weeks he would be disgusted with it. My affection for my charming mistress was just beginning to be endangered, when the regiment to which I belonged, was ordered to the Continent. The fact was, that I met in

Louisa's society a variety of women, of principles as free as her own; and the very jealousy which each lady entertained of her friends, made success with herself the more easy and certain. A little while longer, and Louisa and I had severed; my embarkation, parting us by necessity, saved us probably from a parting by consent.

I left England very poor as to pecuniary means; but rich in every other advantage which (to me,) made life desirable. Youth, O youth! could I but recall the years that I have lived! —I would rather stand now upon the barrenest plain in Europe, —naked—friendless—pennyless—but again sixteen, than possess, as the thing I am, the empire of the world.

Is there a fool so besotted as to trust the cant he utters,—to believe that MONEY can really purchase all the blessings of this life? Money can buy nothing;—it is worth nothing. I have rioted in its abundance; I have felt its total deprivation; and I have enjoyed more, I believe, of happiness in the last state than in the first.

Shall I forget the first event of my career on the Continent, —that event which, in the end, led to its premature termination?—Shall I forget the insolent superiority with which I looked down upon my brother officers,—men to whom play, excess of wine, and mercenary women, seemed, and indeed were, delights sufficient?

Wine, until after thirty, from choice, I seldom tasted. My spirits, when sober, were too vivid for control;—wine only troubled their serenity, without heightening their level. Of play,—I touched it once; and I shall speak of it hereafter. But women? such women as these men could admire? Even my more cultivated sense rejected them;—two years of intimacy with Salvini and her companions had chastened my taste, and made delicate my perceptions. Can I ever, I repeat, forget that exquisite moment,—that moment which secured to me at least one enemy for life—when I, the poorest cornet in our regiment, defeated my colonel in the favour of the first beauty in Lisbon? By heaven, the recollection of that single hour past warms my spirits to high pitch for the hour that is to come! The envy; the hate—the burning hate—which my success engendered in the bosoms of half my acquaintance! The sensation of hating is one which I have never fully experienced; but the pleasure of being hated — oh, it is almost equal to the pleasure of being beloved!

To a man of habits and temperament like mine, the *Peninsula* was a delightful residence in 1808. I remember the gay appearance of the *capital;* which, taken by moonlight from the river, is perhaps one of the most imposing in the world. I remember the striking panoramic *coup-d'œil* of its church and convent spires innumerable; its marble fountains, its palaces, its towers, and its gardens; its streets and squares of white and yellow buildings, each gaudily appointed, from the basement to the roof, with *jalouse* lattices, balconies, and verandahs; — the whole city, too, throwing itself (from the irregular site upon which it rises,) full, at a single glance, upon the eye; and every feature in the prospect, seeming, like an object in a picture, disposed artfully with a view to the general beauty of the scene.

Then the free spirits of the women; — their passions concentrated, almost to madness, by the restraint under which they live! Honour, for aiding the hopes of a lover, be to systems of restriction, severity, and *espionage!* Opportunity, to an English woman, wants the piquancy of novelty. As it is constantly recurring, it is constantly neglected. In Spain, they seize it when it does present itself; for, once rejected, it may never be found again.

But, beyond the beauty of Lisbon as a city; beyond even the brightness of those souls that inhabited it; there was a laxity of law and manner in it at the period to which I speak; a license inseparable from the presence of a foreign force in a prostrate, shackled, and dependent country; an absence as much of moral as of physical police; which, to a disposition such as mine, was peculiarly acceptable. Add to this, the farther fact, that I was fresh in a strange capital; among a people to whose manners, and almost to whose language, I was a stranger; where, little being fully understood, all had credit for being as it ought to be; and where the mere novelty of my situation was a charm almost inexhaustible; — such allurements considered, could I fail to be charmed with the Peninsula?

My stay in this land of delight, then, was something short of three years. I was present at the famous battle of Talavera; and, afterwards, at the desperate contest of Albuera, under Beresford; where the Polish lancers first tried their strength against our English cavalry. I was a sharer, too, in the more partial affair of Busaco; and took part in the duty of covering the retreat that followed; a retreat in which the whole of the southern line of Portugal, from the Spanish frontier to Lisbon, was depopulated and laid waste; in which convents were deserted, cities consumed by fire, and women born to rank and affluence, compelled to seek protection from the meanest followers of the British army.

The evacuation of Coimbra, (the Bath, if I may so call it, of Portugal,) is present to me now, as though it had occurred but yesterday. I see the immense population — men, women, and children, of all ranks and of all ages, — pouring out, at an hour's notice, through the Lisbon gate of the city; and rushing upon a journey which not one in five of them could hope to accomplish. It was little to have abandoned home and property; to have set forth on foot (for the army had seized all conveyance,) — on foot, and unprovided, in a long and rapid march, through a distracted, ravaged, lawless tract of country; if to have suffered this was much, the trial was still to come. I saw these multitudes, spent with travel and with hunger, reach towns in which every hovel — every shed — was filled with troops. I saw families upon families, yet new upon their pilgrimage.— not yet so tamed and beaten down by suffering as willingly to carry their daughters into the guardrooms of an infuriated soldiery — I saw them lying (for even the churches were filled with our sick and wounded) — lying unsheltered all night in the fields and open squares; waiting, with feverish restlessness, the appearance of morning, as though new light (repose apart,) would to them be an occasion of new strength.

The vast column rolled forward on the high road to the capital, collecting the population of the country over which it passed. Behind were left the weak, the aged, and the dying; and some few wretches, of profession, who, tempted by the hope of gain, took their chance (and lost it) of mercy from the enemy.

But though every step over which the mass advanced gave addition to its numbers, there were drains at work, and fearful ones, to counteract the reinforcement. Cold dews at midnight, burning suns by day, scanty provisions, and fatigue unwonted —these ministers did their work, and especially among the females. Towards the close of the second day's march, the women began to fail rapidly. At first, when a girl grew faint, and unable to proceed, her sister would stay by her. This feeling, however, was not fated to last long: soon the sister dashed desperately forward; to sink herself, and meet her own fate, some few leagues farther on.

I saw one company halted between Leiria and Pombal, which must have consisted of eight hundred or a thousand individuals. These people came from the neighbourhoods of Coimbra and Condeixa; some of them from as far up as Mongoalde and Vizeu. There were girls of fourteen or fifteen, clad in their gayest apparel—their only means of carrying, or (as they said) of "saving" it. There were old men, and grandames; peasants, male and female; friars, and artisans, servants, and *religieuses*. After travelling, most of them, more than fifty miles on foot, and passing two or three nights in the open air, they were lying upon the banks of a river, waiting for the sunrise, as I rode past them. I never can forget this scene; and yet I feel that it is impossible for me to describe it. The stream (I believe it was a branch of the Mondego) was dark and swollen, from the effect of recent rains; and it rushed along between the willows, which grew on either bank, as though sharing in the hasty spirit which animated every object about it. On the road, which lay to the right of the river, troops and fugitives were already in motion. It was just dawn when I came up. A light breeze was half clearing off the fog from the surface of the water. I saw the living figures imperfectly as I approached—all white and shrouded, like spectres, in the mist. The light dresses of the girls were saturated with wet. Their flowers and feathers were soiled—drooping—broken. Their hair—(the Spanish women are remarkable for the beauty of that *feature*)—their dark long hair—hung neglected and dishevelled. Their feet, which cardinals might have kissed? were, in many instances, naked—

wounded — bleeding. And, worse than all, their spirit and their strength was gone. Of those whom I saw lying on the banks of that water, a fearful proportion lay there to rise no more. And yet many had gold and jewels; but gold could not help them. And their loveliness remained; and they looked in eloquent, though in mute despair, upon British officers who passed by — and yet those men, who would have fought knee-deep for the worst of them, they could not help them. I overtook, after this, a beautiful girl of fifteen, travelling alone — out of the high road — from apprehension of insult. This girl had been separated from her friends in the general confusion. She had money and diamonds to a considerable amount about her; and had accomplished half her journey, but felt unable to proceed farther. She begged, on her knees, for a horse — for any conveyance; to be allowed to travel near me, with my servants — anywhere, anyhow, to be protected, and to get on. I had not the means of aiding that girl. I could not help her. Every Englishman had already done his utmost. I had then three women under my protection. I see the figure, the countenance, the tears of that girl, at this moment. I thought at one time that I must have staid and been made prisoner along with her. I could not carry her away in my arms. I could not leave her — no man could have left her to her fate. Fortunately an officer came up, who was less encumbered than myself; and she was provided for. — And in such way (and in ways a thousand times more dreadful) great numbers of women got on to the capital. They escaped for a time the lot of their friends and relatives; but, eventually, what was to be their fate? What *was* their fate? What if I saw these women afterwards — women born to affluence — reared in the very lap of luxury and softness — what if I saw many of them begging in the public streets of Lisbon? — I did see them in that state; but it is a subject that I must not dwell upon.

The conclusion of my Peninsular campaign was not favourable to my fortunes. As a soldier, I did my duty in the field; but opportunity for a man to distinguish himself cannot always be commanded. I had a project once, with a few fellows as desperate, or as careless, as myself, for dashing at the enemy's military chest; but our scheme fell to the ground, for we never got a chance of carrying it into execution. In the meantime, as regarded promotion, my general conduct was not such as to make friends. Repeated successes, in one peculiar pursuit, inspired me with an excessive confidence in myself, and with a very contemptuous estimate of most other persons. I saw men, whom, at all points, I ranked far below myself, graced with the favour of superiors, and rich in the gifts of fortune. When a chance did occur for making such usurpers feel their proper place, was it in human nature to resist the temptation? All hope of patronage, under such a *regime*, was of course out of the question. I interfered with everybody and, at last, began to take a pride in doing so. The recompense of these good officers was in due time to be paid.

A Spanish officer, with whom I was associated in the convoy of certain treasure, proposed to me one night, after our halt upon the march, to take a trip down the Tagus, and bring his wife upon the journey. I had met this lady, a short time before, in Lisbon; and (according to my invariable custom in such cases) fancied that she had a liking for my person. It was a fine moonlight evening when we left Villa Nova, and we ran down with the tide to the *Quinta* of my friend; but no sooner had we taken the Signora on board, than the aspect of the weather suddenly changed, and we were exposed, during the whole night, to considerable danger.

From the moment almost that we left Silveira's house, the weather began to be unfavourable. The darkness, after the moon had gone down, was extreme. The wind, which set in squalls across a rapid and contrary tide, seemed to acquire greater force at every successive gust, and was accompanied, from time to time, with heavy showers of rain. Our boat, though capacious enough, was undecked, and slightly rigged—evidently unfit for rough treatment of any kind; and, to make matters worse, our sailors became alarmed, and Silveira, who knew the river, was ill from sea-sickness. How curiously, in the arrangement of the human heart and mind, do our passions balance and compensate each other! A man might reasonably, perhaps, be expected to keep his wits about him in such a dilemma as this.

For myself, I had some little nautical experience; and, besides, my companions were afraid; and it helps a man's valour greatly to see other people frightened. But Silveira's wife, who was as little of a heroine as any woman I ever met with—I was compelled to support her during almost the whole of the night; for the sea kept dashing into our open boat, and her husband, from illness, could scarcely take care of himself; and yet, under these circumstances, while she expected, I believe, to be washed overboard every half minute, I could perceive that I had not been quite mistaken in my suspicion of her good opinion of me.

Whatever interest, however, I might have felt in the progress of this little excursion, its termination was such as I certainly had not contemplated. With the utmost exertions both of the Spaniard and myself, we did not get back to our halting-place until evening on the day after we had started. At daybreak (twelve hours before) a treacherous quarter-master had marched forward with our escort; my friend the colonel did not let slip so favourable an opportunity to get rid of a man whom he doubtless considered as a troublesome coxcomb; and, to avoid the inevitable result of a court-martial, I asked and obtained permission to resign.

CHAPTER II.

UPON home service, my affairs, in a pecuniary point of view, would have been very little affected by the loss of my commission. On service, however, abroad, the consequence was different. As a soldier, I enjoyed many advantages and immunities, which a civil individual could scarcely, even for money, procure. Besides, though no discredit attached to my fault, (for Silveira, indeed, had never been brought to any account,) still I was, up to a certain point, a man placed in the shade. I had not lost my rank dishonourably; but still I *had* lost it, and the military world felt that I had. I missed the visits of some men with whom I had been upon terms of intimacy; and received advances from others, of whose acquaintance I was not ambitious. One friend asked casually when I intended to go to England; another mentioned some new Spanish levies, in which commissions were easily to be obtained. One fellow, to whom I had never spoken in my life, and who had been dismissed from the navy for gross insubordination and misconduct, had the presumption to write to me about "jobs" in "high quarters," "favouritism," "injustice," and "public appeal;" but I horsewhipped him in a public coffee-room, while the waiter read his letter to the company. These, however, were teazing, not to say distressing, circumstances; and, to avoid seeming at a loss, (particularly as I was very much at a loss indeed,) it became necessary to do something, and with the least possible delay.

I could have married Portuguese ladies; but their means were in supposition. Ready money, in Portugal, there was little; rents, in the existing state of the country, were hopeless; and I had not much reliance upon a title to land, which, to-day, was in our possession, to-morrow perhaps in that of the enemy. Misfortunes, as the adage declares, are gregarious. Meditating which course, out of many, I should adopt, I fell into a course which I had never meditated at all.

The Peninsula, during the war, was the scene of a good deal of high play. In quarters distant from the capital, the difficulty of killing time drove all but professed drinkers to gaming; and the universal employment of specie,—for paper was used only in commercial transactions,—gave an aspect peculiarly tempting to the table. Silver, in dollars and Portuguese crowns, was the common run of currency; the army was paid entirely in that metal; and it was no unusual thing to see an officer come down to a gaming house absolutely bending under the weight of a couple hundred pounds which he had to risk; or sending for a servant, (hackney coaches were scarce,) in case of a run of luck, to carry away his winnings.

Hazard and faro were the favourite games. Of billiards people were shy,—people commonly dread faculty in any shape. There was some danger in going home, after being very successful, at night; but the games of chance were in general very fairly played. The bank, of course, had a certain, and a considerable advantage; but as all the houses were public and open, there was little, if any, opportunity for fraud. And it was by no assumed advantage of the table, or by any process so tedious, that my stripping was effected. In luck, I was unfortunate. I lost, at my first sitting, more money than I could afford to part with; and, in hope of recovering it, was compelled to persevere. I have heard, among many dogmas as to the seductiveness of play — (a passion, by the way, no more invincible, though perhaps more rapidly destructive, than most of the other passions to which the human mind is subject,) — that a losing gamester may stop, but that a winning one never can. Perhaps this axiom is meant to apply peculiarly to your gamester *de cœur;* and possibly, (though *de tête* would be the more "germane" illustration,) — possibly, as Gall or Spurzheim would say, the "organ" of winning or losing was not in me strongly developed. As far as my own feeling goes, it certainly negatives the principle. Had I at any time regained my own, I think I should have stopped. — I lost every shilling I possessed, — horses, jewels, and even pistols, in the attempt.

I have stated, I think, that I was an only child; but, up to this point, I have said very little about my parents. Thank Heaven, (for their sakes) they no longer exist. My father died in my arms about seven years since, exhorting me, with his last breath, against the habits he had lived in all his life. I can understand this. My father died what is called "a natural death." Sickness had enervated his mind; terrors, the mere weakness of nerve, oppressed him. The ague of a month effected that change to which the argument of years had been unequal; after fifty years of infidelity, he fancied he died a believer. Were I to live ten years longer, I should probably die as he did.

But I name my relatives in this place, merely for the sake of observing, that, at the time to which I refer, I was very much estranged from them. My father held himself pretty well relieved from anxiety as to the fate of a man over whose conduct he had no control; and it was a draft only for fifty pounds which I received from him in Lisbon after the loss of my commission, accompanied by a letter which determined me never to apply to him again.

So, with twenty guineas only in my pockets, and with experience enough to know how little twenty guineas would do for me, I again landed in England in the year 1812; but I have not time, nor would the world have patience, for the adventures which, in three months, conducted me to my last shilling. I wrote a novel, I recollect, which no bookseller would look at; — a play, which is still lying at one of the winter theatres. Then I sent proposals to the Commander-in-chief for altering the taste of our cavalry accoutrements and harness; next, drew a plan (and seriously too) for the invasion of China; and after these, and a variety of other strange efforts, each suggested by my poverty, and all tending to increase it, the clocks were striking twelve on a dreary November night, as I walked along Piccadilly without a penny in the world.

It is at twelve o'clock this night that my earthly career must terminate; and, looking back to the various changes with which my life has been chequered, I find crisis after crisis connecting itself with the same hour. On the evening to which I allude, I wandered for hours through the streets: but it was not until midnight that I thought very intently on my situation. There is something, perhaps, of appalling in the aspect of London at that hour; in the gradual desertion of the streets by reputable passengers; and in the rising, as it were, from their depths of earth, of forms repulsive, horrible, and obscene. This change of object and association is sometimes peculiarly striking in the Parks. As the evening draws in, the walking parties and well-dressed persons disappear one by one; and the benches become peopled with an array of fearful creatures, who seem to glide from behind the trees, — to be embodied, as it were, out of the air. I have myself turned round suddenly, and seen a squalid shape beside me, which had not been there but the moment before. And I knew not how it came, nor from what quarter it approached; but it came on through the dark like some pale meteor, or unwholesome exhalation, which was not visible till the good light was gone. The closing too (in the town) of the shops, one after the other, — the honester and safer houses first, and so on until the haunts even of guilt and infamy shut up their doors, as seeing no farther prospect through the gloom. — And the few animated objects which break the general stillness, more revolting and fearful even than that stillness itself! Starving wretches, huddled together in holes and corners, seeking concealment from the eye of the police; thief-takers making their stealthy rounds, and eyeing every casual wanderer with suspicious and half-threatening glances. Then the associations which present themselves to the mind in such a situation. Thoughts of burglars, murderers, wretches who violate the sanctity of the grave, and lurking criminals of still darker dye;—the horror being less of injury from such creatures than of possible approximation to them; the kind of dread which a man feels, he can scarcely tell why, of being touched by a rat, a spider, or a toad.

But I wandered on till St. James's bell tolled twelve; and the sound awakened some curious recollections in my memory. A mistress of mine had lived in Sackville Street once; and twelve o'clock (at noon) was my permitted hour to visit her. I had walked up and down a hundred times in front of St. James's church, waiting impatiently to hear that clock strike twelve, which now struck twelve upon my ruin,—my degradation. The sound of the bell fell upon my ear like the voice of an old acquaintance.—My friend yet held his standing; my estate had something changed.

I did wander on, however, after St. James's clock told twelve, and while the rain, falling in torrents, drove even beggars to their shelter. I had neither home nor money. There were acquaintances upon whom I might have called, and from whom a supper and a bed would have been matters of course; but I felt that my spirits were rapidly rising to the right pitch for considering the situation in which I stood. Nothing sharpens the perceptions like the pressure of immediate danger. Had I slept and awoke at daylight, I must again have waited for the hour of darkness. Men succeed, over and over again, upon the spur of emergency, in enterprises, which, viewed calmly, they would never have undertaken.

I strolled onwards down Piccadilly through the wet dark night, (to avoid the hackney-coachmen, who kept teasing me with offers of their services,) and leaned against one of those splendid houses which stand fronting the Green Park. The strong bright glare of the door-lamps below, shewed the princely proportion of the building. Night was now growing fast into morning, but lights were still visible in the show-apartments of the mansion. Presently I heard the sound of a piano-forte, and a voice which I thought was familiar to me. I listened; and, in a moment, the singer went on.

1.

The setting sun with crimson beam
  Now gilds the twilight sky;
And evening comes with sportive mien,
  And cares of daylight fly;
Then deck the board with flow'rs, and fill
  My glass with racy wine;
And let those snowy arms, my love,
  Once more thy harp entwine.

Oh! strike the harp, my dark hair'd love,
  And swell that strain so dear;
Thine angel form shall charm mine eye,
  Thy voice delight mine ear.

Surely, said I, I have heard these words before; but the song continued:

2.

The glasses shine upon the board,
  But brighter shines thine eye;
The claret pales its ruby tint,
  When lips like thine are nigh;
The tapers dim their virgin white
  Beside thy bosom's hue;
And the flame they shed burns not so bright,
  As that I feel for you.

Then strike the harp! each note, my love,
  Shall kindle fresh desire;
Thy melting breath shall fan that flame,
  Thy glowing charms inspire.

It was the voice of a man whom I had known intimately for years. I cast my eye upon the door, and read the name of his family. My old companion,—my *friend*,—was standing almost within the touch of my hand. I thought on the scene in which he was an actor;—on the gayety, the vivacity, the splendour, and the sparkle,—the intrigues and the fierce passions—from which a few feet of space divided me.—I was cold, wet, and pennyless; and I had to choose.

It may be asked, why did not suicide, then, present itself to me as a rallying point? It did present itself at once; and, on the instant, I rejected it. Destitute as I was, I had still a confidence in my own powers—I may almost say, in my own fortune. I felt that, wealth apart, I had a hundred pleasurable capabilities which it would be folly to cast away. Besides, there were relatives, whose deaths might make me rich. I decided not to die.

My next supplies, however, were to arise out of my own personal exertions; and, in the meantime, the approach of light reminded me that I was still wet, and in the street. I had no fastidious apprehensions about degrading myself. If I could have held a plough, or digged in a mine, I should not have hesitated to have performed either of those duties. But, for holding a plough, I had not the skill; and, for the mines, there were none in the neighbourhood of London. One calling, however, there was, for which I was qualified. Within four-and-twenty hours after my dark walk through Piccadilly, I was a private dragoon in the 31st regiment, and quartered at Lymington Barracks.

CHAPTER III.

I HAVE denied, I do still deny, the overpowering influence commonly attributed to rank and fortune; and let me not be accused of offering opinions, without at least having had some opportunities for judgment. If there be a situation in which, beyond all others, a man is shut out from all probability of advancement, it is the situation of a private soldier. But the free, undaunted spirit, which sinks not in extremity, can draw, even from peculiar difficulty, peculiar advantage;—where lead only is hoped for, grains of gold excite surprise;—a slender light shews far, when all is dark around it.

Twelve months passed heavily with me in the 31st dragoons. My apparently intuitive dexterity in military exercises, saved me from annoyance or personal indignity, and might, in a certain way, have procured me promotion. But a halberd, as it happened, was not my object. I looked for deliverance from my existing bondage, to the falling in with some wealthy and desirable woman. And, in the strict performance of a soldier's duty — active, vigilant, obedient, and abstaining — I waited with patience for the arrival of opportunity.

I waited till my patience was exhausted half a dozen times over; but the interim certainly was not passed in idleness. He whose prospect lies straight forward, is seldom content to look about him; but there was matter for analysis and curious investigation on every side of me. As an officer, I had seen little of the true character or condition of the soldiery; and a regiment of cavalry is really a machine of strange constitution — I say, "of cavalry," *par preference*, because there is generally about a dragoon regiment a more lofty, though perhaps not more just style and feeling, than belongs (from whatever cause) to our regiment of infantry.

The 31st regiment was remarkable for the splendour of its uniform and appointments; an attribute rather anything than advantageous to the soldier; but which always, nevertheless, operates powerfully in the recruiting of a corps. We had men amongst us from almost every class of society. There were linen-weavers from Ireland — colliers from Warwickshire and Shropshire — ploughmen, game-keepers, and poachers, from every quarter and county. There were men too of higher rank, as regarded their previous condition; and that in a number very little imagined by the world. There were men of full age, who had run through fortunes — lads who had quarrelled with, or been deserted by, their families — ruined gamblers — *cidevant* fortune-hunters — *ex*-officers, and strolling players. In a company so heterogeneous, it would have been difficult to keep the peace, but for that law which visited the black eye as a breach of military discipline. As men, those who had been "gentlemen" were incomparably the worst characters. Some of them vapoured, or at least talked, about their origin, and so exposed themselves to the ridicule which waits upon fallen dignity. Others made use of their patrician acquirements to seduce the wives or daughters of their more plebeian comrades. They were dissipated in their habits, ribald in their discourse, and destitute even of any remnant of honest or decent principle.

The poachers among us were another party, almost of themselves; for the game-keepers — the same animals domesticated

—never cordially agreed with them. Idle in their habits; slovenly in their appearance; these fellows were calculated, nevertheless, to make admirable soldiers in the field. Their courage was peculiarly of the true English character; slow something to be excited; but, when excited, impossible to be overcome. I remember one of them well—for his anecdotes used to amuse me—who, for two years, had been the *scourge* of every preserve within ten miles of his parish; and who had, with difficulty, escaped transportation, by enlistening as a soldier. He was a strong, muscular lad, about two or three and twenty; not of large stature, or of handsome appearance; but of a resolution, or rather of an obduracy, which nothing short of death could have subdued. I saw him once fight, after repeated provocation, with a fourteen-stone Irishman of the 18th, who was the lion of his troop. The battle lasted, without any etiquette of the prize-ring, in constant fighting, more than an hour. My acquaintance was knocked down in every round, for the first thirty minutes; but the blows made no more impression upon him than they would have done upon a man of iron. That he had the worst of the battle, never seemed to occur to him; he fell, and rose—fell, rose again, and struck on. Nothing but the loss of sight, or of life, could have subdued him; and I firmly believe he would have destroyed himself, if he had been compelled to give up. At length his antagonist's confidence gave way before his obstinacy; and there was something almost staggering to the senses in the appearance of it. The man seemed to get no worse, for a beating that might have destroyed half-a-dozen. He spoke very little; never broke his ground; and rose with a smile, after such falls as might have crushed him to pieces. Both parties suffered severely; my friend rather the most; but, at the end of an hour's fighting, the Hibernian owned himself vanquished.

But whatever might be the qualities of these men individually, taken as a body, they were amenable, reasonable beings. To have made them, individually, discontented, would have been difficult; to have tampered with them, *en masse*, quite impossible. The sound of the word "discipline," had a sort of magical effect upon their minds. Their obedience (from its uniform enforcement) became perfectly mechanical; and severity excited little complaint, for it was understood to be the custom of the service.

We had three different commanding officers during the time of my stay at Lymington; but there was only one who ever disturbed the temper of the garrison; and even he failed to excite any feeling beyond great personal hatred to himself.

The first commandant was a man who had himself been a private soldier; and who had risen, by degrees, to the rank of lieutenant-colonel. Corporal punishment was his reliance. He punished seldom, but severely. And this man, though a strict disciplinarian, was universally popular.

Our second leader was a well-meaning man, but a theorist; and he seemed to have been sent as a punishment for the sins of the whole garrison. He was strongly opposed to the practice of corporal punishment, as tending to degrade, and break the spirit of the soldier; and, being puzzled, as a wiser head might be, in the substitution of other penalties, he actually put his men through a course of experiments upon the subject. For example,—having heard that Alfred the Great made an arrangement by which every man became, to a certain degree, answerable for his neighbour, Major W—— resolved to introduce the same system into his own *depôt;* and whenever, accordingly, any soldier was absent from barracks without leave—and, in a garrison of a thousand men, some one or other was pretty sure to be always absent—he confined the remaining nine hundred and ninety-nine to their barracks, until he returned. Indeed without, I believe, the least feeling of cruelty or malice, this man passed half his time in devising inflictions, and the other half in practising them upon us. And besides this, he fatigued us with eternal inspections; wasted more paper in writing rules and regulations, than might have made cartridges for a whole battalion; and after compelling us, even in cold weather, to go through a tedious parade on a Sunday, was so merciless as always to make a long speech at the end of it.

Our third commandant, and the only one whom I ever dreaded—for the whims of the second hardly passed what might be called vexations—our third commandant was a fool; and, of

course, being a soldier, a martinet. Quite incompetent to the
discussion of any possible matter beyond the polish of a carbine-
barrel, or the number of paces in which a regiment ought to
cross the parade-ground, he gave his full attention to what he
termed the "military" appearance of his troops. A speck upon
a man's uniform—a hair too much or too little in whisker—a
spot, or a drop of water, upon the floor of a room in which
thirty men inhabited, ate, drank, and slept; these were crimes
which never failed to call down heavy retribution. And perfection, with this gentleman, was almost as much a fault as negli-
gence. He lived only upon orders, reprimands, and whippings.
The man who could not do his duty, was to be tortured as a
matter of course; the man who did it well, was corrected as "a
conceited fellow." Every process under his jurisdiction was
conducted at the point of the "damme." He attempted to
make his officers cut their hair in a particular shape. He forbad
a staff-adjutant, who could not afford to give up his place, ever
to quit his barrack-yard without stating where he was going to.
I have known him set three hundred men to pick straws off a
stable-yard, where every fresh puff of wind left them their
labours to begin again. Eventually the fellow joined a regiment
in India; and fell in a skirmish, by a ball, it was supposed, from
one of his own soldiers.

But I was weary of examining characters, and avoiding per-
secutions. I was tired of being a favourite among the nursery
girls of Lymington, and even of enjoying the enmity of the
young gentlemen of the neighbourhood. I had become weary
of the honour and discomfort of endurance—I sighed, in the
midst of exertion, for exertion's reward—I never doubted that
talent must, in time, find its level; but I had begun to doubt
whether man's life would be long enough to afford the waiting,
when the chance that I was hoping, and wishing for, appeared.

How constantly do men ascribe to momentary impulse, acts
which really are founded in deep premeditation. Mistakes, surprises, jokes, and even quarrels, pass current and accidental,
which are in truth matters of *malice prepense*. My object at
Lymington was, to introduce myself to persons of consideration;
and with that view, for months, I carried my life, as it were, in

my hand. Every moment that I could snatch from the routine of military duty, was systematically devoted to searching after adventure. There was not a family of condition within five miles of the depot, but I had my eye upon their motions and arrangements. How often, while watching their gay parties on the river, did I pray for some dreadful accident which might give me an opportunity of distinguishing myself! How often have I wished, in riding night-picket or express, that some passing equipage would be attacked by robbers, that I might make my fortune by defeating them! I saw, by chance, one evening, a mill on fire in the distance; and, making sure it was a nobleman's seat, swam through two rivers to arrive at it. At length, the common-place incident—I had looked for it, though, a hundred times—the common-place incident of two tipsy farmers, on a fair day, affronting an officer in Lymington market-place, who had a lady on his arm, gave me the chance I had so long sought. This affair gave me an opportunity of being useful to Captain and Mrs. Levine.

The honourable Augustus Levine, who had joined the garrison but a few days when this accident befell him, was one of those men of fortune who seem born for no other purpose than to put poor fellows in contentment with their destiny. He was an abject creature, both in heart and mind. Despicable (there be more such) in person as in principle. And yet the worm was brother to an earl—he was master of a fine estate—he commanded an hundred soldiers; and (a man may have too many blessings) he had a young and handsome wife.

When I declare that Lymington Barracks were full of stripling officers, who, in addition to wealth and station, possessed (many of them) all personal advantages, my venture even to think of Mrs. Levine upon the credit of such a service as I had performed, may appear to savour not a little of presumption. Setting the event apart, I should maintain a different opinion. A hundred qualifications, which would only have been of course in a man of rank, in a peasant would excite surprise, and, consequently, interest. My encounter in the market-place, though a vulgar one, had given me some opportunity for display; and a private soldier, who possessed figure, accomplishment, and deportment — who could make verses, make love, and, moreover, fight like a Turk — such a man would secure attention; and love follows very easily. I cannot afford now to dwell upon details; but, whatever be the value of my general principle, consequences, in the particular instance, did approve my dream. Within six months, I had disclosed my real name and rank — eloped with Mrs. Levine — fought a duel with her husband — and had a verdict entered against me in the Court of King's Bench, with damages, by default, to the amount of £10,000.

There is this circumstance, among a thousand others, to attach us to the female sex, that a man can scarce, in any case, whatever the degree of friendship, receive a favour from his fellow man, without some feeling of inferiority; while, from a woman, each new act of kindness, or of bounty, seems but a tribute to his merit, and a proof of her affection.

My encounter with Levine produced very trifling consequences. Both parties were slightly wounded at the first fire, and neither appeared anxious to try the fortune of a second. The penalty of £10,000 was a serious matter to deal with. Mrs. Levine possessed, independent of her husband, an income exceeding £800 a-year; but that property formed no fund for the payment of a large sum in damages. Our only alternative was to quit England immediately.

I enter here with pain upon an epoch in my history, which filled up sadly and wearily a period of five years. Isabella Levine was a woman whose personal charms were perhaps among the weakest of the attractions she possessed. If I had sought her in the beginning from interested motives, I did not long profess a passion without really entertaining it. That she had deserted such a husband as Levine, seemed to me no stain upon her virtue. He had been forced upon her by the command of an uncle on whom she depended; and who himself had felt so little confidence in the man of his selection, that, in giving his niece a large fortune, he reserved it principally within her own control. Was it a crime in Isabella, that she quitted a being whom she could not love? Was she a companion for stupidity — for slovenliness — for brutality? Was she a subject for neglect, and for coarse infidelity? Was it fit that her tenderness, her beauty, and her youth, should be wasted upon a creature who could not appreciate what he was possessing? She did not sell herself to me for title or for fortune. She was not seduced by a fashion or a feather. If she loved me — and I think she did love me — it was for myself alone.

Impressed with these feelings, I left England a second time for Lisbon. The war had now been carried into the heart of France, and a Peninsula had a prospect of sufficient security. If, by law, I was prevented from marrying Isabella, by gratitude, as well as by affection, I held myself bound to her for ever. I took it as an admitted principle, that every man must settle at some time; and deliberately formed my plan of lasting, domestic happiness.

I had not then ascertained that the very thought of a set system is destruction to everything in the nature of enjoyment. I had yet to discover, that it was better even to die at once, than await, in one fixed posture, the wearing of unprofitable vacancy.

I set out with a wish, as well as a resolution, to act well. I had seen the errors of married men, and I determined to avoid them. I will treat a woman, said I, with that attention which she is entitled to demand — I will not render her miserable by my dissipations — I will not insult her by slighting her society — I will love none but Isabella; and with her my hours shall be passed. I now see ill omen in these my first resolutions. A man does not put himself upon the defensive, unless he feels cause to apprehend attack. I suspect that, like the wolf in the fable, the sight of the collar already make me uneasy.

I shall never forget — for my time indeed is almost come — the torture which it cost me to carry my good resolutions into effect — the days, the weeks, the years, that I suffered, of satiety, weariness, indifference, disgust. I am convinced that the decline of my passion for Isabella was only hastened by my efforts to conceal and to resist it. The love of full liberty, which I had been used freely to indulge, acquired now tenfold force from the restraint to which I subjected myself. The company of the plainest woman of my acquaintance would have been delightful to me, compared with the uniformity of beauty.

I bore up against these inclinations until my very brain became affected. My senses grew morbid from excess of inflammation. And, withal, I could perform but half the task I had imposed on myself. I might refuse to love other women, but I could not compel myself to love Isabella. My attentions continued; but they were the attentions of a prescribed duty. The feelings I had once entertained towards her—the letters I had written to her—for I chanced once by accident to fall on some of them—the whole seemed a dream—a delusion—a delirium—from which I had recovered, and the remembrance of which excited wonder.

Steadily to pursue the course upon which I had determined, was not to cheat myself of the conviction that that course was destroying me. In vain did I recollect what I owed to Isabella;—her uniformly excellent conduct,—the sacrifices she had made for me. These images refused to dwell upon my imagination. They were as shadows in the water, which eluded my grasp when I would have seized them. I found only a woman who, now, was in my way; who, no doubt, meant to bestow happiness upon me; but who, in fact, drove me to frenzy. I would again have been left destitute; I would have returned to my ration and my broad-sword; I would have submitted to anything to have been once more a free man, but to desert Isabella, or to be deserted by her;—I was not (Heaven be praised!) quite villain enough to take the first course; my pride could not have endured that she should take the second.

There are limits to the capacity of human endurance. We are none of us so far from insanity as we believe ourselves. My temper had suffered in the course of these conflicts, a shock from which, I think, it never afterwards recovered; when a train of new circumstances, unforeseen and unexpected, broke, for good or ill, the trammels which entangled me.

We had been five years together, and I had been four years miserable, when a habitual depression, which I had perceived, but neglected to speak of—for, in the fever of my own soul, I had no thought for the distress of others—this terminated in the serious illness of Isabella. At first, supposing her indisposition to be transient, I treated it as an affair of domestic routine, taking every precaution for her safety, rather as a matter of course, than from any feeling of anxiety; but an intimation from my physician that she was in a state of real danger, aroused me from that apathy with which I contemplated all passing events.

"Danger? What danger?—There could be no danger; the man must be mistaken."

"He was not mistaken. My wife's complaint was low, nervous fever; brought on, as it seemed to him, by some cause operating upon the mind; and, if her spirits could not be kept up, her peril was immediate."

I never received any intelligence with greater discomposure in my life. A variety of recollections, very like accusations, crowded one after the other suddenly upon my memory. My heart awoke from that lethargy into which long suffering had plunged it. Still, I thought, the thing must be exaggerated.— "Her spirits kept up?"—Why, they must be kept up. "What was to be done to keep them up?"—That, the adviser left to me.

I visited Isabella with feelings which I could scarce acknowledge even to myself. She sent for me as I was going to her chamber; and my purpose of going almost changed. I know not how to describe the sensation which her message produced. I was going to her at the very moment unsummoned; and yet the summons compelled me to turn back. It was not the feeling of a man who is detected in a crime; for that must suppose a previous consciousness that he was committing one. It was the alarm rather of a child who plays with a forbidden bauble, and suddenly discovers that the last whirl has broken it.

I had seen Isabella on the preceding evening; but I found her much worse than I had expected. I leaned upon her bed; it was some time before she could gather firmness to express herself. At length she spoke;—and I hear her accents at this moment.

She spoke, with apparent confidence, of her approaching death. "She regretted it, for my sake, because her fortune would die with her."—"Could she but have secured my future happiness and safety, as she had nothing left in life to hope for, so she would have had nothing to desire."

These are common-place expressions, perhaps I shall be told. The fact may be so;—*Death* is very common-place. But those, who, in the midst of a course decidedly evil, have been cursed with sufficient perception to abhor the guilt they could not abstain from—such only can appreciate my feelings at that moment. The mere mention of Isabella's death, as possible, carried distraction to my soul! She told me, that she had long seen the decline of my affection;—"her only wish was, that it could have lasted while she lived!"—I stood before her a convicted villain. I could not lie—I could not speak;—at last, I wept, or I had died.

I must not dwell upon the particulars of this interview!—She thanked me for the uniform kindness I had shewn her;—for the effort with which I had avoided connections which she had but too plainly seen my desire to form.—"Could I pardon her for the pain that she had caused me? I should be happier after her death; for, if it left me poor, it would at least restore me to my liberty."

Let me do myself justice here, as I have visited justice upon myself elsewhere. I was not quite a wretch. If my passions were habitually fierce and ungovernable, their impulse in the good cause was as powerful as in the cause of ill.

I knelt beside Isabella's bed. I confessed the truth of all she charged me with. I invoked curses on my restless temper;—swore that all my former love for her was rekindled;—that I would not survive her death;—that I should esteem myself her murderer! Nor did I at that moment, so help me, Heaven, utter any sentiment which I did not feel. If I did not at that moment love Isabella passionately, I would have laid my life down with pleasure for her safety—for her happiness. And I trusted that I had in some measure restored her peace of mind; and I was seriously resolving to *like* a peaceful life; when a circumstance occurred well calculated again to put my resolution to the proof.

CHAPTER IV.

Had I been asked for which of my virtues I should ever have a fortune given me, I might have had some difficulty, and should have had, in answering the question. It was my fate, however, for once to be enriched by my irregularities. My grandfather, penetrated on a sudden with admiration of the man who had brought his family-name so much into discussion, died, after making twenty wills in favour of twenty different people; and, passing over my father, bequeathed a property of £4000 a-year to me.

I premised that, about this time, some unforeseen occurrences befell me. Two of these I have already described; the third was, of all, the most unexpected. While I was busy in preparations for returning to England, and devising schemes out of number for pleasures and splendour when I should arrive there —Isabella left me.

It was a blow for which, less than for a miracle, I was prepared. Returning one evening from shooting,—we were then living at Condeixa,—I found a letter in her hand lying sealed upon my table. The sight of the address alone paralysed me. What had happened, flashed in an instant across my mind. The contents of the letter were these:—

"If I have used deception towards you, Charles, believe me it is now for the first time. I wish to spare you the needless agony of bidding me farewell; I wish to secure myself against the danger of being diverted from a course which reflection has convinced me is the best. I can not forget that you have ceased to love me; I have known the fact long, but circumstances have kept me silent. I acquit you, Heaven is my witness! of unkindness, or ingratitude;—esteem,—affection—regard—compassion—I know you gave me these; and love is not at our command. There are men from whom I could be satisfied with kindness and esteem; but I can not fall so low as to accept pity, Charles, from you; you always will—you always must—love some woman; can I know this, and yet live with you, and be conscious that you do not love me?

"For three years I have endured to see you wretched, and to feel myself the cause of your distress. Could I feel this, and yet be happy? What did I gain by depriving others of your heart, when I knew that, to me, your heart was lost for ever? A thousand times have I wished that your scruples would give way, and that you would be happy in a course which could have added nothing to my misery. I have borne all this long; but my motive for bearing it is at an end. Your accession of fortune makes my presence no longer necessary. You have now open before you that career for which you have so long panted; I believe that you are capable of sacrificing it for me; but can I accept such a sacrifice from you, Charles? Can I exact it? Do you think I could value it?

"Farewell! I will no longer continue to hang upon you, interrupting enjoyments in which I am forbidden to participate. Farewell! My pen trembles as I write the word; but be assured that I write it irrevocably.

"Do not distract us both by vain endeavours to recall me. If love were yours to give, I know, I feel, that you would give it to me; but it is not, Charles, at your disposal. Farewell, once more; for I had intended but to say, 'Farewell!' May you be happy, though my day of happiness is over. Thank Heaven, your impetuous temper is no longer likely to be excited by want of means to those enterprises, which might not always be successful;—but, if ever chance should place you again in such emergency, as to make Isabella's fortune—her life—her love—worth your acceptance, then—and then only—will she consent again to hear from you."

She is living yet,—I trust she is! If the last prayers of one who has prayed but too seldom;—if those prayers may be heard which merit nor hearing nor value;—if mercy for another can be granted to him who dares not—can not—ask it for himself—then may every blessing she can wish for—every blessing which can wait on life, be hers; may she know that, in my last hour, my thoughts were upon her; that my latest wishes were breathed for her safety—for her happiness!

How merely is man the creature of events over which he has no control! When I kissed Isabella's forehead, scarce six hours before she wrote that letter, how far was I from imagining that I then beheld her for the last time! and what a turn did our separation give, probably, to my destiny! I despise the pedantic dogma which says, "no one can be missed." Ill as I think of human nature, I think that assertion is a libel upon it. Among creatures who have as little of discrimination as of feeling,—to whom the newest fool is always the most welcome friend,—by such beings it may be true, that "no one can be missed;" but I deny that any man of common sensibility or perception, can part *for ever*, even from a mere companion, without remembrance and regret.

I paused, for my brain was giddy after reading Isabella's letter. My first thought was to follow her; but, on reflection, I abandoned the design. I felt that I could not hope to overcome her fixed belief, that the continuance of our connection would, on my part, be a sacrifice. She had retired into a convent, the Lady Superior of which had long been known to us; and I felt that she must be happier there, or anywhere, than with me. Should it seem that my decision was, under the circumstances, a convenient one, I swear that it was a decision in which my wishes had no part. No honourable or feeling man will doubt my candour in this statement. He will know, if not from experience, from instinct, that, had I listened to my own wishes, I should only have thought of recovering Isabella. He will know that her absence left a blank in my heart; that, spite of philosophy, axiom, or authority, I felt there was a something missing—wanting;—a reliance, a consolation, a *point d'appui* to the mind, which nothing but the society of woman could supply.

And, if I have loved other women, Isabella has not been forgotten. In the maddest moments of gayety, in the wildest hours of license, the doubt of her existence—the certainty of her wretchedness—has dashed across my mind, and poisoned the cup of pleasure at my lips. Before I quitted Portugal, I wrote her letter after letter, intreating, promising, imploring her return. If it was not for my love that I desired to change her resolution, I swear that for my mere quietude, for my peace of mind, I wished to do it. Ah! what have I to regret in being compelled to quit a world, where, to possess feeling or reflection is to be eternally unhappy; where passion leaves its victim no choice, but in his own wretchedness, or in the misery of those whom, at his soul's hazard, he would shield from harm; and where the being who enjoys the most of gratification himself, is the creature who is most callous to the sufferings of all around him!

It was not, however, until I had completed my dispositions as to Isabella's fortune; until I was about to embark for England,—to place distance—seas—between us;—I did not fully, until that moment, feel what it was to part from her for ever. I wrote to her once more, even while my vessel was under sail. Though I was sensible of the folly, I wrote the letter with my blood. I entreated that she would follow me—and follow me without delay. I declared that I should expect her—that I would take no denial—that I should wait for her at the first English port. With that strange confidence which men often have when their hopes are totally desperate, I went so far even as to appoint the hotel at which I should stay. I really did expect that Isabella would follow me to England. I wronged her firmness. The ship in which I had embarked met with contrary winds. A subsequently sailing vessel reached England before us. I found, on landing at Falmouth, a packet from Isabella; but it contained only her picture, and these words—"Do not forget me."

That picture hangs about my neck at the moment while I write. I will die with it next my heart. As the magnet, catching eagerly each particle of iron, lets golden sands roll on unheeded by, so memory treasures up our moments of misfortune, long after those of happiness and gayety are forgotten—Isabella, lost, was to be remembered for ever.

But these are recollections which unhinge me for detail. I have a blow to strike, and almost within this hour, for which every corporal and mental agent must be nerved. And my senses rush along in tide as furious and rapid as my fate! I cannot dwell, amid this whirl of mind and fancy, upon the measures which, in seven years, dispossessed me of £70,000. I am not lamenting that which I have done. I began with a resolution to *live* while I did live. Uncertain of the next moment, the passing hour was all to me. What mattered it, since my course must cease, whether it ceased sooner or later; provided, while it lasted, I was in all things content? I scorned the confined views of men who, possessing means, submitted to let "I dare not" wait upon "I would;" and vowed when I put myself at the head of my fortune, that no expenditure of wealth, no exposure of person, should ever have weight to disappoint my inclination.

Yet my estate lasted longer than, under such a resolution, might be expected. The rich, for the most part, either lavish their money without enjoying it, or, to maintain what is called a certain "state," suffer dependants to lavish it for them. As it happened that I had no wish for commonplace distinctions, nor was very desirous of anything which money alone could buy, I escaped all those rapidly ruinous contests in which the longest purse is understood to carry the day. I saw something of the absurdities of fashion, but I entered very little into them. Curiosity, want of employment, and that natural desire which even the silliest man feels, to laugh at the follies of those about him, made me associate sometimes with fine gentlemen; but I never became a fine gentleman myself.

And yet it was amusing, in the way of *chasse ennui*, to glide along with the frequenters of Bond Street, and with the loungers at the opera; and to observe the excessive—the monstrous—self-delusion of men, who had been born to ample means, and were not incumbered much with understanding. Their talk was such feather; and yet, even in what they uttered, they were generally mistaken. If they were vicious, it was from thoughtlessness; if honest, from accident. Their conversation was so easy, and yet (to themselves) so entertaining. The jest so weak; the laugh so hilarious. Their belief, too, was so facile —I did envy them that faculty! Not one of them ever doubted anything that he was at all interested in crediting. All about them was *fudge;* and yet they never seemed to be aware of it. Their Bond-Street dinners were *not* good. They would talk all day about the fancied merits of particular dishes; and yet at night be put off with such wine and *cuisine* as really was sad stuff, and could not have passed but upon men of fashion.

But the most striking feature in their characters was their utter want of self-respect. I have seen a young man literally *begging* for half-crowns, who but a few months before had driven his curricle, and been distinguished for his insolence. Another would borrow small sums, and never pay them, until not even a servant was left who would lend him a shilling. Others would endure to be insulted by their tradesmen;—to be poisoned at coffee-houses where they could not pay their bills;—to truck and barter their clothes and valuables for ready money with waiters at hotels;—and all this to obtain supplies which in reality they did not want, and because they knew no mode of dissipating time, but in dissipating a certain quantity of specie.

These were the people who went to fights—to races;—wore large hats, and garments of peculiar cut; with little of taste or fancy in their devices; and, of true conception of splendour or of elegance, none.

Then their *hangers-on* were a set of men fit to be classed *per se* in history. Fellows culled from all ranks and stations, but all rascals alike;—their avocations various, but all infamous. There were among them cashiered officers, or men who had left the army to avoid that infliction; fraudulent waiters, and markers from billiard tables; shopkeepers' sons, black-leg attorneys, and now and then the broken-down heir of a respectable name and family.

I recollect one or two of these fellows who were characters for posterity in their way. There was one Mr. M'Grath in particular, a native of the sister kingdom, with whose history in full it fell to my lot to be acquainted. I traced him back to his leaving Dublin, where he had acted as collecting clerk to a distiller; and from whence, on account of some trifling embezzlements, he had come over to England with about twenty pounds in his pocket. This man on his arrival had not a friend nor a connection to back him; his address was bad; his person not prepossessing; and he had an unconquerable aversion to anything like honest labour; but he began with a little, and, by industry, rose.

His first step in London was into a second floor lodging in Jermyn Street, Piccadilly,—for he laid himself out as an appendage to men of fortune from the beginning. The woman of the house dwelt herself in a single apartment; waited upon her guests as a servant; and fleeced them, because her house was "in a situation!"

This woman had a hump-backed daughter, who stood a grade above her mother. I saw her afterwards in a workhouse, to which I went for the purpose of ascertaining the truth of M'Grath's history. She did the better kind of labour, while her mother attended to the drudgery: and, by parsimony, and great exertion, they had acquired near £2000.

M'Grath's second step in life, having heard of the £2000, was to marry his landlady's humpbacked daughter; and, with part of the money, he bought a commission in the Guards. Here he remained but a short time, his real character being discovered. Within twelve months he deserted his newly acquired wife. The furniture of the mother's house was next seized for his debts. The two miserable women then came for support upon the parish; and, with the wreck of the £2000, M'Grath commenced gentleman.

And, with the appointments of respectable station about him, this fellow had gone on for more than twenty years when by accident I met with him;—the most handy, and universally applicable creature in the world. Latterly he had found it convenient to call himself a conveyancer; and undertook to act as an agent on all occasions. He was a money lender;—an assistant in borrowing money, or in investing it. He bought or sold a horse; could obtain patronage (upon a deposit) for a curacy or a colonel's commission. Then he dealt among the bankrupts; could indorse a bill;—get it cashed. He would arrange a provision for a distressed lady;—wait upon a betrayer at the hazard of being kicked down stairs;—threaten law proceedings; —introduce a new face;—in short, wherever there was distress and helplessness, there, as if by instinct, you were sure to find M'Grath.

I met with the gentleman under circumstances (for him) peculiarly unlucky. He had been settling with a certain peer the terms upon which he was to be freed from the importunity of a female, from whom importunity ought not to have been necessary. I chanced, shortly afterwards, to fall in with the lady; and (she really had been unfortunate) to become interested for her. M'Grath in this case had gone to work with less than his usual prudence. He had received at the end of his negotiation

£500 from the nobleman in question, upon a written promise that the applicant should trouble him no more; of which £500 he accounted for £200 in cash, giving his own note to his client as security for the rest. This was a safe £300 gained; but M'Grath was not content. Distress within a short time obliged the same woman to dispose of some jewels and other personal property which she possessed; and this property, with a fatuity apparently unaccountable,—even after what had happened— she employed M'Grath to find a purchaser for. The monstrous apparent folly of such an act, made me doubt the truth of the whole story when I heard it. In *heaven's name*, I asked, why had she trusted such a fellow as M'Grath even in the first transaction?—" And who but such a man," was the answer, " would have undertaken such an office?"

M'Grath, however, probably had his necessities as well as other people; for, on this occasion, he took a measure of very questionable safety. Relying upon the lady's dread of public exposure, he pawned the whole of her jewels, and converted the money to his own use. I caused him merely to be arrested, although his offence was, I believe, a criminal one; and eventually he was liberated from prison by the Insolvent act; for he had judged rightly so far—the exposure of a prosecution could not be borne; but, by a singular coincidence, I had afterwards to kick him out of my own house, on his calling for the particulars (he did not know upon whom) of a next presentation to a living advertised for sale.

Women, however, of course, among the true spendthrifts of my acquaintance, were the principal objects of discourse and of attention. But their arrangements even upon this point were of so odd a description, that the ridiculous overpowers every other feeling when I think of them. I forget the man's name who told a certain king that there was no royal road to the knowledge of mathematics. I doubt he would have failed to impress my acquaintances with that truth. *On achete le tout*, seemed to be their conviction. One loved, in order that he might be affirmed a person in the world. Another, for the fashion of a particular lady. A third, because a mistress was a good point to shew " style" in. And a fourth, because it was necessary to have one. *The non-chalance* of this last set was the most exquisite thing in nature. They affected (and I believe felt) a perfect indifference towards their *protegées;* introduced all their acquaintance, without a jot of jealousy, at their houses; and I saw a letter from a peer to a French woman, who transacted love affairs for him, stating that he meant to form an attachment of some duration when he came to town; and describing (as to person) the sort of lady upon whom he should wish to fix his affections.

The nature of such connections may well be imagined. No regard was ever dreamed of for the feelings of the women; the men were, of course, appreciated and abused. It was a sacrifice on both sides; but the sacrifice of the man was merely a sacrifice of money, of which he did not know the value; and that sacrifice neither obtained nor deserved any gratitude; for the same individual who would ruin himself in keeping a splendid *etat* for his mistress, would lavish nothing upon her that did not redound to his own "fashionable" notoriety.

For myself, if I did not enter into the spirit of what was called *ton*, it did not arise from any want of general good reception. As soon as it was found that I cared about no *coterie*, all *coteries* were open to me. But, if it was much to be one of the few, I thought it would be even more to stand alone. And therefore, although I kept fine horses, I did not race them to death. I had a handsome furnished house, but I refused to have a *taste;* that is to say, I did not lie awake fourteen nights together, imagining a new scroll pattern for the edge of a sofa; nor decide, (still in doubt,) after six weeks perplexity, which was the properest tint of two-and-twenty for the lining of a window curtain. In short, my private arrangements were no way guided by ambitious feeling; whether I rode, drove, drank, or dressed, I did the act merely because it was an act gratifying to myself, not because it had been done by Lord Such-a-one, or was to be done by Mr. So-and-so; and, although my fortune was small, compared with the fortunes of some of my companions, yet, as it mattered not how soon the whole was expended, I generally seemed, upon emergency, to be the richest man of the circle I was moving in.

And a race for some to envy has my career been to this moment! If the last few months have shewn note of coming evil, that evil could not terrify me when I was prepared to elude it. If I have not enjoyed, in the possession of riches, that absolute conviction, (my solace under poverty,) that what tribute I did receive was paid entirely to myself, yet the caution and experience which poverty taught me has preserved me from gross and degrading imposition. Let me keep up my spirits, even with egotism, in a moment like this! I have not been quite an object to court imposition. The same faculties and powers, which availed me when I was without a guinea, continued at my command throughout my high fortune. I have not been, as an old man, wasting property which I could not spend; I have not been a wretched pretender, by purchase, to place and to circumstance, to which desert gave me no title; I have not been the thing that I am, to die, because I will not be.

Gold is worth something, inasmuch as it gives certain requisites for continued enjoyment, which can be obtained from no other source. Apart from all pretension to severe moral principle, I had ever this feeling, in its fullest extent—that the man was thrice a villain, a wretch thrice unfit to live, who could plunge any woman that trusted him into poverty, into disgrace. To this principle, I would admit neither of exception nor evasion. I do not say that every man can command his passions; but every man can meet the consequences of them. Again and again, in my days of necessity, did I fly from connections which seemed to indicate such termination. Money, however, as society is constituted, can do much—my subsequent wealth relieved me from all obstacles.

Yet, let me redeem myself in one point—I shall not attempt it in many—my power was in no instance (as I believe) employed cruelly. For my fellow-men, I had little consideration. I knew them merciless—I had felt them so. Still, upon man, if I recollect well, I never wantonly inflicted pain; and in no one instance—as Heaven shall judge me!—did I ever sacrifice the feelings of a woman.

A portion of my wealth was given to relieve my father from debts which he had incurred in expectation of the whole. Another portion, I trust, will have placed in security beings whose happiness and safety form my latest wish on earth. A third portion, and a large one, has been consumed in idle dissipation; but, if I have often thrown away a hundred guineas, I have sometimes given away ten.

The whole, however, at last, is gone. Parks, lordships, manors, mansions—not a property is left. As my object was always rather pleasure than parade, this change in my circumstances is little known to the world. I am writing—and I shall die so—in elegant apartments; with liveried servants, splendid furniture—all the paraphernalia of luxury about me. The whole is disposed of, and the produce consumed. To-morrow gives the new owner possession. A hundred persons make account to nod to me to-morrow. I have, for to-morrow, four invitations to dinner.—I shall die to-night.

Let me not be charged with flying this world, because I fear to meet the loss of fortune. Give me back the years that I have spent; and I can deem lightly of the money. But my place—my station among my fellow-men?—It totters; it trembles. Youth, hopes, and confidence—these are past; and the treasure of the unfathomed ocean could not buy them back.

Life of life—spirit of enjoyment—to what has it not fallen! Does it still spring in the heart, like the wild flower in the field—the native produce of a vigorous soil, which asks no tillage, defies eradication, and rears its head alike amid the zephyr and the storm? No; it is this no longer. It is an exotic now—a candle-light flower—the sensitive plant with the hue of the rose; love is its sunshine—wine the dew that cherishes it; it blossoms beneath the ray of the evening star, and blooms in the illuminated garden at midnight; but, in the cool breeze of morning, it droops and it withers; and day, which brings life to all else, destroys it for ever.

Then, if I had the Indies still in my grasp, would I endure to descend in the scale of creation? Would I join the class of respectable old men; and sit spectator of a mellay which I am no longer able to engage in? Would I choose the more disgusting course of some I see around me; and let the vices of manhood degenerate into the weaknesses of age? Would I struggle to maintain a field in which victory is past my hope; dispute a palm which, of necessity, must be wrested from my hand? Would I endure to have men, whom I have been accustomed to see as children, push me insolently from the stage of life, and seize the post which I have occupied?

If I could not bear this, still less could I endure the probable, the inevitable consequences of living to extreme old age. To be, if not distasteful to my own depraved and doting sense, conscious of being distasteful to all the world beside! To die worn out with pains and aches! Helpless in body — feebler still in mind! The tottering victim of decrepitude and idiotcy, cowering from that fate which by no effort I can avoid!

I will not come to this. I will not make a shirking, ignominious end of life, when I have the power, within myself, to die as may become a man. To this hour I have had strength to keep my station in the world. In a few moments it would be gone — but I shall go before it. And what do I lose by thus grappling with my fate? A few years at most of uncertainty or uneasiness. That man may die to-morrow, I know afflicts him little; but let him reflect, in his triumph, that he *must* die on the next day. Let him remember, that when he has borne to hear people inquire after his health, listen to his answer with impatience, and go to be happy out of his reach — when he has borne to close the eyes of the last friend of his youth, to lose all his old connections, and to find himself incapable of forming new ones — when he has endured to be a solitary, excommunicated wretch, and to read, in the general eye, that he is an intruder upon earth — he is still but as a ball to which a certain impetus is given; which, moving in a fixed track, can neither deviate nor pause; and which has but (to an inch) a marked space to pass over, at the end of which comes that fall from which the world's worth cannot save it.

I can write no more. My hour is fast approaching. — Now am I greater, in my own holding, than an emperor! He would command the fate of others; but I command my own. This is, in very choice, the destiny which I would embrace. There is something sublime in thus looking in the face of Death: he sits over against me as I write; and I view him without terror. If

I have a predominant feeling at this moment, it is a feeling of curiosity.

One full glass more, and I am prepared. Wine is wanting only to aid the nerve, not to stimulate the courage or the will. My pistols lie loaded by my side. I will seal this packet, nevertheless, with a steady hand; and you who receive it shall bear witness that I have done so.

Now, within this half hour, I will forget even that care must be the lot of man. I will revel for a moment in the influence of wine, and in the smile of beauty — I will live, for one moment longer, the being I could wish to live for ever.

The clock strikes eleven. — Friend, whom I have selected to receive my parting words, I must conclude. I shall send this letter to you instantly. You will receive it while I still exist; and yet you will be unable — the world would be unable — to prevent the act I meditate. Do me justice — and farewell! When the chimes tell twelve to-night, I shall be uppermost in your mind. You will wonder — you will be troubled — you will doubt. And, when you sit at breakfast to-morrow morning, some public newspaper, recording my death, will give you perhaps the real name of

TITUS.

END OF THE ODOHERTY PAPERS.

J. S. REDFIELD,
110 AND 112 NASSAU STREET, NEW YORK,
HAS JUST PUBLISHED:

EPISODES OF INSECT LIFE.

By ACHETA DOMESTICA. In Three Series: I. Insects of Spring.—II. Insects of Summer.—III. Insects of Autumn. Beautifully illustrated. Crown 8vo., cloth, gilt, price $2.00 each. The same beautifully colored after nature, extra gilt, $4.00 each.

"A book elegant enough for the centre table, witty enough for after dinner, and wise enough for the study and the school-room. One of the beautiful lessons of this work is the kindly view it takes of nature. Nothing is made in vain not only, but nothing is made ugly or repulsive. A charm is thrown around every object, and life suffused through all, suggestive of the Creator's goodness and wisdom."—*N. Y. Evangelist.*

"Moths, glow-worms, lady-birds, May-flies, bees, and a variety of other inhabitants of the insect world, are descanted upon in a pleasing style, combining scientific information with romance, in a manner peculiarly attractive."—*Commercial Advertiser.*

"The book includes solid instruction as well as genial and captivating mirth. The scientific knowledge of the writer is thoroughly reliable."—*Examiner*

MEN AND WOMEN OF THE EIGHTEENTH CENTURY.

By ARSENE HOUSSAYE, with beautifully Engraved Portraits of Louis XV., and Madame de Pompadour. Two volume 12mo. 450 pages each, extra superfine paper, price $2.50.

CONTENTS.—Dufresny, Fontenelle, Marivaux, Piron, The Abbé Prevost, Gentil-Bernard, Florian, Bouflers, Diderot, Grétry, Riverol, Louis XV., Greuze, Boucher, The Vanloos, Lantara, Watteau, La Motte, Dehle, Abbé Trublet, Buffon, Dorat, Cardinal de Bernis, Crébillon the Gay, Marie Antoinette, Made. de Pompadour, Vadé, Mlle. Camargo, Mlle. Clairon, Mad. de la Popelinière, Sophie Arnould, Crébillon the Tragic, Mlle. Guimard, Three Pages in the Life of Dancourt, A Promenade in the Palais-Royal, the Chevalier de la Clos.

'A more fascinating book than this rarely issues from the teeming press. Fascinating in its subject; fascinating in its style; fascinating in its power to lead the reader into castle-building of the most gorgeous and bewitching description."—*Courier & Enquirer.*

"This is a most welcome book, full of information and amusement, in the form of memoirs, comments, and anecdotes. It has the style of light literature, with the usefulness of the gravest. It should be in every library, and the hands of every reader."—*Boston Commonwealth.*

"A BOOK OF BOOKS.—Two deliciously spicy volumes, that are a perfect *bonne bouche* for an epicure in reading."—*Home Journal.*

REDFIELD'S NEW AND POPULAR PUBLICATIONS.

SKETCHES OF THE IRISH BAR.

By the Right Hon. RICHARD LALOR SHEIL, M. P. Edited with a Memoir and Notes, by Dr. SHELTON MACKENZIE. Fourth Edition. In 2 vols. Price $2 00.

"They attracted universal attention by their brilliant and pointed style, and their liberality of sentiment. The Notes embody a great amount of biographical information, literary gossip, legal and political anecdote, and amusing reminiscences, and, in fact, omit nothing that is essential to the perfect elucidation of the text."—*New York Tribune.*

"They are the best edited books we have met for many a year. They form, with Mackenzie's notes, a complete biographical dictionary, containing succinct and clever sketches of all the famous people of England, and particularly of Ireland, to whom the slightest allusions are made in the text."—*The Citizen (John Mitchel).*

"Dr. Mackenzie deserves the thanks of men of letters, particularly of Irishmen, for his research and care. Altogether, the work is one we can recommend in the highest terms."—*Philadelphia City Item.*

"Such a repertory of wit, humor, anecdote, and out-gushing fun, mingled with the deepest pathos, when we reflect upon the sad fate of Ireland, as this book affords, it were hard to find written in any other pair of covers."—*Buffalo Daily Courier.*

"As a whole, a more sparkling lively series of portraits was hardly ever set in a single gallery. It is Irish all over; the wit, the folly, the extravagance, and the fire are alike characteristic of writer and subjects."—*New York Evangelist.*

"These volumes afford a rich treat to the lovers of literature."—*Hartford Christian Sec*

CLASSIC AND HISTORIC PORTRAITS.

By JAMES BRUCE. 12mo, cloth, $1 00.

"A series of personal sketches of distinguished individuals of all ages, embracing pen and ink portraits of nearly sixty persons from Sappho down to Madame de Staël. They show much research, and possess that interest which attaches to the private life of those whose names are known to fame."—*New Haven Journal and Courier.*

"They are comprehensive, well-written, and judicious, both in the selection of subjects and the manner of treating them."—*Boston Atlas.*

"The author has painted in minute touches the characteristics of each with various personal details, all interesting, and all calculated to furnish to the mind's eye a complete portraiture of the individual described."—*Albany Knickerbocker.*

"The sketches are full and graphic, many authorities having evidently been consulted by the author in their preparation."—*Boston Journal.*

THE WORKINGMAN'S WAY IN THE WORLD.

Being the Autobiography of a Journeyman Printer. By CHARLES MANBY SMITH, author of "Curiosities of London Life." 12mo, cloth, $1 00.

"Written by a man of genius and of most extraordinary powers of description."—*Boston Traveller.*

"It will be read with no small degree of interest by the professional brethren of the author, as well as by all who find attractions in a well-told tale of a workingman."—*Boston Atlas.*

"An amusing as well as instructive book, telling how humble obscurity cuts its way through the world with energy, perseverance, and integrity."—*Albany Knickerbocker.*

"The book is the most entertaining we have met with for months."—*Philadelphia Evening Bulletin.*

"He has evidently moved through the world with his eyes open and having a vein of humor in his nature, has written one of the most readable books of the season."—*Zion's Herald.*

REDFIELD'S NEW AND POPULAR PUBLICATIONS

MOORE'S LIFE OF SHERIDAN.

Memoirs of the Life of the Rt. Hon. Richard Brinsley Sheridan by THOMAS MOORE, with Portrait after Sir Joshua Reynolds. Two vols., 12mo, cloth, $2.00.

"One of the most brilliant biographies in English literature. It is the life of a wit written by a wit, and few of Tom Moore's most sparkling poems are more brilliant and fascinating than this biography."—*Boston Transcript.*
"This is at once a most valuable biography of the most celebrated wit of the times and one of the most entertaining works of its gifted author."—*Springfield Republican.*
"The Life of Sheridan, the wit, contains as much food for serious thought as the best sermon that was ever penned."—*Arthur's Home Gazette.*
"The sketch of such a character and career as Sheridan's by such a hand as Moore's, can never cease to be attractive."—*N. Y. Courier and Enquirer.*
"The work is instructive and full of interest."—*Christian Intelligencer.*
"It is a gem of biography; full of incident, elegantly written, warmly appreciative, and on the whole candid and just. Sheridan was a rare and wonderful genius, and has in this work justice done to his surpassing merits."—*N. Y. Evangelist.*

BARRINGTON'S SKETCHES.

Personal Sketches of his own Time, by SIR JONAH BARRINGTON, Judge of the High Court of Admiralty in Ireland, with Illustrations by Darley. Third Edition, 12mo, cloth, $1 25.

"A more entertaining book than this is not often thrown in our way. His sketches of character are inimitable; and many of the prominent men of his time are hit off in the most striking and graceful outline."—*Albany Argus.*
"He was a very shrewd observer and eccentric writer, and his narrative of his own life, and sketches of society in Ireland during his times, are exceedingly humorous and interesting."—*N. Y. Commercial Advertiser.*
"It is one of those works which are conceived and written in so hearty a view, and brings before the reader so many palpable and amusing characters, that the entertainment and information are equally balanced."—*Boston Transcript.*
"This is one of the most entertaining books of the season."—*N. Y. Recorder.*
"It portrays in life-like colors the characters and daily habits of nearly all the English and Irish celebrities of that period."—*N. Y. Courier and Enquirer.*

JOMINI'S CAMPAIGN OF WATERLOO.

The Political and Military History of the Campaign of Waterloo from the French of Gen. Baron Jomini, by Lieut. S. V. BENET U. S. Ordnance, with a Map, 12mo, cloth, 75 cents.

"Of great value, both for its historical merit and its acknowledged impartiality."—*Christian Freeman, Boston.*
"It has long been regarded in Europe as a work of more than ordinary merit, while to military men his review of the tactics and manœuvres of the French Emperor during the few days which preceded his final and most disastrous defeat, is considered as instructive, as it is interesting."—*Arthur's Home Gazette.*
"It is a standard authority and illustrates a subject of permanent interest. With military students, and historical inquirers, it will be a favorite reference, and for the general reader it possesses great value and interest."—*Boston Transcript.*
"It throws much light on often mooted points respecting Napoleon's military and political genius. The translation is one of much vigor."—*Boston Commonwealth.*
"It supplies an important chapter in the most interesting and eventful period of Napoleon's military career."—*Savannah Daily News.*
"It is ably written and skilfully translated."—*Yankee Blade.*

REDFIELD'S NEW AND POPULAR PUBLICATIONS.

NAPOLEON IN EXILE ;

Or, a Voice from St. Helena. Being the opinions and reflections of Napoleon, on the most important events in his Life and Government, in his own words. By BARRY E. O'MEARA, his late Surgeon, with a Portrait of Napoleon, after the celebrated picture of Delaroche, and a view of St. Helena, both beautifully engraved on steel. 2 vols. 12mo, cloth, $2.

" Nothing can exceed the graphic truthfulness with which these volumes record the words and habits of Napoleon at St. Helena, and its pages are endowed with a charm far transcending that of romance."—*Albany State Register.*

" Every one who desires to obtain a thorough knowledge of the character of Napoleon, should possess himself of this book of O'Meara's."—*Arthur's Home Gazette.*

" It is something indeed to know Napoleon's opinion of the men and events of the thirty years preceding his fall, and his comments throw more light upon history than anything we have read."—*Albany Express.*

" The two volumes before us are worthy supplements to any history of France."
Boston Evening Gazette.

MEAGHER'S SPEECHES

Speeches on the Legislative Independence of Ireland, with Introductory Notes. By FRANCIS THOMAS MEAGHER. 1 vol. 12mo, Cloth. Portrait. $1.

" The volume before us embodies some of the noblest specimens of Irish eloquence ; not florid, bombastic, nor acrimonious, but direct, manly, and convincing."—*New York Tribune.*

" There is a glowing, a burning eloquence, in these speeches, which prove the author a man of extraordinary intellect."—*Boston Olive Branch.*

" As a brilliant and effective orator, Meagher stands unrivalled."—*Portland Eclectic.*

" All desiring to obtain a good idea of the political history of Ireland and the movements of her people, will be greatly assisted by reading these speeches."—*Syracuse Daily Star.*

" It is copiously illustrated by explanatory notes, so that the reader will have no difficulty in understanding the exact state of affairs when each speech was delivered."—*Boston Traveller.*

THE PRETTY PLATE,

A new and beautiful juvenile. By JOHN VINCENT. Illustrated by DARLEY. 1 vol. 16mo, Cloth, gilt, 63 cts. Extra gilt edges, 88 cts.

" We venture to say that no reader, great or small, who takes up this book, will lay it down unfinished."—*Courier and Enquirer.*

" This is an elegant little volume for a juvenile gift-book. The story is one of peculiar instruction and interest to the young, and is illustrated with beautiful engravings."—*Boston Christian Freeman.*

" One of the very best told and sweetest juvenile stories that has been issued from the press this season. It has a most excellent moral."—*Detroit Daily Advertiser.*

" A nice little book for a holyday present. Our little girl has read it through, and pronounces it first rate."—*Hartford Christian Secretary.*

" It is a pleasant child's book, well told, handsomely published, and illustrated in Darley's best style '—*Albany Express*

REDFIELD'S NEW AND POPULAR PUBLICATIONS.

LAS CASES' NAPOLEON.

Memoirs of the Life, Exile, and Conversations of the Emperor Napoleon. By the COUNT LAS CASES. 4 vols. 12 mo. Cloth, with eight Portraits on Steel, two Maps, and ten Illustrations, $4; half calf or morocco, extra, $8.

"The earlier American editions of these fascinating memoirs have long been out of print. Of all the works relating to Napoleon by his personal friends and associates, this is the best and most important."—*N. Y. Herald.*

"In no other work can be found so full and truthful a statement of the private qualities or natural disposition of the soul of the greatest general which the world has ever produced, as in Las Cases' Journal."—*Christian Secretary, Hartford.*

"A work which for minuteness of detail, keenness of description, and interesting information in regard to one of the greatest soldiers that ever lived, is not surpassed, if equalled. The author, favored as he was with constant companionship of the Emperor, for years, possessed peculiar advantages for collecting material for such a volume."—*Buffalo Express.*

HISTORY OF LOUISIANA.

The History of Louisiana—Spanish Domination. By CHARLES GAYARRE. 8vo., cloth. $2 50.

The History of Louisiana—French Domination. By CHARLES GAYARRE. 2 vols., 8vo, cloth. $3 50.

"Its author is an accomplished scholar, a fine writer, and has devoted himself to his subject with commendable fidelity and zeal. His work is an important and valuable addition to the local and early history of an interesting portion of our country, and deserves a place in every library in which works of American history form any part."—*Boston Post.*

"There is little need of looking beyond Gayarre, who rests his narrative on authentic documents."—*Bancroft's History of the United States, Vol. VI.*

"It includes, among a variety of interesting passages, the war of 1776; the politics and intrigues of the West, for the navigation of the Mississippi; the intrigues of WILKINSON, M'GILLIVRAY, and others; the Yazoo scheme; the curious episode of WILLIAM AUGUSTUS BOWLES; and a variety of interests, adventures, experiments, and politics, all of which are luminously stated, logically arranged, and argued to just conclusions of history."—*W. Gilmore Simms.*

FRANCHERE'S NARRATIVE.

Narrative of a Voyage to the Northwest Coast of America, in the years 1811, '12, '13, and '14; or the First Settlement on the Pacific. By GABRIEL FRANCHERE. Translated and Edited by J. V. Huntington. 12mo, cloth. Plates. $1 00.

"Of all the narratives of travel and adventure in our Northwestern wilderness, there is none that gives a more vivid and picturesque description of the events, or in which the personal adventures of the narrator are told with more boldness, yet, freer from all egotism, than in this unpretending work of Mr. Franchere. It is truly a fragment of our colonial history, saved from oblivion."—*Philadelphia National Argus.*

"The great value of this work, as an authentic and decisive narrative of critical events was strongly attested by Colonel Benton, in the great debate of 1846, on the Oregon boundary question. It is a pleasant narrative, simply told. Irving made much use of it in his Astoria."—*Boston Atlas.*

"The De Foe-like simplicity of the style, its picturesque descriptions of personal adventure, and of the features of the countries traversed by the author, confer an interest on this narrative, apart from that which springs from its historical value."—*New York Evening Post.*

REDFIELD'S NEW AND POPULAR PUBLICATIONS.

SATIRE AND SATIRISTS.

By JAMES HANNAY, Author of "Singleton Fontenoy." 12mo. Cloth. 75 cents.

"As respects nice analysis of character, sharp penetration, general culture and knowledge of the times of which he speaks, Mr. Hannay deserves to be classed among the best modern essayists."—*Christian Enquirer.*

"A more entertaining, useful, and reliable volume upon the important and comprehensive subject of which it treats, we have never had the pleasure of reading."—*Charleston Weekly News.*

"These lectures are very much after the fashion of *Thackeray*'s brilliant series, and we pay Mr. Hannay the highest possible compliment when we say his sketches do not suffer by comparison with those of the author of Pendennis."—*Savannah Journal and Courier.*

"The anecdotes of the satirists, with which the work abounds, furnish a wholesome seasoning to the dish and add increased interest to this well-digested little volume."—*Christian Secretary, Hartford.*

FINGER RINGS.

The History and Poetry of Finger Rings. By CHARLES EDWARDS, Esq. With numerous illustrations. 12mo. Cloth. $1 00.

"A publication even more unique in its text than peculiar in its title. It is issued in beautiful style, displays a remarkable industry in exploring so novel a field of research, and contains much that is both curious and interesting."—*Boston Atlas.*

"It is remarkable how much authentic history, antiquarian lore, pleasant anecdote, and true poetry may be drawn through a ring. The author writes *con amore*, and has given us one of the pleasantest and most useful books of the season."—*Arthur's Home Gazette.*

"The book is richly interspersed with anecdotes and is certainly one of the most noticeable publications of the day for novelty and interest."—*Boston Journal.*

FULL PROOF OF THE MINISTRY.

By REV. J. N. NORTON, A. M., Rector of Ascension Church, Frankfort, Ky., author of "The Boy Trained to be a Clergyman." 12mo. Cloth. 75 cents.

"Those who have read 'The Boy who was trained up to be a Clergyman,' from the pen of the same gentleman, need only be told that this is a sequel to that tale. For others we will add that this volume is crowded with incident, is racily written, and of course full of interest."—*Lowell American Citizen.*

"The author must be a preacher of short sermons, for his book makes a short story of what might have been, with the usual spinning out and amplifying, an ambitious work of two volumes."—*Worcester Palladium.*

"All Christians may obtain from it some valuable hints to direct them in their religious duties."—*Hartford Religious Herald.*

"The style is chaste and concise, and the teachings of the book of the highest moral worth."—*Detroit Democrat.*

"It is unnecessary for us to recommend it to parents and teachers. Its influence will be excellent upon any mind, particularly if young."—*Buffalo Democracy.*

REDFIELD'S NEW AND POPULAR PUBLICATIONS.

COSAS DE ESPAÑA.

(Strange Things of Spain.) Going to Madrid, via Barcelona. 12mo. $1 00.

"We commend this volume as a most charming one, written with elegance and ease, full of vivacity and wit, and describing the old customs of quaint old Spain in the most spicy and delightful manner."—*Boston Evening Telegraph.*

"The history of the Spanish pig would not be unworthily placed with the famed essay of Elia. The volume is instructive, humorous, a model of style, in short, a most remarkable book that will bear many readings. Anybody who knows what a good book is, we advise to buy this."—*Newark Daily Advertiser.*

"The author is a gay fellow, never out of spirits, no matter what may be the annoyances around him, and he compels his reader to enter with zest into all the scenes he describes. The volume is altogether a most agreeable one."—*Philadelphia Eve. Bulletin.*

"This racy volume contains a series of pictures of Spanish life, painted by an artist whose pencil is both skilled and practised."—*Zion's Herald, Boston.*

"The author is of the rollicking school of travellers, and is a pleasant companion. He has a charm in his method of handling his subjects which can not fail to fascinate his readers."—*Louisville Journal.*

SOUTHWARD HO!

A Spell of Sunshine, by WILLIAM GILMORE SIMMS, author of "The Partisan," &c. 12mo. Cloth. $1 25.

"This is one of Simms's works that readers will be most pleased with. It is sprightly and full of variety, serving up southern life, character, and scenery, with the fidelity and force of a master."—*Worcester Palladium.*

"There is a great deal of literary excellence in this work. It embraces a series of continuous tales of the most interesting and lively nature, written in an admirable manner, and calculated to please all tastes."—*Daily Times.*

"This is one of the ablest, most entertaining, and popular productions of the above-named author. It abounds in striking delineations of character, and is pervaded throughout with a truly American and patriotic spirit."—*Christian Intelligencer.*

"'Southward Ho!' has modern life for its theme, and with the gleaming wit, and graphic descriptive powers of the writer, abounds with entertainment."—*Baltimore Sun.*

HOSMER'S POETICAL WORKS.

The Poetical Works of W. H. C. HOSMER. Now first collected. With a Portrait on steel. 2 vols., 12mo. $2 00.

"Imagination, poetic spirit, and diction, are patent in these polished compositions. The first volume is chiefly devoted to the legendary lore of Indian tradition, and abounds in picturesque descriptions of Nature's wildest scenery. Occasional poetic effusions, evoked by some incident of the hour, or suggested by the teeming travail of a glowing imagination, make up the second volume. The work constitutes a body of lyrics, and of rich specimens of almost every metre in English poesy."—*National Intelligencer.*

"The poems designed to perpetuate the traditions of the Indian race particularly, are of a high order, the subject being evidently suited to the author's peculiar genius. Some of the "Bird Notes" also are exquisitely beautiful, and so too are many of the Miscellaneous pieces. The volumes are highly creditable to the author and to the country."—*Puritan Recorder.*

"He has certainly written a great deal of agreeable and flowing verse, abounding in smooth descriptions of nature, and illustrated by apt and pleasing imagery.—*New York Tribune.*

REDFIELD'S NEW AND POPULAR PUBLICATIONS.

LIFE OF SEWARD.

Life of the Honorable William H. Seward, with Selections from his Works. Edited by GEORGE E. BAKER. 12mo. Cloth. Portrait. $1 00.

"The work presents, in a form well adapted for popular circulation and perusal, some of the most striking evidences of the genius and statesmanlike ability of Mr. Seward. It is ornamented with a well engraved portrait of Senator Seward."—*Boston Journal.*

"In short, it embraces all that the general reader could desire in regard to the history of the great statesman of New York."—*Christian Secretary, Hartford.*

"All agree that Mr. Seward is a man of remarkable powers, and that the productions of his pen are generally highly honorable both to the intellect and the literature of the country. The present volume contains a very felicitous epitome of the history of his public career, and a selection of some of his best discourses, illustrative of his character both as a statesman and a scholar."—*Puritan Recorder.*

"To any person who wishes to know about William H. Seward, all that the public have a right to know, we recommend this book. It contains the cream of his speeches and the history of his life."—*New Bedford Mercury.*

THE YOUTH OF JEFFERSON;

A Chronicle of College Scrapes at Williamsburg, in Virginia, A. D. 1764. 12mo. $1 00.

"Few of cultivated taste who take the volume up, will fail to read it through at a sitting. The originality of its construction, the correctness and easy flow of its style, and the reader's consciousness that he is enjoying, with the author himself, the gay moments of a learned, thoughtful, and observing man, make the book one of the most delightful of the day."—*N. Y. Courier and Enquirer.*

"It recounts some of the college pranks of Jefferson and a few of his fellow-students. It is really a delightful little volume, written in a dashing, brilliant style; and it can not possibly be read in an ill humor."—*Christian Freeman.*

"This is a little volume, the title of which fully explains its contents. It is full of capital stories of student life, and rollicking, youthful experiences in the early days of the 'Old Dominion.'"—*Buffalo Democracy.*

TOM MOORE'S SUPPRESSED LETTERS.

Notes from the Letters of Thomas Moore to his Music Publisher, James Power, (the publication of which was suppressed in London) with an Introductory Letter from Thomas Crofton Croker, Esq., F. S. A. With four Engravings on Steel. 12mo. Cloth. $1 50.

"The present work is intended to correct misapprehensions naturally arising from a perusal of the 'Memoirs' of Moore by Lord John Russell. No one can hesitate to convict his Lordship of very gross breaches of historic truth, in the suppression of portions of the letters he pretended to edit; his entire aim appearing to be the withholding of any thing in Moore's letters inconsistent with the opinion his Lordship wished the public to entertain of his author. The publication of these suppressed letters and fractions, will set right these misapprehensions. Here Moore is presented to the world under his own hand and seal."—*Winchester Democrat.*

REDFIELD'S NEW AND POPULAR PUBLICATIONS.

TRENCH'S PHILOLOGICAL WORKS.

THE STUDY OF WORDS.

By Rev. RICHARD CHENEVIX TRENCH, B. D. One vol., 12mo, price 75 cents.

"He discourses in a truly learned and lively manner upon the original unity of language, and the origin, derivation, and history of words, with their morality and separate spheres of meaning."—*Evening Post.*

"This is a noble tribute to the divine faculty of speech. Popularly written, for use as lectures, exact in its learning, and poetic in its vision, it is a book at once for the scholar and the general reader."—*N. Y. Evangelist.*

"It is one of the most striking and original publications of the day, with nothing of hardness, dullness, or dryness about it, but altogether fresh, lively, and entertaining."—*Boston Evening Traveller.*

ENGLISH, PAST AND PRESENT.

By Rev. RICHARD CHENEVIX TRENCH, B. D. 12mo, price 75 cts.

"An able work by an able author. The subject is treated under the several heads of, the English a composite language; its gains; its diminutions; the changes in its meaning; and the changed spelling."—*Hartford Courant.*

"The entire work is so clearly and simply written, and the information imparted is of so interesting a nature, and is so pleasantly given, that it may be read with zest by the most careless and amusement-seeking."—*Boston Post*

"In its most vivid and charming sketches of the component parts of the English language, it will give us much pleasure as instruction."—*Philadelphia Episcopal Recorder.*

THE SYNONYMS OF THE NEW TESTAMENT.

By Rev. RICHARD CHENEVIX TRENCH, B. D. 12mo, price 75 cts.

"The nice distinctions between words of nearly the same significations, and the shades of different meaning often applied to the same word, render a book of this kind not only convenient, but in fact necessary. All may be enlightened by its perusal."—*Christian Herald and Messenger.*

"It shows great exactness of thought, and a wide range of philological training; and we can hardly imagine how the subject could have been treated at once more concisely and more luminously. Every biblical student, especially every clergyman, ought to be in possession of the volume."—*Puritan Recorder.*

"This book is well worth the perusal of every thorough theological student. Like all the works of Mr. Trench it evinces marks of great scholarship. As an exegetical aid in the solution of the meaning of the New Testament, the work under notice is invaluable."—*Saturday Evening Gazette.*

ON THE LESSONS IN PROVERBS.

By Rev. RICHARD CHENEVIX TRENCH, B. D. 12mo, price 50 cts.

"It is a book at once profoundly instructive, and at the same time, deprived of all approach to dryness, by the charming manner in which the subject is treated."—*Arthur's Home Gazette.*

"It is a wide field, and one which the author has well cultivated, adding not only to his own reputation, but a valuable work to our literature."—*Albany Even. Transcript.*

"The work shows an acute perception, a genial appreciation of wit, and great research. It is a very rare and agreeable production, which may be read with profit and delight."—*New York Evangelist.*

REDFIELD'S NEW AND POPULAR PUBLICATIONS.

LORENZO BENONI;

Or, Passages in the Life of an Italian. Edited by a Friend. One vol., 12mo; price $1.00.

"The author of the volume is Giovanni Ruffini, a native of Genoa. Being implicated in the attempt at revolution in 1833, he was compelled to seek safety in flight, and has since that period resided in England and France. Under fictitious names he gives an authentic history of real characters and true incidents. It is a graphic picture of Italian life and habits; and a true, though mournful exhibition of the baneful effects of despotic rule, and priestly control in education."—*Norfolk (Va.) Herald.*

"From the first page to the last, it absorbs the reader's faculties with the intensity of its interest, and leaves him little consciousness outside the circle in which its characters have their being. Yet over the whole work there broods such a terrible shadow of despotism and the suffering it has caused, that its fascination is of a strange and painful kind."—*New York Daily Times.*

"This is one of the books occasionally met with, having a species of Tarantella power, charming the reader, and admitting of no cessation in its perusal, until the volume is entirely completed, leaving him even then like little Oliver, 'asking for more.'"—*Ev. Post.*

GRISCOM ON VENTILATION.

The Uses and Abuses of Air: showing its Influence in Sustaining Life, and Producing Disease, with Remarks on the Ventilation of Houses, and the best Methods of Securing a Pure and Wholesome Atmosphere inside of Dwellings, Churches, Workshops, &c. By JOHN H. GRISCOM, M. D. One vol. 12mo, $1.00.

"This comprehensive treatise should be read by all who wish to secure health, and especially by those constructing churches, lecture-rooms, school-houses, &c.—It is undoubted, that many diseases are created and spread in consequence of the little attention paid to proper ventilation. Dr. G. writes knowingly and plainly upon this all-important topic."—*Newark Advertiser.*

"The whole book is a complete manual of the subject of which it treats; and we venture to say that the builder or contriver of a dwelling, school-house, church, theatre, ship, or steamboat, who neglects to inform himself of the momentous truths it asserts, commits virtually a crime against society."—*N. Y. Metropolis.*

"When shall we learn to estimate at their proper value, pure water and pure air, which God provided for man before he made man, and a very long time before he permitted the existence of a doctor ? We commend the Uses and Abuses of Air to our readers, assuring them that they will find it to contain directions for the ventilation of dwellings, which every one who values health and comfort should put in practice."—*N. Y. Dispatch.*

HAGAR, A STORY OF TO-DAY.

By ALICE CAREY, author of "Clovernook," "Lyra, and Other Poems," &c. One vol., 12mo, price $1.00.

"A story of rural and domestic life, abounding in humor, pathos, and that naturalness in character and conduct which made 'Clovernook' so great a favorite last season. Passages in 'Hagar' are written with extraordinary power, its moral is striking and just, and the book will inevitably be one of the most popular productions of the season."

"She has a fine, rich, and purely original genius. Her country stories are almost unequaled."—*Knickerbocker Magazine.*

"The Times speaks of Alice Carey as standing at the head of the living female writers of America. We go even farther in our favorable judgment, and express the opinion that among those living or dead, she has had no equal in this country; and we know of few in the annals of English literature who have exhibited superior gifts of real poetic genius."—*The (Portland, Me.) Eclectic.*

REDFIELD'S NEW AND POPULAR PUBLICATIONS.

SIMMS' REVOLUTIONARY TALES.
UNIFORM SERIES.

New and entirely Revised Edition of WILLIAM GILMORE SIMMS' Romances of the Revolution, with Illustrations by DARLEY. Each complete in one vol., 12mo, cloth; price $1.25.

I. THE PARTISAN. III. KATHARINE WALTON.
II. MELLICHAMPE. IV. THE SCOUT.
V. WOODCRAFT.

"The field of Revolutionary Romance was a rich one, and Mr. Simms has worked it admirably."—*Louisville Journal.*

"But few novelists of the age evince more power in the conception of a story, more artistic skill in its management, or more naturalness in the final *dénouément* than Mr Simms."—*Mobile Daily Advertiser.*

"Not only *par excellence the* literary man of the South, but next to no romance writer in America."—*Albany Knickerbocker.*

"Simms is a popular writer, and his romances are highly creditable to American literature."—*Boston Olive Branch.*

"These books are replete with daring and thrilling adventures, principally drawn from history."—*Boston Christian Freeman.*

"We take pleasure in noticing another of the series which Redfield is presenting to the country of the brilliant productions of one of the very ablest of our American authors—of one indeed who, in his peculiar sphere, is inimitable. This volume is a continuation of 'The Partisan.' "—*Philadelphia American Courier.*

ALSO UNIFORM WITH THE ABOVE

THE YEMASSEE,

A Romance of South Carolina. By WM. GILMORE SIMMS. New and entirely Revised Edition, with Illustrations by DARLEY. 12mo, cloth; price $1.25.

"In interest, it is second to but few romances in the language; in power, it holds a high rank; in healthfulness of style, it furnishes an example worthy of emulation."—*Greene County Whig.*

SIMMS' POETICAL WORKS.

Poems: Descriptive, Dramatic, Legendary, and Contemplative. By WM. GILMORE SIMMS. With a portrait on steel. 2 vols., 12mo, cloth; price $2.50.

CONTENTS: Norman Maurice; a Tragedy.—Atalantis; a Tale of the Sea.—Tales and Traditions of the South.—The City of the Silent—Southern Passages and Pictures.—Historical and Dramatic Sketches.—Scripture Legends.—Francesca da Rimini, etc.

"We are glad to see the poems of our best Southern author collected in two handsome volumes. Here we have embalmed in graphic and melodious verse the scenic wonders and charms of the South; and this feature of the work alone gives it a permanent and special value. None can read 'Southern Passages and Pictures' without feeling that therein the poetic aspects, association, and sentiment of Southern life and scenery are vitally enshrined. 'Norman Maurice' is a dramatic poem of peculiar scope and unusual interest; and 'Atalantis,' a poem upon which some of the author's finest powers of thought and expression are richly lavished. None of our poets offer so great a variety of style or a more original choice of subjects."—*Boston Traveller.*

"His versification is fluent and mellifluous, yet not lacking in point of vigor when an energetic style is requisite to the subject."—*N. Y. Commercial Advertiser.*

"Mr. Simms ranks among the first poets of our country, and these well printed volumes contain poetical productions of rare merit."—*Washington (D. C.) Star.*

Memoirs of a Distinguished Financier.
FIFTY YEARS
IN BOTH HEMISPHERES;
OR, REMINISCENCES OF A MERCHANT'S LIFE.
By VINCENT NOLTE. 12mo. Price $1.25. [Eighth Edition]

The following, being a few of the more prominent names introduced in the work, will show the nature and extent of personal and anecdotal interest exhibited in its pages:—

Aaron Burr; General Jackson; John Jacob Astor; Stephen Girard; La Fayette; Audubon; the Barings; Robert Fulton; David Parish; Samuel Swartwout; Lord Aberdeen; Peter K. Wagner; Napoleon; Paul Delaroche; Sir Francis Chantry; Queen Victoria; Horace Vernet; Major General Scott; Mr. Saul; Lafitte; John Quincy Adams; Edward Livingston; John R. Grymes; Auguste Davezac; General Moreau; Gouverneur Morris; J. J. Ouvrard; Messrs. Hope & Co.; General Claiborne; Marshal Soult; Chateaubriand; Le Roy de Chaumont; Duke of Wellington; William M. Price; P. C. Labouchere; Ingres; Charles VI., of Spain; Marshal Blucher; Nicholas Biddle; Manuel Godoy; Villele; Lord Eldon; Emperor Alexander, etc. etc.

"He seldom looks at the bright side of a character, and dearly loves—he confesses it—a bit of scandal. But he paints well, describes well, seizes characteristics which make clear to the reader the nature of the man whom they illustrate."

The memoirs of a man of a singularly adventurous and speculative turn, who entered upon the occupations of manhood early, and retained its energies late; has been an eye-witness of not a few of the important events that occurred in Europe and America between the years 1796 and 1850, and himself a sharer in more than one of them; who has been associated, or an agent in some of the largest commercial and financial operations that British and Dutch capital and enterprise ever ventured upon, and has been brought into contact and acquaintance—not unfrequently into intimacy—with a number of the remarkable men of his time. Seldom, either in print or in the flesh, have we fallen in with so restless, versatile and excursive a genius as Vincent Nolte, Esq., of Europe and America—no more limited address will sufficiently express his cosmopolitan domicile.—*Blackwood's Magazine.*

As a reflection of real life, a book stamped with a strong personal character, and filled with unique details of a large experience of private and public interest, we unhesitatingly call attention to it as one of the most note-worthy productions of the day.—*New York Churchman.*

Our old merchants and politicians will find it very amusing, and it will excite vivid reminiscences of men and things forty years ago. We might criticise the hap-hazard and dare-devil spirit of the author, but the raciness of his anecdotes is the result of these very defects.—*Boston Transcript.*

His autobiography presents a spicy variety of incident and adventure, and a great deal of really useful and interesting information, all the more acceptable for the profusion of anecdote and piquant scandal with which it is interspersed.—*N. Y. Jour. of Commerce.*

Not the least interesting portion of the work, to us here, is the narration of Nolte's intercourse with our great men, and his piquant and occasionally ill-natured notice of their faults and foibles.—*N. Y. Herald.*

It is a vivid chronicle of varied and remarkable experiences, and will serve to rectify the errors which too often pass among men as veritable history.—*Evening Post.*

The anecdotes, declamations, sentiments, descriptions, and whole tone of the book, are vivacious and genuine, and, making allowance for obvious prejudices, graphic and reliable. To the old it will be wonderfully suggestive, to the young curiously informing, and to both rich in entertainment.—*Boston Atlas.*

As an amusing narrative, it would be difficult to find its superior; but the book has peculiar interest from the freedom with which the author shows up our American notorieties of the past forty years.—*Courier*

Milton Keynes UK
Ingram Content Group UK Ltd.
UKHW011105200224
438164UK00004B/536